MACINTOSH WINDOWS INTEGRATION

Integrating Your Macintosh with Windows 95/98 and Windows NT Environments

MACINTOSH WINDOWS INTEGRATION

Integrating Your Macintosh with Windows 95/98
and Windows NT Environments

JOHN RIZZO

MORGAN KAUFMANN
ACADEMIC PRESS, a Harcourt Science and Technology Company
San Diego   San Francisco   New York   Boston
London   Sydney   Tokyo

Academic Press
A Harcourt Science and Technology Company
525 B Street, Suite 1900, San Diego, CA 92101-4495 USA
http://www.academicpress.com

Academic Press
24-28 Oval Road, London NW1 7DX United Kingdom
http://www.hbuk.co.uk/ap/

Morgan Kaufmann
340 Pine Street, Sixth Floor, San Francisco, CA 94104-3205 USA
http://www.mkp.com

Library of Congress Catalog Card Number: 99-63440

International Standard Book Number: 0-12-589325-6

Printed in the United States of America
99 00 01 02 03 IP 9 8 7 6 5 4 3 2 1

For Adriana,
who brightens my days with games of Pooh and Mr. Foot.

Contents

Chapter 6   Exchanging Files Electronically Between Mac and Windows   119

Part Three Cross-Platform Networking Infrastructure   145

Chapter 15   Cross-Platform Printing   407

Acknowledgments

No one writes a book like this alone. It takes the active cooperation and assistance from numerous people and organizations.

I'd first like to thank Richard Birchall, a professional engineer at the Atomic Energy of Canada Limited who really knows how to integrate Macintosh and Windows. Richard began sending me tips and leads to chase down as soon as I put MacWindows.com on line late 1997. He has been a great help as a technical reviewer for this book, providing tips and information, and more leads to chase.

I am also grateful to Nathan Garcia for providing helpful insight in his technical review and for pushing on with this project despite some difficult personal circumstances.

Much of this book grew out of the MacWindows.com web site, and owes its foundations to the many MacWindows readers of who have sent in leads and tips. Some of the contributors include John Wolf, Henry Norr, Nate Caplin, Bill Reynolds, and Darryl Lee, though there are many others. I'm also grateful to Ric Ford for helping promote MacWindows in its early days.

Thanks to my former editors of MacWeek and eMediaweekly, who helped me with the BackPanel column I wrote for the magazines. David Morgenstern deserves a great deal of credit for making possible this book's appendix at a time when he had his hands full.

Most of the companies whose products are mentioned in this book have helped in one way or another. Michael Conrad of Microsoft was a great help in providing answers about Windows NT and Windows 2000. Several people at Apple where helpful in answering many picky questions, and I'd like to thank Staci Sheppard for getting me in touch with most of them. There were also some kind people at Adobe, Citrix, Connectix, Data Viz, Insignia Solutions, Open Door Networks, Xinet, and other companies who provided assistance.

Finally, thanks to my editor, Thomas Park, who has been very supportive throughout the project, and to Shawn Brown for lending her considerable expertise during the book's production cycle.

Foreword

Networks exist for one reason and one reason only: to move data from one place to another. Sometimes it's simple. Sometimes it's not. Very seldom is moving data impossible. Luckily, it's easy when you know how.

The most popular, or at least fastest growing, network operating system is from Redmond, Washington. Some of the most tenaciously loyal users rely on equipment designed and distributed out of Cupertino, California. It's always taken extra effort to bridge data between the two.

Universal, even basic, compatibility and support for the Mac environment among foreign disk operating and network operating systems has been spotty at best. Most of the time, network administrators have had to rely on unrelated products among several vendors, if tools were indeed available, to make things work. Worse, network admins are often forced to support unfamiliar foreign-protocol products on short notice. Mergers and acquisitions pair inherently incompatible systems, leaving it to the support staff to make it all work together.

Marching orders, after all, are marching orders. Survival, both corporate and personal, revolves around adaptation and quick response. So, it falls on the resourcefulness, wiles, good luck, and a free exchange of ideas among support veterans to make hastily wedded networks work together well enough to not impede mission-critical processes. In the absence of tools and utilities, they've (we've) have had to network among themselves (ourselves) for tips and tricks on how to make unrelated platforms interoperate smoothly. It's in this spirit that the contents of this volume are offered. Within these covers resides the results of many years' experience and global networking among users and vendors who refuse to be denied use of their preferred OS. These details are focused through the lens of the author's honed knack for being in the right place at the right time to ask the right questions and apply proper analysis.

The good news is that cross support among the several systems is improving almost every day. The Internet has been a catalyst in unifying and conforming disparate flavors of networks. This trend has also brought new attention to legacy tools for integrating unrelated protocols and data formats. Which are chosen to solve individual dilemmas depend on analysis of the details.

Three fundamental questions apply to how data is handled:

> Who needs the data?
> How important is the data?
> What is the data's most efficient handling?

Any company that wishes to succeed must answer these questions and base handling of each bit of data through impediments to implementation. Companies that wish to succeed must put the good of the many over the convenience of the few. So say support staff's directives, anyway, driven by expedience, pragmatism, and/or the bottom line. That may be interpreted as making the users' jobs as easy as possible without regard for the trouble a few must endure to make it so. Efficiency, you see, is in the eye of the beholder. Sometimes users don't wish to change (and have enough clout to avoid changing) from hardware and software to which they've grown accustomed. On the other hand, there is often neither time nor resources to convert from existing, uncoordinated equipment into something either standardized or otherwise easier to administer.

At the heart of the matter is connectivity and compatibility. Data might be needed around the world, just across the room, or in an alternate format on the machine right in front of you. In the easiest cases, the sending and receiving equipment are cut from the same cloth. Yet, end users don't care whether the system they're using is homogeneous or not. For them, it must work as if it were. It's the system administrators, those on the front line, who take the heat when the hardware or software does not work that way. That's whether the problem is avoidable or inevitable, support's fault or a design flaw. Seldom do system admins hear praise for a job well done. The best strategy is to gather enough tools to oil those wheels before they squeak.

Applying the studied advice offered on the following pages to one's own circumstances will help keep the ship going. There's no such thing as too much connectivity or too many tricks to keep it under control.

Nathan Garcia
March 1999

Nathan Garcia hosts On Computers, *a weekly tech-oriented call-in talk show, and is the* How Does it Work *correspondent on* Beyond Computers. On Computers *is syndicated domestically by SNP Communications;* Beyond Computers *is syndicated through Public Radio International. Both programs may be heard internationally over the Armed Forces Network and in archives at www.oncomputers.msn.com and*

www.beyondcomputersradio.msn.com.

Introduction

This book is dedicated to two great computer platforms—Windows and Macintosh—and how to use them together. Using either one of them can produce good results, but using the two together can be even more powerful. Just how you do this has been problematic. You might find a way to move files between Mac and Windows described in the back of a software manual. A book on Windows NT Server might give you a few tips on using Macs, and book on the latest version of Mac OS might give you a sidebar on dealing with PCs. This book won't tell you everything there is to know about Windows and Mac OS, but focuses on the parts you need to know when using them together.

The goal of this book is to enable you to accomplish what you need without having a library of books on a lot of different topics. It could even enable you to avoid hiring a consultant. The book should serve as an introduction to various subjects related to Macintosh–Windows integration and as a resource for finding solutions to specific problems.

Who Should Read This Book

Traditionally, you were either a Mac person or a Windows person. In becoming one or the other, you learned a lot of techniques, but not much that applies to both platforms. Because the execution of technology can be so different, you may not be aware that the other platform uses some of the same or equivalent technology. I've found that basic assumptions by PC experts are sometimes unknown to Mac experts, and vice versa. It's sometimes difficult for the two groups to even talk to each other, as even the language of the two systems is different. (For example, Windows networks have *permissions*; Mac networks have *privileges*. Both describe a similar concept.) Additionally, using Macintosh and Windows together brings up new issues that neither expert is familiar with.

Understanding that both Mac and Windows people need this information, I've included information that may be old hat to one group, and a new revelation the other. For this reason, you probably won't read the book from cover-to-cover like a novel. Instead, you'll pick chapters, skip over some sections, and probably use the index to find related topics. There are explanations of how each platform accomplishes tasks, and comparisons between the two, so the that you'll know what the "equivalent" is on the other platform.

All this is to say that this book is written for both Windows and Macintosh people. Here is a sample of who this book was written for, in no particular order:

- Experienced Windows NT administrators who need to support Macs
- People of either Mac or PC backgrounds who aren't NT experts, but who want to support Macs with Windows NT
- Experienced Mac administrators who want to support Windows
- Business workers, home users, professional users, students, network users, and administrators who need to work with

both platforms because they have a Mac in one location and a PC in the other
- ◆ Managers who want to get a handle on what's involved with making the two platforms work together
- ◆ Users of either operating system who want to know what to do with files they get from users of the other platform

What's in This Book

Many chapters begin with a section called *Differences* that gives a comparative explanation of how a technology works on Macintosh and Windows. From there, the chapters often go on to describe the problems that arise from these differences, and how to fix them. There are separate chapters on Macintosh and Windows networking for those who are familiar with one but not the other. There are chapters on technologies that both platforms use, focused, of course, on how to use them together.

The book is divided into five sections:

- ◆ **Part 1: Integration Basics.** We start with management and planning issues, and an introduction to technical issues. These are mostly organizational issues that should be considered before you start investing in equipment and software. If you are looking for a way to use your home and work computers work together, you can skip to Part 2.

- ◆ **Part 2: Exchanging Files.** This section offers several chapters on issues related to moving and using files, either on a network or off. These topics are common to most people integrating Windows and Macs, regardless of their situation. There's also a look at common disk storage problems and solutions.

◆ **Part 3: Cross-Platform Networking Infrastructure.** These chapters cover the basics of how Mac OS and Windows do networking and their similarities, differences, and areas of compatibility. There is also a discussion of TCP/IP—the universal network language—and issues related to cross-platform environments.

◆ **Part4: Macintosh and Windows NT and Other Servers.** This section focuses on solutions for cross-platform network services, including file service, printer sharing, and remote access. Windows NT plays a prominent part of this section, as it does in the real world. Chapter 11 provides an introduction to Windows NT Server, as well as a more specific look at the techniques for supporting Macs. For many people, Chapter 11 will be the core of this book. There's also a discussion of the alternatives to Windows NT Server in Chapters 13 and 14.

◆ **Part 5: Using Foreign Operating Systems.** Sometimes the best way to solve integration problems is to run a Windows program on a Mac, of vice versa. There are several ways to do this, both on the individual level and the corporate network level. The book concludes with a chapter on sharing monitors and keyboards between a group of Macs and PCs.

What's on the CD-ROM

The CD-ROM at the back of the book contains Windows and Mac software that enables cross-platform integration. The purpose is to give you a first-hand look at some of the top utility and networking solutions described throughout the book. There is freeware, which is yours to use, as well as shareware, written by authors who ask for a modest fee if you find the software useful. There's also demonstration software that is fully or partially functional for a limited time after you install it. Regardless of what machine you use, take a look inside the folders of both the Mac and Windows software. Many contain electronic manuals in PDF format that will give you a further idea of what the software can do for you.

Using MacWindows: The Web Site for Macintosh–Windows Integration

It's common these days for people to create web sites to accompany books, movies, and all sorts of products. In this case, the opposite occurred—the book grew out of the MacWindows web site (http://www.macwindows.com). You can use MacWindows as the companion web site to this book. Things that are impossible to keep current in a book—the latest bugs, new solutions, Internet URLs, new versions of products, contact information for companies—you'll find these at the MacWindows web site. Throughout the book, you'll see notes called Web Update Links. These are URLs for regularly updated web pages at MacWindows where you can get current information on a topic.

The MacWindows web site provides daily news, tips, and information about products, bugs, and fixes that have to do with all aspects of integrating Macs and Windows. (There's also some Linux and UNIX coverage.) MacWindows includes the topics in this book, such as networking, Macintosh and Windows integration, Windows emulation, and cross-platform file issues.

I first started thinking about doing a web site during the summer of 1997. I had been writing about the subject for a decade in books and magazines, and had accumulated a lot of information. Yet, when I needed a specific piece of information, I had to search for it. Some of it was in notes, some of it was in stories I had written, some of it was buried deep in stacks of paper. I had hoped the Internet would solve the problem, but only found scattered pieces of information.

I started putting MacWindows together in the summer of 1997, and it went on-line in November of 1997. The idea was not only to create a resource with everything that I knew about integrating Macs and PCs, but to share the experiences of the readers. Today, MacWindows contains over 70 web pages of information and links.

The purpose of MacWindows is the same as that of this book—to provide information to both Mac and Windows users and network administrators on how to deal with each other. You won't find any "Macs rule" or "Windows is best" propaganda at MacWindows. You won't find news about how well or poorly Apple is doing, or about the latest lawsuits against Microsoft. MacWindows is not an evangelist site for either platform. Like this book, MacWindows assumes that its readers already have both Macs and Windows machines, and want to get them to work together better.

MacWindows News. The MacWindows home page contains daily news related to integrating Macs and Windows. This includes announcements of new bugs and their solutions, new integration-enabling products and updates, and anything of interest to people working with two platforms. MacWindows News also reports on items related to Linux and UNIX and Macintosh.

MacWindows Solutions. This department contains lists of products that enable Macintosh and Windows integration. Solutions contains short descriptions of products, as well as links to product web pages and manufacturers' home pages. Solutions also contains contact information, such as phone numbers.

MacWindows Tips. This section contains information on how to solve some very specific problems, including working around buts. Many of the tips included in this book are at the site. However, the Tips section is updated to include the most current information.

MacWindows Tutorials. This department contains some of the information contained in these book on how to accomplish standard tasks, such as translating a file or setting up Windows NT Services for Macintosh. You'll find more how-to information in this book than in MacWindows Tutorials. The coverage is also more detailed in this book.

Special reports. These are similar to product reviews, but with a platform-integration focus. You'll find test data and notes on how products behave, as well as some information on how to accomplish certain tasks.

Part One

Integration Basics

What's in This Section:

Chapter

What's in This Chapter:

♦ *The benefits of mixing Macs and PCs*

♦ *What cross-platform integration tries to accomplish*

♦ *Defining cross-platform goals*

1

The Goals of Cross-Platform Integration

Making Macintosh and Windows PCs work together might seem like a natural enough endeavor. They're just computers, and computers should be able to communicate, right? But then you look closer at the operating systems. People who know Macs open the Windows control panel and don't see anything that looks familiar. People who know Windows can't find a Registry to edit in Mac OS. Getting the two platforms to work together is a mystery to both groups, who often assume it can't be done.

More often than not, it can be done. There are ways to get a Macintosh to send a file to a Windows machine in a readable, editable form. There are ways to connect a Mac to a particular Windows server. There are ways to run a particular program on a Macintosh. A solution here, a technique there, and soon you're talking real integration.

3

Computer integration is more than single networking or software technology. It's about lot of technologies and issues in a workflow situation, and it's about training and knowledge of both platforms. Integration is not about Macintosh versus Windows. It's about Macintosh and Windows.

The goal of integration is what you want it to be. It could be as simple as being able to use your home Mac as an extension of your Windows PC at work. Or it could mean having Macs and Windows as part of a large company network and workflow. Either way, platform integration requires the two types of computers to work together smoothly at all levels.

The ideal goal of platform integration is to create a situation where no one needs to ask which computer a person in an organization is using to accomplish a task. We're not quite there yet, but every year, the technology gets closer and closer to achieving complete integration. But even now, practical integration is achievable. It's not magic, and it's not rocket science.

Why Integrate?

But why bother at all? Why shouldn't Mac devotees stay all Mac? Why not replace all the Macs with Windows machines? After all, it is easier to stay with one platform.

Imagine for a moment that you're a carpenter hanging a door frame. You've used a saw to cut the wood, shims and a level to get the sides straight, and a hammer and nails to fix it in place. Now you're ready to notch out the spots in the frame where the hinges will go. You ask your partner to hand you a wood chisel. Your partner gives you a screwdriver.

"We've gone to all Acme tools and got rid of all our Stanleys," your partner explains. "It simplified our inventory and maintenance procedures. However, Acme doesn't make a wood chisel. But next year, they're going to come out with this really great wood chisel that will blow away all the other wood chisels. For now, here's a screwdriver."

Computers are also tools. They're more complex and more difficult to use together than carpenters' tools, but they are tools nonetheless. Like a carpenter, you want the best tool for the job. Sometimes that's Macintosh, and sometimes it's Windows. And once in a while it might be UNIX, too. Each platform—the combination of an operating system and hardware—has its own particular strengths and weaknesses.

The Right Tool for the Right Job

The idea that one platform has the best tools for every job is simply unrealistic. For instance, Macs are well suited to certain tasks in the publishing industry, such as Postscript output and ligatures. Publishing software tends to be more mature on the Mac than on Windows. On the other hand, database tools using ODBC and DDE tend to be more mature on Windows than on Mac. This doesn't mean Windows can't do publishing or Macs can't do databases, but they may not be the best tools for the job.

Often, there is a piece of software that is particularly well suited for your situation and that only runs on one platform. Having an all-Mac shop would rule out a specialized map-creation tool that is available only for Windows. On the other hand, an all-Windows shop eliminates the possibility of using GoLive CyberStudio, a highly acclaimed web page designer with some unique capabilities.

There are many benefits to keeping both operating systems around and enabling them to work with each other. Here are a few of them:

- ◆ **Keeping up with innovation.** The right tool today may not be the best tool six months from now. Being cross-platform allows you to try out the latest software and techniques, regardless of whether they come out on Windows or Mac

OS first. If you've got both, you don't have to wait for innovative new tools to be ported from one platform to another.

♦ **Flexibility.** There's no doubt that using multiple operating
systems is more flexible than being a 100 percent Mac or
Windows shop. A mixed platform shop lets you better react
to the changing requirements of your customers and your
suppliers. It lets you focus on your workflow and your business, not on a platform.

♦ **Freedom in hiring.** Having both platforms at hand lets you
hire employees based on their work skills in your field, not
their computer skills.

♦ **Consistent Web Publishing.** If you're a Web publisher,
being cross-platform means you can create sites for everyone. It enables you to check both the appearance of the
content and technology (Java, CGI scripts, an so forth) on
both platforms. Mac web surfers get really annoyed when
they are told a site doesn't work with Macs, or when they
get an apparently meaningless error message such as "Java
script didn't execute." Similarly, designing a site with only
Macs in mind might give you some colors and fonts that
look awfully strange on Windows browsers.

♦ **Mac advocates can keep their Macs.** Integration is the single best strategy for keeping Macintoshes in a corporate
environment. If you can get the Macs to play nice with
everybody else, and they do their job, many management
teams have been inclined to let them stay.

♦ **Going from two networks to one.** For computer administ-
trators, integrating Macintosh into the mainstream computing environment and workflow eliminates the
headaches of maintaining separate systems.

Drawbacks to Going Mixed-Platform

All these benefits don't come for free. The fact is, it is easier to run a mono-platform shop. A cross-platform system adds complexity to your processes and to their management, as well as some potential expense. There will be more technology issues to be aware of, and more potential problems to crop up. They can also add personnel requirements. There's also additional training that will be required, not only for the new technology, but in the do's and don'ts of making them work together. You may run into opposition from users or network administrators.

This doesn't mean you shouldn't integrate, of course, as the benefits can outweigh the drawbacks. What it does means is that you need to be aware of the problems and the solutions, preferably before you integrate. If you can extend this awareness to the staff, you're enlisting allies.

Defining Your Goals

Part of knowing what you're in for is knowing what you want. Your integration goals aren't going to be the same as someone else's, and may even change over time. You can integrate Macs and Windows at many different levels of operation and of technology. Know what you want to accomplish.

Many people focus on enabling Macs and Windows to both use a particular product. In many cases, this is an important goal, one that has many valid reasons. In other cases, however, it's just an assumed goal, when in actuality, it's the performance of a task that is important, not the use of a particular piece of software. You should decide from the start if replacing your current software will be better in the long run.

What follows are descriptions of some typical cross-platform compatibility goals at different levels.

Use Disks Interchangeably

The goal of sharing Zip, floppy, CD-ROM, and other storage media is a fairly easy one to accomplish, requiring some basic knowledge and possibly some extra software.

Exchange and Use Files Interchangeably

This is where a Mac user sends a file to a Windows user, who works on it, maybe adds another set of files, and perhaps sends it back to another Mac user. The files may be interchanged directly or via a server that both platforms access.

To accomplish this goal, you need to consider the software applications you use and how you move them. What is the more important goal, using files on both platforms or using a certain piece of software? You may need to decide which is more important, as the best enabling technology may differ.

You should also take a look at the file formats you use and consider their cross-platform implications. Some file formats will be more difficult to work with on a cross-platform basis and may result in higher training costs. For example, some graphics file formats are much easier than others to move across platforms without having to edit the result. You need to decide if using the particular format is the goal, or if the task of using some format is more important.

Network Connectivity

This is such a broad area that you really need to break down your networking goals into smaller functional areas. For instance, one networking goal might be to go to a single transport protocol for everyone. Usually, this means eliminating NetBEUI and AppleTalk, and standardizing on TCP/IP. A mostly Mac shop might want to go all-AppleTalk for Macs and Windows, however.

Another goal might be to use Windows NT Servers. Again, this is multifaceted, since there are multiple types of network services that come with NT, and even more that you can add. Be aware that file sharing isn't the end of the question. There's also e-mail, web service, and services that provide your local network access to the Internet. Special-purpose server software, such as OPI and RIP servers, are also becoming increasingly popular. You might need Macs to access some of these services, but not all.

You also need to decide if your goal is to use a particular server platform or server software on that platform, or if your goal is more functional.

Overall, the goal of a network should be to provide tools for your workflow. The network should not be a goal in itself.

Share Peripherals

This goal often applies to printers, but it can also apply to monitors and keyboards. Not only does sharing peripherals cut down on costs, but it can conserve space in situations where you have a lot of computers in a small space.

Framing the Decision

When coming up with your own goals, you should identify the benefits you foresee from replacing one platform with another, or merging separate Mac and Windows groups. Are they perceived or real? It helps to look at it from the perspective of your workflow. Identify and prioritize the problems in your work flow that you want to solve. Do you need software that won't run on Mac? Would you like better security? Or perhaps a faster workflow could reduce your time cycles.

When framing your goals, it's also important not to be a cockeyed optimist. Going to a mixed-platform system will introduce new problems. Try to identify these before you decide what you want to do, so you can weigh the alternatives. You'll find that most of the problems that will crop up aren't unique to your setup.

What's Next

Once you've clearly defined just what you want to accomplish by mixing Macs and Windows PCs together, you can move on to how. But before I get to the nuts and bolts of combining Windows and Macintosh into a system, you should look at a higher level of *how*—your philosophy of integration. Philosophy is part science, part religion. Understanding your own can help you narrow down the choices.

Chapter

What's in This Chapter:

- ◆ What's an integration philosophy?

- ◆ Creating your integration philosophy

- ◆ Cross-platform myths

2

Integration Philosophies

Throughout this book, you'll find alternative methods of solving particular platform integration problems. While I've provided the pros and cons of these solutions, I've tried stay away from judging one method as "the best." That's because there is no one way to integrate Windows and Macintosh that is best for everyone.

Before you buy any products, before you even create a plan, it's a good idea to consider your philosophy of integration. If defining your goals are the "what do I want to accomplish," the philosophy is "how do I want to accomplish this." Not "how" as in "what software do I buy," but "how" as in "which technology route do I want to take."

For instance, you might have a question: "How do I get the Macs to access the Internet using Microsoft Proxy Server." There are answers to this question, but the question itself already has an integration philosophy built into it. It assumes you are going to use Microsoft Proxy Server as your Internet gateway. But the broader question of "How do I get Macs and Windows machines to access the Internet using a Windows-based proxy server?" has additional solutions that may provide extra benefits.

I'm not passing judgment on any particular integration philosophy—there are good reasons for holding each one. However, you should realize that you may have a particular philosophy in mind. There are many different ways to accomplish a particular goal, and there is no single best way to integrate. Knowing what your integration philosophy is going to be will help you narrow down the choices.

What Goes Into an Integration Philosophy

There's a lot you bring to the drawing board that makes up a group's integration philosophy. This includes the particular mix of people—workers, administrators, and managers—and their backgrounds and computing situations, and their past experiences with various technologies. You should also realize that a philosophy includes attitudes towards Macintosh, Window 95/98, Windows NT, and UNIX. It's okay to have preferences, but try to give up an attitude of OS Wars. It's okay to prefer to work with hammers, as long as you remember that screwdrivers can do some useful things, too.

Your platform preferences can also determine your own course of action. It is often up to Mac people in a large Windows-based organization to jump-start integration. If you are a Mac user and want to keep your Macs in this type of a situation, it will be up to you to learn the details of integration, and their impact on the overall system.

Your integration philosophy also includes your knowledge base, and what you don't know. You're reading this book to expand your knowledge base, but don't assume something can't be done because you don't know what the answer is. An organization's knowledge base also influences integration decisions. If a group accomplishes a particular task very well, you may not need to institute a completely new process because of the new software features touted by a manufacturer.

Who you are—or who your organization is—also goes into the decision making process. For instance, what's best for small networks is not necessarily what's best for big networks.

Sometimes the philosophy is imposed on you, and it's your job to implement it. It's better if some thought is put into it, but even if you had no part in coming up with the integration philosophy, knowing what it is will help you come up with better solutions.

A Look at Integration Philosophies

By integration philosophies, I do mean methods of implementing goals—the larger "how-to's." The following pages describe some of the more common integration philosophies, but this is by no means a comprehensive list. There are also philosophies that are combinations of one or more of these approaches. The main point here is to illustrate how different cross-platform solutions can be. Each approach presents its own benefits and challenges.

Integrating a Little at a Time

The "little-by-little" philosophy advocates a conservative approach. You might already have Macs and PCs, but they exist in different departments. Now you want to start using them together, but you don't want to make any drastic changes. You want to keep the workflow going with as little interruption as possible.

This type of implementation will include periods of overlapping methods and intermediate solutions. For instance, if you were replacing server platforms, such as replacing Mac-based servers with Windows NT or UNIX, and you wanted to take it slow, you might need interim methods of allowing clients to talk to both types of servers. You might even want to enable the servers to communicate with each other. If you were switching network protocols, you might want to have a multiprotocol period.

This approach allows for some experimentation. You can try out different solutions and approaches on small parts of the group. If your organization is big enough, you might consider investing in some hardware and software and setting up an integration lab, where you can test out solutions before you employ them on the real network. However, the experimentation shouldn't be open-ended. An overall plan and a timetable should include any evaluation periods.

A challenge to the little-by-little approach is in implementing large-scale changes, such as network architecture redesigns or major shifts in workflow. For instance, it is difficult to install new cross-platform application software a little at a time.

Designing Cross-Platform from the Ground Up

Designing (or redesigning) a network and a workflow system from the ground up has the potential of getting the best end result, if you make the right design decisions. A danger here is that you may overlook some aspect of cross-platform workflow that could cause a serious problem. A strict all-at-once approach requires a lot of planning and considers a lot of different factors at different levels. To make sure you don't forget anything, your planning process should include various people involved in the workflow, not just technical experts.

If you go this way, you should keep in mind that nothing in the computer industry is set in stone, and new solutions can crop up at any time that might prove beneficial.

"Make the Macs Connect, but Don't Touch My NT Server"

The "Connect the Macs, but don't touch the NT server" philosophy is where the IS group will permit Macs, but doesn't want to do anything to support them. Shops with this philosophy don't even want to run Microsoft's Windows NT Services for Macintosh on the server. Organizations with this philosophy usually have NT Server at the heart of the network architecture.

The types of solutions for this approach often involve adding Macintosh software. This can be client software, or gateway software, or utilities that run on a Mac. Running Windows applications on the Macs via an emulator or coprocessor card can be an important piece of the equation in this situation.

If you are in a situation where you're the one who wants to keep Macs in the face of a hostile IS group, it's going to be up to you to learn about compatibility issues with Windows. It's likely that the Mac users will have to change some of their habits, such as the way they name files, if they are to be integrated into the mainstream.

"Nobody Ever Got Fired for Buying Microsoft"

This philosophy is one where you decide that all of your integration enabling products are going to have a Microsoft logo, a common one in business. Adherents to this approach have no problems installing Services for Macintosh (SFM) on Windows NT Servers, but don't want to consider alternatives. But this philosophy is more than just specifying SFM. It requires Microsoft server solutions for all network services, including file service, email, and Internet proxies.

There are perfectly valid reasons to go this way, such as having a single vendor to deal with, having Microsoft-trained network administrators, or believing that the Microsoft solutions are the best for your Windows users. However, you do need to consider the drawbacks before jumping into this. If you don't know why you are going all Microsoft, you should consider that there are alternative Windows-based products from smaller companies that do a better job in supporting Macintosh on Windows NT networks. Going the all-Microsoft route won't solve all your cross-platform problems and will require some additional helper utilities—from companies other than Microsoft. It also may require some trade-offs, and living with Macs that can't do everything that the Windows clients can. For example, before Windows 2000 Server, there was no way to provide file service to Macs without AppleTalk except by going to a non-Microsoft product. If the benefits of staying all-Microsoft outweigh these issues, then by all means, go for it.

Keeping a Mostly Mac Shop, Sprinkle with Windows

This is a Macintosh-based office that wants to stay that way, but would like the benefits of a few Windows machines. The solutions here are very different from those of a mostly PC environment. Here, you can make the PCs adapt to the way you are doing things. For instance, you can install software to enable the PCs to read Macintosh disk storage, or install AppleTalk networking software.

If this is your integration philosophy, you don't have to make drastic changes to the way things work now. In this type of situation, you should look for solutions that give the best services for Macintoshes. You might consider UNIX as a server platform, which can offer Mac file service over TCP/IP. A group interested in ease-of-use and Mac familiarity can go with AppleShare IP, which supports native Windows file sharing as well as Mac clients. Windows NT Server can play a role here as well, though it doesn't necessarily have to be the only server platform.

Cross-Platform Myths

Part of an integration philosophy is attitude, but you should use objective reasoning to drive decisions, or you probably won't end up with the best solution. It's important to take a scientific viewpoint. Just because you or someone you know doesn't have an answer doesn't mean there isn't one. And just because "everyone" says it's true doesn't make it so.

A case in point: In 1998, I started seeing a tip about running Connectix Virtual PC, a Windows emulation environment for Macintosh. The tip being reported on the web and in email lists was a supposed method to speed up performance of Windows under emulation, which isn't particularly fast because of the nature of emulation. According to this information, you could get great speed gains by removing the Finder and configuring the Mac so that it would boot up with Virtual PC and Windows instead of the Finder. Some of the reports even attributed the tip to Apple cofounder Steve Wozniak.

It all sounded great, so I contacted one of the creators of Virtual PC at Connectix for details on how it worked. It turns out it didn't. He told me that there wasn't any basis in fact to the claim that this technique improved performance by any amount. It was a myth.

So while your integration philosophy can and should reflect personal attitudes, it shouldn't based on myths. There are a lot of myths about cross-platform integration floating around. Just because a myth is false doesn't mean the opposite is true. Here are some of the more general myths I run into:

Myth: Macs and Windows Are the Same

Anyone who has gotten inside the guts—installed and removed hardware and software from Mac and Windows machines—knows that the two platforms are not the same. If they were, there wouldn't be any need for integrating the two. The point is not promote one over the other—the danger in this myth is that it can lead to overlooking the deficiencies in both platforms. It also assumes you'll get the same results on either platform, or have no problems when you move something from one to the other.

Myth: Only Macs Can Do Publishing

The fact is that companies do publish on Windows. Publishing software is more mature on Macs, but the level is rising on Windows. Additionally, print houses are learning how to deal with Windows.

Myth: Publishing on Windows Is Just Like Publishing on Macs

Quark XPress may look the same on both platforms, but there are still several publishing tasks that Macs are better at. Postscript output on Windows is improving, but still lags behind that on Mac. Windows can't handle ligatures—special spacing of certain characters. Move a file with ligatures from Mac to Windows, and the ligatures disappear. Once again, assuming that both platforms are equivalent oversimplifies the situation. For instance, in publishing, retaining fonts is a problem when moving files between Windows and Mac machines.

Myth: There's No Software for the Mac

There is Windows-only software, but there is also software that is available for Mac only. (This is one of the reasons for going mixed-platform.) If one company doesn't make a Mac version of its software, some other company may have an equivalent package.

Of course, there are Windows products that have no Mac equivalent. These include specialized server software, such as raster image processors (RIPs) and database servers, as well as specialized client and workstation software.

Myth: Windows Networking Is Black Magic

Some Mac people hold the idea that getting Windows networking to function requires a very specialized skill set and a lot of configuring and tweaking. This was true before Windows 95 and Windows NT, but today, Windows networking is an elegant, reliable system that works very well. Windows networking has some capabilities that Mac networking does not.

As you'll see in Chapter 9, one way that Windows networking differs from Mac networking is that some features of Mac peer-to-peer networks require servers in Window networks. The role of the server in a traditional Mac network was mostly ancillary, though this is changing with the advent of TCP/IP. Windows networking is a still a bit more complex than Macintosh networking, but it is not beyond the reach of the average Mac networking administrator to learn.

Myth: Windows NT Is the Only Server You Can Have

Technically, a mixed-platform network can mix servers as well as workstations. Windows NT Server can communicate with other server platforms. As server software becomes more and more specialized, we will be seeing more of this.

Untrue Truisms

In addition to myths, there are also truisms that aren't true. These usually take the form of predictions that become assumptions. Here are some untrue truisms of the past:

The future of networking is OSI. If you didn't follow networking in the late 1980s you probably never heard of OSI. But at one point, it was accepted as fact that everyone running PCs, Macs, and UNIX would be communicating over the OSI network protocols, the universal network language. While a worldwide standards group in Geneva labored over the minutiae of OSI standards, TCP/IP and the Internet swept the computer world and conquered it.

The future of networking is IPX. This was back when Novell was king of corporate networking and IPX was the next big thing. Novell abandoned IPX in favor of TCP/IP in NetWare 5.

The Mac OS will be replaced in 18 months—by OS/2. I heard Bill Gates himself make this prediction at a conference in the late 1980s.

Macintosh is dead. This one is still around. People have been saying this since about 1987 or so. This is perhaps the longest-running unfulfilled prediction in the computer industry. We've also heard this about Sun, Novell, and for a while in the early 1990s, even IBM. Predictions about the computer industry must be taken with a large grain of salt.

What's Next

The next chapter provides an overview of the issues involved with integrating Windows and Macintosh. This includes technical issues and personnel issues.

Chapter

What's in This Chapter:

- ♦ **Personnel and training issues**

- ♦ **An overview of integration technology issues**

- ♦ **Differences in PC and Mac terminology**

- ♦ **Areas of compatibility**

3

View from the Top

The purpose of this chapter is to introduce the areas you may need to invest in as part of your integration plan. One part of your investment will be enabling technology, including software, hardware, and networks. The software includes utilities that, because of their relative low cost, are easy to overlook in the planning process. However, not all of your mixed-platform problems are based in technology, and neither will your investments be. There are personnel and training issues related to integrating Macintosh and Windows as well. Training people to use the utilities and other cross-platform enabling solutions can go a long way toward a smooth workflow. There's also value in training users in how the other guy does his job—enabling your Mac people to at least understand the ABC's of Windows, and training your support people to understand both platforms.

Personnel and Training

Integrating Macs and Windows is very much about people, as it mixes users and information services (IS) groups. People bring their own attitudes and knowledge to any organization. Though this book is mostly about technology, going from a single-platform to a mixed-platform organization will bring personnel issues. Ignore them at your own peril.

The basic situation in many organizations is that users would rather stay all-Macintosh, while IS and network administrators would rather go all-Windows. This is a generalization, but rings true in many organizations. Mixing platforms may at first appear to be a lose–lose proposition, as both users and IS people whine about all the trouble you're making. If you simply implement the cross-platform technology without giving people the whys and hows, you're looking at a clash of cultures, an us-versus-them attitude. "*They* are trying to take our Macs away." "*They* are Mac fanatics." "*They* just don't get it." There are already enough "us's" and "thems" in any organization—managers and workers, department X and department Y, union and salaried—that you don't need to layer "Mac heads" and "Windows bigots" on top.

Training can ease a culture clash. The goal is to have both users and IS groups compromise, to learn to accept the other platform. They can only do that with a little knowledge.

What to Teach People

There are several ways you can get training, but you should first know what you want in a curriculum. There are five areas of training that will help your cross-platform workflow to function effectively:

- Information about the other platform
- Information about cross-platform utilities and workflow
- Training for your IS group
- Training for self-supporting Mac groups
- General knowledge of common technology

Information about the Other Platform

An understanding of how the other platform works can help a user accept the other side and be willing to work with it. It also gives them an understanding of problems between the platforms that are likely to occur. The ideal situation is where you don't have Mac users and Windows users, just computer users—a "bilingual" staff, able to work on both Mac OS and Windows, depending on what's needed at the moment. Being about to shift personnel between both tools adds a good deal of flexibility to your organization. However, even if the users aren't proficient at both platforms, they should be aware of the limitations of each platform to prevent workflow problems. Some of the things a user should know about the other platform:

- ♦ How each operating system recognizes what application to open (Windows file name extensions, Macintosh type and creator codes).
- ♦ File naming rules
- ♦ How to access the network
- ♦ How to use removable storage
- ♦ How to send files over e-mail so that the user at the other end receives a usable file instead of garbled text.
- ♦ Basic information about how the network works

Both Windows and Mac users should be aware of the file formats of the application software they are using and whether the formats are cross-platform. All of these topics are discussed later in this book.

Information about Cross-Platform Utilities and Workflow

Don't limit training to application software—users need to know how to use integration-enabling utilities, which are often left out of the planning process. For instance, a simple networking utility can often help a Mac user access a part of a Microsoft network or a database. Windows and/or Mac users should be trained in converting file formats on booth platforms, using MacLinkPlus, Conversions Plus, DeBabelizer, and others tools discussed in Chapter 5. File renaming utilities can help ensure that no illegal characters slip by onto Windows machines. Running a Windows emulator on a Mac might enable a Mac user to use one piece of proprietary Windows software. Windows users might need utilities to decode or decompress Mac files.

Also, cross-platform workflow takes some teamwork. Users, especially new employees, should know what happens to a file when it leaves their desk. They should know if it goes to another platform, and what is done with it. The publishing industry has its own set of cross-platform issues, such as fonts, ligatures, and graphics previews, with which both Mac and Windows users should be acquainted. The network administrators or information services groups also need to be aware of these issues, which leads us to the next section.

Training for Your IS Group

Training the users about cross-platform issues is only half the job. Your IS group needs to learn about Macintoshes as well. Even if you use an outside consultant to integrate your computers, you'll want the support and opinions of your IS group. They can only support your consultant if they have an idea of what's going on.

The basic problem is that the Microsoft certification (MCSE) program is very light on Mac issues and doesn't even say much about Microsoft Windows NT Services for Macintosh. Out of this lack of knowledge, an IS support person will often respond to a question about integration with "it can't be done," when a simple solution will solve a cross-platform issue. The lack of knowledge about things Mac and integration with Windows is often the reason why IS groups tend to lobby for going all Windows.

It helps to understand their point of view. An IS professional with primarily MCSE training has invested a large amount of time in learning the Microsoft way of doing things. If things are done differently by another platform, by their comfortable definition, it is "wrong." Your training task is not to counter their knowledge set, but to add to it.

Your IS groups need to know how the Mac works, and why cross-platform problems occur, and what the various solutions are. Without the proper training, IS groups often assume that the Mac OS is an inferior, incompatible operating system that isn't worth bothering with. I once heard an IS professional describe the Mac as an "Etch-a-Sketch." However, once equipped with the facts, I have seen people with this attitude change their position to see Mac OS as a *different* operating system, with strengths and weaknesses, and with many areas of PC compatibility.

If you are in the publishing industry, your IS people *must* learn the traditionally Mac-based processes and technologies of publishing. This includes Postscript, color separation, and fonts. The proper training allows your IS group to support your users and the workflow, but it also allows them to tune the network infrastructure to meet the needs of the workflow. You shouldn't have to change your workflow to meet the needs of the network.

MacWindows Tip

If you're looking for cross-platform talent, try searching or posting an ad on a web-based job board. One of the largest is Monster Board (http://www.monsterboard.com), which holds well over 100,000 advertisements for positions across the United States.

On the other side of the fence, Mac support personnel also need to learn how to support Windows. Mac support people who are not well versed in Windows will often lobby to keep Mac and Windows groups and networks separate, a position that will be backed up by Windows IS groups. Separate Mac and Windows networks and groups is not cross-platform integration and doesn't let you reap the benefits of using both platforms together. Teaching them about Windows will help Mac support people solve and prevent cross-platform issues from the Mac side.

Self-Supporting Mac Groups

Mac support people often emerge from self-supporting Macintosh groups within a larger Windows environment. Self-supporting Mac groups often evolve out of necessity—the IS group doesn't have the knowledge required to support Macs and isn't interested. Sometimes the attitude of the information services group is "you can keep your Macs if you don't bother us about them."

It is still best to train your IS group to understand Macs, but when you do, you still may want to keep your self-supporting Mac groups. If people in the Mac group are willing to do it, and you are ready to permit it, this is something you can take advantage of. However, the idea is not to ignore the Mac groups—train them. Train a few Mac people not just about taking care of the Macs, but about cross-platform issues. I'm not saying that you should turn everyone into a network administrator. But having a higher-level view of the overall system will lead to better decisions.

Teach Basic Technology

Teaching how things work can give people a deeper understanding of issues than just memorizing techniques. General knowledge makes it easier to troubleshoot problems. It gives a person a useful perspective on the technologies employed by one platform or another. If one knows how common technologies are configured and used in Macs and PCs, then one can see the differences in the platforms.

This applies to users as well as IS professionals. I'm not talking about teaching how to write code or analyze network packets, but a higher-level knowledge of the systems involved.

I once wrote a book called *How Macs Work* and participated in the PC version, *How Computers Work*. They were both unusual computer books, in that they didn't teach what most people think of as "practical knowledge." There were no tips, no techniques. They just explained the principles of operation in layperson's terms. People in the book publishing industry were skeptical, yet both books were bestsellers. An understanding of how computers work can help people in their work with computers.

The ironic aspect of this is that training people in multiple platforms will give them a deeper understanding of the basic principles involved. This happens when one sees and understands how there are two or more ways of doing almost anything. For instance, it is easier for a multilingual person to grasp new languages than it is for a person who is unilingual. With a few languages under your belt, you realize that English is just one instance of a language, and that other methods of communication are possible.

How to Do Cross-Platform Training

A good strategy to start with is to find out which of these areas your organization needs to know about. Have your top technical Mac and Windows users and support people meet to discuss the issue. Find out who the experts are and where the holes in people's knowledge lie. Once you know what it is you need your group to know, you can look for the training sources to meet your needs.

Training Sources

Your organization can do some of the training itself. If people have the technical and people skills, you may be able to have different groups train each other on some issues concerning Macs and Windows. Where integration-enabling utilities are concerned, you may have to first have at least one person get up to speed before deciding how to teach it. You can also try a self-paced CD-ROM course to get people started on learning the other platform.

For purely cross-platform issues that don't crop up with either type of user, you can hire a consultant to design a special training course, or pick an off-site course from a catalog. If you identify cross-platform utilities, you may be able to find trainers who can add the utilities to their curricula. Either way, you'll want to carefully question potential outside consultants and trainers to see if they are covering areas of

cross-platform integration that you've decided are important. Consultants can be just as ignorant of cross-platform issues as your own staff.
If a consulting company advocates an all-Mac or all-Windows position, it's probably because it doesn't have enough expertise in Macintosh–Windows integration itself.

Industry trade shows and conferences are also good sources of cross
platform training, as many are now offering sessions on integration.
(I've taught at some of them myself.) Encourage people from your
group attending these conferences to speak up and ask questions about
their specific problems. There is often a question-and-answer period at
these sessions where you can ask specific questions about your situation. You'll also find that speakers are often receptive to one-on-one
questions from audience members right after a sessions ends. Don't be
afraid to walk up to the podium and introduce yourself. Conferences
are also a good place to find consultants. You get to "preview" your
potential trainers and consultants by listening to what they have to say.

Keep It Up

It's important to follow up a training session by applying the newly
gained knowledge to your particular situation. A one-day training session isn't going to stick if the participant doesn't practice it on the job.

Once personnel are introduced to cross-platform issues, it's a good
idea to renew the training periodically. As with other computer technologies, cross-platform solutions evolve and change fairly rapidly.
And as other technologies change, the issues that are important in
integration of different platforms change. For instance, database access
by different platforms is less important than it used to be, since web
clients now provide the universal database client. E-mail attachments
are more important than they used to be. A decade ago, people would
move a 5-Mb CAD file from a workstation using a reel of tape. Today,
a 50-Mb e-mail enclosure is not uncommon. Looking to the future,
many of the issues now important to work with Mac clients of Windows NT Server will disappear as Windows 2000 Server takes its
place. Undoubtedly, new issues will arise.

Integration Technology Issues

This section presents an overview of the technological issues involved with integrating Windows and Macintosh, issues that are tackled in more depth the remaining part of this book. Here, we'll look at the technological aspects of mixing platforms in different ways. I'll first describe the basic cross-platform issues by looking at the systems involved. Then I'll describe the problem by considering the tasks you might want to accomplish. Looking at both views of the same basic problems and solutions can be helpful in zeroing in on what you need.

A System View of Cross-Platform Issues

Macintosh–Windows integration can occur at many levels of the platforms. There's hardware, software, file formats, several levels of software (such as drivers and applications), and several levels of networking (including protocols and server software). Often you'll need to integrate at multiple levels at once. That is, a solution for one of these systems isn't necessarily a complete solution to accomplish your task.

Hardware

In Mac–Windows integration, the relevant hardware systems are the ports and input/output interfaces of each platform. The differences need to be overcome when you need to share peripherals—printers, scanners, keyboards, monitors, and so forth. There are some ports and interfaces that both platforms have in common. These include the PCI expansion slots, Ethernet networking ports, and Universal Serial Bus (USB) ports.

Disk Filing Systems

Macintosh, Windows 95/98, and Windows NT all use different methods of writing data to storage disks. These differences are easily overcome with software utilities that enable Macs and Windows to share disks. However, these utilities also require a common hardware interface, which is SCSI in the case of external storage devices.

Device Drivers

This is low-level software that enables computer hardware to communicate with peripherals, drives, and expansion cards. Device drivers are very specific to the hardware and operating system and never move across platforms. You can move a printer, graphics card, or Zip drive from one machine to the other, but you need an OS-native and/or processor-specific device driver for each.

Application Software

Generally, the application software running on the computers isn't as important as the file formats they output. Running the same application on Mac and Windows can sometimes enable integration when both versions output the same, cross-platform file format. However, you can often get the same result (a common file format) by using different applications on each platform. Generally, you can't run any Windows executable file—one that ends in .exe—on a Macintosh, and vice versa. The exceptions to this rule—and sometimes an integration solution—are the emulators or coprocessor cards (described in Chapter 16).

File Formats

This is one of the core issues making the two platforms work together. You need to use file formats that can moved between Macintosh and Windows with little or no degradation in the content or formatting. You can also choose file formats that can be easily translated, or converted, between Mac and PC formats with little or no degradation.

Fonts and Text

Fonts are an issue in publishing. The basic problem is that you use one set of fonts in a document on one platform, move the document to the other platform, and the fonts are substituted. If you want the same font in a document, you generally need the font installed on both machines—the Mac version on the Mac, and the Windows version on the PC. There's also the issue of what type of fonts to use. Postscript is more prevalent in publishing, but TrueType is more prevalent in Windows. (Some applications include both PostScript and True-Type fonts, especially when they are available on both platforms.) A new font type, OpenType, has been designed to be cross-platform, but has its own issues.

A separate issue from fonts is text itself. Mac OS and Windows both define the English alphabet in the same way, but the use of special characters, such as accents, umlauts, and just about anything that requires the use of the Mac option key, results in garbled text when moved across platforms. Avoiding these characters can help in many situations, but the gradual adoption of Unicode by software manufactures promises to fix this problem.

Server Applications

Server applications running on Windows need to support Macs. Sometimes you can enable a Mac to access a certain type of software by adding software on the Mac. A server software package often includes multiple network services, the features that servers provide to Macs and Windows—file service, e-mail, web pages, and so forth. Different server software can support Macs in varying degrees, sometimes providing Mac and Windows clients with the same features, sometimes favoring Windows clients. The best server software from an integration point of view supports Macs and Windows PCs equally, with no differences in how the user accounts are administered.

Client Software

This is the network software that users work with to access network services. Often the solution is similar to that of application software— find a client that has both Mac and Windows versions. However, sometimes Mac and Windows versions of client software from the same company are not equal. A good case in point is Microsoft's Outlook e-mail client software, which is not only unequal in the Mac and Windows versions, but has limited communications between the two platforms.

Network Protocols

Any two computers communicating over a network need to run the same network protocols, which you can think of as network languages. There are several levels of protocols. The first is the basic transport protocol (such as TCP/IP). Other protocols perform specific tasks, such as authentication, communications over a telephone line, or communications with a specific server. Network problems can occur here when the client software on users' computers doesn't support a protocol used by a server.

A Task-Based View of Cross-Platform Issues

A systems-based view of Windows-to-Macintosh integration issues looks at individual layers of technology, starting with the hardware as the foundation. You can think of the system-based view as building a lasagna layer-by-layer. It looks at a horizontal layer, which isn't completely uniform, with globs of cheese here, some sausage there, and overlapping pasta there.

A task-based view of integration is a vertical view that cuts down through the layers. What you get in your piece of lasagna depends where you decide to cut down (you don't always need sausage). You might not cut down through every layer, stopping halfway, or you might decide to go from the bottom up.

Getting out of the kitchen and back into the office, what this means is that to accomplish a particular cross-platform task often requires a number of solutions in many of the systems discussed in the last section. For instance, I'm often asked a simple sounding question which has quite a complex answer: "How do I move a file from a Mac to a PC over a network?" There are many ways to enable this task of moving files, so there is no one right answer.

This view—looking first at what you want to accomplish rather than at the systems involved—is actually the place to start designing a cross-platform environment, which goes back to what I said in Chapter 1. Given that this chapter is an overview of integration issues, I'll list some of the more common cross-platform tasks people want to accomplish without listing every type of solution. Since the task of "moving files" takes up most of the lasagna, I've broken it up into several categories.

Moving a File across a Network

You first need some hardware, such as Ethernet adapters (or ports) and cables. You need a common protocol, such as TCP/IP or AppleTalk, and you need software that can move the file across the wire. You can use a file server, though it's not required. You might also need software to convert the file between formats. The issue of fonts (described in the previous section) also comes into play here as well.

Handling File Naming Differences

The fact that Mac OS is more liberal with how you can name a file than is Windows can cause all sorts of problems in a cross-platform environment. I mentioned this earlier in the section on training, but I can't overemphasize how important this is. Misnaming files on the Mac side can cause all sorts of problems on the Windows side. There are software solutions at the server level and as utilities, but the best answer is training for the Mac users.

E-mailing Files

Moving files over e-mail from one platform to another often results in files that are unintelligible gibberish. The solutions are easy with the right software and a little knowledge about encoding and compression methods. Some e-mail client software handles cross-platform enclosures better than others. Utilities can also help. Other issues related to e-mail include enabling a network of Macs and Windows PCs to share a common Internet connection.

Using Windows Files on Macs

A common problem here is that files that did not originate on Macintosh appear with generic icons and are unrecognizable to Mac OS, even if the file is of a format the Mac software can read. This has to do with basic differences in Mac and Windows files. Graphic files moving in either direction can have their own problems. For instance, image previews in Mac files don't cross over to Windows.

Using Printers of the Other Platform

Cross-platform printing usually requires a network running TCP/IP or AppleTalk. There are many different ways to get printers attached to networks, some involving servers and some not. The main issue centers around the Postscript page description language. Both Macs and PCs use it, but some PC printers don't. There are some ways to enable Macs to print to non-Postscript printers. Also, the particular Postscript driver you use on a Windows machine can make a big difference in the output quality.

The Effects of Upgrades

When running a mixed platform environment, you need to approach the upgrading of any software conservatively. Upgrading application software or the operating system of a client or server can introduce unexpected cross-platform problems that can be difficult to trace. It's a good idea to keep the previous version of software around just in case an unexpected problem occurs that forces you to revert.

For instance, when Mac OS 8.1 was introduced, Mac users connected to Windows NT Server 4.0 noticed that the file icons of the network drive would bounce around. This made it difficult for users to select a file. (The so-called "jumping-icon bug" also happened to a lessor degree with OS 8.0.) A typical initial reaction was that it was a bug in Apple's operating system. A future version of Mac OS would fix it, right? The problem with this answer was that though the jumping icons occurred with Windows NT servers, they did not with Mac servers. Eventually, Microsoft issued a fix (a "hotfix"), which was later included in the Service Pack 4 upgrade to Windows NT 4.0. Mac OS 8.1 was considered a minor upgrade, but Apple had changed one aspect of how the Finder updates icons—a change that turned out to be permanent.

Before you upgrade software, you should test it on a spare (nonproduction) machine. Test the software in relation to your workflow— exchange files, log on to servers, send e-mail, and so forth. (It isn't realistic to have a test network, but you could have a test machine to install upgrades of server software.) You may already be testing out new software on a spare machine. In a cross-platform situation, one test machine usually won't cut it, as you need a Mac and a Windows machine.

Your test Windows machine can sometimes be a "virtual" Windows machine running on a Macintosh, in the form of a Windows emulator or a Pentium card on the Mac. This approach works for higher level functions, such as working with applications, file formats, and networking at the client level. However, what happens on an emulator or Pentium card usually isn't indicative of what will happen on a real PC at the hardware and drive levels.

Differences in Terminology

One of the aspects of using Macs and Windows together is getting to know the language of each platform. Often, each platform refers to the same thing with a different term. At other times, there are features that are roughly equivalent, though not exactly the same. Table 3.1 is a brief list of some of the differing terms listed alphabetically by their Windows names.

Table 3.1 A guide to Windows and Macintosh terms

Windows	Macintosh	Comment
ALT key	Option key	Equivalent keys
ALT-F4 (terminate program)	Command-control-escape (force quit)	Equivalent keyboard command
Control (CTL) key	Command key	Equivalent keys
Control Panel item	Control panels	Settings and configuration
CTL-F4	Command-W	Closes a window
Dial-Up Networking window	Remote Access or PPP control panel	Remote networking
Directory	Folder	Windows uses both terms, "directories" in DOS
Device drivers	Extension files	Software that connects to peripherals
DLL	Shared library, as extensions files	Files with code used by multiple applications
Domain	AppleTalk zone	A logical subdivision of a network
Network Neighborhood	Chooser	Method of viewing and selecting network devices
Network share	Shared network resources	A shared network folder or printer
Permissions	Access privileges	Limits server access
Registry	Preference files	Storage location for settings
Right click	Control click	Activates pop-up menus
Shortcuts	Aliases	A pointer file to another file or folder

Areas of Compatibility

Windows PCs and Macintosh aren't completely different. Both are computers with a processor, RAM, and a hard drive, and both even use some of the same hardware subsystems. Apple also builds a certain degree of PC compatibility into Macs. The PC compatibility has been increasing over time, as Apple adopts PC hardware standards. Apple adds software to Mac OS for working with PC disks, files, and networks. By adding third-party products, you can extend the Mac's Windows compatibility or add Macintosh compatibility to Windows PCs (see MacWindows Solutions, http://www.macindows.com/solution.html.) The following is a summary of the PC compatibility features built into each Macintosh. These topics are covered in more depth in later chapters.

Hardware Expansion

Both hardware platforms use PCI (Peripheral Component Interconnect) expansion slots. This means that you can use the same expansion card in both machines as long as you have the driver software for each. Manufacturers often supply drivers for both platforms for products such as graphics cards, network interface cards, and I/O cards for motion video.

Universal Serial Bus (USB) is a hardware standard that both Apple and Microsoft have recently begun to adopt. A consortium of companies including Intel, Microsoft, and Apple designed USB to replace the serial and keyboard ports of both computers. USB peripherals such as printers, keyboards, mice and trackballs, scanners, and secondary storage devices can be run on both Windows and Mac, as long as there is a proper driver installed on the machine.

Microsoft supports USB in Windows 95 OSR2 B and Windows 98. Windows 2000 (the successor to Windows NT 4.0) will also support USB. The iMac was the first Macintosh to support USB, followed by the "Blue and White" Power Mac G3. Apple has said that all Macintosh models will eventually have USB ports.

Using PC Disks

Macs can read, write, and format PC floppy disks and can read and write to PC SCSI disk media. Mac OS software (called PC Exchange in OS 8.1 and earlier and File Exchange in 8.5 and later) mounts the PC disks on the Finder desktop. With PC Exchange/File Exchange turned on, you can mount PC floppies, Zip and Jaz cartridges, and Syquest cartridges on the Finder desktop and copy files to and from Macintosh disks. It also mounts DOS-formatted storage PC Cards (PCMCIA) in PowerBooks. Using another set of system files, Mac OS can also mount and read PC CD-ROM disks. (See Chapter 4 for details.)

Using Windows Files

File Extension Mapping of the PC Exchange Control Panel (File Exchange in OS 8.5 or later) enables Mac applications to launch PC files when you double-click Windows and DOS files in the Finder. The Mac OS Easy Open control panel (part of File Exchange in OS 8.5 and later) enables you to select a Mac application or translation path when you double-click Windows and DOS files in the Finder.

Mac OS could at one time also translate files between Windows and Mac formats through the included DataViz MacLinkPlus translators. Apple de-bundled it from the operating system in July of 1998. MacLinkPlus is now available separately from DataViz. Mac OS does come with QuickTime translators, which let you convert between some Mac and Windows graphic and multimedia file formats. (See Chapter 5 for details.)

Networking

Networking has areas of compatibility between PCs and Macs at the lower levels. The Mac's Ethernet port and a PC's Ethernet adapter can be connected to the same segment of Ethernet cabling. Both Macs and Windows come with software that enables them to communicate with each other using TCP/IP, the most popular network transport protocol.

In network printing, the common technology is Postscript. Both platforms come equipped to print to networked Postscript printers.

File sharing between Mac and Windows is not as easy. The standard file-sharing software on Mac and Windows client machines is not compatible. You'll need to add the third-party software to either Mac or Windows clients to move files between them using the standard methods. However, you can move files between PCs and Macs using Personal Web Sharing, a feature that enables any computer with a web browser to access Mac files and folders. Mac can act as a mini web server as well as serve ordinary (non-HTML) files over TCP/IP (Mac OS 8.0 and later).

Windows NT Server and its successor, Windows 2000 Server, both come with software you can install to support Macintosh clients. The same is true for Novell NetWare before version 5.0, and you can add file sharing software to the Mac for NetWare 5.0 and latter. There is also software for UNIX servers that supports Macs and Windows clients.

As you will see later in the book, there is a lot more to networking than printing and file sharing over Ethernet and TCP/IP. But with the basic networking technologies already compatible, enabling other cross-platform networking tasks is usually a matter of adding third-party software to one machine or the other.

Integration Is Getting Easier

Mixing Macs and Windows machines used to be more difficult, and it's going to be easier in the future. The technology has been evolving toward better integration. Today there are more and better solutions coming from software and hardware manufacturers than ever before.

Microsoft and Apple have realized that people want each platform to work with the other. (For Apple, integration is a survival strategy.) In recent years, both companies have been adopting each other's standards in their products. For instance, Windows NT Server 5.0 is adopting some Apple networking standards for support of Mac clients, and Apple has adopted Microsoft networking standards in its AppleShare IP server product.

Both companies have been slowly moving toward adopting some of the same industry standards. For instance, Microsoft and Apple have made TCP/IP the default networking transport protocol in their operating systems. Both companies have also adopted support for Unicode (in Windows 98 and Mac OS 8.5), a cross-platform definition of text that will eventually replace ASCII text. The World Wide Web is probably the best example of successful cross-platform integration. There are some limitations and cross-platform glitches, but in the 1980s, no one predicted the emergence of a worldwide network of Windows, Mac, and UNIX computers sharing graphics, sound, and animation.

Part Two

Exchanging Files

What's in This Section:

Chapter

What's in This Chapter:

♦ **Drivers and disk formatting in Mac OS and Windows**

♦ **Using and formatting PC floppies on Macs**

♦ **Using Windows SCSI drives on Macintosh**

♦ **Reading PC CD-ROM and DVD-ROM disks on Macs**

♦ **Using DOS-formatted PCMCIA cards in PowerBooks**

♦ **Using Macintosh disks on Windows PCs**

4

Sharing Storage Media

Sneakernet was an effective way to move data between Macs and PCs long before the web and Windows NT Servers made the scene. In today's age of networks, using portable storage media to move data is still useful, and more practical than ever. You can share a wide variety of storage media between Macs and Windows machines, including floppy diskettes, external hard drives, Zip, Jaz, "mega" floppies, Syquest, PC cards, magneto-optical, and CD-ROM.

This can come in handy. For instance, if you wanted to download a large file from the Internet to your home Mac and modem, you could save time by downloading it to the PC at your office, which might have a fast Internet link. You can then move the file to your home on one or more removable disks. (Chapter 6 covers issues of cross-platform file compression and segmenting.)

Sharing disks means that an operating system must be able to mount, read, and write files to foreign disks. Mac OS comes with a set of software that can mount PC disks in the Finder. PC Exchange does much of this disk-mounting work and can format floppies in DOS format. PC Exchange also enables you to work with foreign data files. (You'll find information about PC Exchange's file-launching capabilities in Chapter 5.) Other software picks up the rest of the duties.

Windows doesn't come with any built-in abilities to read Mac disks, but with the addition of one of many utilities programs, your PC can be as bilingual as your Mac.

Still, there are limitations to using Windows storage media on Macs and Macintosh media on Windows machines. Except for floppies, the foreign storage devices must use a SCSI or USB interface. And although you can add a utility to Windows NT that will enable it to access Macintosh disks (described later in this chapter), there are no products as yet that enable Macs to read Windows NT NTFS formatted drives. And, of course, mounting a foreign disk on a Mac doesn't necesssarily mean you'll be able to open files or run PC software—you can find answers to those types of problems in Chapter 5 and later in Part 4.

Before we get into the hows and whys of using foreign disks, let's take a look at what makes Macintosh and Windows disk storage different.

Web Update Link: *For the latest product information about the topics covered in this chapter, check http://www.macwindows.com/disks.html.*

Differences:
Mac and Windows Drivers and Formatting

There are two aspects of disk storage that can differ in Macintosh and Windows—disk device drivers and formatting standards used on the disk. The drive hardware and media are identical in many cases. Storage device drivers are specific to an operating system and can never be cross-platform. Formatting, however, can be the same on Mac and Windows in some storage media.

Mac and PC Drivers

Storage device drivers on Mac and Windows work differently. A Macintosh storage driver is a piece of software located in a hidden partition on the drive media itself. Normally, in order for a Macintosh to recognize the disk media, Mac OS must be able to read the device's driver and load it into memory.

MacWindows Tip

When you use La Cie's SilverLining driver for your Mac-formatted drives, you must disable the SilverLining control panel if you want PC Exchange to read PC-formatted disks. That's because Silver-Lining loads its own driver into RAM.

PCs, on the other hand, don't use a driver on the media. Instead, code in the motherboard's BIOS chip initially controls the IDE hard drive and floppy drive. A SCSI adapter card (which allows booting from a disk drive) has its own BIOS. At the beginning of the boot process, the BIOS reads a piece of code called the master boot record at the beginning of the boot drive, which tells the PC which partition to boot from. The drivers for the hard drive, CD-ROM, and other devices, then load from the boot disk as the operating system boots.

When you use a removable Windows disk on a Mac, there won't be a Mac driver. In this case, PC Exchange must load its own Mac driver for the device from the startup disk into RAM. Similarly, when using a Macintosh disk on a PC using a utility, Windows must use a Windows-compatible driver supplied by a utility, not the standard Windows driver.

Mac and PC Disk Formatting

Loading a driver into RAM gets the operating system communicating with the disk drive, but that's just the first step. The operating system must also be able to understand the disk's formatting—the physical layout of the data on the disk—in order to read the information on the disk. In the cases where formatting differs between Macintosh and Windows, a bit of software can enable the operating system to understand the foreign format. Mac OS comes with PC Exchange and a set of extension files for this purpose.

With older disk technologies, the formatting on Macintosh and Windows differs. This is true for floppy disks, hard drives, and certain removable media. Newer removable disk technologies, such as CD-ROM and DVD, use the same formatting standard for both Macintosh and Windows.

Most Macintosh hard drives are formatted using HFS (Hierarchical File System). Starting with Mac OS 8.1, a more efficient disk format, HFS+, became an option as well. DOS and Windows 3.1 use a hard drive formatting standard called FAT (file allocation table), which comes in variants called FAT12 and FAT16. Windows 95 can use a couple of additional variants, VFAT and FAT32. That latter became available with Windows 95 OSR2 and Windows 98. FAT32 and HFS+ have one thing in common—they both allow for smaller blocks on larger volumes, which gives you more storage space.

Windows NT can use the FAT format or its native format, NTFS (NT File System). Removable media , such as Zip, Jaz, Syquest, and magneto-optical cartridges, most often use the most popular drive format for each platform, HFS for Macintosh and FAT for Windows.

CD-ROM disks can be formatted in any one of several standards, including HFS on Macintosh and FAT on PCs. However, most CD-ROMs for Windows are formatted in a standard called ISO 9660, which Macs can read when the appropriate extensions files are loaded (see Reading PC CD-ROM Disks later). The CD-ROM included with this book is formatted in ISO 9660. You can also find dual-formatted CD-ROMs, which typically contain an ISO 9660 partition and another partition. A slightly older version of ISO 9660, called High Sierra (developed in 1986), can also be read by Mac OS.

One of the more recent popular technologies for mass storage, DVD, uses a cross-platform formatting standard called Universal Disk Format (UDF). CD-ROM disks can also be formatted using UDF. Windows 98 and Mac OS 8.1 and later come with drivers to read UDF-formatted DVD-ROM (read-only) and CD-ROM disk.

Mounting PC Disks with PC Exchange

In Mac OS, the ability to use most Windows disks is provided by PC Exchange, a control panel up to Mac OS 8.1, and part of the File Exchange control panel starting with Mac OS 8.5. (CD-ROM access is provided by another set of files in the Extensions folder of the System folder.) PC Exchange loads a driver for a PC floppy disk or a SCSI or USB storage device. You don't need to do anything—just let the file sit in your Control Panels folder. Turn PC Exchange off or remove it from the Control Panels folder in the System folder, however, and the Mac loses its ability to mount PC disks.

PC Exchange Version History

In the years before PC Exchange, you could not mount PC disks on the Finder desktop, even though the Mac's floppy drive supported PC floppies. Instead, you had to either use the old Apple File Exchange utility to move file between PC floppies and the Mac hard drive, or access the floppy from within an application's Open dialog box.

Apple wasn't the first to come up with the idea of enabling Macs to read PC disks. The first utility was DOS Mounter, created by Dayna Communications, which has since been acquired by Intel. However, DOS Mounter is still around (see sidebar). Another utility, Insignia Solutions Access PC (now discontinued), also predated PC Exchange.

Apple first offered PC Exchange as an add-on to Mac OS to System 7.0. These versions (1.x) could only mount DOS-formatted floppies. PC Exchange first became a part of the Mac OS system software in 1994 with System 7.5, which shipped with PC Exchange 2.0. This was the first version to support PC SCSI devices, such as hard drives and removable disk storage. Subsequent versions got better at mounting certain types of data and added features. The last version of PC Exchange that was a separate control panel shipped with Mac OS 8.1. This was version 2.2, shown in Figure 4.1.

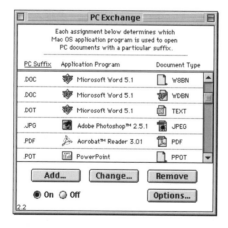

Figure 4.1 PC Exchange in Mac OS 8.1 and earlier

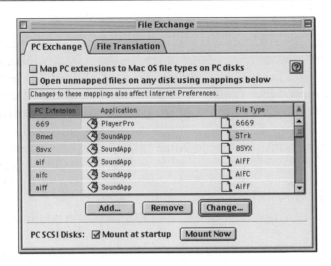

Figure 4.2 PC Exchange tab in the File Exchange control panel of Mac OS 8.5

In Mac OS 8.5, PC Exchange was combined with the Mac OS Easy Open control panel into a single control panel called File Exchange. PC Exchange is now available as the PC Exchange tab in the File Exchange control panel (Figure 4-2). At this time, Apple added the Mount Now button. You can use this button to help mount a disk that is having trouble showing up on the desktop. Another feature is that you can now script File Exchange using AppleScript.

Throughout the rest of this chapter, you'll see references to different versions of PC Exchange and their capabilities. You can usually run any version of PC Exchange in any Mac OS. You can upgrade PC Exchange just by dragging the newer version to the System folder. However, the File Exchange control panel won't run in versions of Mac OS before 8.5.

DOS Mounter

Before there was PC Exchange, there was DOS Mounter, the first utility to enable the Mac to mount floppy disks in the Finder. The original program is still around in the form of DOS Mounter 98 from Software Architects (http://www.softarch.com/). DOS Mounter 98 still does a few things PC Exchange does not. In addition to mounting PC floppies and any PC SCSI media, it lets you view both the full Windows 95 file name and the 8.3 DOS file name.

Mounting PC Storage Devices with PC Exchange

When PC Exchange is installed and turned on, it will load a driver into RAM for a PC floppy or removable SCSI or USB disk you insert, or for a PC SCSI hard drive connected. (CD-ROM disks are treated separately; see later section.) The PC disk will appear on the Finder desktop with an icon identifying it as originating from a PC:

You can drag and drop Mac and PC files between the PC disk and any Mac volume.

The files on a mounted Windows disk will each be represented by a generic PC icon (Figure 4.3), unless you have specified an application and its icon to open the file. You configure this in the PC Exchange control panel. (This is called extension mapping, a feature discussed in Chapter 5.) PC Exchange gives files with the generic PC icon a Mac type code of TEXT and a Mac creator code of dose, regardless of the type of file. (Chapter 5 goes into detail about Macintosh type and creator codes.)

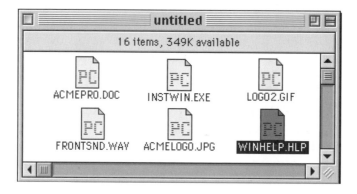

Figure 4.3 PC files on a PC disk mounted in the Finder

MacWindows Tip

When you insert a locked PC floppy diskette containing non-U.S. English characters in the names of files and folders or in the diskette name, the disk won't mount. Instead, you get the error message: "This action could not be completed because the file could not be found." The message is in English, even when you run a non-English version of Mac OS.

The solution is to unlock the disk and reinsert it. When non-U.S. English characters (those ASCII values above X'7F') are used in the names of files, folders or the diskette, PC Exchange needs to write information on the disk in order to mount it. (It builds the invisible files Finder.dat and Desktop, and an invisible Trash folders on the PC floppy.) However, PC Exchange can't write to a locked disk.

Software Architects' DOS Mounter also has this problem, but Insignia's Access PC (discontinued July 1, 1996) did not.

Using and Formatting PC Floppies on Macs

Since 1989, the Mac's 3.5-inch floppy drive has had the ability to read, write, and initialize 1.44-MB PC floppies, known as DOS-formatted floppy diskettes. Macs of the past several years also have the ability to recognize Windows 95 1.6-MB floppies.

The Mac floppy drive is known as the SuperDrive or FDHD (pronounced fud-hud), short for floppy drive, high density. The only Mac models that didn't have a SuperDrive were the original Mac 128K, the Mac 512K, the Mac Plus, and older Mac SEs (the SuperDrive was added in the middle of the SE's production run). The iMac, introduced in 1998, is the first model since the SE not to have a FDHD—the iMac and the "blue and white" Power Mac G3 do not contain any floppy drive.

With PC Exchange installed and turned on, you can reformat any 1.44 MB floppy in either Mac or DOS format. To initialize a floppy disk in DOS format, select the disk in the Finder, pull down the Special menu, and choose Erase Disk. Select "DOS 1.4 MB" and click Erase, as shown in Figure 4.4. You can also select "Macintosh 1.4 MB" to reformat a DOS disk as a Macintosh disk. The selection "Pro-DOS 1.4 MB" is a format for the old Apple II machine.

Figure 4.4 Initializing a floppy in PC floppy format

Using 1.6 MB Windows Floppies (DMF) on Macs

Most DOS-formatted floppies hold 1.44 MB, like Mac floppies. However, Windows 95 introduced a new type of floppy: the 1.6 MB Distributed Media Format (DMF) floppy. While the Mac's floppy drive can't format 1.6 MB DMF floppies, it can read and write data to them. You can mount DMF floppies in the Finder if you have PC Exchange 2.0.7 or later installed and turned on.

With versions of PC Exchange earlier than 2.0.7, you can access 1.6 MB floppies only from within applications. If you insert a DMF floppy when the Finder is active, the Finder will ask you if you want to initialized the disk. You should say no, unless you want to completely erase the floppy and turn it into a 1.44 MB floppy.

To get a version of PC Exchange that mounts DMF floppies, you need Mac OS 7.6 or later, which included PC Exchange 2.1.1. Users with earlier versions of Mac OS can mount DMF floppies if they have PC Exchange 2.0.7, which came with Apple's now-discontinued PC Compatibility Card. However, version 2.0.7 does not work on some older Mac models, including the Power Macintosh 7100, 8100, 7300, and many Mac models with 680x0 processors.

MacWindows Tip

You can make a disk image file of any PC floppy with Apple's Disk Copy. However, to make a disk image of a 1.6 MB DMF floppy, you need PC Exchange 2.1.1 and Disk Copy 6.1 or later. (Disk copy is a free download from Apple's support updates web site.)

Corruption of PC Floppy Disks

Can merely reading a floppy disk corrupt the data? It can in this case. Apple reports a problem with the PC Exchange version 2.1.1, which shipped with Mac OS 7.6 through Mac OS 8.0. (It was fixed with File Exchange 2.2 in Mac OS 8.1.) This version has problems reading certain DOS-formatted floppies and, in some cases, can corrupt the data on the disk. The problem causes parts of files to appear garbled.

The problem occurs with floppies formatted on certain PCs that use FAT16 in the floppy's boot records, but which actually contain FAT12 directories. PC Exchange 2.1.1 reads and checks the FAT field, decides that the floppy is of FAT 16 format, and reads the data incorrectly from the clusters on the disk.

The corruption of all the data on the disk can occur when PC Exchange 2.1.1 writes anything to a disk that contains a FAT12 format, but that it thinks is a FAT16 format. Apple reports that merely inserting and browsing the contents of an unlocked DOS formatted disk can corrupt the DOS disk. The Finder can create or update a FINDER.DAT file on an unlocked floppy disk, even when you're just reading the disk.

One way to fix one of these disks is to reformat the PC disk as a Mac-intosh disk, then reformat the disk as a PC disk. The Finder's Erase Disk command (see above) will create a DOS disk that is completely FAT12. As the name implies, this procedure completely erases any data on the disk.

You can "fix" PC Exchange 2.1.1 with Apple's free DOS Format Fixer utility (available at http://swupdates.info.apple.com/cgi-bin/lister.pl?Apple_Support _Area/Apple_Software_Updates/US/Macintosh/Misc/). DOS Format Fixer prevents corruption, but doesn't fix corrupted disks.

It's better just to get another version of PC Exchange. In addition to upgrading to at least PC Exchange 2.2, you could also downgrade your version of PC Exchange to 2.0.7 and earlier. These versions ignore the field in the boot record. However, if you are going to con-tinue to use PC Exchange 2.1.1, it's a good idea to set the tab lock to write-protected on PC floppies before inserting them into Macs, in order to prevent loss of data.

Using Windows SCSI and USB Drives on Macs

When you connect PC-formatted hard drives and removable storage drives to a Mac's SCSI port, PC Exchange will be able to recognize them as long as you turn them on before starting up the Mac. For removable storage, the cartridges need to be ejected before turning on the Mac. (If you leave a PC-formatted cartridge in the drive before starting up, you may get a "Sad Mac" icon at startup time.)

PC Exchange can mount PC SCSI hard drives that use FAT format-ting. Which FAT variant can be mounted depends on the version of PC Exchange, but by version 2.2 (included in Mac OS 8.1), PC Exchange could mount FAT12, FAT16, VFAT, and FAT32 volumes. There currently is no method to mount IDE hard drives in any PC format on a Macintosh, nor is there any way to mount a Windows NT NTFS drive on a Macintosh.

Versions of PC Exchange previous to 2.2 had problems mounting PC formatted 160 MB Quantum hard drives as well as certain Maxtor drives. Version 2.2 fixed these problems.

Volume Size Limitations

PC Exchange versions before 2.2 (from Mac OS 8.1) cannot mount PC volumes larger than 1 GB. Version 2.2 can mount PC volumes up to 4 GB if they are formatted as FAT32 or as DOS FAT. However, PC Exchange still cannot mount FAT16 volumes bigger than 1 GB. If you try to mount a FAT16 volume bigger than 1 GB with PC Exchange 2.2 or later, you'll get the following message:

> PC Exchange cannot mount this volume because its allocation block size is greater than or equal to 32k.

It's not the most meaningful error message for most users.

Mounting PC Removable Cartridges in the Finder

The procedure for mounting removable media in PC formats on a Macintosh can vary, depending on which drive technology you are using and whether you are using PC Exchange or Software Architect's DOS Mounter.

PC Exchange will mount DOS-formatted Zip or Jaz media using the Iomega Driver extension file that came with the drive. You won't have to do anything differently when using PC-formatted cartridges than you would for Mac cartridges. The Zip or Jaz extension file will load a driver for PC-formatted cartridges. (Because the Zip driver is aware of and works with PC Exchange, the Zip drive is not included in the list of drives when you press PC Exchange's Option button.) However, PC Exchange must be installed and turned on in order to mount DOS-formatted Zip or Jaz media.

For non-Zip removable media drives (such as Syquest or magneto optical), don't use the device driver that came with the drive when using PC disk media. If you've been using the drive for Mac cartridges, you'll need to disable the driver extension file by turning it off in the Extensions control panel, or by removing it from the Extensions folder in the System folder. Next, open the PC Exchange control panel, click Options, select the SCSI or USB device from the list (as shown in Figure 4.5), and restart your Mac. During startup, PC Exchange will load its own device driver for that SCSI device.

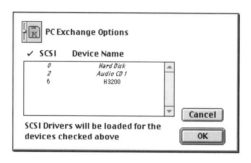

Figure 4.5 The Options dialog box of the PC Exchange control panel

In Mac OS 8.5, the Options button was removed. If you don't want to use the device driver, you can shut off its extension in the Extensions Manager control panel.

If you replace the PC Exchange control panel with the more full-featured DOS Mounter from Software Architects, the procedure is different for Zip and Jaz drives. With DOS Mounter 95 installed, you must remove the Iomega driver when using either DOS or Mac or DOS Zip or Jaz cartridges. DOS Mounter's MultiMounter extension will supply the device driver.

PC Exchange 2.2 improved support for removable media, such as Jaz, Zip, and magneto-optical, in that these cartridges can mount with less trouble. It also fixed problems with mounting Pinnacle's magneto-optical DOS-formatted cartridges.

PC Exchange will also eject a Mac-formatted Zip cartridge if it has bad formatting. You may or may not get a warning message. To reformat the disk as a Mac (HFS) disk, you'll have to first turn PC Exchange off before using the Zip formatting tools. In the Zip Tools program, use Erase Disk with Surface Verify.

NOTE: A damaged DOS-formatted disk may be unreadable. Never try to repair a DOS-formatted disk with a Macintosh disk repair program, or you may destroy information on the disk. Repair DOS-formatted disks on Windows using SCANDISK or other PC disk repair program. You can do this on a PC, or from a Mac running a Windows emulator or coprocessor board (see Chapter 16).

Mounting Multiple-Partition Cross-Platform Disks

PC Exchange can mount SCSI or USB disks containing multiple partitions. PC Exchange will mount each Mac or DOS-formatted partition as a separate volume on the desktop.

However, PC Exchange may not be able to recognize the PC-formatted partitions of a multiple-partition disk if the disk was originally formatted as a Macintosh volume. This is caused by residual Macintosh boot block information remaining on the drive after the PC partitions were created. PC Exchange sees this Mac boot block information and assumes the entire disk is Macintosh-formatted, ignoring the PC partitions.

You can prevent this problem from occurring when you create a multiple partition drive from a Mac formatted drive. First, you'll need to erase the Mac boot block information by doing a low-level format of the Mac disk with a DOS or Windows utility. You can then add a non-Mac partition.

You can use the DOS FDISK utility, but simply creating a new partition does not erase the Mac boot block info. You need to use an undocumented FDISK command called MBR, which stands for master boot record—another name for the master boot block. This is the first sector of a disk. The FDISK/MBR command recreates the master boot block, deleting the Mac information. At the DOS prompt, the command looks like this:

```
C:\>FDISK /MBR
```

Microsoft warns that this utility should not be used on disks with more than four partitions, as it can erase some of the partition information. The FDISK /MBR command will also make a disk unusable if the disk has been partitioned using the Storage Dimensions Speed-Stor utility with its /Bootall option.

Formatting PC SCSI or USB Disks

Both Windows and Mac OS have the ability to format SCSI or USB disk in a DOS FAT format (assuming the machines have SCSI or USB ports or adapters). Windows doesn't necessarily mean PC here, as you can format FAT partitions from a PC emulator on a Mac. We'll first look at this process on the Mac, and then on Windows.

FAT Formatting in Mac OS

To format FAT partitions on non-floppy media on a Mac, you'll need a third-party utility. The Mac's PC Exchange can't create or reformat DOS partitions and does not let you reformat Mac partitions as DOS partitions. You can, however, erase existing DOS partitions mounted on the desktop. To do this, select the DOS volume mounted on the Finder's desktop and choose Erase Disk from the Special menu. You'll notice that you don't have the option to create a Mac volume, as you do with floppy diskettes. (See Figure 4.6.)

Several Macintosh disk utilities are available that let you format and partition FAT volumes. Software Architect's DOS Mounter comes

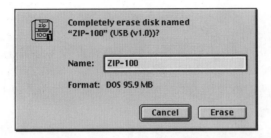

Figure 4.6 Unlike with floppies, the Finder's Erase command won't reformat FAT-formatted SCSI or USB media as a Mac disk.

with a utility called MultiFormatter that not only can format DOS partitions, but can create both Mac and DOS partitions on a single SCSI disk.

Software Architect's Formatter Five goes even further and can format SCSI drives in FAT, HFS, and UDF formats. It can test and verify the media. Formatter Five also includes the mounting ability of DOS Mounter.

For Zip and Jaz media, you can use Iomega's Tools utility to reformat a FAT-formatted cartridge in Mac format and to reformat any Zip or Jaz in FAT format.

FAT Formatting in Windows

Of course, you can also format a SCSI hard drive or removable cartridge on a Windows machine with a SCSI adapter board. (For USB, you need Windows 95 OSR2 or Windows 98.) But you can also do this from within a Windows emulator or coprocessor card running on a Mac. (See Chapter 16.) You can use the standard DOS FDISK (short for Fixed Disk Setup) utility to remove or create the partition.

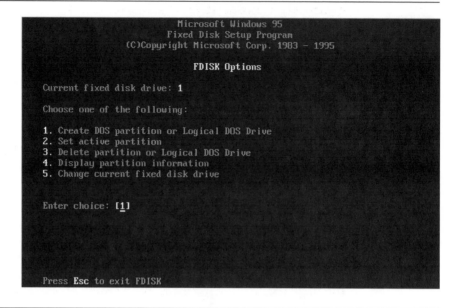

Figure 4.7 The DOS FDISK utility to create a partition

To access the utility, type FDISK at the DOS command prompt. Next, you'll have to select the drive you want to work on by selecting Option 5 (see Figure 4.7). If you only have one partition on the disk, and you only want one partition, you have to delete the existing primary partition before adding a new one by using option 3. After you reboot, you'll need to format the partition using the DOS FORMAT command to format a hard drive. Instead of FORMAT, you can also use the drive setup and partitioning software that may have come with the PC's SCSI controller board.

When initializing and formatting a removable SCSI cartridge on a PC, such as a Zip disk, you should not use the DOS FDISK command. Instead, use the disk preparation utilities that came with the removable drive or the SCSI controller board. (If you don't completely erase a cartridge that was originally formatted as a Macintosh volume, PC Exchange may not recognize it. This problem was discussed earlier in the section called Mounting Multiple-Partition Disks.) You also can use the DOS FORMAT command.

If you are using Windows NT and are formatting a disk for use on a Mac, remember to format in FAT, since PC Exchange can't mount NTFS volumes.

Using PC SCSI Devices with x86 Coprocessor Cards

When running Windows on a Mac through the use of an x86-based coprocessor card (described in Chapter 16), it is sometimes useful to connect PC-formatted SCSI devices to the Mac in order to make them available to Windows. If you want to use the SCSI drive as the Windows C: or D: drive, you'll need to prevent PC Exchange from loading the driver for this drive. Otherwise, PC Exchange will mount the drive in the Finder, making it unavailable to the coprocessor card.

To prevent PC Exchange from loading a driver, open the PC Exchange control panel and click the Options button. Make sure the SCSI driver for the device is unchecked, then click OK. If you have Mac OS 8.5 or later, you'll have to turn the File Exchange control panel off in the Extensions Manager; the Options button is no longer available. (In OS 8.5 and later, PC Exchange is a tab in the File Exchange control panel.) Software Architect's DOS Mounter does not work with Apple DOS or PC Compatibility cards, or with Reply cards. It does work with Orange PC cards from Orange Micro.

Reading PC CD-ROM and DVD-ROM Disks on Macs

Mac OS has the ability to mount DOS and Windows CD-ROM disks on the Finder's Desktop, but PC Exchange doesn't play a role here. Instead, there are a set of extension files in the System folder:

 Apple CD-ROM (or Apple CD/DVD if you have a DVD-ROM drive instead of a CD-ROM drive)

Apple Photo Access (if you plan to use PhotoCD formatted files)

 Audio CD Access

 Foreign File Access

 High Sierra File Access

 ISO 9660 File Access

UDF Volume Access (Mac OS 8.1 and later)

Most Windows CDs use the ISO 9660 format. In order to mount these on the Finder desktop, you need at least the Apple CD-ROM, Foreign File Access, and ISO 9660 File Access extension files in the System folder. Turning these extensions off in the Extensions Manager control panel disables the Mac's ability to read most PC CD-ROMs.

The High Sierra File Access file enables the Mac to mount CDs in High Sierra format, an older version of ISO 9660. Apple Photo Access is required to mount the CDs in the Kodak Photo CD format. The Audio CD Access file enables the Mac to mount and play audio CDs. The UDF Volume Access file enables access to UDF-formatted DVD and CDs. The Foreign File Access file is also required to mount any of these formats, as well as the ISO 9660 format, as it converts calls from Mac OS to non-HFS CD discs.

As with other types of disks, reading a Windows CD-ROM doesn't necessarily mean you can open the files on the disk, play PC games, or use Windows software. The ability to mount Windows CD-ROMs is useful only if:

   ♦ Your Mac applications can read the Windows files on the CD-ROM, or
   ♦ You can convert the files to Mac format with MacLinkPlus, QuickTime, or other translation software, or
   ♦ You can run Windows using an emulator or coprocessor card

Known Problems with ISO 9660 CD-ROMs

It's likely you'll run into dual-format, dual-partition CD-ROMs, which have both Mac HFS and ISO 9660 information. A problem with older versions of Apple CD-ROM driver software prevented the Windows partition from mounting on the desktop, with only the Mac partition being mounted. This problem was fixed in 1996 with version 5.1.5 of the Apple CD-ROM software.

A more recent ISO 9660 problem occurs with QuickTime 2.5 when it's run with Mac OS 8.0 or Mac OS 8.1, both systems that shipped with this version of QuickTime. A bug in QuickTime 2.5 causes the Mac to crash when you try to play QuickTime movies from an ISO 9660 CD-ROM. You can avoid a crash if you copy the QuickTime movies to your hard drive. However, the better solution for Mac OS 8 or 8.1 users is to upgrade to QuickTime 3, which fixed the bug.

Using DOS-Formatted PCMCIA Cards in PowerBooks

The credit-card-sized PC Cards (also know as PCMCIA cards) used in laptops come in all kinds of functional types, including data storage. Mac PowerBooks can use DOS-formatted PC Cards. In fact, most storage PC Cards come preformatted as DOS volumes. The PC Exchange control panel version 2.0.2 or greater (included with System 7.5 and later) enables most PowerBooks to mount these volumes. (These models include the 190 500, 5300, 2400, 3400, and all of the PowerBook G3 models.) As with disk media, PC Exchange enables the PowerBook to write and read to data and from the DOS-formatted PC card, as well as delete files.

Reformatting a Storage PC Card

A Mac can't reformat a Mac PC Card as a DOS/Windows volume, but it can reformat a DOS/Windows PC Card as a Macintosh volume.

To do this, you must first eject the PC Card. Then turn off PC Exchange. Then open the PC Exchange control panel and select the

Off option. In Mac OS 8.5, PC Exchange (the tab in the File Exchange control panel) no longer has an Off button. You'll have to turn File Exchange off using the Extensions Manager control panel, and restart.

To format, insert the PC card. A message will ask you if you want to reformat the PC card as a Macintosh volume. Click Initialize.

Once the PC card is reformatted, you can turn PC Exchange back on by opening the PC Exchange control panel and selecting the On option.

Using Macintosh Disks on Windows PCs

Windows doesn't have built-in Macintosh disk compatibility, but third-party products can enable Windows users to work with Mac disks. These software utilities can read Mac CD-ROMs and read and write Mac floppies and SCSI drives, including Zip, Syquest, magneto optical, and hard drives.

The best products integrate the use of Macintosh disks into the Windows user interface, allowing Windows users to access Mac disks from the Open dialog boxes of applications, the Windows Explorer, the My Computer icon, and the ordinary places from which disks are accessed. Here are just a few of the products available.

Web Update Link: *For a complete and current list of products that enable Windows PCs to use Mac disks (with links to manufacturers' web sites), see http://www.macwindows.com/disks.html.*

MacDrive98

Media4 Productions
2800 University Avenue, Suite H1B-101 West
Des Moines, Iowa 50266-12585

800-528-7440
http://www.media4.com/

MacDrive98 integrates with Windows 95, Windows 98, and Windows NT (both Intel and Alpha versions), so that Windows users can access Mac disks of all types from the desktop, the Explorer and from any software. MacDrive can read, write, and format Mac disks, as well as decode MacBinary (.bin) and BinHex (.hqx) files. It enables Windows to use Macintosh floppies, external SCSI drives, and removable media on a SCSI bus or parallel-port, including Zip, Jaz, Bernoulli, Syquest, magneto optical and CD-ROM. MacDrive98 also works with Macintosh multisession CD-R or dual-format disk.

MacOpener

DataViz
55 Corporate Drive
Trumbull, CT 06611
800-733-0030
203-268-0030
http://www.dataviz.com

MacOpener is from the same company that produces the MacLinkPlus file translators that once came with Mac OS (see Chapter 5). MacOpener is integrated with Windows 95 and Windows NT, so that Windows users can access Mac disks wherever they access PC disks. It also lets you preview Mac text and graphic files before you open them. MacOpener supports Mac floppies, CD-ROMs, and any SCSI media.

Here and Now

Software Architects
19102 North Creek Parkway, Suite 101
Bothell, WA 98011
425-487-0122
http://www.softarch.com

One of the oldest of the Mac disk mounters for Windows, Here and Now is basically a Windows version of DOS Mounter on the Mac side. It is integrated with Windows 95, so that Windows users can access Mac disks wherever they access PC disks. Here and Now works with Mac floppies and CD-ROMs and any SCSI media, including hard drives and phase-change disks. It presents full Mac file names in Windows 95 without truncation and will add the appropriate Mac Type and Creator codes to Mac files. Here and Now is available for DOS, Windows 3.1, and Windows 95/98.

Just the First Step

Of course, just because you can get a foreign disk onto your machine doesn't guarantee that you'll be able to use the files on it. You might have to first decompress it or combine segments from multiple disks. This will be discussed in Chapter 6.

You then might need a way to open the files. PC Exchange can also help guide you to a Mac application that can open your PC files. The next chapter, Working with Foreign Files, will tell you how you can open and edit foreign files on both Macs and Windows PCs.

Chapter

What's in This Chapter:

- ♦ *Viewing Windows long file names on Macs*

- ♦ *Working with Mac files on Windows:*
  Mac type and creator codes

- ♦ *Opening Windows files on Macintosh*

- ♦ *Translating files*

- ♦ *Using fonts with Macs and PCs*

5

Working with Foreign Files

Foreign files can arrive on your hard drive through a variety of methods—from a disk cartridge, the local file server, e-mail, or U.S. mail in the form of a CD-ROM. The objective now is to make use of these files—open them, read them, edit them, and perhaps save them in a foreign format.

Some applications use file formats that are cross-platform. For example, Word for Windows can open Word for Mac files, and PageMaker running either platform can read PageMaker files created on the other platform—provided you have the correct versions running on each platform. Other applications, such as Adobe Photoshop, Equilibrium DeBabelizer, and AppleWorks (formerly ClarisWorks), can open and sometimes save documents in a variety of Macintosh and Windows formats.

73

If none of your applications can correctly read the foreign file, you may be able convert it to a format you can use with file translation software. Mac OS comes with file translation software that converts between Windows and Mac file formats, and you can augment these tools with products that focus on graphics and multimedia formats. Windows users can buy third-party file translation software to do the same on PCs. Some companies, including Microsoft, provide utilities (sometimes called *filters*) that can translate between two specific formats.

If no translation solution exists, Mac users have the option of running Windows software on a Macintosh through the use of a software emulator or an x86 coprocessor card. These solutions are discussed in Chapter 16.

This chapter deals with issues of files as they exist in their uncompressed form. Chapter 6 covers issues concerning the use of compression and encoding in cross-platform environments.

Web Update Link: *For the latest product information about the topics covered in this chapter, check http://www.macwindows.com/filetran.html.*

Differences: Macintosh and Windows Files

Although some software manufacturers use the same file format in the Macintosh and Windows versions of their applications, the files on the two platforms still differ in several other ways. The most obvious difference is the file naming conventions that Mac OS and Windows use. File names on Macintosh and Windows differ in two ways: the characters that you are allowed to use in a file name, and the maximum number of characters in the name. The Macintosh PC Exchange control panel (part of the File Exchange control panel in OS 8.5 and later) is one tool that can work with the differences in file names in Mac OS and Windows. There are also converter utilities that can fix naming problems. These are discussed later in the chapter.

But Macintosh and Windows files differ on a deeper level as well. Mac files consist of two parts, a data fork and a resource fork. Windows files are "flat," in that they don't have two forks. When a Mac file is moved to Windows, the resource fork is often lost. Mac application files keep much of their important information in the resource fork. For Mac data files, much of the resource fork is empty, but other information about the file is lost, including the *type* and *creator codes*. These codes tell Mac OS what type of file it is, what application created it, and what icon it should have.

There's also a difference in the way the operating systems use text, which can sometimes cause problems with sending e-mail and when editing HTML code created on another platform. Mac OS and Windows use the same 128 ASCII characters, called the "lower ASCII." These include the roman alphabet, numbers, and punctuation marks. Problems occur with the so-called upper 128 ASCII—characters with accents, markings, and special characters—which can differ between Mac and Windows. When one of the upper 128 ASCII characters is used, it can appear as a box or blank space on another platform. Windows and Macs also use different a ASCII character to indicate the end of a line of text. Macs use a carriage return (CR), while PCs and UNIX use a line feed (LF).

You can fix these types of problems manually with a word processor, or automatically with a file translators (discussed later in the chapter). You can also use text editing utilities, such as the shareware ASCII Converter (http://www.geocities.com/SiliconValley/Network/7185/software.html). More are listed at:

http://www.macwindows.com/filetran.html#filetools.

I'll start by discussing file names conventions and solutions. We'll then dive in into the intricacies of type and creator codes.

Viewing Windows Long File Names on Macs

The DOS naming convention consists of a maximum of 8 characters followed by a dot and the 3-character extension. The "8.3" file names are required in DOS, in Windows 3.1, and in Windows NT before version 4, but are commonly used by users of all versions of Windows.

Windows 95 introduced the so-called long file name, which can have up to 253 characters. Long file names are also used in Windows 98 and in NT 4 and later. When you view a Windows 95 file with a long name in DOS, you'll see an 8.3 version of it. That's because Windows 95 and 98 store two versions of a file name, a long file name and a truncated version that Windows creates. The truncated version automatically includes the 3-character extension indicating the type of file and application that created it. Spaces are removed, and the first 8 characters end in a tilde (~) indicating that characters have been removed, followed by a 1 (or 2 or 3 if other files begin with the same first 6 char-

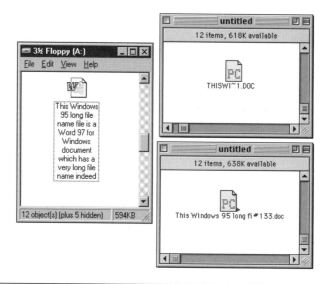

Figure 5.1 A Windows 95 long file name (left) is truncated to 8.3 in Mac OS 8.0 or earlier (upper right), but is truncated to 31 characters in OS 8.1 (lower right).

acters). For example, a Word file called "My mother's favorite cookie recipes" in Windows 95 appears as "MYMOTH~1.DOC" in DOS.

Since Mac OS only permits 31 characters in a file name, PC Exchange does a similar truncation when you bring Windows 95/98/NT files or folders with long file names to the Mac on a disk. In Mac OS 8.0 or earlier, PC Exchange truncates a Windows long file name in the same way that Windows does for DOS, so "My mother's favorite cookie recipes" appears as "MYMOTH~1.DOC" in the Finder. In Mac OS 8.1 and later, PC Exchange truncates the long file name to 31 characters, using a pound sign (#) to indicate that characters have been removed, followed by a unique number to prevent duplicate file names. Our Word for Windows file appears as "My mother's favorite cookie#133" in Mac OS 8.1. You can see another example in Figure 5.1.

Just as in Windows, the Mac's PC Exchange software doesn't permanently alter the file name, but stores two copies, this time for display in Windows 95 and Macintosh. If you are using Software Architects' DOS Mounter 95 to mount a PC disk on a Mac, you can see the entire 253-character Windows 95/98 file name. In the Finder, DOS Mounter 95 also shortens the name to 31 characters, but you can view a file's Windows 95 long name and DOS 8.3 name by opening the DOS Mounter 95 control panel and dragging your file to the File Information icon. (See Chapter 4 for more on DOS Mounter.)

Windows 95/98 Long File Names on CD-ROM

The original ISO 9660 CD-ROM format standard supports only file names in the DOS 8.3 format. (For more on ISO 9660, see Chapter 4.) Microsoft expanded ISO 9660 to add limited support for Windows 95 long file names. These extensions are called Romeo and Joliet. Romeo uses file names of up to 64 characters. Joliet stores two sets of file names, one in DOS 8.3 format, and another using the first 32 characters of the Windows 95/98 long file name. The Mac system file responsible for accessing PC CD-ROMs, the Foreign File Access extension, does not recognize these long-file-name additions to ISO 9660. Thus, Macs can only read the 8.3 names of Joliet-formatted CD-ROMs.

Converting Mac File Names to Windows File Names

When Mac users are working with files that will be passed on to Windows users, it's safest to get in the habit of using the DOS 8.3 naming convention for your files. Windows 3.x and earlier require 8.3, and Windows 95, 98, and NT need the three-character extension. Mac users also need to take care not to use characters that are illegal in Windows file names. Mac OS only has one character that cannot be used in a file name—the colon (if you try to type a colon in a file name in the Finder, you get a hyphen.) The illegal DOS and Windows file name characters are as follows:

$$? \quad [\quad] \quad / \quad \backslash \quad = \quad + \quad < \quad > \quad : \quad ; \quad " \quad ,$$

The most common offender is the forward slash, illegal in Windows file names but popular with Macintosh users who like to include a date in the file name, as in *Reports 12/1/98.*

In addition to these illegal characters, there are some further restrictios. For instance, it's not a good idea to use periods other than before the three-character extension. You also don't want to have file names that end in a period or a space. If you move a file like this to a server, the Windows clients won't be able to access the files. Spotting a file name that ends in a space can be tricky to do by eye, but the utilities described on the next page can help check for these problems.

If you are moving Mac files to Windows PCs using a disk, PC Exchange can help with file names. When you copy a file to a PC disk mounted on the Finder, PC Exchange strips out characters that are illegal in PC names and replaces them with underscores. It also deletes spaces or periods at the end of file names.

However, if you are moving files from Macs to PCs over a network or the Internet, PC Exchange does not intervene. Manually checking and editing a few file names isn't too much trouble, but when you're moving dozens or hundreds of files to PCs, you can save a lot of time by using a utility to do this for you.

NameCleaner

Sig Software
http://www.sigsoftware.com/

NameCleaner is a Macintosh utility can manipulate file names for
DOS, Windows, UNIX, NetWare, and other foreign file systems. It
can add Macintosh type/creator codes to files with definable
PC/UNIX extensions. NameCleaner can remove nonviewable characters, such as "smart" quotes, and pad out punctuation marks. It also
lets you append information (size, date, and type) about individual
files and apply a dictionary for type phrases. (You'll find NameCleaner on the CD-ROM included with this book.)

Drop Rename

Chaotic Software
http://www.chaoticsoftware.com/

Drop Rename performs many different types of renaming operations
on files and folders. It lets you create custom self-running scripts called
"Renamelets" to change names to DOS/Windows formats. The scripts
can include conditional renaming (if–then procedures), wild card
search and remove, file numbering, and more.

A Better Finder Rename

Frank Reiff
http://www.publicspace.net/ABetterFinderRename/

A Better Finder Rename is a low-cost shareware utility that can
remove illegal Windows characters from file names. It is implemented
as a contextual menu plug-in for the Macintosh Finder (Mac 8.0 and
later) and lets you rename batches of files at once. With A Better Finder Rename, you can do a search and replace on file names, but the utility won't recognize illegal characters—you have to know what to
search for.

Web Update Link: *For the latest web links and product information about these and other file name converters, check
http://www.macwindows.com/filetran.html#filetools.*

Opening Windows Files on Macintosh

Both Mac OS and Windows will launch a platform-specific application when you double-click on a data file icon. However, the two operating systems use different methods to identify which application should be launched. Windows looks in part at the file name, specifically at the three characters after the dot, called the file name extension. (The file name extension is often not displayed in Windows, but you can see the full file names with extensions in DOS.) Microsoft Word for Windows files, for instance, use the .DOC file name extension. In Windows 95 and 98, changing the name of a text file by ending it in *.DOC* will give it a Word 97 icon, and double-clicking it will launch Word.

NOTE: You can only open foreign data files, not applications or other programs. If a Windows file ends in .EXE, it is a program. (EXE stands for executable.) You can only run a Windows program on a Mac with PC emulation software or a coprocessor card, described in Chapter 16. Similarly, Windows can't open Mac applications without a Mac emulator.

By contrast, Mac OS completely ignores the file name. It instead uses a file's four-character type and creator codes to launch an application when the file is double-clicked. The creator code (FMP3 for FileMaker Pro 3.0, for example) tells the Mac which application to open when you double-click on the file. The Mac type code designates the format of the file. This can be a generic format standard, such as TEXT or PICT, or an application-specific format such as CWWP for a ClarisWorks word processing file. Files that are applications have the type code APPL. (Other codes are displayed in Table 5.1.)

generic file

Together, the type and creator codes also tell the Finder what icon to display for the file. If the application indicated by the creator code is not installed on the Macintosh, the file will be displayed with a generic icon.

Table 5.1 Macintosh creator and type codes for common applications and files. Codes are case sensitive.

Application	Creator code
Adobe Acrobat	CARO
Adobe Illustrator 6	ART5
Adobe Photoshop	8BIM
ClarisWorks	BOBO
FileMaker Pro 4	FMP4
Home Page	BlWd
Microsoft Excel	XCEL
Microsoft Word	MSWD
Now Contact	NIC!
Quark XPress 3.x	XPR3
SimpleText	ttxt

File format	Type code
Application file	APPL
ClarisWorks word processing	CWWP
Excel 5 worksheet	XLS5
GIF	GIFf
HTML	TEXT
PICT	PICT
Quark XPress document	XDOC
JPEG	JPEG
Text	TEXT
TIFF	TIFF
Word 6 document	W6BN
Word 8 document	W8BN

Windows and DOS files that you bring to a Mac have either no type and creator codes or codes that are garbled. These files will have a generic icon. This means that at first, Mac OS won't know what to do with a Windows file when you double-click on it, even if it is a file that your Mac applications can read.

MacWindows Tip

Although you can see the full names of PC files from within DOS, Windows often hides the file name extension. You can configure the Windows Explorer to show the extensions in any Explorer view. Open Windows Explorer, select the View menu, click Options, and unclick the option called "Hide MS-DOS file extensions for file types that are registered."

There are three ways to deal with files with no or unrecognizable type and creator codes. You can change the codes manually. You can set up PC Exchange to automatically add type and creator codes based on the three-character extension of the file name. And you can use the Mac OS Easy Open control panel in Mac OS 8.1 and earlier, and the File Translation tab of the File Exchange control panel in Mac OS 8.5 and later. Mac OS Easy Open is also discussed later in this chapter. We'll first consider changing type and creator codes yourself.

Viewing and Editing the Type and Creator Codes

Here's a typical scenario: Someone sent you a Quark Xpress file, but Quark didn't recognize it. Not only that, but your fancy utilities don't recognize it either. You might think it's time to throw the file away, but taking two minutes to change the type and creator codes of the file can render it complete usable.

In an integrated Macintosh–Windows environment, Mac users can make much better use of files that originated on Windows machines if they know how to view or change the type and creator codes of the files. Sometimes simply adding a type code can change a file from a garble of ASCII characters into an editable text or graphic file. (Other times you might need to decode or decompress a file, as discussed in Chapter 6.)

Type and creator codes are normally invisible, but you can see them with a number of utilities, including the Finder's own Find File or Sherlock, as well as with the MacLinkPlus File View utility that came with Mac OS until mid-1998.

To change the type and creator codes of a file, you can use ResEdit (freeware from Apple), Norton Utilities' Fast Find, and BBEdit. MacLinkPlus 10 will change type and creator codes automatically.

Keep in mind that type and creator codes are case-sensitive. When adding a code, you must correctly use upper- or lowercase, or the code won't work.

Viewing File Codes with Find File

Viewing a file's type and creator codes with Find File or Sherlock is a quick and easy first step when you receive a file that nothing will open. Figure 5.2 shows Find File, but the procedure is the same in Sherlock:

1. From the Finder, hit Command-F.
2. In the pop-up menu, choose File Type.
3. Click More Choices and choose Creator in the next pop-up menu.
4. Simply drag and drop the file you want to learn about to the Find File Window. The type and creator codes will appear.

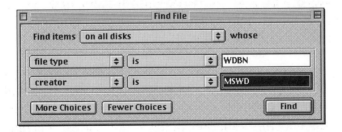

Figure 5.2 Viewing a file's type and creator codes in Find File

Viewing File Codes with DataViz FileView

It's even easier to look at the codes with FileView, the DataViz utility that came with the Mac OS CD-ROM before July of 1998, when Apple stopped bundling MacLinkPlus. FileView is installed with MacLinkPlus and is located in the MacLinkPlus folder. To check a file's type and creator, simple drag and drop the file on top of the DataViz FileView icon. The window that opens will display the type and creator codes in the upper right. As with Find File, FileView can only display a file's type and creator codes; it can't alter them.

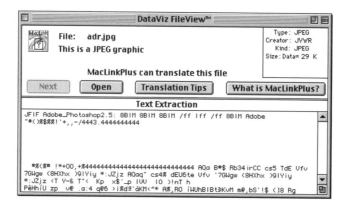

Figure 5.3 FileView displays type and creator in the upper right.

Viewing and Editing File Codes with MacLinkPlus 10

With DataViz' MacLinkPlus 10 and later (a separate product not bundled with Mac OS), FileView functionality has been rolled into the MacLinkPlus utility. Not only does it let you view the type and creator, but MacLinkPlus 10 can look inside the file, determine what the correct codes should be, and reset the codes to the correct codes when you click a button.

You can drag and drop a file on top of the MacLinkPlus icon in the Finder, or launch the utility and drag one or more files into the utility window from the Finder. MacLinkPlus will display the type and creator codes on the lower right (see Figure 5.4) and will tell you if they aren't correct. Click the Fix button to have MacLinkPlus reset the codes.

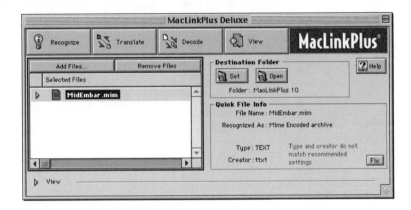

Figure 5.4 MacLinkPlus 10 can determine when a file has incorrect Mac type and creator codes.

Although MacLinkPlus 10 makes good guesses, it isn't always correct. If it doesn't get it right, or you know what the type and creator codes should be, you can manually set the codes. Go to the File menu and select "Set Type and Creator." The following window appears:

Figure 5.5 Editing type and creator codes with MacLinkPlus 10

Viewing and Editing Type Codes with Norton Utilities

You can also change the file codes with a copy of Norton Utilities from Symantec. The utility to use is Fast Find, located in the Norton Tools folder of the Norton Utilities folder.

1.   Drag and drop your file to the Fast Finder icon in the Finder.
2.   In the file window, click on your file (see Figure 5.6).

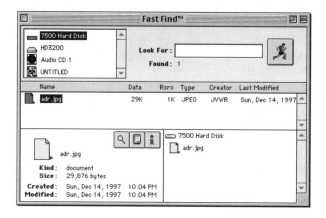

Figure 5.6 Selecting a file to edit in Norton Utility's Fast Find

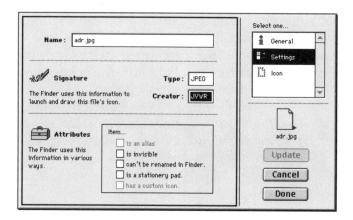

Figure 5.7 Entering new type and creator codes with Norton Fast Find

3. Click on the "i" (for information) icon.
4. In the new window that appears, click on the word Settings in the upper right (see Figure 5.7).
5. The type and creator fields will appear. You can type in the desired type and creator codes. Save and quit.

MacWindows Tip

Need to change codes by the batch? The shareware utility Mini Conversion by Tom Riley (http://members.xoom.com/tsha/tom/) can add type and creator codes of groups of files. Windows files moving to Mac often have no type and creator code, or often non-useful type and creator codes. Mini Conversion presents you with multiple windows (called pads*) onto which files can be dropped and changed. Mini Conversion can also make files invisible, stationery, or name locked.*

Editing Type Codes with ResEdit

Apple's free ResEdit utility (http://swupdates.info.apple.com/) has the reputation of being a dangerous tool in the hands of the non-programmer. This is because ResEdit opens up a file's resources; accidentally deleting or changing a resource can damage the file. However, the ResEdit window you use to access the type and creator codes is safe for anyone, since it doesn't give you access to anything that could seriously damage a file.

1. Open ResEdit. If an open dialog box appears asking you to choose a file to open, close it.
2. Go to ResEdit's Edit menu and open Get File/Folder Info. Select your file from the dialog box that appears.
3. Enter the appropriate type and creator codes in the fields at the top of the window that appears (see Figure 5.8). Save and quite ResEdit.

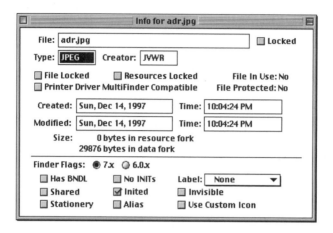

Figure 5.8 Changing a file's type and creator codes in ResEdit

Extension Mapping with PC Exchange

Editing the type and creator codes can turn a mystery file into something you can deal with, as well as launch a Mac application when you double-click it. Fortunately, this doesn't mean you need to manually add type and creator codes for every file you receive from a Windows user. As I mentioned earlier, Mac OS has two pieces of software that will help you with double-clicking a foreign file. In Mac OS 8.5, both are represented in the File Exchange control panel as two tabs: PC Exchange and File Translation. Before Mac OS 8.5, they were two separate control panels, PC Exchange and Mac Easy Open, and had fewer features. I'll discuss PC Exchange in this section, and Mac Easy Open/File Translation in the next.

PC Exchange uses a technique called extension mapping to specify an application to open when you double-click a Windows file. PC Exchange lets you specify Mac type and creator codes that will be given to Windows files based on the 3-character extension in the file name. It also comes with preset mappings, which you can alter. Figure 5.9 shows PC Exchange (pre–OS 8.5) configured to assign Mac applications to open several types of text, graphics, and sound files. Figure 5.10 shows the Mac OS 8.5 version.

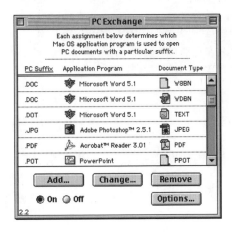

Figure 5.9 Extension mapping in PC Exchange

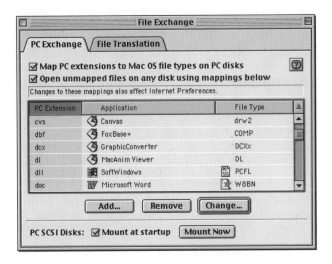

Figure 5.10 In Mac OS 8.5, PC Exchange is part of the File Exchange control panel and offers more options.

There are several limitations to PC Exchange you should be aware of:

◆ In versions before Mac OS 8.5, PC Exchange only works with files on PC disks—not for files received from e-mail, from the Internet, or from a LAN. Starting with Mac OS 8.5, you have the option of enabling PC Exchange to open a file. You need to check the box labeled "Open unmapped files on any disk using mappings below" (see Figure 5.10).

◆ PC Exchange does not translate files. Your application needs to know how to open the file you are mapping.

◆ Extension mapping does not consider the type and creator codes a file type can have. For instance, mapping a Word file extension, .DOC, to a Photoshop type and creator does not give Photoshop the ability to open a Word file. If you did such a mapping, Photoshop would launch when you double-clicked a .DOC file, but give you an error message.

MacWindows Tip

In versions before Mac OS 8.5, PC Exchange doesn't work for files you've downloaded to your startup hard drive. You can get around this by copying the file to a DOS-formatted floppy or removable cartridge, ejecting the disk, and reinserting it. Copy the file back to your hard disk. The PC file now has the type and creator codes of the application you want to open, as you indicated in the PC Exchange control panel.

The ability to map files on your own hard drive that was added with Mac OS 8.5 is not turned on by default: You need to turn it on yourself. This particular feature of PC Exchange is superseded by Mac OS's QuickTime 3 and later, which has it own method of opening multimedia files called QuickTime Exchange. When you double-click a PC multimedia file on your hard drive that QuickTime recognizes, QuickTime Exchange will take action before PC Exchange does.

QuickTime Exchange is normally turned on, but you can turn it off in the QuickTime Setting control panel (shown in Figure 5.11). You need to click the pop-up menu and select QuickTime Exchange. You might want to turn it off if you are working with a particular type of PC file that you wanted to open in a particular, non-QuickTime-enabled application.

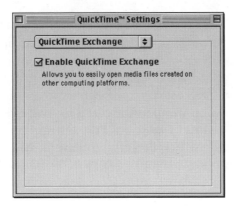

Figure 5.11 QuickTime Exchange acts to open PC multimedia files before PC Exchange.

Another PC Exchange feature that began with Mac OS 8.5 is to have files on PC disks treated as generic text files, but continue to have files on Mac disks (such as your hard drive) opened based on their file extension. In this case, you'd unclick "Map PC extensions to Mac OS File types on PC disks," but click "Open unmapped files on any disk" like this:

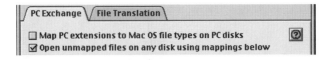

PC Exchange also displays the icon for the select file type that the file will be opened as. If no file type is selected, OS 8.5 displays no icon (Figure 5.10) while earlier versions display a generic icon (Figure 5.9). Mac OS 8.5 also added mappings not only for PC files, but for Mac files as well, including many applications that you probably don't have. These do not have an icon displayed next to the file type. You can change this mapping to an application that is on your hard drive, as discussed in the next section.

Configuring PC Exchange

To configure PC Exchange to recognize a particular file name extension with a particular application, click the Add button. (To edit an existing extension map, just double-click it.) Next, in the field called PC Suffix, type the three-character file name extension you desire and select a Mac application to open the file. This will give the PC file a Mac creator code. You can also select a document type from the pop-up menu, which will give the file a type code and a Macintosh file icon belonging to the application you've selected. (See Figure 5.12.)

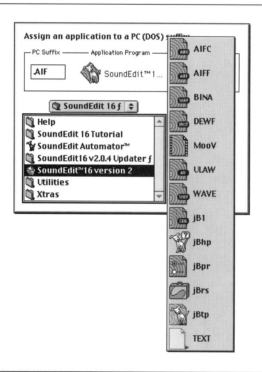

Figure 5.12 The pop-up menu to assign the file type code and icon

These selections are stored in the PC Exchange preference file in the Preference folder in the System folder. Starting with Mac OS 8.1, the system software comes with a preference file that already contains extension mappings, which you can alter to suit your needs using the control panel. You can also move or copy this preference file to other Macs to copy the same extension maps and settings. In Mac OS 8.5 or later, the file is called File Exchange Preferences. Before OS 8.5, it's called PC Exchange Preferences. In both cases, the file resides in Preference folder inside the System folder.

Configuration Options Added in Mac OS 8.5

In OS 8.5 and later, PC Exchange has some additional configuration options, including some Internet features. When you click the Options button in the Change Mapping window (Figure 5.13), the

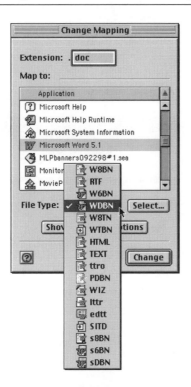

Figure 5.13 Assigning a type code in PC Exchange, Mac OS 8.5 and later

window expands to show new options (Figure 5.14). Some of the new settings allow for the fact that you can now use extension mapping with Mac files, as well as PC files. The Map Outgoing option will assign Mac type and creator codes to a file you are sending or copying. The Data Format options let you select Macintosh if you know the type of file is a Mac file (as it is in the case of Figure 5.14). The Binary Data selection is for when you don't know what format a particular extension represents. The Plain Text option are for text files (including HTML files).

The Handle By pop-up menu tells the Mac how files with a particular extension (in this case .MOV) should be handled by a web browser. The *Processing with Application* selection lets you set which application will open it automatically once it is downloaded. Notice in Figure 5.14 that we have SimpleText as the mapped application on the left, and MoviePlayer selected in the *Handle by* pop-up on the right. That means SimpleText will open .MOV files that come in by disk, and Movie Player will open and play the file when the web browser accesses it, like a web browser plug-in. The *Saving to File* option saves the file to the disk instead of playing it when it is downloaded.

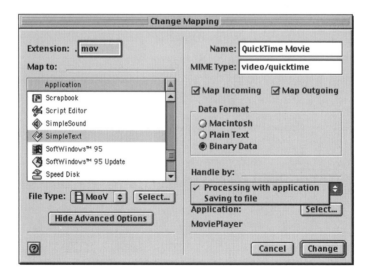

Figure 5.14 PC Exchange configuration options in Mac OS 8.5 and later

Opening PC Files with File Exchange/Mac OS Easy Open

The other way Mac OS helps you find a Mac application to open a DOS, Windows, or Mac file when you double-click it is with the File Translation tab of the File Exchange control panel. Before Mac OS, this was called Mac Easy Open and was a separate control panel. Both versions share many features, but the updated version adds some new capabilities.

In addition to helping you locate an application to open a file, Mac Easy Open and File Translation also helps you select a *translator* to convert the file into a format one of your applications can open. (The next section discusses more about the translators themselves.)

When you double-click on a PC file and you have "Automatic document translation" turned on (in the Mac OS Easy Open control panel or the File Translation tab of the File Exchange control panel), you are presented a list of your applications and translators that can possibly open or convert the PC file (see Figure 5.15). This dialog box comes up when the file you double-click has a creator code that does not match that of any of your applications. You then choose a Mac application to open the file, or choose an application with translation by MacLinkPlus or QuickTime. In the latter case, the translator will create a new file in a converted format before launching the application.

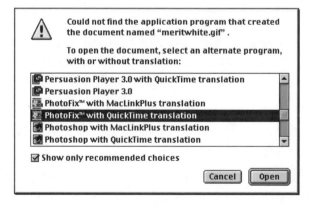

Figure 5.15 Applications and translators appear when you double-click a PC file.

If you click off the "Show only recommended choices" check box, all of your applications will appear—even those that cannot open the file. This is sometime desirable, as the recommended choices don't always pick a solution you want. For instance, Microsoft Word can open plain text documents you download from the Internet, but the only choice that would work in the recommended list is "Word with MacLinkPlus Translation." Translating the file will also work, but is unnecessary in this case. Turning off "Show only recommended choices" will let you select Word without translation.

MacWindows Tip

If you double-click an application in Mac OS 8.1 and earlier, you may get an error message, "The application that created this document cannot be found" instead of the list of applications and translators. If this happens, check the Mac Easy Open control panel to make sure it's turned on.

Once you make a selection and click Open, the application you selected will launch and attempt to open the file, with or without translation, depending on your selection. Mac OS will remember your choice, so that the next time you double-click on this type of file, your chosen application will launch and open the file without bringing up the Easy Open dialog box.

Configuring Mac OS Easy Open/File Translation Control Panel

If you prefer to have the dialog box come up every time you double-click a Windows file, you can select the appropriate check box in the control panel. In Mac OS 8.1 and earlier, this the *Always show dialog box* selection in the Mac OS Easy Open control panel (Figure 5.16). In Mac OS 8.5 and later, this is the *Always show choices when translating files* selection in the File Translation tab of the File Exchange control panel, shown in Figure 5.17.

The OS 8.1 Mac Easy Open control panel lacks one feature that the OS 8.5 File Exchange control panel has—the ability to edit the translation preferences, as well as add some of your own. In OS 8.1 and

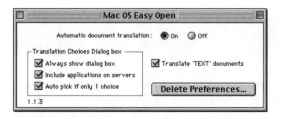

Figure 5.16 The Mac OS Easy Open control panel in Mac OS 8.1 and earlier lets you delete preferences, but doesn't let you see them or edit them.

earlier, translation preferences are merely the application choices you've already made, which Mac Easy Open "remembers." For instance, if you double-clicked a Windows JPG file and chose Photoshop in the window that came up, the translator preferences would skip the window and launch Photoshop again the next time you double-clicked a Windows JPG file. If you *don't* want Photoshop to launch, you can make Mac Easy Open "forget" the translation preferences. You can click the Delete Preferences button in the Mac OS Easy Open control panel to make Mac OS Easy Open "forget" all of the choices you've made previously. (See Figure 5.16.)

Unlike Mac Easy Open, the OS 8.5's File Translation tab of the File Exchange control panel displays all translation preferences loaded, and allows you to add your own. And instead of having to delete all the preferences, you can selectively delete individual preferences by selecting one and clicking the Remove button.

To add a translation preference to the File Translation tab, click the Add button (Figure 5.17). In the window that comes up, browse through the hard disk until you find the type of file for which you would like to set a preference. Select the file and click the Continue button to select an application or and application with a translator to open a file with the type and creator code of the file you've selected.

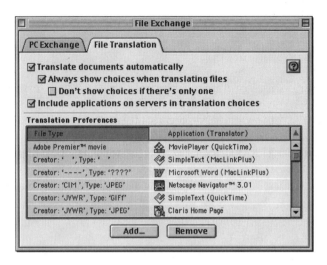

Figure 5.17 The File Translation tab of OS 8.5 lets you edit translation preferences.

Unlike PC Exchange, the File Translation/Mac Easy Open preference setting does *not* look at the file name extension, but looks at the type and creator code of the file. You also cannot edit the type and creator code here. For files with type and creator codes that are empty or garbled, adding a preference here won't be helpful. Remember, adding a preference only helps automatic translation. If you don't have a preference, you'll get the list of applications and translators shown in Figure 5.15.

MacWindows Tip

If you have multiple versions of Microsoft Office applications, including Office 98, you may have a problem when you double-click a Word 98 or Excel 98 file—Easy Open/File Exchange launches and asks MacLinkPlus to translate the file. The problem seems to occur when the different versions of the applications are on different volumes, and the newest version is not on the startup drive. DataViz recommends fixing the problem by moving all of the versions to the startup drive or by keeping only the newest version of the applications on the startup drive, and keeping the older versions on other drives.

Translating Files

When your applications can't open a foreign file, you need to translate the file into a format one of your applications can read. File translation converts a file's formatting information as well as the basic data. Mac OS comes with translation software, some of which can be accessed through the File Translation/Easy Open dialog box, as described in the last section. In addition, there are several other ways to use the Mac's translation software. And while the File Translation/Easy Open dialog translates only from Windows to Mac formats, you can use the translators to go the other way, from Mac formats to Windows formats.

Windows users can also translate files between Mac and Windows formats, using software from DataViz and other vendors. For better translation of graphics file formats, both Windows and Mac users can take advantage of several graphics editing packages that do a good job. A description of some of these third-party translation products for Windows follows a discussion of the Mac OS products.

Whenever you translate a file on either platform, a new file is always created during the translation process, keeping the original intact. This lets you experiment with translating into different formats while still preserving the original. File translation isn't always cross-platform, either. On both Windows and Mac OS, you can translate a Mac file into another type of Mac document and create a Windows file from another type of Windows file.

Web Update Link: *For the most recent information on translator products for Macintosh and Windows, see http://www.macwindows.com/filetran.html.*

Mac OS Translators

Mac OS has come bundled with file translator software for many years. Currently, it comes with QuickTime translators that can convert between a variety of multimedia formats. For many years Mac OS also included MacLinkPlus translators from DataViz. (You now have to purchase MacLinkPlus from DataViz.) MacLinkPlus translators convert word processor, spreadsheet, database, and some graphics formats. They can also translate word processor files that contain embedded graphics. You use QuickTime and MacLinkPlus translators the same way, which is indirectly, through other software. QuickTime translators are part of the QuickTime extensions files in the Extensions folder. MacLinkPlus translators are located in the DataViz folder in the System folder.

You never interact with MacLinkPlus and QuickTime translator files directly—you access them transparently through other software, where you simply choose the file format you want to translate to. These methods include:

♦ The Easy Open window, as explained in a previous section
♦ The document converter file
♦ In Mac OS 8 and later, the Finder contextual pop-up menu (MacLinkPlus 10 and later)
♦ In Mac OS 8.5 and later, from the Open and Save dialog boxes and the Find File command

MacLinkPlus Translators

MacLinkPlus began shipping with some Mac models with OS 7.5. Apple stopped bundling MacLinkPlus translators with Mac OS in July of 1998, near the end of the run for Mac OS 8.1. This means most OS 8.1 system CDs contain it, but some do not. Mac OS 8.5 does not contain MacLinkPlus translators. In September of 1998, DataViz began shipping a MacLinkPlus 10, which included file translators and a new utility. Some versions of ClarisWorks and AppleWorks also shipped with MacLinkPlus translators.

If you don't have MacLinkPlus, it's worth looking into. I have found MacLinkPlus to be an essential tool for cross-platform environments for many years. It can process hundreds of different types of text-based and graphic file conversions.

Whether you have the free version of MacLinkPlus or a more current version that you purchased, you can purchase additional translators. For instance, MacLinkPlus 9.0, the version bundled with Mac OS 8.0 and 8.1, does not come with translators for Microsoft Office 97 for Windows. An inexpensive upgrade to MacLinkPlus 9.7 or later adds the translators for Office 97 for Windows and for several formats used on the Internet, including HTML and GIF.

Whatever version of MacLinkPlus you have, you'll find three major groups of files related to translation:

- Document Converter file (located in the MacLinkPlus folder). You use this to translate files.
- Translator files (MacLinkPlus translators are located in the DataViz folder in the System folder. QuickTime translators are part of the QuickTime extensions files in the Extensions folder.)
- MacLinkPlus Setup control panel.

In addition to these files, MacLinkPlus 10 comes with an application.

The Document Converter

You use the Document Converter to create a file that will translate one or more documents to a specific Mac or Windows file format. The Document Converter works with both MacLinkPlus and QuickTime translators.

Document Converter

To create this converter file, first make a copy of the Document Converter file, located in the MacLinkPlus folder. Then double-click the copy. A window will appear, as shown in Figure 5.18.

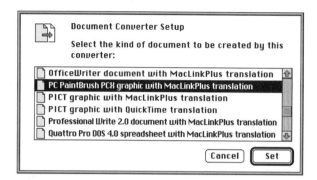

Figure 5.18 Selecting a translation for a document converter file

From this window you select the file type you want to create. As with Mac Easy Open, you can choose file formats translated with MacLinkPlus or QuickTime translation, depending on the format.

When you click Set, the window closes and the Document Converter file takes on the name of the format you want to create.

to Microsoft Word Windows 6.0,

In the Finder, you can translate a document to the format you've selected by dragging and dropping your document on top of the converter file. You can also convert batches of files by dragging a folder with the files on top of the converter file. You can make copies of the document converter file and place them anywhere on your hard disk, or create multiple converter files that translate to a variety of formats. You can also change the format of a converter file over and over again. To change the format that a converter file creates, just double-click the converter file and select a new file format.

Translating with MacLinkPlus 10 or Later

You can use the previously discussed translation methods with MacLinkPlus 10, as well as several new methods. MacLinkPlus 10 also added more translators, a new application, and the ability to decompress and decode files. (The decoding feature is discussed in Chapter 6.)

If you have Mac OS 8.0 or later, MacLinkPlus 10 lets you translate files from the Finder's contextual pop-up menu. To translate a file this way, control-click on the file in the Finder to bring up the Mac OS 8 contextual menu. When you select the MacLinkPlus item at the bottom of the menu, you have several choices, as shown in Figure 5.19. The menu item called Recognize will tell you the file's format. Quick Preview lets you view the file from the contextual menu without opening an application. You can also open the MacLinkPlus application, or translate the file right on the spot by selecting a file format. At this point, the MacLinkPlus translators have already recognized the files and present only the file formats that are pertinent. These means you don't have to scroll through dozens of word processor formats to translate a graphics file.

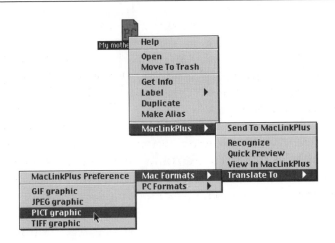

Figure 5.19 File translation with Contextual menus with MacLinkPlus 10

The MacLinkPlus 10 application lets you translate the file and edit the type and creator codes. You can also view a file, including graphics. MacLinkPlus will also act upon batches of files, so that you can translate them together. To work with a file, you can drag a file or folder over the MacLinkPlus icon, or drag a file or folder from the Finder to the open application, or load files from within the application. The files you add to MacLinkPlus don't have to have the same format, either. You can add Mac and Windows files of various types, as shown in Figure 5.20.

Figure 5.20 The MacLinkPlus 10 application, previewing a file

MacLinkPlus Setup Control Panel

The MacLinkPlus Setup control panel is used for making minor changes, some for specific file translations. There are two pop-up menus. You choose from among several categories from the first pop-up, and make your selection in the second.

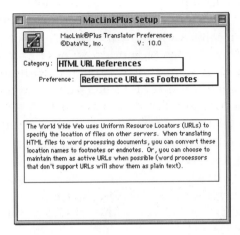

Figure 5.21 MacLinkPlus Setup control panel

The categories vary depending on the version of MacLinkPlus, but all let you set the parameters of translation. The first category, Languages, determines which alphabet will be used during translation. The Multi-national selection uses most American and European alphabets.

The PC Text Translations category lets you select between DOS text and Windows text for creating PC documents. The main difference is the so-called extended ASCII characters. Windows and Mac OS can make use of more characters than can DOS. The DOS text selections converts characters that are forbidden in DOS into permitted characters. The PC File Naming category in later versions lets you choose between 8.3 (eight-character file name with three-character extension) and Windows file names for newly created PC documents.

The AutoBullet, AutoNumber, and Outlines category gives you a choice of maintaining the automatic renumbering and bulleting feature of some word processors, or translating these into fixed numbers and bullets.

Translating Files on Windows

Windows doesn't come with translation software, but you can use third-party software to convert between Windows and Mac file formats on Windows machines. On the Windows side, file translators are sometimes referred to as filters or converters.

The most comprehensive cross-platform translator utility for Windows is Conversions Plus, DataViz' version of MacLinkPlus for Windows 3.1, 95, 98, and NT. Like the Mac OS version, Conversions Plus translates a variety of Mac and PC word processor, spreadsheet, database, and graphics file formats. The software can recognize a variety of file types automatically and works with e-mail. The Name Doctor feature will fix problems related to the differences in Mac and PC file naming conventions, removing illegal characters or wrong extensions. A nice bonus is that it includes the functionality of MacOpener, DataViz' utility for using Mac floppy and SCSI disks (including HFS+ formatted disks) on a PC. Conversions Plus can also can decode and decompress e-mail attachments from Mac users.

Web Update Link: *For the latest product information about the translator products for Windows, check http://www.macwindows.com/filetran.html#WindowsTransProducts.*

A more basic package is TransferPro from Digital Instrumentation Technology (http://www.dit.com/). It translates Mac and PC graphics file formats and contains graphics and text viewers for many file formats. Transfer Pro also has character filters that can convert the end-of-line characters in a text file, the carriage return for Macintosh and line feed for PC. Like Conversions Plus, Transfer Pro enables Windows and UNIX to read and write Mac disks.

KeyView Pro from Verity Canada (http://www.keyview.com/) allows users to view, convert and compress/decompress documents. It supports a variety of Windows file formats, including MS Office 97, Lotus Suite 97, and Corel Word Perfect 8. There are fewer Mac formats, including Microsoft Word, Word Perfect, and PICT, but it also works with e-mail and does file compression/decompression and decryption.

Single-Purpose Translators

Several software vendors offer their own single-purpose file translators for converting between Mac and Windows versions of their own applications. Although the file formats of many applications work on both Macs and Windows, files are usually only compatible with particular versions of the application. The problem occurs when a user of an older version on one platform wants to open files created by a new version on the other platform.

Application manufacturers often offer these single-purpose translators free on their web or FTP sites. These translators are typically one-way, in that they can import files, but can't save files to the other platform. Some of these translators run on Macs, others run on Windows.

Microsoft

Microsoft offers translators for Office that run on Mac OS and convert from Windows to Mac formats only. For instance, the Word 97/98 Import Converter for Word for Mac 5.1 or 6 enables users of Word 5.1 or 6 for Mac to import files created in Word for Windows 7.0, 97. It does not enable Mac Word to save in Word for Windows 7.0, 97 formats.

You can find the Word 97/98 Import Converter for Word for Mac at http://www.microsoft.com/macoffice/prodinfo/office/coexist.htm. A good jumping off place when you're looking for Office converters is http://www.microsoft.com/macoffice/.

There is also a Word 6.0 Converter for Word 5.x for Mac. It enables users of Word 5.x for Mac to import files created by Word 6.0 for Windows, Window NT, and Mac. It does not create Word 6.0 files. You can find Word 6.0 Converter for Word 5.x for Mac at http://www.microsoft.com/macoffice/work_wd_fs.htm.

Adobe

Adobe's Cross-Platform PageMaker Converter is a utility for Windows 95 and NT that translates publications and templates created in Page-Maker 5.x and 6.0x for Macintosh to PageMaker 6.0 for Windows. After translating the files, you can open them in PageMaker 6.5 for Windows. You can translate one Mac publication at a time, or convert a batch of files.

You can download Cross-Platform PageMaker Converter from the Adobe web site at:
http://www.adobe.com/supportservice/custsupport/LIBRARY/4cd2.htm

Translation Problem Areas

The goal of file translation software is not only to be able to read the text in a file, but to retain document formatting, such as columns, margins, and font size and style. With most translation software, the success of conversion is usually good, particularly for text-based files created by word processors, spreadsheets, and databases. Graphics embedded in word processor files are usually converted without problems. However, there are some formatting areas that may need tweaking after translation.

This section covers the translation of text-based files. Graphics file translation is discussed in the next section.

Fonts

When doing a translation, you should decide if retaining the same font in the translated document is important. If it isn't, good. Unless the computer doing the translation has exactly the same fonts that were specified in the document, the translator will substitute another font for the one specified in the document. If it is important that the fonts be the same, you should try to get the same fonts installed on the Mac and Windows machines.

Font substitution is a hit-or-miss situation—sometimes the font used is close to the original font, while other times there is no relation between the two. Besides changing the look, substituting a font can reflow the text, drastically changing a document. For instance, a font that is slightly wider can turn one-line sentences into two-line sentences. As a result, résumés that fit nicely on a single page may spill over to a second page in the translated document.

Keep in mind that both Mac OS and Windows come with TrueType fonts, which makes them a safe bet to use in documents that you're sending off to users of other platforms.

Fonts can be a problem even when you're not translating files, but simply moving files between compatible platforms. For more on these issues, see the section on fonts later in the chapter.

Column widths

The width of columns can sometimes vary slightly from that in the original document. This could mess up text flow in a page layout. Unfortunately, there's not much you can do about it except to watch out for it and to correct it after the translation.

Tables

Success at translating tables varies with the type of application that created the original file. Using tab-delimited text instead of a table can make it easier for users of other platforms, particularly if the file you are giving them isn't in the final format. For instance, tab-delimited text is useful if you give a Word file to someone who intends to pour the text into a page layout program such Quark XPress. Tab-delimited text is also the best format to use when moving data from a database, spreadsheet, or other table-based data file.

Graphics Translation

On either platform, trouble-free translation of graphics files can be trickier than that of text-based files. In general, the more complex the graphics image and the file format, the more difficult it will be to translate accurately. Graphics file formats can be categorized into two technologies: *bitmap* (or raster), which uses dots to define an image, and vector, which uses objects and curves to define an image.

Bitmap graphic formats are the easier to translate, particularly if a version exists for both platforms. GIF and JPEG are completely cross-platform bitmap formats and don't require translation at all when moving between Windows, Mac, and UNIX machines. The differences between Windows .TIF and Macintosh TIFF are minor (the byte order is reversed), which makes it a good cross-platform format. Other bitmap formats tend to translate fairly accurately, even though they exist on only one platform another. These include CGM and BMP on Windows, and PICT on Mac.

Strictly speaking, the modern version of PICT, PICT2, is not a bitmap format, but a metafile. A metafile is a hybrid of bitmap and raster, basically a bitmap image that can contain some objects. However, as far as translation is concerned, metafile formats are treated as bitmap images. Windows MetaFile (WMF) is similar in concept to PICT2, but is a completely different file format. One cannot say that "WMF is the Windows version of PICT." In fact, WMF files are not as easily translated to and from as PICT images.

Vector formats, such as EPS, FreeHand, and Illustrator, are more complex and have more problems translating exactly, especially if you want to translate them into a bitmap form. As with bitmap graphics, the best results occur when you translate between similar formats on Mac OS and Windows. Some problem areas include:

PICT Previews. Whether you are translating a Mac file to a Windows format, or just moving a cross-platform file, you will lose its PICT preview. Windows can't read PICT. Some applications have the ability to provide other types of previews. For instance, you can often choose to create a TIFF preview for an EPS file. This is a good choice. JPEG and the WMF (the Windows equivalent to PICT) are also okay to use as preview formats, if your software supports them.

Line thickness. Delicate lines can thicken or darken during translation. This is particularly true when converting from a vector format to a bitmap format.

Blends. Blends can sometimes drop out altogether on more complex translations. Other than fixing the problem after the translation, the best method is to use formats that are similar on both platforms, such as the Mac and Windows versions of EPS or TIFF.

Embedded fonts. Fonts in vector graphics are difficult to move between Mac and Windows. If the Mac and Windows machines don't have exactly the same font, font substitution can have effects that are even worse than in text-based files. For instance, you can end up with text that overlaps itself so that it is illegible, and text that spills out of the block where it is supposed to remain. Your best bet is to convert the editable text into outlines before it leaves your machine. Adobe Illustrator and other vector drawing programs have this ability, as do some translation utilities.

Colors. Colors can shift during the conversion process. However, before you start correcting the color, be sure that a color shift is real and not due to a different color depth setting on a monitor display.

Graphics Translator Products for Mac and Windows

If you need to go beyond the graphics translation capabilities of the translators that come with Mac OS or the Windows products mentioned earlier, there are some tools that not only do an excellent job at translating graphics formats, but also have tools that let you clean up translation problems.

Equilibrium's DeBabelizer

DeBabelizer (http://www.equilibrium.com/) is a batch processing image editing application that is also very useful for translating between Mac and Windows bitmap formats. For one, it can translate between more than 100 Mac and Windows graphics file formats, including Animated GIF, Kodak FlashPix, and PNG, a format used on the Internet. Though DeBabelizer was originally a Mac product, the Windows NT version now supports more file formats than the Mac version.

DeBabelizer is also a great tool for editing a file after translation to correct for any deficiencies or unintended alterations. Not only does it have good editing tools, but once you figure out what is needed, you can automate the process using scripting tools so that you can translate and correct multiple files at the same time. DeBabelizer also includes tools for creating cross-platform color palettes to use when working on Web images.

MacWindows Tip

Macintosh and Windows displays have slightly different aspect ratios. They are closer than the difference between movie and television ratios, but they still differ. This means that if you create a full-screen image on one platform and move it to the other, it won't be exactly full screen—there will be some black banding. DeBabelizer for Mac OS or for Windows has a command to convert the aspect ratio between the two platforms. From the Image menu, select Scale, and then select one of the following: "IBM to Mac Aspect Ratio" or "Mac to IBM Aspect Ratio." You can also script this command to apply to a batch of files, or as a step in a longer script including several editing steps.

TechPool Software's Transverter Pro

Transverter Pro (http://www.techpool.com/) is a tool that focuses on Postscript functions. It works well for converting vector graphics formats, such as EPS, Illustrator, and PDF (Acrobat), and rasterizing vector formats (including Postscript) to bitmap formats, such as GIF,

JPEG, and TIFF. It also includes tools for fixing problems and can handle the problem of fonts embedded in a file. Transverter Pro is available for Windows and Macs.

Flattening Mac Multimedia Files for Windows

Apple QuickTime technology is completely integrated across Mac and Windows users. Both platforms can view the same multimedia files with QuickTime-enabled applications or browser plug-ins. Nevertheless, if created on a Macintosh, self-playing (or "self-contained") files, such as QuickTime movies and some other cross-platform multimedia files, must be "flattened" before being moved to Windows or posted to the Internet. (If created on Windows, these files need no modification to be played by either platform.) The reason goes back to the discussion of Mac files at the beginning of this chapter—Mac files consist of a data fork and a resource fork. (See the section called Differences: Macintosh and Windows Files.)

Unlike most Mac data files, self-playing movies, such as QuickTime .MOV files, QuickTime VR movies, and MPEG movies, contain significant information in the resource fork of the file. Flattening a file combines the data and resource forks so that Windows users can play the movies, but doesn't disable the files for Mac users.

You must flatten Mac-created self-contained files on a Mac. You can use versions of Apple's Movie Player that have the editing functions enabled. This includes versions that come with Mac OS 8.x, and QuickTime 3 Pro. The Movie Player that comes with the free QuickTime 3 has the editing features disabled. To flatten a file in Movie Player, open the file, go to the Save As dialog, and check "Mac Movie Self-Contained" and "Playable on non-Apple computers."

Other Mac programs that can flatten movies include DeBabelizer, Adobe Premiere, and several shareware utilities, including Flattmoov and Movie Converter. You can find these at web sites, such as ZDnet, that offer Mac shareware.

Using Fonts with Macs and PCs

For people doing ordinary office activities, fonts aren't much of an issue when moving documents back and forth between Windows and Macintosh. However, for people in print publishing, the use of fonts in mixed-platform environments presents problems of its own. There are font problems with text reflows, ligatures, and styles. These problems are in addition to the differences in ASCII characters described at the beginning of the chapter. Because of these problems, you'll need to proofread a file after it is moved between platforms.

Each of these problems has its own possible solutions, but there is a general solution if you are distributing a file that doesn't need to be edited. You could distribute it in a format that embeds the fonts in the document. The most common format is Adobe's PDF (Portable Document Format), which you can create with Adobe Acrobat. Windows and Mac users will see the exact same layout, fonts, and graphics, as everything is contained in the file. The drawbacks are that PDF files aren't editable and can be large because of all the embedded information.

Another possible solution to many of these problems is a new type of font, OpenType, being developed by Microsoft and Adobe. It supports ligatures and font styles on both platforms. It also supports Unicode characters, which fixes the problem ASCII has with different characters on Mac and Windows. However, at the time of this writing, OpenType had not been adopted by a significant portion of the publishing market, so it remains only a potential solution at this time.

Text Reflow due to Different Fonts

The reflow of text occurs when the fonts called out in the document aren't installed on the computer you move the file to. Different fonts have different thicknesses, so a carefully designed four-page brochure on a Mac could takes up up four and a quarter pages on a PC. Text reflow can also occur between two Macs or two Windows machines that don't have the same font, but Macs and a PCs are less likely to have the same fonts.

You can prevent reflow problems by installing the same font set on both Macintosh and Windows machines. "The same font" means the same font product from the same manufacturer. Fonts with the same name from different font companies are not the same. TrueType and Postscript Type 1 fonts of the same name are will also differ. Although Postscript Type 1 fonts are popular with professional print publishers, don't assume that the target PC for your document will have Post-script fonts. As with Mac OS, Windows comes with TrueType fonts, but use of Type 1 fonts is not as prevalent on Windows as it is on Mac.

If you don't require the exact same text flow on Mac and Windows, you can select fonts on each platform that are similar. You have to be careful with this approach. Frequent print samples from both plat-forms are advisable. For instance, the Mac TrueType fonts Times, Hel-vetica, and Courier are called Times New Roman, Arial, and Courier New on Windows. Although the fonts look the same, they don't have the exact same spacing characteristics. A safer bet would be to use Mac versions of Times New Roman, Arial, and Courier New, which Microsoft posts at its web site.

The use of Type 1 fonts can maks it easier to get the printed results of complex Word tables and forms to look the same on each platform. This is because more often, the Mac and Windows Type 1 fonts have exactly the same names and spacing characteristics.

MacWindows Tip

If you're having trouble finding the same font for both Mac OS and Windows, make your own. On the CD-ROM included with this book, you'll find the shareware Windows utility CrossFont, which converts between PC and Mac PostScript Type 1 or TrueType fonts. The shareware Mac utility TTConverter can convert True-Type fonts between Macintosh and Windows. You can find it at several web sites, including ZDnet at http://www6.zdnet.com/cgi-bin/texis/swlib/mac/infomac.html?fcode=MC13911. If you want to modify a font and output Type 1 fonts for Mac and Windows, use Macromedia's Fontographer (http://www.macromedia.com).

Font Families and Styles

Professional print publishers on the Mac use a font family containing four separate fonts for the font styles *plain, bold, italic,* and *bold italic,* instead of altering a plain font with the italic and bold commands in an application's menu. Using specially designed fonts yields more readable bold and italic text than using the bold and italic commands, which just arbitrarily thicken or slant text.

A cross-platform problem with a Mac document can occur when a font family contains more than the standard four style typefaces. For instance, some families include a heavy or ultrabold font, which means the family would contain an ultrabold italic. Windows doesn't support a font family with more than four fonts, so it will sometimes substitute another font for one or more fonts in the family.

Ligatures

If you move a file to a PC and are getting strange characters where your f's and l's should be, chances are you've been using ligatures on the Mac. A ligature is a typographic feature that runs two or three characters together.

For instance, ﬂ and ﬁ are ligatures, while fl and fi are not.

You many not even realize you are using ligatures. In some software, such as Quark XPress, ligatures are a simple preference setting that you can turn on or off. The problem is that ligatures don't move over to Windows when you move a file created on a Macintosh. Windows doesn't support ligatures and will substitute a character for the ligature.

There is a similar problem with numerical fractions created on Windows—they don't cross over to Mac OS, which will substitute characters. Mac publishers often use superscripts and subscripts (or a "baseline shift" in Quark XPress) to manually set fractions.

If you decide that you want to use ligatures and fractions, one solution is to choose a so-called "expert" font set that has a Mac and Windows version. The down side to using expert fonts is that you will be limitted in your selection of typefaces. Adobe offers expert font families in some popular typefaces, including Garamond, Bodoni, and Formata. (See Adobe's on-line type browser at http://www.adobe.com/type/browser/main.html).

Another solution is to add special ligature and fraction characters to your Mac and Windows fonts using Macromedia Fontographer, a font editing program. Fontographer gives you a vector drawing environment similar to FreeHand in which you can create or modify characters. You can then save the font as Mac and Windows versions to install on your workstations.

What's Next

Learning how to work with common files can go a long way toward integrating Mac OS and Windows machines in a work environment. However, there is more to cross-platform sharing of files than file formats. Sending files via e-mail can also add cross-platform file problems not discussed in this chapter. Most e-mail problems are caused by the use of encoding and file compression. These problems are often compounded by e-mail software that isn't aware of these common problems. The next chapter looks at problems related to moving files via e-mail.

Chapter

What's in This Chapter:

- ♦ *Attaching files to cross-platform e-mail messages*

- ♦ *Encoding files for Windows users*

- ♦ *Decoding enclosures from Windows users*

- ♦ *Working with foreign file compression formats*

- ♦ *Receiving foreign encoded or compressed files*

Exchanging Files Electronically between Mac and Windows

As the most popular Internet service, e-mail is also the most common form of communication between Mac and Windows users. It is also a common source of cross-platform problems. A Windows user receives an enclosed file from a Mac user, but all the Windows user sees is a garble of random characters. A Mac user receives messages from Windows users that contain mysterious boxes that have to be stripped out. These problems can also occur when downloading files from web or FTP sites and can occur even on the most "integrated" networks. Trouble with moving files can occur not only with Internet (POP/SMTP) e-mail and Internet FTP sites, but with proprietary LAN-based e-mail systems and file servers.

You may wonder why a chapter on moving files over wires wasn't included in the networking section of the book. The reason is that

cross-platform file transfer problems are not usually network problems, but are most often file problems, related to the issues described
in Chapter 5. File transfer problems typically originate with the users
and their e-mail client software, not with the servers or gateways.
These problems can be prevented or fixed afterward by the users
themselves, or by network administrators setting up e-mail client software. (Chapter 12 describes solutions to file problems that are sometimes seen with Macintosh clients and Windows NT Server.)

Web Update Link: *For the latest product information about
the topics covered in this chapter, check http://www.macwin-
dows.com/compress.html.*

Differences: Attaching Files to E-mail Messages

The biggest electronic file transfer problem between Mac OS and
Windows users is attaching, or enclosing, files to an e-mail message.
Users receive a file that looks like garbled text or a file they can't open
at all (see Figure 6.1). Most often this problem occurs with Mac messages going to Windows users, but it can occur the other way around.
This problem has nothing to do with the format of the file (see chapter 5) and can occur with completely cross-platform files.

Files consisting of garbled text have been encoded, and sometimes
compressed, by the sender's e-mail software, but the receiver's e-mail
software has been unable to decode or decompress it. Often it's
because the sender used an encoding or compression scheme the
receiver's e-mail software doesn't recognize.

Despite the fact that you can attach highly formatted documents, pic-
tures, and multimedia to e-mail messages, the only thing that actually gets transmitted is plain, unformatted ASCII text. When you attach
a file to an e-mail message, the e-mail software encodes it—turns it
into ASCII text—and appends it to the body of the message. The
receiver's e-mail software recognizes that the appended text is an

encoded file and decodes the file. If the receiver's e-mail software (or web browser plug-in or utility) doesn't recognize the encoding format, the file remains gibberish text.

Figure 6.1 This encoded text gibberish could be anything from a color picture to a spreadsheet.

There are multiple encoding and compressing formats available to any user with the right software. Some formats are more popular on Windows; others are more commonly used on Mac OS. There are UNIX-based encoding and compressing formats as well.

The differences between the Mac and Windows formats for encoding and compression stem from the differences in Mac and Windows files discussed in Chapter 5. Macintosh encoding and compression schemes try to save the Mac file's resource fork and the type and creator code, which in turn determines the icon of a file used in Mac OS. When you use a Windows or UNIX encoding or compression format to send a Mac file, the resource fork is lost. When a Mac user encodes or compresses a file with a Mac scheme, chances are the Windows software won't know what to do with it.

Encoding: From Mac to Windows Users

The most common reason that Windows users receive unusable files from Mac users is that most Mac e-mail software defaults to the Bin-Hex encoding scheme, which is rarely supported in Windows software. BinHexed files posted on a web or FTP server usually have file names ending in .hqx, but BinHex-encoded e-mail enclosures often don't include this suffix.

Mac e-mail client software defaults to BinHex encoding because it transmits a Mac file's resource fork along with the data fork. Since a Mac file's resource fork isn't used by Windows, there is no point in trying to preserve it for a Windows user, and no point in using BinHex encoding. If a Mac user is e-mailing a file to both Mac and Windows users, then BinHex makes sense, but you'll need to install Bin-Hex decoding software on the Windows machines. Aladdin's free Expander for Windows can decode BinHex and MacBinary (see sidebar), as well as decompress Mac archive formats. Expander for Windows can be found on the CD-ROM included with this book and is available from http://www.aladdinsys.com. (Expander for Windows is discussed in more detail in the section called .SIT Utilities for Windows later in the chapter.) The WinZip utility (http://www.WinZip.com) can also decode BinHex.

Base64 in Eudora

Base64 doesn't ordinarily save a Mac file's resource fork, but Qualcomm's Eudora for Macintosh has a way of including the resource in a Base64-encoded message. Eudora for Mac calls this method "AppleSingle." PC users won't be able to decipher files sent to them in Eudora's AppleSingle format.

Eudora for Macintosh calls ordinary Base64 encoding "AppleDouble." This sends a Mac file's data fork and resource fork as separate files. Windows users can then discard the resource fork.

On the Mac, you set Eudora's encoding in the Settings window, which you select from the Special menu. You then click the Attachments button, which brings up the selection of encoding schemes. You'll have to bring up this window every time you want to change the encoding format.

Most Mac e-mail client software will let you change the encoding scheme used for file enclosures, though users may not realize it. Mac users sending files to Windows users should use choose UUencode (also called UUcode) or Base64, which most Windows e-mail software supports.

Despite its name, UUencode—short for UNIX-to-UNIX encoding —does not require UNIX for encoding or decoding. UUencoded files posted at web and FTP sites often have names that end with the .uu extension. Occasionally, UUencoded file names end with .uue or .uud. UUencode files attached to an e-mail message often do not have a file extension.

Base64 is an encoding scheme used by MIME-compliant e-mail soft-ware. For this reason, Base64 encoding is sometimes referred to as "MIME encoding." MIME (Multipurpose Internet Mail Extension) is actually a more general e-mail message standard that specifies e-mail messaging aspects such as the formatting of the body of an message, as well file attachments. The names of Base64-encoded files sometimes end with the .MIM extension.

It is somewhat surprising that Mac e-mail software doesn't do more to help Mac users send files to Windows users. CE Software's QuickMail Pro Client (available for Mac and Windows) is one Internet e-mail client that does (Figure 6.2). It keeps track of encoding schemes to by user, so that once you set up the address book, enclosed files will be encoded correctly according to what computer each recipient uses. You identify people in the address book as users of Windows, Mac

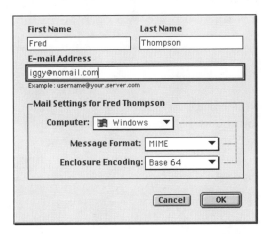

Figure 6.2 QuickMail Pro assigns the right encoding scheme for each e-mail recipient's operating system.

OS, or UNIX. When you enclose a file to a Mac user, BinHex encoding is selected (ensuring that the Mac file's resource fork and type and creator codes will be kept). QuickMail Pro Client chooses UUencoding for UNIX users and Base64 for Windows users. It also lets you change the encoding preferences.

MacBinary Encoding

MacBinary is another Mac-only encoding method that should not be used for files intended for Windows users. Aladdin's Expander for Windows can decode MacBinary, but most Windows software can not. Most Mac e-mail software does not support the MacBinary option, but you find it in some compression utilities and file transfer software. Because MacBinary (.bin) files are up to 30 percent smaller than BinHex (.hqx), you'll also find MacBinary files posted on Macintosh-related web and FTP sites. For instance, Apple now posts its software update files in MacBinary format at its FTP sites.

MacBinary puts a file's resource fork into the data fork to protect it during transmission. Unlike UUencode and Base64, MacBinary doesn't encode a file as plain text; MacBinary files are transmitted in binary code—zeros and ones. This means that you can't use a text editor—or any other software—to open a MacBinary encoded file. Your only option is to decode it with a utility that supports MacBinary.

To complicate matters, there are several versions of MacBinary. The most common is MacBinary II, created in 1990 to save the information in the Comments field of a Mac file's Get Info Window. MacBinary III was created to save certain file information added with Mac OS 8 and has become standard with OS 8.5. Older versions of software won't be able to decode newer versions of MacBinary.

Decoding Enclosures from Windows Users

Most Mac e-mail software supports UUencode and Base64 (MIME). Current versions of stand-alone e-mail clients, such as Eudora Pro, Internet Outlook Express, QuickMail Pro, and the now discontinued but popular Claris Emailer, all will decode UUencode and Base64 attachments automatically. Web browsers and America Online use helper applications, such as StuffIt Expander, to decode attachments encoded in these formats.

However, even with support of UUencode and Base64, e-mail software can sometimes fail to decode the attached file for one reason or another. It could be that an e-mail server or gateway altered the header, rendering the enclosure unrecognizable to the e-mail client. The same can happen when characters are accidentally lost during transmission.

Whatever the reason, if your e-mail software doesn't recognize the encoding, the text encoding of the attached file may show up in the body of the message, or it can show up as an attached file that looks like gibberish when you open it. On a Mac, the encoded file has a generic icon and empty type and creator codes, or may have gibberish type and creator codes. (See Chapter 5 for an explanation of type and creator codes).

Either way, the file is a plain text file, which means you can open it with a text editor to view the gibberish and find out what type of encoding was used. (Keep in mind that many enclosures will be too large for viewing with Simple Text.) You might have to separate the encoded text from the other parts of the e-mail message. Then you can use one of many Macintosh utilities you can use to decode the file, including MacLinkPlus 10 or later, StuffIt Deluxe 5 or later, or some of the compression utilities that also decode, which are described later in the chapter.

(For Windows users decoding Mac files, see the section on Windows utilities later in the chapter.)

Automatic Decoding with MacLinkPlus

The easiest utility to use to decode files on a Mac is DataViz' MacLinkPlus 10 or later, which eliminates many of the steps just described. It can automatically recognize the encoding scheme, even when the text file contains the e-mail message and the message header. MacLinkPlus 10 can detect where the encoded file starts and ends, strip out the header information, recognize the encoding scheme and decode the file or files, and decompress it (if compressed), all in one step. (Earlier versions of MacLinkPlus, including those that came with Mac OS, cannot decode files.)

Before you decode an e-mail enclosure, MacLinkPlus lets you look inside of it. As shown in Figure 6.3, you can see files that are encoded within a file, and see what's in them. MacLinkPlus will tell you what the file names are and what type of files they are (in this case, Word for Windows). From this window, you could choose to decompress one or more of the files in the enclosure, as well as translate selected files to a Macintosh file format.

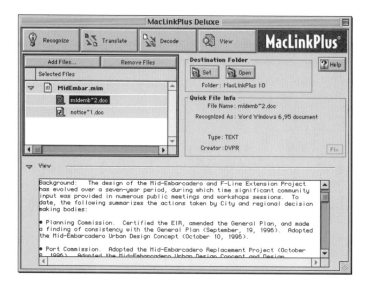

Figure 6.3 MacLinkPlus 10 gives you a preview of the files encoded inside an e-mail attachment.

Cracking Open Encoded Files

You may sometimes have to take things into your own hands. If your e-mail software didn't decode the enclosed file, you may find that other utilities, such as StuffIt Expander or StuffIt Deluxe, also won't recognize the file as something they can decode. (MacLinkPlus 10, though better at recognizing encoded files than most, still doesn't work 100 percent of the time.) You'll need to determine if or how the file was encoded and then tell your utility what it is. Here's how:

1. Open the file with a text editor or word processor to determine how the enclosure was encoded.
2. Strip out any extraneous text, such as the e-mail message body and header.
3. Save the file as a text file.
4. Change the type and creator codes of the file to enable the utility to recognize the file.

When you open the file with a text editor, the encoded file will include some text that identifies it. A UUencoded file starts with the characters "begin 644," as shown in Figure 6.4. The e-mail message or header

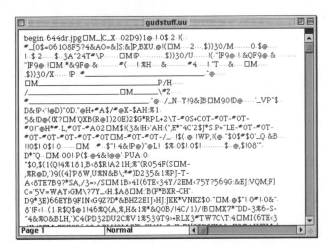

Figure 6.4 The beginning of a UUencoded file

information would come before the "begin 664." The next few characters indicate the name of the encoded file. In this case, although the encoded enclosure is called "gudstuff.uu," we can see from Figure 6.4 that the enclosed file is called "dr.jpg." The encoded file ends with the word "end." After that , you might see more data from the e-mail message. To make the file recognizable to a decoding utility, this file would need to delete everything before "begin 644" and after "end," and save the file as text.

Base64 (or MIME)-encoded files start with several lines that provide information about the encoded file, such as the file name. One of the first lines will contain these characters:

```
Content-Transfer-Encoding: base64
```

Figure 6.5 An e-mail message with a Base64-encoded file at the bottom

Base64 encoded text files from Windows users sometimes have file names that end in .mim, the extension for MIME. Figure 6.5 shows such a message opened in a text editor. Notice that it includes the e-mail message before the encoded file. Above the e-mail message is a snooty warning that provides absolutely no help.

To decode the file yourself, you'll have to remove the snooty message, the e-mail message text, and any headers. In this case, you can keep the first line with the file name (the one that ends "name='SVA-MARL.RTF'") and everything below it. If you are saving the encoded portion as a new file, be sure you save it as a text-only file (not a in a word processing format).

If your word processor has given the file its own icon, then it may have assigned the file its own creator code, or a type code of something other than TEXT, and your decoding utility may refuse to open the file. In this case, you'll have to change the file's type code to TEXT and creator codes to ttxt, using ResEdit, Norton Utilities, MacLinkPlus, or another utility (as described in Chapter 5).

You probably won't get BinHex-encoded files from Windows users, but if you do, you can identify them by the line "This file must be converted with BinHex 4.0." The actual encoded file begins and ends with a colon.

StuffIt Expander, the free utility that acts as a helper application for decoding files downloaded with some web browsers and e-mail software, probably won't be able to decode an enclosure that your e-mail program couldn't. However, Aladdin's StuffIt Deluxe product might. With either utility, you'll probably have to open or decode the text file from within the utility, rather than double-clicking the file.

Web Update Link: *For the latest information about utilities that can decode text-encoded files, check http://www.macwindows.com/compress.html.*

Working with Foreign File Compression Formats

Before a file is encoded, the e-mail software will often compress it (or "archive" it) to make it smaller in order to shorten the transmission time. When you enclose files in an e-mail message, you (or your software) can compress them before encoding. (Encoding does not make a file smaller. In fact, encoding often makes a file bigger.)

Compression can be more of a cross-platform problem than encoding, as a lot of Mac and Windows software doesn't support the format popular on the other platform. Unlike encoding, compression is not required to send a file via e-mail, so when in doubt, turn compression off.

The predominant compression format among Windows users is .ZIP (no relation to Iomega's Zip drives), while the StuffIt .SIT format is most prevalent in the Mac world. If you must compress, one strategy is to use a utility that will compress in the other platform's popular compression format. However, utilities that decompress a variety of formats are easier to find than compression utilities. For instance, there are free utilities that decompress .ZIP on Mac and .SIT on Windows. (These are discussed later in this section.)

Another strategy is to compress files in a format other than .ZIP and .SIT, such as the many UNIX compression formats available, such as GNU zip (.gz). Table 6.1 lists the common Mac, Windows, and UNIX compression formats.

A Cross-Platform .SIT

The .SIT compression format has become more cross-platform recently. With StuffIt Deluxe 5, Aladdin Systems created a new .SIT format, known as the StuffIt 5 archive format. The new .SIT format is easier to move to Windows machines and across the Internet because it is now a *flat file* format, similar to some QuickTime movies (see Chapter 5). A StuffIt 5 archive doesn't put important information into the Mac resource fork, as did the previous SIT format. Information about the files contained in the archive and any encryption are now stored in the data fork of the file. The new format also compresses up to 20 percent tighter. However, you can only create or decompress a StuffIt 5 archive if you one of the version 5 or later products for Windows and Mac, such as Expander and DropStuff (both included on this book's CD-ROM). You should also be aware that the archives of the very old StuffIt 1.5 and earlier are not supported in current software.

Table 6.1 Compression formats

Format	Description
.ARC	Less common PC format
.ARJ	Less common PC format
Compact Pro (.CPT)	Less common Mac format
GNU zip, or GZIP (.gz)	Popular UNIX format (older format)
.SIT (StuffIt)	Popular Macintosh format
.SIT (StuffIt 5)	Newer SIT format
UNIX Tape Archive (.TAR)	UNIX format
UNIX Compress (.Z, always uppercase)	Compression built into most versions of UNIX. Compress a single file only.
.ZIP	Most popular Windows, DOS format

Which compression format you choose depends on to whom you are sending the files. The trickiest situation is when a Mac user sends a file to both Mac and Windows users, wants to preserve the type and creator of a Mac file for the Mac user, and doesn't know what software is installed on the Windows users' PCs. Compressing with .ZIP is a good choice for Mac users sending a file to Windows users, but can be problematic, depending on the software used.

To get around this problem, you could simply send two e-mail messages: one with a zipped enclosure for the Windows users, and another with .SIT archive for Mac users.

ZIP Compression/Decompression for Mac OS

Using ZIP to compress files works well for Mac users sending files to Windows users. It is also handy for Mac users to be able to unZIP files received from Windows users. However, if you are e-mailing a file to a group of people that includes Macintosh users, you may run into some limitations.

For one, zipped archives can't contain files whose names use characters outside the so-called 7-bit ASCII characters. This includes file names with non-English characters, such as umlauts and accents. This is a separate issue from characters prohibited in Windows file naming (discussed in Chapter 5). This is a ZIP limitation, and also applies to files being sent from one Mac to another.

Another restriction is that no Macintosh implementation of ZIP saves all relevant Macintosh-centric data. If you use the ZIP utility correctly, you can manage to keep the resource fork of a Mac file and the type and creator codes. Zipping a file, however, loses other Mac information, such as custom folder icons and file attributes associated with Mac OS 8 or later.

(Folders with custom icons contain an invisible file called "icon\r," where the \r is a carriage return. There is also a some information that tells the Finder to use this icon file. Zipping preserves the invisible file, but loses the Finder information.)

The biggest problem with ZIP and Macs is that each ZIP utility uses a completely different method to preserve the resource forks of Mac applications. Mac users using different ZIP utilities can lose type and creator codes, or worse, may not be able to unzip the files. The most popular Mac unzipping tool, the free StuffIt Expander, ignores "Mac-centric" info in ZIP files.

The next few pages will look at some of the most popular zipping and unzipping utilities for Macintosh. Several of these utilities can decode or encode files as well.

Web Update Link: *On the next few pages, you'll find web sites listed for the utilities described. Since URLs can become out of date, check MacWindows to find current links and the latest information on these and other utilities at http://www.macwindows.com/compress.html.*

PKZIP Mac, Ascent Solutions Inc. (ASi)

Ascent Solutions
http://www.asizip.com

Ascent offers PKZIP Mac at its web site as shareware, though it is one of the more expensive ZIP utilities for Mac. The price has something to do with the fact that Ascent also sells one of the most popular ZIP utilities for PCs, PKZIP for Windows.

You can both compress and decompress (or zip and unzip) files with PKZIP Mac. The utility will retain the resource fork and type and creator codes of Mac files. However, because PKZIP uses a proprietary format to save the resource fork, Mac users decompressing with another unzipping utility will lose this information. A benefit to Ascent's proprietary format is that keeping the resource does not prevent Windows users from using the Zip file. This is useful for sending the same Zip archive to both Mac and Windows users, and is an advantage over ZipIt, described next.

ZipIt

Created by Thomas Brown
http://www.awa.com/softlock/zipit/zipit.html

The shareware ZipIt utility is one of oldest zipping utilities for Mac. Like PKZIP Mac, ZipIt both compresses and decompresses ZIP, is easy to use, and generally works well. ZipIt is included on the CD-ROM that you'll find at the back of this book.

ZipIt includes an option for using MacBinary for retaining resource forks and type and creator code when Mac files are transferred to Mac users (see previous sidebar on MacBinary). However, with the MacBinary option turned on, Windows users will not be able to decode the files. Neither will Mac users without a MacBinary decoder (though they can use any MacBinary decoder, not just ZipIt). At the time of this writing, the ZipIt shareware utility for Mac OS supports MacBinary II, but not MacBinary III.

StuffIt Deluxe

Aladdin Systems
http://www.aladdinsys.com

StuffIt Deluxe is Aladdin Systems' commercial utility for compression/decompression and encoding/decoding. It's a good Macintosh tool with a fair number of cross-platform abilities. It can decompress ZIP archives, though it can't create them, which is its biggest deficit. StuffIt Deluxe can also decompress Compact Pro (.CPT), .ARC, gzip (.gz), TAR, UNIX Compress (.Z). And, of course, you can create and unstuff in the StuffIt (.SIT) format. With StuffIt Deluxe 5.0 and later you can create archives in the newer, more cross-platform SIT format (see page 130), as well use the old SIT format.

StuffIt Deluxe also encodes and decodes a variety of PC, UNIX, and Mac formats, including Base64/MIME, UUencode (.UU), BinHex (.HQX), .LHA, and MacBinary (.BIN). Version 5.0 and later supports the newer MacBinary III encoding format. It can also decrypt documents encrypted with Private File, Aladdin's cross-platform encryption tool. You can segment a big StuffIt archive into smaller pieces for copying to floppy disks, or join segments you've received.

MacWindows Tip

If the drag and drop ability of StuffIt Expander or DropStuff stops working, but you can still launch DropStuff manually, chances are you need to rebuild your desktop. Just hold Command-Option when starting or restarting the Mac.

One reason to own StuffIt Deluxe is that it contains usability features that are integrated with Mac OS, which let you use StuffIt Deluxe without opening the utility. With the proper extensions installed, you can encode a file in BinHex just by typing .hqx at the end of the file name. Similiarly, you can decode and decompress a file simply by removing .hqx and .SIT from file name. StuffIt Delex also has its own Magic Menu in the Finder. You can also access the Magic Menu by clicking on a file or folder while holding down the Control key to open the Mac OS 8.x contextual menu list.

StuffIt Expander

Aladdin Systems
http://www.aladdinsys.com/expander/

Most Mac users already have the StuffIt Expander, as it comes with Mac OS. (Just in case you don't, StuffIt Expander is included on this book's CD-ROM.) You can find newer versions of the free utility at the Aladdin web site. StuffIt Expander 5.0 or later is required to decompress StuffIt 5 archives. On most Mac hard drives, StuffIt Expander is found in the Internet folder, as it is the web browser helper that unstuffs, unzips, and decodes. The free utility does not create archives or encode. In addition to ZIP and SIT, StuffIt Expander can decompress gzip (.gz and .tgz). It can decode UUencode (.uu, .uue, .enc), BinHex (.hqx), and MacBinary (.bin), but does not decode Base64/MIME (.mim). StuffIt Expander can decrypt Private File (.pf) documents created by Aladdin's security software.

StuffIt Expander has no user interface. It works automatically with a web browser, or you decode and decompress by dragging the archive on the StuffIt Expander icon in the Finder. If StuffIt Expander fails to decode a file when you download it, drag-and-drop isn't going to force it to recognize the file—you have to manually clean it up, as described earlier in the chapter.

DropStuff

Aladdin Systems
http://www.aladdinsys.com/

Aladdin's DropStuff falls in between the free StuffIt Expander and the commercial StuffIt Deluxe. It is more useful than Expander, because it lets you create SIT and self-extracting (.sea) archives, but is classified as shareware, with a modest cost. It can't create a .ZIP archive, but it can unzip files. DropStuff works by dragging a file on top of the icon. It won't join segmented archives together. DropStuff is also on the CD-ROM at the back of this book.

MindExpander

MindVision
http://www.mindvision.com/Consumer/

MindExpander is a another free unzipper and unstuffer, a competitor to the free StuffIt Expander, though not quite as versatile. It also decodes MacBinary and BinHex, but not PC or UNIX encoding schemes at this time. MindVision makes the cross-platform developer installation program Installer Vise.

MacGzip

Created by Jean-loup Gailly http://persephone.cps.unizar.es/General/gente/spd/gzip/gzip.html.

MacGzip is a free Mac utility that both compresses and decompress the GNU zip (.gz) format, popular on UNIX and the Internet. In fact, it's the only Mac program I'm aware of that creates GNU zip archives. The program and the source code are both free.

UnZip

Info-Zip
http://www.cdrom.com/pub/infozip/

UnZip is another free decompression utility. The web site includes versions for multiple operating systems, as well as the Mac version. UnZip does not compress files.

Windows Utilities That Decompress/Compress Mac Archives

The main problem with using the SIT compression format for Windows files is that it isn't widely used on Windows. However, once you get a SIT decompresser for a Windows machine, you won't run into any of the problems that Mac users can have with ZIP. There are several Windows freeware or shareware utilities that can compress or decompress SIT files, some of which are described next.

I'll start with Aladdin, the creator of the SIT format and maker of the Macintosh StuffIt software. The company has two Windows compression utilities, Expander for decompressing SIT archives, and DropStuff for creating SIT archives, which is useful for sending compressed files to Macintosh users.

Web Update Link: *For the latest information on these or other cross-platform compression/decompression utilities for Windows, see http://www.macwindows.com/compress.html#WinCompression.*

Aladdin Expander for Windows
Aladdin Systems
http://www.aladdinsys.com/

Another utility you'll find on this book's CD-ROM is the freeware Expander for Windows, the most advanced SIT unstuffer for PCs. Like the Mac version, Expander for Windows decompresses files, but does not compress them. Expander for Windows is a 32-bit utility for Windows 95/98/NT 4.0. There is also a 16-bit version for DOS Windows 3.x called Unstuff/PC, which has capabilities similar to those of Expander for Windows, but is generally behind Expander in terms of updates.

Expander for Windows supports a variety of compression and encoding formats. In addition to decompressing SIT files, Expander can decompress ZIP, ARC, ARJ, and GZIP (.gz). Expander will also decompress self-extracting archives created in SIT, ZIP, and ARJ, but does not decompress Compact Pro (.CPT) archives.

Expander for Windows is also handy if you're receiving e-mail from Macintosh users, since it decodes MacBinary (.bin), BinHex (.hqx), and UUencode (.uue) encoding formats. You can also use Expander to join segmented archives created with StuffIt Deluxe for Macintosh. (Segmenting is used to copy a large file onto several floppy disks.)

It's worth it to have at least version 5.0, which updated its Macintosh compatibility and cross-platform features. Most importantly,

Expander 5.0 added the ability to decompress StuffIt 5.x archives, the newer version of the SIT compression format. (Expander went from version 2 to version 5.0—there were no versions 3 or 4.) Expander for Windows 5.0 and later also can decompress self-expanding .SEA archives, something that no other PC software can do. Also new in version 5.0 was the ability to decode the newer MacBinary III encoding format used by Mac OS 8.5 and other software. Expander 5.0 was the first version to support Unicode (the cross-platform, multilingual alternative to ASCII text), and the first version to be able to decompress Arc (.arc) archives that include folders within folders.

The Expander for Windows interface is very simple—you drag and drop a file or folder from Windows into the open Expander window. Expander then decompresses the files and stores them in a location that you determine. (See Figure 6.6)

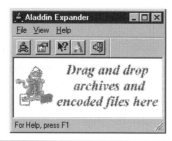

Figure 6.6 Expander for Windows

Aladdin also offers a cross-platform encryption product called Private File, which can compress files in .SIT archives before it encrypts them. Private File can provide 128-bit encryption of files (with 40-bit encryption available for outside the Unitied States). Drag and drop files and folders to encrypt with password. When you buy Private File, you get the Windows and Mac OS versions together in the box.

Aladdin DropStuff for Windows

Aladdin Systems

http://www.aladdinsys.com/

Since StuffIt Expander for Macintosh comes with every copy of Mac OS, compressing files with DropStuff for Windows guarantees that any Mac user will be able to decompress your archive. DropStuff for Windows is a versatile, all-around compression utility, since it also can compress in .ZIP format, and comes with Expander for Windows (which decompresses .SIT and .ZIP archives). No other Windows utility compresses and decompresses both .SIT and .ZIP. (DropStuff for Windows 1.0 does not create StuffIt 5 archives. At the time of this writing, Aladdin was working on StuffIt 5 support in a future version.)

DropStuff works by dragging a file on top of an icon. It also supports Windows contextual menus (the right mouse button), which lets you click on a file, compress it, and enclose it in an e-mail message without launching a utility.

DropStuff for Windows is shareware that is included on this book's CD, and can also be downloaded from the Aladdin's web site. It is not expensive, and if you register, Aladdin will provide on-line technical support.

MindExpander

MindVision

http://www.mindvision.com/Consumer/

MindExpander for Windows is a free decompresser for that supports SIT and ZIP. It also decodes MacBinary and BinHex. (There is also a Macintosh version of MindExpander.) MindVision makes the cross-platform developer installation program Installer Vise.

ExtractorPC

Cyclos

http://www.cyclos.com/extractorpc.htm

If you need to decompress a Macintosh Compact Pro (.CPT) archive on Windows, you can use Cyclos' free ExtractorPC. Cyclos is the maker of the Compact Pro compression shareware for Macintosh. ExtractorPC is a one-trick pony, but it does the job, and the price is right.

WinArj

Tony Lichtenegger
http://www.hotfiles.com

WinArj is a full-featured, shareware module for Visual Basic that can both compress and decompress Mac, Windows, and UNIX formats. It will also let you add files to an existing archive, a handy feature if you are passing an archive back and forth between Windows and Mac users. You can also use WinArj to create self-extracting archives. In addition to SIT, Win Arj supports ARC, ZIP, ZOO, LHA, PAK, TAR, and Microsoft compression formats. WinArj is a shell that requires THREED.VBX, the Visual Basic 3.0 runtime module, and Windows 3.x.

When Not to Decompress Mac Files on Windows Machines

There are times when you might prefer to download Macintosh files to a Windows PC, not for use on the PC, but for the purpose of moving the file to a Macintosh by disk. It could be that the Macintosh doesn't have a modem, so you can't download the file directly. In another scenario, you have a Windows machine with a fast T1 connection to the Internet at work, and a Mac with a modem at home. In this case, you don't want to use any of the Windows unstuffing tools that have just been described.

If you are using a Windows machine to download Macintosh files for use on a Macintosh, it is best to *avoid* decoding or decompressing the file on the Windows PC. Instead, move it to the Macintosh in its encoded or compressed form, and process it there. Once again, the reason is to prevent the loss of the file's resource fork. For a data file, this a minor problem resulting in the loss of an icon, and the inability of Mac OS to recognize the file upon double-clicking it (see Chapter 5). However, if the file is a Macintosh executable—that is, an application, system software, or utility software, the loss of the resource fork will disable the program once it gets to the Macintosh.

Avoiding decoding or decompression of a Macintosh file on Windows can sometimes be problematic with e-mail software, but easy with Web browsers, which don't support Mac formats. Many e-mail clients for Windows do not support these Mac formats either, which in this case, is a good thing. They will simply receive an unrecognizable file that you can then move to a Macintosh. The is problem is with e-mail programs that do support these formats, such as Eudora, because they rarely let you disable the decoding of Mac encoding and compression formats. In this case, your only solution is to use an e-mail client that does not support BinHex or SIT to retrieve the message.

The solution is easier when you download Mac files with a web browser. If your Windows web browser supports the Mac file formats, you have a helper application, such as WinZip or Expander for Windows, installed. You can prevent BinHex (.hqx) decoding and SIT decompressing of a Mac file by disabling a helper application. How you disable it differs with the browser and the version. Here's a quick look at how to do this in Microsoft Internet Explorer and Netscape Navigator.

Disabling Auto Decoding/Decompression in Internet Explorer

To temporarily disable BinHex decoding or SIT decompression in Microsoft Internet Explorer for Windows, you need to locate the helper applications from within Internet Explorer.

1. Go to the View menu and select Options.
2. In the Options menu, select the Programs tab (shown in Figure 6.7).
3. Click the File Types button.
4. Scroll through the Registered File Types list until you find the format you want to turn off. The SIT compression format is listed as "StuffIt Archive." The .hqx encoding format is listed as "BinHex File."

5.   Select a format (see Figure 6.8).
6.   Click the Edit button to bring up the Edit File Type window. In the Actions field, select "open." (See Figure 6.9.)
7.   Click the Remove button to remove the "open" action.

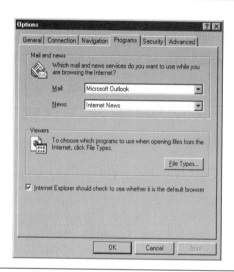

Figure 6.7 The Internet Explorer Programs window

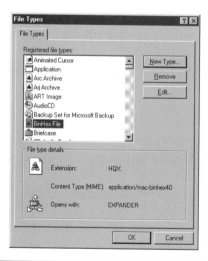

Figure 6.8 Locating the BinHex file type in Internet Explorer

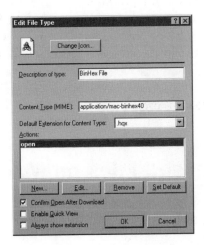

Figure 6.9 Disabling BinHex decoding in Internet Explorer

8. Should you desire to enable decoding or decompression of this file type, go back to this Window, click the New button, and type "open" in the Action field. Then click on Browse to locate your helper program on the hard disk.

Disabling Auto Decoding/Decompression in Navigator

Disabling BinHex encoding or SIT decompression in Navigator for Windows is similar to the process in Internet Explorer.

1. Go to the Options menu and select General Preferences.
2. Click on the Helpers tab
3. Scroll through the list and select Macintosh StuffIt Archive or BinHex Archive.
4. Click the Edit button. In the new window that appears, click either the Save to Disk button or the Prompt User button.

With Prompt User chosen, when you try to download a Mac file, a message will appear asking if you want to use the helper application, cancel, or save to disk. Choose Save to Disk.

When you move the file to your Mac, your Mac decoding or decompression software may not recognize the file as an archive. You may have to open the file from within the utility software.

Receiving PC Compressed Files on Macintosh

Situations opposite to the one described in the previous section are easier to work with. That is, you can download a Windows file on a Macintosh, and then move it to a Windows machine without problems. You can also safely decode and decompress the Windows file on the Mac before moving it to a PC, or for use on the Mac running Windows emulation or a coprocessor card (see Chapter 16).

Some Windows compressed files you'll see on the Internet have file names that end in *.exe*, which indicates that the file is Windows software code. These files are little installer programs that contain the compressed files and the code to decompress the files and install them in their proper location. Microsoft and other Windows software companies often post update files at web sites as .exe files. Mac users can download .exe files, but they cannot expand these files on a Mac without the use of Windows emulation software or a coprocessor card.

What's Next

So far we've skirted around the issue of networking. The next part of the book turns to the issues of building a cross-platform network. This includes hardware and protocols, as well as Mac networking for Windows people and Windows networking for Mac people.

Part Three

Cross-Platform Networking Infrastructure

What's in This Section:

- ◆ **Chapter 7 Network Interface Hardware**

- ◆ **Chapter 8 Macintosh Networking Basics**

- ◆ **Chapter 9 Windows Networking Basics**

- ◆ **Chapter 10 TCP/IP on Macintosh and Windows**

Chapter

What's in This Chapter:

- ♦ *Network interface hardware on Mac and PCs*

- ♦ *Setting up Ethernet in cross-platform networks*

- ♦ *Setting up LocalTalk in cross-platform networks*

- ♦ *Other network interface hardware*

- ♦ *Wireless networking*

- ♦ *Configuring the network interface in Mac OS and Windows*

Network
Interface Hardware

Installing network interface hardware and cabling is the first and probably easiest step in creating a cross-platform network. Windows PCs and Macintoshes can be connected to the same wire segment using the same network interface hardware and cables. At this level, only the driver software for the hardware is platform specific.

All Macs come with at least one type of network interface, Ethernet or LocalTalk, and many models have both on the motherboard. Networked PCs usually have Ethernet adapters. Ethernet is the most common network type, and LocalTalk, while on the decline, is still used for small Mac networks. You can also add network interface cards for other types of networks, such as Fast Ethernet and token ring.

Along with the network interface hardware, each computer runs low-level driver software that comes with the computer or the network interface card. This driver enables the computer to recognize the hardware. PCs and Macs also use higher-level drivers that enable network protocols to be used.

This chapter covers some of the technology of the network interface, pointing out the differences between Macintosh and Windows.

Differences: Network Interface Hardware

The differences in network interfaces for Macintosh and Windows PCs are small. Networking at the hardware level is a data pipe, and is even more platform-agnostic than is Internet technology at higher software levels. Because of this, there should be few cross-platform problems at the network interface level.

One major difference between the platforms is that Mac OS can only communicate over one network interface at a time, while Windows can make use of several. When Apple put two Ethernet connectors on some Mac models, it was to give you a choice of plugs, not to enable connection to two different Ethernet networks. With a PC server, you can use two Ethernet cards connected to the same network to split the data load of each card. On a Mac, you can only do this with special software, such as the AppleShare IP server.

Network interface cards of the past few years fit in a Peripheral Component Interconnect, or PCI, slot. PCI has been a standard slot in PCs since the mid-1990s. Apple adopted PCI as its standard in 1995 with the introduction of the Power Macintosh 7500 and 8500. Before PCI, the standard expansion slot in Macs was NuBus. Some older Macs also had a processor direct slot (PDS), but network interface cards for PDS slots were rare.

Most Macs and PCs of recent years contain PCI expansion slots, which means you can use the same network interface card in both machines. This means you could find a working Fast Ethernet card in a PC, pull it out, and install it in a Mac. You will also need driver software written specifically for the operating system and hardware.

PCI cards come in two sizes, 12 inches long and 7 inches long. Some PC and Mac models only have room for the 7-inch type, but network interface cards can usually fit in the smaller slot.

Ethernet

Ethernet is the most popular network interface for PCs and Macs. It is the first choice for a cross-platform network because of its wide availability, relatively low cost, and good performance, and because it can support multiple network protocols at once. Ethernet, as defined by the IEEE 802.3 specification, broadcasts data over the network at a rate of 10 Mbits per second. The actual throughput is less, slowing as the numbers of computers and the traffic rates increase. Throughput also depends on other facts, such as the network protocols used.

There are several types of Ethernet, each with its own type of cabling schemes and connectors. Every Mac and PC on a network segment must use the same Ethernet type. The most common variant of Ethernet is 10BaseT, which uses unshielded, twisted-pair cabling containing two pairs of wires. The 10BaseT cable (also known as *category 3* cable) plugs directly into the port on the computer or network interface card, without the need for a transceiver box. 10BaseT cables use an RJ-45 connector, which looks like a thicker version of an ordinary telephone cable.

10BaseT Ethernet usually makes use of a star topology, so that every computer and network printer connects directly to a piece of connecting hardware called a hub. Macs and PCs can connect to the same hub. For small Ethernet networks, you can buy inexpensive hubs for as little as $30, such as Asanté Technologies' FriendlyNet 10TS, which networks five devices. You can also use Farallon EtherWave products, which break the usual 10BaseT rules, and let you daisy-chain Macs and PCs without the use of a hub, like LocalTalk networking on Macs.

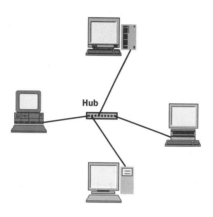

Figure 7.1 The star topology of 10BaseT Ethernet

Other types or Ethernet are no longer in wide use, mainly because they cost more to install and are often less reliable performers. The most expensive type, 10Base5 Ethernet (also called "thicknet"), requires 0.4-inch thick coaxial cable that has two layers of shielding between the layers. 10Base5 cabling is still found in network backbones—a network that connects smaller networks—though fiber optic cable has been replacing thicknet for backbone uses. Another Ethernet type not often installed today is 10Base2, also called "thinnet" because it used a 0.2-inch coaxial cable with a single layer of shielding. Because the shielding protects signals from outside interference, thinnet and thicknet Ethernet don't require hubs—these networks are laid out in a string, called a bus configuration. Thinnet and thicknet Ethernet cables connect to the computers through the use of a small transceiver box.

Making Ethernet Connections

At least one Ethernet port is built onto most Macintosh desktop and PowerBook motherboards and is also found on the motherboards of a few PC models, as well as on many network printers. An Ethernet network interface card can be added to older Mac models where it is not built in, such as the on Performa models, some Motorola StarMax models, and pre–PowerPC Macs from the 1980s. Most PCs get Ethernet connectivity through the use of an Ethernet network interface card.

Power Mac G3 Ethernet Driver Problems

The first-generation (platinu-colored) Power Mac G3s have some problems with the extension file called *Ethernet (Built-In)* version 2.0, and to a lesser degree, versions 2.0.1, 2.0.2, and 2.0.3. The problems occur the Power Macintosh G3 Desktop 233, 266, and 300 and Power Macintosh G3 Minitower 233, 266, and 300. (You'd also see the problems with later G3 models, but these models shipped with later versions of the driver.) Version 2.0 was the wort offender—it could corrupt files being transferred on a network with heavy traffic. It also prevented the Power Mac G3 from connecting to a network when the 10BaseT port was attached to an autosensing 10/100 Mb Ethernet hub or switch. Versions 2.0 through 2.0.3 of the driver can cause the Mac to lose network services, such as file sharing and printing. With any Power Mac G3, you should run at least version 2.0.4 of the Ethernet (Built-in) driver file. You can download a current driver from Apple's web site (http://www.info.apple.com/swupdates). The problems are limited to these machines—version 2.0 of the Ethernet driver does not cause a problem on other Mac models or with the PowerBook G3 models.

The built-in Mac Ethernet ports and 10BaseT cards for PCs use a standard RJ-45 jack, into which you plug the 10BaseT cable directly. However, some older Power Macs, such as the 6100, 7100, and 8100, as well as some NuBus-slot Ethernet cards, used a second type of connector, the AAUI (Apple Attachment Unit Interface) jack. Some Mac models, such the Power Mac 8500, gave you both the RJ-45 and the AAUI jacks. The AAUI jacks require you to use a $30 transceiver, which contained an RJ-45 jack. You could then plug a 10BaseT or other type of cable into the transceiver. The AAUI jack was Apple's version of the AUI jack (Attachment Unit Interface) used on the even older Ethernet cards for both Macs and PCs. (Some Ethernet cards for PCs still give you both AUI and an RJ-45 jacks.) All of these jacks can be used in computers on the same 10BaseT Ethernet segment.

Several models, such as the Power Mac 8600, came with two Ethernet ports, 10BaseT and AAUI. However, only one port can be used at a time.

Ethernet Crossover Cables

If you need to network one PC and one Macintosh, you can connect their 10BaseT ports without using a hub, but you must use a crossover cable, also know as a "Category 5 Crossover" or a "patch cable." Any network software that works over Ethernet will work over a crossover cable. You can also use a cross-over cable with two PCs or two Macs.

You can buy a crossover cable inexpensively, often for under $10, but if you need one right away, you can make one from a standard Ethernet cable. A 10BaseT cable has four wires two pairs). The RJ45 connector has eitht pins. You need to reverse pins 1 and 3, and pins 2 and 6, as in Figure 7.2. (The other pins aren't used.) If you hold the connector with the cable running away from you and the tab down, pin 1 is the right-most pin. The wire colors can differ, but you can note the colors of the wires by looking through the RJ-45 connector. Cut the cable, strip the wires. and rejoin the wires in the right combination. (Solder would be good, but you can twist the wires together.) If you really want to do it right, you can buy new RJ-45 cable connectors and insert the wires into the tiny holes. This takes some practice, so buy several RJ-45 connectors.

Factory-made Ethernet crossover cables will work well at lengths from 3 to 300 ft. Without a hub to regenerate the signals, they will degrade with longer cables, which could lead to communication problems.

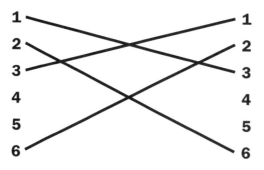

Figure 7.2 The pinouts for an Ethernet crossover cable

LocalTalk

LocalTalk has been around almost as long as the Mac has. LocalTalk was originally designed as a way to share laser printers, which cost $7000 in 1985. Since that time, LocalTalk ports have been used in hundreds of network printers from Apple, Hewlett Packard, and other vendors. Easier to set up and less expensive than 10BaseT Ethernet, LocalTalk reigned as the Mac user's *network-interface-for-the-rest-of-us* for a decade. In fact, the iMac of 1998 was the first Mac not to have a LocalTalk port since Mac networking was introduced in 1985.

Today, limitations in LocalTalk have reduced it's role in networks. One problem is that LocalTalk is useful only in small networks with moderate amounts of network traffic. A single unaided LocalTalk cable can have a maximum of 32 nodes (computers and printers). A LocalTalk network that uses a series of hubs, switches, and repeaters can support 254 nodes. However, with the rise of 10BaseT Ethernet, the use of LocalTalk hubs is no longer common.

LocalTalk also has a much smaller bandwidth than Ethernet, transmitting at 230.4 kbits per second. This is a quicker way to move a file than a 56k modem, about the same as an ISDN connection, but it is slower than Ethernet's 10 Mbits per second bandwidth. In terms of actual data transmission rates, Ethernet runs about 4 to 5 times faster than LocalTalk, not the 40 times that the transmission rate would indicate.

As a cross-platform network medium, LocalTalk is limited by the fact that it can only run the AppleTalk protocol. (The AppleTalk protocol, on the other hand, can run on any network interface and cabling scheme, including Ethernet and token ring.) This means you usually need to install third-party AppleTalk software on your Windows machines (see Chapter 14) if you want to create a cross-platform LocalTalk network. However, if you need to, you can run TCP/IP on LocalTalk by "encapsulating" TCP/IP inside of AppleTalk using a MacIP server. (See Chapter 10.)

LocalTalk Connections in Macs

Despite its limitations, LocalTalk has benefits that make it a sufficient network for a handful of computers, as well as a good ad-hoc network for laptops on the go. Small LocalTalk networks can be set up and running minutes after new Macs are unpacked from their boxes, which makes it an inexpensive temporary network until a more permanent Ethernet network can be put together.

LocalTalk is cheap and easy because of the cabling. LocalTalk uses ordinary unshielded, stranded telephone wire with standard RJ-11 telephone plugs and jacks, the same as you use to plug a telephone or modem into a wall jack. LocalTalk can also use the twisted pair telephone wire used in walls, which is a higher grade than the stranded wire outside of walls.

Each RJ-11 connector plugs into a LocalTalk transceiver, which connects to the computer. LocalTalk transceivers are known generically as "PhoneNET connectors," after the PhoneNET brand name popularized by Farallon. (The original LocalTalk transceivers from Apple used a different wiring scheme, but have long since disappeared.) LocalTalk transceivers are inexpensive, often less than $20 a pair.

You plug a LocalTalk transceiver into the Mac printer port or a PC's LocalTalk interface. On a Mac, you can use either the Printer port or

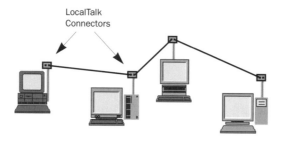

LocalTalk
Connectors

Figure 7.3 A LocalTalk daisy-chain requires terminating resistors at either end.

the Modem port for LocalTalk. (PowerBooks usually have a single serial port.) The transceiver also has to RJ-11 jacks. You connect one computer or printer to the next in a daisy chain, much like a SCSI chain, as in Figure 7.3. (You can configure LocalTalk using a hub, but this has become uncommon since the advent of 10BaseT Ethernet.) Also like a SCSI chain, a LocalTalk chain requires a terminating resistor at either end. Usually, the 120 ohm terminating resistor is fitted into an RJ-11 plug, which you pop into the extra RJ-11 socket of the first and last nodes. You can also use Farallon PhoneNET Pocket Connectors, which come with built-in terminating resistors and only a single RJ-11 jack. These small terminators are easy to carry around.

LocalTalk for PCs

LocalTalk network interfaces for PCs are neither common nor inexpensive—a LocalTalk Network Interface card can cost more than a 100BaseT card. However, there are some situations where it might make sense to use LocalTalk for a cross-platform network. For instance, if you were adding a single PC to a Mac LocalTalk network, it would be less expensive to add a LocalTalk card to the Windows PC than to replace the LocalTalk cabling with Ethernet cabling. If the LocalTalk network contained several LocalTalk printers, upgrading to Ethernet would require LocalTalk-to-Ethernet adapters for the existing printers. You could also add a LocalTalk network interface card to a Windows NT server or a Novell NetWare server to service an existing LocalTalk network of Macs.

Currently COPS (http://www.copstalk.com) is the only company still making LocalTalk cards for PCs (the COPS LT) card. Another company, Apexx Technology (http://www.apexxtech.com/), offers a parallel port LocalTalk adapter. Both COPS and Apexx offer AppleTalk software for Windows 95/98 an NT, which is required, as LocalTalk only runs AppleTalk protocols.

Web Update Link: *For current information on LocalTalk network interfaces for PCs, see http://www.macwindows.com/Network.html.*

Other Network Interface Hardware

Macs and PCs can also participate on other types of network interfaces, such as Fast Ethernet, Gigabit Ethernet, and token ring, with the addition of a network interface card and driver software.

Fast Ethernet

Fast Ethernet, also known as 100BaseT Ethernet, is a higher-speed variant of 10BaseT Ethernet with a top theoretical bandwidth of 100 MB per second. To take advantage of the throughput, you should use TCP/IP protocols. (AppleTalk is a much slower protocol.) With TCP/IP, file transfer from a network volume can in some cases be faster than access of a hard drive, in the 5-to-7 MB per second range. (This has been shown to be the case with UNIX file servers, clients running Windows 95 or NT and Mac OS 8.5 or later. Mac OS 8.5 greatly boosted the speed of Mac client file transfers.)

Almost every aspect of 100BaseT is the same as 10BaseT, except for the bandwidth. As specified in the IEEE 802.3u standard, 100BaseT uses the same type of data frames (or packets) to send data as 10BaseT. Also like 10BaseT, Fast Ethernet is set up in a star configuration with a hub or switch in the center. Fast Ethernet uses a category 5 cable.

Because of these similarities, 100BaseT hardware is usually backward-compatible with 10BaseT. This means that most 100BaseT network interface cards can run on a 10BaseT network at 10 Mbits per second. The 100BaseT port on the iMac's motherboard can also operate on 10BaseT networks. Additionally, auto-sensing 10/100BaseT hubs can detect whether a computer is using a Fast Ethernet or 10BaseT interface and communicates with that computer at the appropriate speed. This makes it easy to upgrade a network from 10BaseT to 100BaseT, as you can install 100BaseT network interface cards a few at a time, on an as-needed basis, and still keep the network running.

The main difference between the two Ethernet variants is that 100BaseT requires a higher grade of cable than 10BaseT. Fast Ethernet requires at least category 5 unshielded twisted pair cable while 10BaseT can use category 2, 3, or 4.

PCI 100BaseT Ethernet network interface cards are available from a wide variety of vendors, including 3Com, Asanté, Farallon, Intel, and NetGear. Many companies sell both Mac and Windows drivers.

MacWindows Tip

Some Power Mac G3s with 10/100BaseT network interface cards in them came with a driver extension file called Apple 10/100 Fast Ethernet. *This file must be installed separately, as it is not part of the standard installation. The driver resides on the System CD-ROM, in a folder named "Important Extra System Software." You can install it simply by dragging it to the Extensions folder in the System folder.*

Gigabit Ethernet

There is another variant of Ethernet, known as Gigabit Ethernet, or 1000BaseT, which has 10 times the bandwidth of Fast Ethernet. (As with Fast Ethernet, you'll want to run TCP/IP to get the most out of the bandwidth.) Network designers began installing Gigabit Ethernet first on network backbones, a part of a network that connects other network segments together, but usually doesn't connect directly to user workstations. Recently, the standard has begun to garner some support from operators of high-volume networks, such as in prepress publishing and large production houses.

Gigabit Ethernet PCI cards and hubs have been available for several years, though at high cost, and at first only for PCs. Macintosh drivers for Gigabit Ethernet adapters only started becoming available in late 1998. Apple gave Gigabit Ethernet in Macs a push in early 1999 when it began offering Gigabit Ethernet adapters as an option for the so-called "Blue and White" Power Mac G3, the second-generation Power Macintosh G3. Asanté was one of the first cross-platform Gigabit providers with its GigaNIC cards. Asanté provides GigaNIC drivers for Windows 95/98, Windows NT (Intel and Alpha), and Mac OS.

At the time this book was written, Gigabit Ethernet was still in the early stages of adoption. For the next few years, Gigabit Ethernet costs are likely to remain high in comparison to Fast Ethernet, and it is not likely to be widely adopted.

Token Ring

Token ring (IEEE 802.5) is an older network interface developed by IBM. It was once dominant in environments that networked PCs and IBM mainframes. Macintoshes can participate on token ring networks as well. Instead of using a broadcast method of transmitting data, such as one used by Ethernet, token ring only allows one computer to transmit data at a time. Because of this, token ring is more efficient than Ethernet and can carry heavier loads. However, use of token ring networks has been declining in recent years as low-cost 10BaseT Ethernet has become pervasive.

At one time token ring cards for Macintosh were available from half a dozen vendors. Today, there is only one known vendor providing a Mac OS driver for a token ring card. The company is Madge Systems and the card is the Smart 16/4 PCI Ringnode card. The Macintosh driver is not provided with the board, but you can download it from the Madge web site (http://www.madge.com).

NOTE: In case you want to get technical, Ethernet's method of broadcasting packets on a network is known as CSMA/CD—carrier sense, multiple access, with collision detection. When Ethernet hardware detects packet collisions, it resends the packets.

Wireless Networking

The promise of networking without the expense of cabling has always been intriguing, but has been hampered by slow speed and competing technologies and standards. Wireless networking interfaces have been around for a decade or so, using a variety of frequencies, but haven't gained much popularity. There are several much-hyped wireless home networks products, but even for small networks, they offer higher cost, lower bandwidth, and more hassles than simple 10BaseT Ethernet.

The closest thing to a popular business wireless technology at this point is the IrDA (Infrared Data Association) standard, an infrared method that has been adopted in many Intel-based and Apple notebook computers, as well as in the Apple iMac, and in some printers.

Several PowerBook models have infrared communications panels, but not all of them support IrDA. There are two types of infrared network interfaces used in PowerBooks, IrDA and IRTalk. Some models support both, and older models support only IRTalk. If they don't support IrDA, they cannot communicate with PC notebooks or other IrDA devices.

IrDA has a bandwidth of 4 Mbit per second—quite a bit slower than Ethernet, but still faster than LocalTalk. It can run both TCP/IP and AppleTalk.

IRTalk is Apple's wireless version of LocalTalk. It runs at 230.4 Kbit per second, the same as wired LocalTalk. Also like LocalTalk, IRTalk can run only the AppleTalk protocols. However, IRTalk has one advantage over IrDA, in that it is a multipoint technology, in that several PowerBooks pointed in the right direction can use it simultaneously. IrDA is point-to-point technology, in that a notebook computer must be aimed directly at another IrDA device.

The iMac, the PowerBook G3 and G3 series, and the PowerBook 3400 have both IrDA and IRTalk. The PowerBooks 190, 5300, 1400 only have IRTalk, and cannot communicate with PC notebooks.

With either IrDA or IRTalk, you can communicate directly with another computer to transfer files, or connect to a wired network by aiming the laptop at an infrared transceiver connected to the network. As with the wired network interfaces, a PC and a Macintosh communicating over wireless must be using the same protocol.

Configuring Infrared in PowerBooks

Macintosh PowerBooks that support IrDA come with three driver files: the Infrared control panel, IrDALib extension, and IrLanScannerPPC extension. The Infrared control panel (Figure 7.4) will tell you whether IrDA and IRTalk is selected, and which Infrared devices are in range to communicate with.

To switch between IrDA and IRTalk, click the Options button to bring up the Options window (Figure 7.5). The check box labeled "Notify me if the Infrared connection is interrupted" only works for IrDA. With this check box selected, a message will tell you if the other computer moves out of range or shuts down during communications.

The PowerBook will not go into sleep mode by itself when the IrDA option is selected in this window and in the AppleTalk control panel with AppleTalk on. In this case, you can still put the PowerBook into sleep mode manually.

MacWindows Tip

The IrDA setting can sometimes interfere with the establishment of a dial-up PPP connection using the Remote Access or PPP control panel, presenting an error message that says the modem port is in use. Switching the Infrared control panel's setting to IRTalk will enable the PowerBook to establish a PPP connection.

Figure 7.4 The PowerBook's Infrared control panel

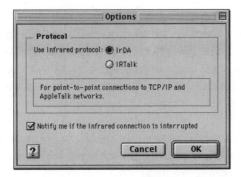

Figure 7.5. Switching between cross-platform IrDA and Apple-only IRTalk

IRTalk's multipoint ability can interfere with creating an infrared connection with another PowerBook that is directly behind it or too close. Moving the PowerBooks farther away and skewing the angle can enable the connection.

Installing Network Interface Cards

Macs and Windows machines differ in the way you install a network interface card, even though you may be installing the same card in each.

Ethernet (Built-In)

To install a card in a Mac, you place it in a PCI slot and copy an extension file—the driver file that came with the card—to the Extensions folder in the System folder. As far as the low-level installation goes, that's it. With PCs, there are some additional issues and procedures.

In a PC, expansion cards communicate with the processor and memory on the motherboard using several lines of communications known as system resources. (PC resources have no relation to the resource fork of a Macintosh file, by the way.) One PC resource is an interrupt request (IRQ), which forces the processor to stop what it's doing to look at a request from the card. The direct memory access (DMA) channel is a link to the PC's memory. There is also a memory address that must be set. Each device in the PC, including cards, drive controllers for floppy disk, hard drive, and CD-ROM, COM ports, and LPT ports for printing, must be set to use a unique set of these resources. If two devices try to use the same IRQ line or DMA channel, there's a conflict. With Windows 3.x and earlier, you have to set these system resources for each device you add. If you picked an IRQ line that the floppy disk controller happened to be using, you'd be in for some serious troubleshooting time.

Microsoft and Intel's Plug and Play technology, introduced with Windows 95, automates the configuration of these system resources. If the network card, PC hardware, and drivers are Plug and Play compatible, the PC's BIOS will work with the hardware to allocate unique IRQ addresses, DMA channels, and so on, to each device. Plug and Play devices can also share certain resources. Windows 95 and 98 will handle these configuration issues for you. The allocation of resources occurs when the PC boots up with an unrecognized or yet-to-be-configured device. Windows 95, 98, and NT will also help with configuration by trying to find a Plug and Play device driver that works with your card. If it can't find one, Windows will tell you that it can't find a driver for the device and will ask you to install one from a distribution disk that came with the new hardware.

After you install driver software, you should check to make sure that Windows is communicating with the card. Open the Network icon in the Control Panel. If this installation was successful, you'll see your network interface card listed.

If you don't see the card in the Network window of the Control panel, you'll need to do some manual configuring of the driver by clicking the Add button and following the instructions. If this doesn't work, go back to the software disk that came with the network interface card and run the installer wizard.

You can add multiple network adapter cards to PCs to communicate with one or more networks, though getting them to working can be tricky. Macs can only make use of one network interface at a time.

Reconfiguring an IRQ Setting in Windows 95/98/NT

Even with Plug and Play, you may need to reconfigure the IRQ setting of a network interface card manually. Depending on which hardware from which manufacturer happens to be in the PC, a network interface card might work better at one IRQ setting than another. IRQ settings are described by numbers, IRQ2, IRQ3, IRQ4, and so forth. To reset an IRQ address, perform the following:

1. Open the System icon in the Control Panel. Click the Device Manager tab to get a list of hardware (Figure 7.6).

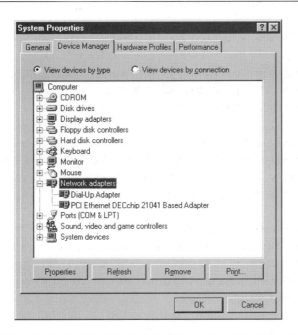

Figure 7.6 The Windows System Properties window

2. Double-click the Network adapter icon to bring up the Properties window for that device.
3. Click the Resources tab to display the resource settings, as shown in Figure 7.7.
4. Uncheck Use Automatic Settings and double-click the Interrupt Request listing to change the IRQ line.

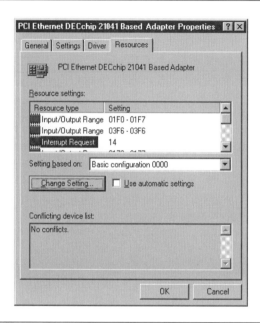

Figure 7.7 Changing the IRQ line for a NIC in the Properties window

If you are working with older hardware that is not Plug and Play compatible, you'll have to configure the system resources manually. If you don't have a list of the every system resource setting for every device in the PC—and most people don't—avoiding conflicts can be a matter of trial and error. Older network interface cards uses jumpers on the cards to set IRQ and memory addresses. Other cards used special setup software that came with the cards. You'll also need to change the driver software to match the IRQ and memory address settings.

Selecting Network Interfaces in Software

When you have more than one network interface installed, Windows and Mac OS give you a way of selecting the interface or interfaces to use. In Windows, you can select several. In Mac OS, you can only select one at a time, but you can go back and select a new network interface at any time without restarting the computer. With either system, a modem connection to a network is also treated like a network interface alternative.

In most versions of Windows, you choose select the network interface and the network protocols from the Network dialog box (Figure 7.8), located in the Control Panel. If you don't see your adapter in the list, click the Add button, and then click Adapter and Add. This will bring up a list of network interface cards from which you can choose. Clicking the Have Disk button will prompt you for the manufacturer's driver installation diskette or CD-ROM.

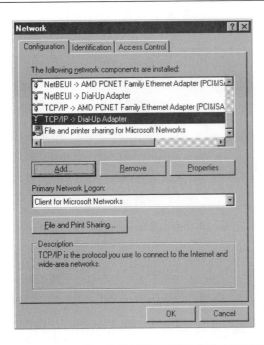

Figure 7.8 Selecting network interfaces with Windows' Network dialog box

The Windows 95/98 Network dialog box will present choices, such as Ethernet, that are not present in the machine. On a Mac, you won't get the Ethernet choice if the Mac doesn't have an Ethernet port or network interface card. You can also configure protocols and networking software from the Network window. I'll have more to say about those in future chapters.

In Mac OS, you choose the network interface used for a particular protocol. There's a TCP/IP control panel for selecting the network interface for TCP/IP, and an AppleTalk control panel for doing the same with AppleTalk. For Macs using the IPX/SPX protocol on Novell NetWare networks, the NetWare Client for Macintosh includes a MacIPX control panel to choose the network interface.

Although you can't network over two network interfaces at once, you can use two protocols at the same time. For instance, you would use AppleTalk and TCP/IP at the same time if you were browsing the Web while printing a Web page to a network printer.

To select a network interface in the TCP/IP control panel, you click on the Connect Via pop-up menu at the top of the window. Figure 7.9 shows three choices, Ethernet, PPP (which is a dial-up modem

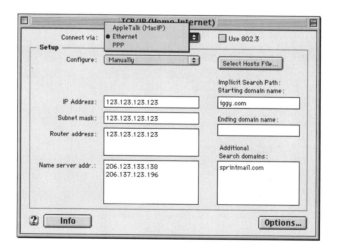

Figure 7.9 Choosing a network interface in the Mac TCP/IP control panel

connection), and AppleTalk (MacIP). I've already mentioned that TCP/IP cannot travel over LocalTalk. MacIP is an method that encapsulates TCP/IP packets inside of AppleTalk packets, enabling them to travel over LocalTalk. (There is further discussion of MacIP in Chapter 10.) In a PowerBook, the TCP/IP Connect Via pop-up menu would have an additional choice of Infrared Port (IrDA), if that option were enabled in the Infrared control panel. Any other network interfaces, such as 100BaseT or token ring, would automatically show up here as well, as long as the proper driver extension files were in the Extensions folder.

You choose a network interface in the AppleTalk control panel in the same manner as the TCP/IP control panel, via a Connect Via pop-up menu (shown in Figure 7.10). There are two choices for LocalTalk, the Printer Port and Modem Port. (In PowerBooks, which have a single serial port, there is a single LocalTalk choice called Modem/Printer Port.) As with the TCP/IP control panel, any additional network interfaces will show up here. In current PowerBooks, one of the choices will be either Infrared Port (IrDA) or Infrared Port (IRTalk), depending on which you have selected in the Infrared control panel.

You'll notice that the AppleTalk control panel contains no fields to accept typed information. That's because the AppleTalk protocol is self-configuring.

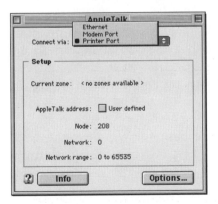

Figure 7.10 Choosing a network interface in the Mac AppleTalk control panel

You can also run AppleTalk on Windows with the addition of software. AppleTalk solutions for Windows also come with network services software that enables Windows PCs to participate in AppleTalk-based file sharing and printing. In addition, the Windows NT Server comes with AppleTalk file sharing support of Macintosh clients. Chapter 14 will discuss AppleTalk for Windows solutions.

Building on Infrastructure

With the network hardware installed, you have a system on which to broadcast messages and move files. But setting up the network infrastructure is just the first step in getting the Macintosh and Windows platforms to communicate. There are two other important pieces you'll need to create an effective cross-platform network:

1. Network protocols. These include TCP/IP, AppleTalk, and NetBEUI. Protocols are the network languages used by the computers. Machines must speak the same protocol in order to communicate.
2. Network services. These are the user applications and server software that provide user functions such as file sharing and email.

Windows and Mac OS include software that provides some protocols and network services, but they aren't necessarily compatible—you may need to add software. But even when they are compatible, setting up protocols and services on each platform is very different. Chapter 8 is a primer on Macintosh networking for Windows people who don't know Macs, or for Mac people who don't know networking. Chapter 9 describes the basics of Windows networking, information you'll find helpful when setting up a cross-platform network.

Chapter

What's in This Chapter:

- ◆ **Mac OS network software: Open Transport**

- ◆ **Configuring TCP/IP software**

- ◆ **Configuring AppleTalk**

- ◆ **Configuring printing and file sharing**

8

Macintosh Networking Basics

For over a decade, network software has been an integral part of Mac OS. Drivers, libraries, and applications installed on every machine have enabled networking at every level. Mac OS includes the low-level network interface drivers that run the built-in Ethernet and LocalTalk network hardware described in Chapter 7. Mac OS includes network transport protocols, the languages that computers use to communicate with each other. On the network services level, Mac OS includes drivers for network printing, as well as file sharing client software and peer-to-peer server software over AppleTalk and TCP/IP protocols.

For many years, Macintosh networking was focused around AppleTalk, designed for connecting Macs to other Macs and to printers. The Mac-only focus changed in 1995, when Apple completely rewrote the networking portion of Mac OS and renamed it Open Transport.

The new networking software took the emphasis off of AppleTalk and made TCP/IP an equal partner as a communications vehicle. Mac OS 8 introduced Personal Web Sharing, a feature that lets other users on a TCP/IP network access a Mac's files using a web browser. Cross platform networking with AppleTalk is also possible. Macs can use AppleTalk and TCP/IP at the same time, as you might if you were browsing the Web while printing a Web page to a network printer.

The built-in features still lack many cross-platform capabilities at the network services level. However, there are many third-party solutions that can augment the Mac's native network abilities. Most of these are built on the lower-level services of Open Transport. Other chapters will discuss some of those approaches. The purpose of this chapter is to provide a brief look at the networking components of Mac OS, and their cross-platform abilities and implications. With an understanding of what Mac OS offers and what it lacks, one can better evaluate the efficacy of add-on solutions.

Mac OS Network Software: Open Transport

Open Transport is the collective name for the Mac OS files that enable networking of all types. Open Transport is also a set of APIs (application program interfaces) that developers use to create networking software for Mac OS. Open Transport consists of a set of drivers and other files located in the Extensions and Control Panel folders in the System folder. A few of the networking system files, such as those that enable printing and file sharing, are not part of Open Transport and can function with pre–Open Transport software known as *Classic Networking*.

Mac OS 8.5 added some non–Open Transport files related to net-woring, including Sherlock (which lets you search the Internet), an Internet control panel (a front end to the Internet Config settings program), and the DNS Plugin extension. These are not depicted in Figure 8.1.

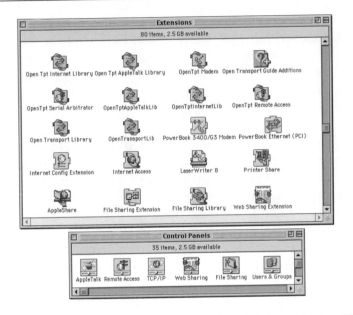

Figure 8.1 The Mac OS networking software

Most Open Transport files don't load into RAM at startup, but instead load when a user accesses a network. When Open Transport files are loaded, such as when you initiate a dial-up Internet connection to the Internet, the memory partition of Mac OS increases. (You can see this in the About This Computer Command in the Apple menu.) If virtual memory is on, the increase in the Mac OS RAM partition can be as little as 200K. With virtual memory off, it can be as much as 1.2 MB. When the network connection is terminated, the memory is released.

Open Transport is a multiprotocol system. It comes with two transport protocols, TCP/IP and AppleTalk. Classic Networking was basically AppleTalk networking, with TCP/IP tacked on to the edge. Open Transport put TCP/IP on an equal footing with AppleTalk in terms of access to the operating system, which improved the speed and stability of TCP/IP networking. Developers have developed drivers for other protocols, such as IPX/SPX and NetBIOS Over TCP/IP, using the Open Transport APIs. These add-on protocols also get access to the operating system services available to AppleTalk and TCP/IP. Developers of networking software have access to several types of efficient network communications methods, including UNIX STREAMS and DLPI. (Open Transport was based on something called MENTAT STREAMS, which caused some file serving problems in early versions of Open Transport.)

Open Transport gives users the ability to switch between different network interfaces, including serial (LocalTalk), dial-up, and network interface cards, without having to restart the Mac or quit network applications. It also provides a consistent interface for configuring protocols and network services.

Running Open Transport

Today, Open Transport is standard on all Mac models, including PowerBooks. Apple introduced Open Transport in the first Power Macs to use PCI expansion slots, the 7500, 8500, and 9500. Older Power Macs can also run Open Transport, which supports network interface cards in NuBus slots and SCSI-attached network adapters. It also supports network interface cards in PC Card slots in PowerBooks. You can run Open Transport on System 7.1 or later, though Apple recommends using System 7.5.3 or later. Open Transport has its own installer, so you can install it without doing a complete Mac OS upgrade.

Still, there are ways to run Classic Networking. In addition to simply using an older version of Mac OS, there used to be a program called Network Selector, which shipped with non-PCI Macs. Network Selector let users switch between Open Transport and Classic Networking.

If you are considering running Classic Networking on an older Mac, consider this: Classic Networking was a hodge-podge of Apple files and freeware that had been collected separately over the years. Classic Networking is slower and generally less stable than Open Transport and is incompatible with some of today's third-party networking software. However, it does use a megabyte less memory than Open Transport, which might be a consideration for older Macs.

That being said, it should be noted that it took a little time for Apple to get Open Transport right. I recommend using at least version 1.2 or later. However, you should not under any circumstances use any version of Open Transport earlier than version 1.1, which was the first stable release. Earlier versions were slow and prone to crash during Internet connections and while printing. There were also problems establishing PPP connections. Version 1.2 (which first shipped with Mac OS 8.0) fixed some more TCP/IP problems, including a famous bug called the "ping of death."

To see what version of Open Transport is installed in a Mac, open the AppleTalk control panel and click the Info button. The Open Transport version is displayed above the AppleTalk and AppleTalk driver version numbers (Figure 8.2).

You can also find the version of Open Transport by selecting the Get Info command in the File menus of the AppleTalk, TCP/IP, and PPP control panels.

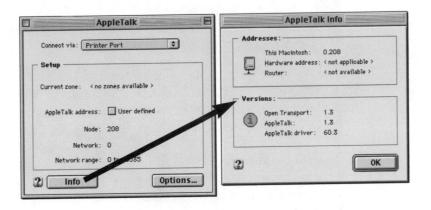

Figure 8.2 The AppleTalk control panel will show you what version of Open Transport is installed.

Creating Multiple Configurations

The TCP/IP, PPP, and AppleTalk control panels share common features. The File and Edit menus of each is identical in all three control panels. The main features are user modes and multiple configurations.

There are three user modes, shown in Figure 8.3:

♦ **Basic.** Minimizes the displayed fields by hiding some, and making others read-only.
♦ **Advanced.** Displays all fields (the Remote Access/PPP control panel does not have an Advanced user mode).
♦ **Administrator.** Lets you choose to lock out individual settings or fields so that uses can't change them, except by going into Administrator mode. You can lock users out of Administrative mode with a password.

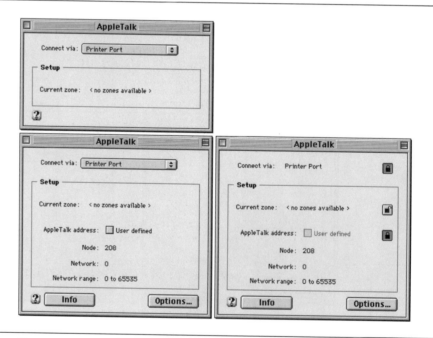

Figure 8.3 Basic, Advanced, and Administrator views of Apple networking control panels. The TCP/IP and Remote Access control panels have similar views.

You can also create multiple, different configurations and switch between them at any time, without having to restart the Mac. For instance, a traveler with a PowerBook might configure several different PPP settings (with different telephone numbers and ISP settings) and TCP/IP settings. Someone accessing several different TCP/IP networks regularly might create several TCP/IP configuration settings. A PowerBook user might create several configuration settings to access the same network from different places, such as a home, an office, and while traveling.

To create a new network configuration for AppleTalk, TCP/IP, or PPP, you choose Configurations from the File menu of the control panel. Select a configuration (if you only have one, select Default) and click the Duplicate button. Then rename the new configuration and alter the settings. To choose a configuration to use, click on the configuration and click the Make Active button, as shown in Figure 8.4.

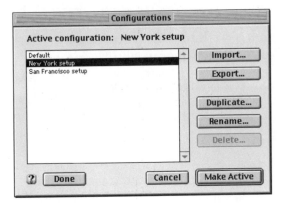

Figure 8.4 Creating multiple configurations in the TCP/IP, PPP, and AppleTalk control panels

TCP/IP Software

This section looks at the basic functions of the Macintosh Open Transport TCP/IP software, and some of the configuration aspects that are common to all network situations. More detailed information on configuring specific IP situations is included in Chapter 10, where the settings are compared to those in Windows.

Mac OS now includes not just TCP/IP transport protocols, but services as well. You can access an AppleShare file server over TCP/IP—this is described in the later section called AppleTalk and AppleShare. Mac OS 8.1 introduced TCP/IP printing. Personal Web Sharing turns a Mac workstation into a peer-to-peer web server. In Mac OS 8.5 and later, you can use Mac OS's Find File utility to contact and do a look-up on one or more Internet search engines without opening a web browser.

Troubleshooters should be aware that Apple's old MacTCP Ping utility is not compatible with Open Transport, and Apple is not planning to upgrade it. There are several Ping utilities for TCP/IP that are compatible with Open Transport. These include MacPing from Dartmouth (ftp://www.dartmouth.edu/pages/softdev/), OTTool from Neon Software, (ftp://ftp.neon.com) and Mac TCP Watcher v2.0 from Peter N. Lewis & Stairways Software (ftp://ftp.share.com).

TCP/IP Control Panel

The Connect Via pop-up is where you choose the network interface method for connecting to a TCP/IP network. (See Chapter 7 for more details.) You get a choice of Ethernet, PPP, and AppleTalk encapsulation—MacIP (MacIP is discussed in Chapter 10). The pop-up menu will also display any other types of network hardware you have installed, such as token ring.

The Configure pop-up menu (Figure 8.5) is where you set the method of obtaining an IP address. There are four choices:

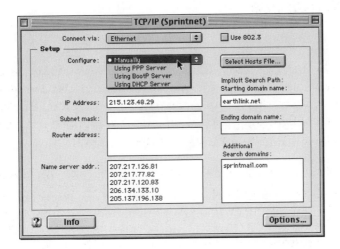

Figure 8.5. The TCP/IP control panel

◆ Manually—used when you type in an IP address
◆ Using PPP Server—often used with a modem connection
◆ Using BootP Server—a server that gives out IP addresses
◆ Using DHCP Server—a more common IP address server in cross-platform networks.

With each different setting, the control panel will gray out irrelevant fields and enable relevant fields.

Mac OS 8.5 shipped with Open Transport 2.0, which added a new self-configuring feature for the IP address. When the TCP/IP control panel is set to DHCP and no DHCP server responds, the Mac will set its own IP address and check the network to make sure that no other nodes have the address. This is similar to the way AppleTalk has always worked. This makes it easier to set up a small TCP/IP network with a DHCP server. (Windows 98 has a similar feature. For more details on IP self-addressing and other TCP/IP issues, see Chapter 10.)

Remote Access (or PPP) Control Panel

The Remote Access control panel was called PPP in versions of Mac OS before 8.5. Both look nearly identical, and perform the same main function—to let you dial, disconnect, and monitor PPP (Point-to-Point Protocol) connections over a telephone line. You can use other software to dial a PPP server, but the Remote Access or PPP control panel must be located in the Extensions folder. You can also dial a telephone manually, by selecting the Dial Manually command from the Remote Access menu.

A PPP connection behaves differently in one respect on desktop Power Macintosh and notebook PowerBook models. When you choose Sleep from the special menu or control strip on a PowerBook, Open Transport will close the PPP link. However, on a desktop Mac, the link is not terminated. A sleeping desktop Mac can keep an active network link going, so it's okay if sleep mode initiates during a big file transfer.

The Remote Access control panel used to be part of a separate Apple product, Apple Remote Access. It has some abilities that the older PPP control panel does not. Most notably for cross-platform environ-

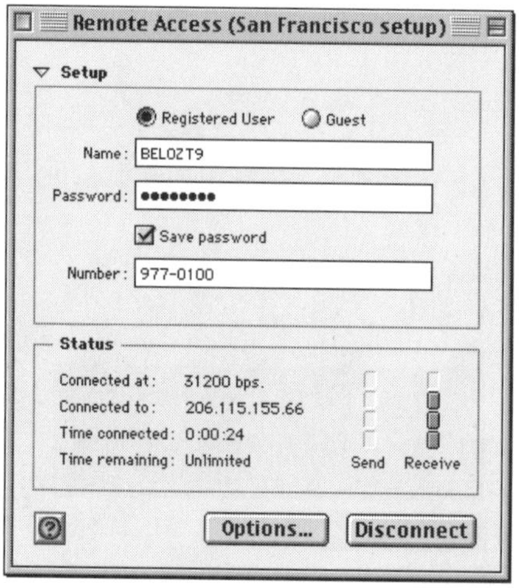

Figure 8.6 The Remote Access control panel

ments, it can use the MS-CHAP (challenge handshake authentication protocol) protocol to dial into Microsoft Remote Access Servers. It can create a dial-up AppleTalk link using the Apple Remote Access Protocol (ARAP), which you select through the Options button.

For more on dial-up networking, see Chapter 12.

Alternatives to Remote Access and PPP Control Panels

There are Internet service providers who still instruct their Macintosh customers to use FreePPP or MacPPP, shareware control panels for dial up connections that predated the Open Transport PPP control panel. At this point, there is no reason use these older freeware PPP implementations instead of the Remote Access or PPP control panel that comes with Open Transport. If your ISP asks you to use the older software, it's likely that the ISP hasn't bothered to look into Mac OS networking in the past several years, or hasn't upgraded its installation CD-ROM.

If you insist on running FreePPP or MacPPP instead of OT/PPP, make sure you use version 2.5 or later of each. Earlier versions of each have problems when virtual memory is turned on and tend to crash when Open Transport is installed.

There are a few Open Transport–compatible PPP alternatives that have added features. Network Telesystems' NTS PPP (you need 2.0 or later) enables a Mac to connect to Windows NT Servers using Microsoft's PPTP (point-to-point tunneling protocol) and MS-CHAP. PPTP creates a secure encrypted "tunnel" over the Internet to your LAN, while MS-CHAP is Microsoft's authentication protocol for Windows NT Remote Access Servers (RAS). NTS PPP also supports AppleTalk over PPP for getting to printers and AppleShare servers on the network. NTS PPP comes bundled with Ping under the name TunnelBuilder or in a bundle of Internet applications and utilities called TCP Pro. (http://www.ntsi.com/).

If you need to make a SLIP connection, you'll have to add third-party software, as Open Transport does not come with a SLIP driver. LinkUPPP! by FCR Software (http://www.fcr.com) can create SLIP as well as PPP connections. It's also a multilink PPP client, in that is supports the use of two 56K modems together over one phone line to double the bandwidth to 112K. It also supports AppleTalk over TCP/IP connections.

MacWindows Tip

The long-time MacSLIP, created by Hyde Park Software, is no longer available except as part of Qualcomm's Eudora Pro e-mail software. If you do have an old copy of MacSLIP, you'll need version 3.0.3 or later to be compatible with Open Transport.

TCP/IP Printing

Macs can print over TCP/IP to printers that support the LPR/LPD (Line Printer Remote/Line Printer Daemon) protocol. LPR/LPD originated in BSD UNIX, but is now supported in printers from Apple, Hewlett-Packard, and other manufacturers.

Figure 8.7 Configuring IP printing on a Mac with the Desktop Printer Utility

In order to print over IP, the Mac needs the LaserWriter printer driver 8.5.1 or later installed. LaserWriter 8.5.1 first shipped with Mac OS 8.1, but you can enable IP printing on Mac OS 7.5 through Mac OS 7.6.1 by copying the LaserWriter 8.5.1 or later file to the Extensions folder (in the System folder. You can download a current LaserWriter driver from Apple's Software Update web site (http://www.info.apple.com/swupdates), or simply copy it from the Extensions folder of a Mac with Mac OS 8.1 or later.

You configure IP printing through the Desktop Printer Utility that comes with Mac OS (Figure 8.7). This will create a desktop printer icon. From the list of printer types, select "Printer (LPR)" and click OK. Next select a PPD for the printer from "Postscript Printer Description (PPD) File." Click "Change in the "Internet Printer" area. Now you'll need to enter the printer's IP address or domain in the "Printer Address" field. You can enter a queue name, if the printer is set up to use one. The Verify button will check to see if the Mac can locate the printer.

For more on TCP/IP printing, see Chapter 15.

Sharing Files with TCP/IP: Personal Web Sharing

For people who need to move files between Macs and PCs but don't want to buy any software, Mac OS's Personal Web Sharing feature is a good solution. Personal Web Sharing gives users of any operating system access to files on Mac workstation, and can also enable the Mac to server HTML pages. Users can download files from the Mac using a web browser.

MacWindows Tip

Personal Web Sharing first shipped with Mac OS 8.0. You can also run Personal Web Sharing on Mac OS 7.6 and 7.6.1, but if you do, be sure to update Open Transport to version 1.2 or later to avoid the crash-causing bug known as the Ping of Death and other problems.

Personal Web Sharing works much like AppleTalk file sharing, and in fact makes use of the File Sharing control panel (called Sharing Setup before Mac OS 8.0), which is where you turn on AppleTalk file sharing. Turning File Sharing on enables both AppleTalk and IP file sharing. You can then use the Web Sharing control panel (Figure 8.8) to assign a folder to be shared via TCP/IP. If you want to allow one or more users to make changes to the folder, you click a button that uses the access privileges you've set in the Users & Groups control panel,

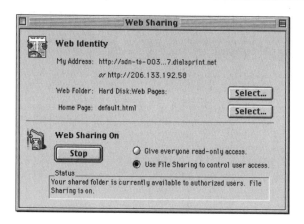

Figure 8.8 The Web sharing control panel

the same place you set access privileges for AppleTalk file sharing (described later in this chapter).

You can use Personal Web Sharing in two ways. The first is to turn a folder containing HTML files into a mini web server. (Mac OS 8.x installs a folder called "Web pages" with some samples.) In this folder you can do things that dedicated web servers do, such as use CGIs to gather and distribute data using forms.

Web Sharing can also enable users to access your non-HTML files, such as word processor, graphics, and desktop publishing documents. Web browser users see your files with a Finder-like interface called Personal NetFinder, which represents documents with their application icons and folders with folder icons (Figure 8.9). The Web Sharing control panel sets this up automatically when you select a file to share. The only difference in creating a mini-web server and a Personal NetFinder folder is that for the latter, when the window comes up saying "Select a document in the web folder to use as your home page," you hit the None button.

Personal Web Sharing has limitations. It's not as fast as a dedicated Web server and isn't recommended for dial-up connections. The problem is that a loss of the IP connection could cause the host Mac to freeze. If you want to use Personal Web Sharing over the Internet, you

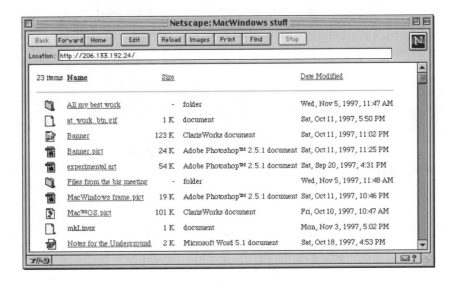

Figure 8.9 With Personal NetFinder enabled, a Mac folder appears like this in another user's web browser.

should use a LAN-based connection to the Internet or intranet with a static IP address.

AppleTalk and AppleShare

Although TCP/IP is the universal network language, AppleTalk is still quite popular with Macintosh users and is even used in cross-platform networking. Because of its ease of use and auto-configuration properties, anyone can quickly set up an AppleTalk network without typing in a single number anywhere.

The first AppleTalk network service was network printing. Since 1987, Mac OS has had peer-to-peer AppleTalk file sharing ability through the use of the Apple Filing Protocol (AFP). Windows NT Services for Macintosh employs AFP over AppleTalk networks.

For dial-up connectivity to AppleTalk networks, Open Transport supports Apple Remote Access (ARA) version 2.0.1 or later. ARA enables Macs to access file servers and other AFP volumes and print over a dial-up connection.

AppleTalk Addressing

AppleTalk has the somewhat undeserved reputation of being a "chatty" protocol. This reputation stems from AppleTalk's default ability to configure AppleTalk node addresses automatically, without a server, through negotiation. This dynamically assigned addressing is facilitated by the AppleTalk Address Resolution Protocol (AARP). When an AppleTalk node joins the network, it checks its parameter RAM for the last AppleTalk node address it use, and sends out a message asking of another node has the address. If another node does, it picks another address at random.

If needed, Macs and printers can also change their address, without any intervention. This is possible because the Macs and printers identify each other by names. This is the Computer Name in the File Sharing control panel (called Sharing Setup before Mac OS 8). Printer names are assigned with a utility from a Mac. The Name Binding Protocol (NBP) queries AppleTalk devices and asks for their names. When you open the Chooser and look for printers or file servers, NBP locates these devices on the network and displays their names. Unlike the naming schemes of other networks, such as WINS and DHCP on Microsoft networks, NBP does not require a server.

Manual AppleTalk Addressing

The total bandwidth used by AppleTalk self addressing is small, along the lines of the traffic generated on TCP/IP networks with server-assigned addressing schemes such as DHCP and the WINS name resolution servers on Microsoft networks. Still, if you don't go for self-configuration, you can shut off AppleTalk's self-configuration feature and manually assign addresses to AppleTalk nodes (Figure 8.10). The Macs will need Open Transport to do this. However, Open Transport AppleTalk will still check for duplicate protocol addresses on the LAN even when static addressing is configured.

Figure 8.10 Manually configuring an AppleTalk node address

To manually assign an AppleTalk address, open the AppleTalk control panel. Next to *AppleTalk Address*, click the check box labeled *User Defined*. You can now type in a node number and network number. The node number for each computer, printer, or router must be unique on a given AppleTalk subnet. (A subnet is a cable segment with a unique network number or range of network numbers.)

Node numbers can be any number from 1 to 254. Network numbers can be any number from 1 to 65,536. (There are no "dots" as in IP addressing.) If you have an AppleTalk router (such as the software router available in Windows NT Server), you can set the network numbers there. Typically, you assign a range of network numbers for each routed cable segment.

You'll need to configure every AppleTalk node in the same manner—either with dynamic addressing or with manually assigned AppleTalk node numbers. As with the TCP/IP control panel, you can prevent users from changing an AppleTalk address by locking the Address field in the AppleTalk control panel while in Administrator mode, and then switching to Advanced or Basic mode.

AppleTalk Printing

Network printing for Macintoshes is still largely done with AppleTalk, though Mac OS 8.1 introduced TCP/IP printing via the LPR/LPD protocol. AppleTalk printing is carried out by the Printer Access Protocol (PAP). AppleTalk printers from all vendors use the Postscript page description language. Mac OS cannot access PC printers without added software, or special server support (as in Windows NT Server).

AppleTalk PAP printing has some advantages over LPR/LPD on TCP/IP. It is easier to set up, in that network printers are detected by the system automatically. With IP printing, you need to type in a printer's IP address or domain. PAP also returns more status and error information back to the user, telling you if a printer is idle, busy, out of paper, has a Postscript error, or is missing a tray, among other things.

To select a network printer, open the Chooser in the Apple menu. You click the LaserWriter icon to bring up a list of Apple and non-Apple Postscript laser printers on the network. (The LaserWriter icon is created by the LaserWriter driver file in the Extensions folder.) Some laser printer models have their own driver, which gives the user access to

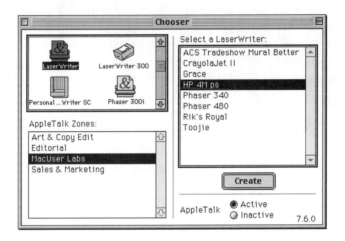

Figure 8.11 Selecting an AppleTalk printer from the Chooser

special features, such as tray handling. Non-network printers are also represented in the Chooser, each by its own individual icon.

If the network has an AppleTalk router, it might be divided up into logical zones. Clicking on a zone in the lower left of the Chooser brings up a list of printers in that network, as shown in Figure 8.11. To select a printer, click the name of a printer and close the Chooser. The printer will stay selected when the Mac is turned off, and will change only when you select a new printer.

AppleShare and AFP

AppleShare is Apple's file server product based on the Apple Filing protocol (AFP). Server products that use AFP are said to be AppleShare-compatible, or AFP-compatible.

Mac OS includes both AFP client and AFP server software, so that Mac users can access each other's machines for file sharing. AFP network volumes mount on the desktops of Mac users and PC users with AFP client software installed. The AFP software in Mac OS is not considered part of the Open Transport suite and can run on Classic Networking. There are also AFP-compatible non-Mac servers, including those running Windows NT and UNIX.

In recent years, the AppleShare server has provided AFP service on TCP/IP, in addition to AppleTalk, and is now called AppleShare IP. This enables traditional Macintosh file service without the use of the AppleTalk protocol. AppleShare IP 6.0 went a step further, supporting native Windows clients using the Microsoft SMB/CIFS file services over TCP. (For more information, see Chapter 13.) Mac clients can access AFP file service over TCP/IP through the Chooser's Server IP Address button (Figure 8.12).

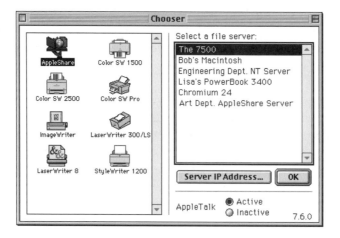

Figure 8.12 The Chooser shows AFP network servers.

Logging on to AFP-compatible Servers

Logging on to an AFP compatible network volume begins with the Chooser, accessible from the Apple menu. (The Chooser, originally designed to select printers, is showing its age as an interface and may be replaced in the future version of Mac OS.) The AppleShare extension file is actually a driver for the Chooser and shows up in the upper left field in the Chooser. If the AppleTalk Active button is selected and the Mac is connected to an AppleTalk network, clicking on the AppleShare icon will bring up a list of AFP-compatible file servers.

The computers listed aren't necessarily AppleShare servers running on Macintoshes. They can be any type of computer, server or workstation, running AFP-compatible server software. This includes a Mac workstation with File Sharing turned on, a Windows NT Server running Services for Macintosh, a Windows 98 workstation running PC MacLAN from Miramar Systems, a Linux server running Netatalk services, or a Novell NetWare server.

Figure 8.12 shows a network without AppleTalk zones. If the network has AppleTalk routers configured with zones, the Chooser will display a zone list in the lower left, as in Figure 8.11. When you click on a zone, the AFP-compatible servers in that zone will be displayed.

If the network has an AppleShare IP server or some other server that supports AFP over TCP/IP, you can also connect to it using TCP/IP. Click the AppleShare icon, click the Server IP Address button, and type in an IP address or alias.

After selecting the server and volume you wish to mount on the desktop, you'll be asked for a password (Figure 8.13). If guest access is enabled on the AFP server, you can click Log on as a Guest and log on without a password. Click OK, and another window will come up with a list of volumes available on the AFP server. You can choose to mount one or more volumes at once.

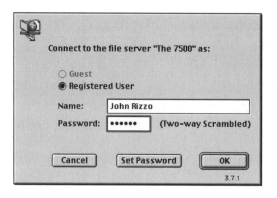

Figure 8.13 Entering a user name and password for a file server connection

Click OK and the network volume appears on the right side of the desktop as a network drive icon. You can drag and drop files to and from the volume if you have the privileges.

You can simplify the process of logging onto an AFP network volume, whether connected locally or over a telephone connection via Apple Remote Access, by making an alias of a file or folder on the mounted volume. (Select the file, folder, or volume and choose Make Alias from the File menu.) When you double-click an alias of a network volume, the alias will bypass the Chooser and log on for you, prompting you for passwords. Double-clicking an alias of a remote volume brings up the Apple Remote Access client.

Sharing Files with AppleTalk

File Sharing enables a Mac workstation to become a peer-to-peer AFP file server, accessible by any Macintosh or a PC with AppleTalk/AFP software installed.

The first step is to open the File Sharing control panel (called Sharing Setup in versions of Mac OS before 8.0), shown in Figure 8.14. The Network Identity section is where you give the Mac a password and a

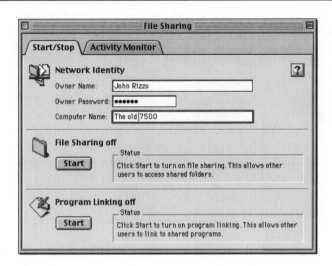

Figure 8.14 The File Sharing control panel

name. This Computer Name appears in other Mac users' Choosers when they click on the AppleShare icon, and is used by a variety of network software to identify the Mac.

Typing in a name in the Owner Name field will create a user with the name in the Users and Groups control panel. Next, click the start button to turn on File Sharing.

After turning on File Sharing, you create a shared volume by selecting (clicking once) a folder on a hard drive, removable cartridge, CD-ROM, or DVD-ROM. You now need to bring up the Sharing window for the selection item. How you do that depends on what version of Mac OS you have. In Mac OS 8.5 or later, you bring up the selected item's Get Info box (choose Get Info from the File menu). You then click the pop-up menu labeled Show, and select Sharing. In versions before Mac OS 8.5, you choose the Sharing command from the File menu. In either case, you get a window that looks similar to the one in Figure 8.15.

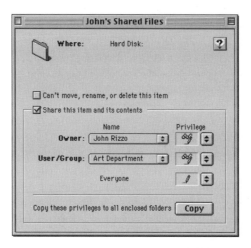

Figure. 8.15 Setting access privileges in the Sharing window

In both versions, you'll click the box labeled *Share this item and its contents*. In addition to sharing a folder, you can share an entire disk. Removable cartridges become non-removable (that is, the Mac won't let you eject them) if they contain a shared item. Floppy disks cannot be shared.

The Sharing window is also the place you can limit access by other users on the network. There are three levels of access privileges you can set, read and write, read only, and write only. Read and write lets users copy files to and from the folder over the network. Read only lets users open the mounted volume, view its contents, and copy files to their local hard drive; they cannot copy files to the folder. A write-only AFP folder is called a drop box. Users can copy items into the mounted folder, but they can't open it.

You can set different privileges for different network users. You usually set the first pop-up menu, called Owner, to read and write. The bottom pop-up menu, called Everyone, is often set to a lower level of privilege, or to None for no access. The middle pop-up, User/Group, lets you set access privileges for a single individual or a group of users.

When you close the Get Info window (for OS 8.5 or later) or the Sharing window (earlier than OS 8.5), your folder icon turns into a shared icon:

Reports from March

Creating Users and Groups

You create the individual user or group in the Users and Groups control panel (shown in Figure 8.16) by clicking the appropriate button. Clicking New User brings up a New User window, where you enter the user's name and password. It's convenient for the user if you use the same that is typed in the user's Owner Name from his or her File Sharing control panel. This way the user's name will automatically appear in the logon window when they log onto your Mac.

You can edit an existing user or group by double-clicking the icon in the Users and Groups list. This brings up the New User window again, except this time, it's named after the user. Here you can change the user name and password. You can also add the user to one or more

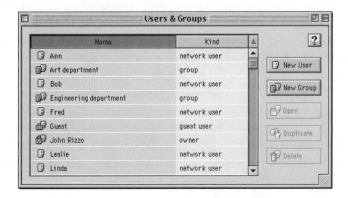

Figure 8.16 The Users and Groups control panel

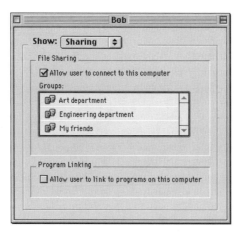

Figure 8.17 The Users and Groups control panel, Sharing window

groups. Select the Sharing item in the pop-up menu (Figure 8.17). You can add this user to groups by simply dragging the Group icons here from the main Users and Groups window (Figure 8.16). You can also do the opposite, and drag users' icons into a Group window.

Monitoring Access

People who are copying files to and from the shared folders on your hard disk can slow down your Mac, so you may notice some jumpiness while you're typing. The more people accessing your Mac, the greater the slowdown.

You can check to see who is accessing your Mac in the Activity Monitor tab of the File Sharing control panel, shown in Figure 8.18. (In Mac OS 7.6 and earlier, this is a separate control panel called File Sharing Monitor.) If the spirit of sharing gets to be too much for your Mac to handle, you can disconnect one or more users accessing your Mac. Just select the name from the list of connected users and click the Disconnect button.

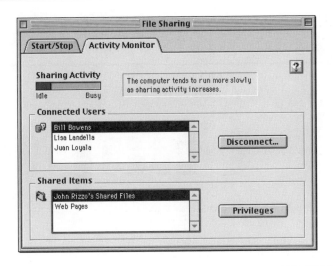

Figure 8.18. The Activity Monitor lets you see who is accessing your Mac.

A View from the Other Side

This chapter took a brief tour of the built-in network protocol and network services software of Mac OS, including how to set up basic file sharing and network printing. Later chapters will return to some of these topics in greater detail. The next chapter discusses some of these same topics as they apply to Windows, the other half of our integration story.

Chapter

What's in This Chapter:

♦ *An overview of Windows networking capabilities*

♦ *Installing and configuring Windows network software*

♦ *Using Windows network protocols*

♦ *Sharing files and printers*

Windows
Networking Basics

When it comes to the acronym-filled world of Windows networking, Mac experts not familiar with the area are often in the same boat as Windows users unfamiliar with networking. The concepts are foreign, and knowledge of a few terms doesn't seem to go very far. Some of the Windows networking concepts have no Macintosh equivalents.

Windows networking may not be high art, but it's not black magic either. Since the advent of Windows 95, networking on PCs has gotten easier for both the user and the person installing the network. Windows networking is also robust and full-featured. Windows 95, Windows NT, and Windows 98 come with network software ranging from low-level drivers to file sharing and print services. Unlike Mac OS, the networking software isn't all installed automatically. You install and configure it through the Network dialog box.

199

This chapter is not meant to be a complete guide to Windows networking, but is an introduction for Mac people, or for Windows people without networking experience. You'll find what network capabilities come with Windows, and how to get them up and running. And of course, I'll point out the cross-platform ramifications where they occur.

Chapter 7 covered the installation of a network interface card in PCs. This chapter picks up where Chapter 7 left off.

A Brief History of Windows Networking

Windows 3.1 didn't come with much built-in networking software, and installing and configuring it was a chore, particularly when you were using different pieces from different vendors. With Windows for Workgroups, Microsoft began bundling all the software you needed for file sharing, as well as the infrastructure to support network applications, such as e-mail. However, it was still difficult to install and configure. Conflicts were common: conflicts with port addresses, interrupt lines, drivers, and memory addresses.

Windows 95 was a big step forward in terms of networking. The software was more complete, and Plug and Play removed much of the trial-and-error that previously accompanied setting up a Microsoft network. Not only does Plug and Play prevent many of the conflicts seen with earlier versions of Windows, but there are fewer lower-level items to configure. Windows 95 beefed up support of multiple network protocols, enabling the same type of networking services to run on top of each protocol.

Windows 95 also added software for the user. The Network Neighborhood enables users to browse their network to look for and connect to servers and printers. Windows 95 also included the Microsoft Exchange e-mail client and the Internet Explorer Web browser.

Today, Microsoft networking is very similar in Windows 95, Windows 98, and Window NT 4.0 Server and Workstation. Windows 98 improved dial-up networking and the software for TCP/IP, which was upgraded from an optional protocol to being the default protocol.

The Network Dialog Box

The Network dialog box is where you install and configure most Microsoft and third-party network software in Windows. To open the Network dialog box, double-click the Network icon in the Control Panel. You can open the Control Panel either from the Start button (select Settings) or from the My Computer window.

MacWindows Tip

Another way to open the Network dialog box is to right-click the Network Neighborhood icon and select Properties from the pop-up menu.

The Network dialog box is where you install and configure four types of networking software: Network adapter cards (or rather, their drivers), protocols (again, the drivers for the protocols), client software, and service software (for peer-to-peer file and print sharing). The basic procedure is to install the software and "bind" the adapter, protocols, and client and server software together. Most of the configuration action occurs in the Properties dialog of each individual piece of software. The Properties dialog is contextual, so that the Properties dialog for the TCP/IP differs completely from that of IPX/SPX.

The four software categories are laid out slightly differently in the Network dialog box of Windows 95/98 and that of Windows NT. The Network dialog box in Windows 95 and 98 has three tabs, while it has five tabs in Windows NT 4.0. The goal in both versions is to get to the Properties dialogs for a piece of networking software, but 95/98 and NT organize it differently. In Windows 95/98, almost everything starts from one tab, the Configurations tab. Here you see a list of adapters, protocols, and services that are installed (see Figure 9.1). You can select one, and click the Properties window to configure it. To install a piece of network software, you click the Add button, and then click through a series of windows

The Network dialog of Windows NT has separate tabs for adapters, protocols, and services, as shown in Figure 9.2. You access the Properties dialog from one of these tabs.

Both versions have an Identification Tab. This is where you give your computer a name (the NetBIOS name) to identify it to other computers on the network. Windows NT has a Bindings tab at the top level of the Network dialog box. Windows 95/98 puts a Bindings tab in the Properties dialog boxes. Windows 95/98 also has an Access Control tab. This is where you set passwords for network access to the PC. In Windows NT you set new user privileges with other tools, such as the User Manager for Domains.

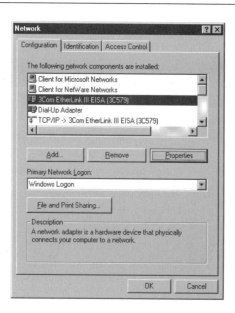

Figure 9.1 The Network dialog box of Windows 95/98

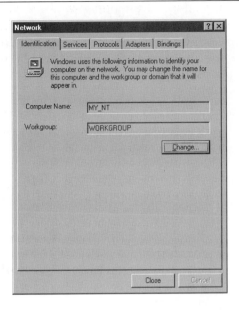

Figure 9.2 The Network dialog box of Windows NT 4.0

Standard Microsoft Networking Protocols

Windows networking makes use of three core transport protocols, NetBEUI, TCP/IP, and IPX/SPX. NetBEUI is an old standard PC protocol confined to use on small, single-segment networks. IPX/SPX came from the Novell NetWare operating system and is rarely used outside of a NetWare environment. TCP/IP came from the UNIX networking environment and is the protocol of choice in corporate environments. Microsoft's file and print sharing software in Windows will run over any of the three core protocols, as can third-party client or server software. Windows also comes with a few other protocols that aren't as popular, such as the old DECnet and Banyan VINES. You install and configure these in the same way you would the others.

With some protocols, there is a naming protocol that runs on the transport protocol. Naming associates the names of computers with network address numbers. There is often a naming server associated with the naming protocol. (By comparison, AppleTalk, has a built-in naming service that doesn't require configuration or a server.) There are several naming protocols that you can use in Windows, including NetBIOS, WINS, and DHCP.

Installing Protocols

When you installed and configured a network adapter card in Chapter 7, you also configure the protocol to work with it. You can install and configure additional protocols later using the Network tool in the Control Panel. The procedure for Windows 95/98 goes like this:

1. Open the Network icon of the Control Panel.
2. Click the Add button. A window called Select Network Component Type will open (Figure 9.3).
3. Click Protocol. A new window opens listing protocols and software manufacturer (Figure 9.4).
4. Click Microsoft for the standard Windows protocols. You see the set of protocols that comes with Windows.
5. Double-click the protocol you want to add. You should see the protocol in the Configuration tab of the Network window.

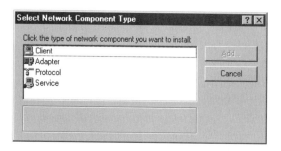

Figure 9.3 Selecting a category of network software to add

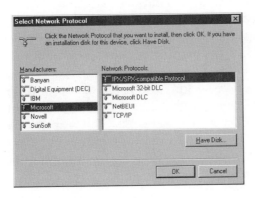

Figure 9.4 The Protocol window

Its name will be listed with the network interface adapter in the PC, as shown in Figure 9.5. The network adapter by itself will be another entry. When you close the Network dialog box, the Windows may

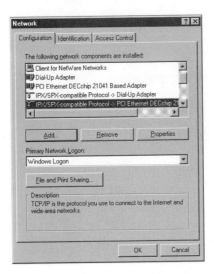

Figure 9.5 The installed protocol

prompt you to insert the Windows 95/98 installation disk, to install the driver software.

You can check for the binding of network adapter to protocols in the Bindings tab of the Properties window of the card, which you can bring up by double-clicking the name of the card. (See Figure 9.6.) Windows also needs to bind the protocol to the client software, such as the Client for Microsoft Networks. The Properties window for each protocol has a Bindings tab that you can check. You use the Properties window for a protocol to do any remaining configuration tasks, as is described in the following sections.

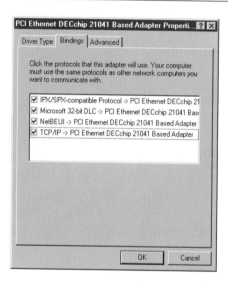

Figure 9.6 Checking protocol bindings

A Brief Word about AppleTalk

As one would expect, the AppleTalk networking protocols don't play much of a role in Windows networking. Windows 95 and 98 do not come with any AppleTalk abilities. You can, however, add third-party AppleTalk networking software to Windows 95/98, but you don't use the procedure just described. (Third-party AppleTalk products for Windows are covered in Chapter 14.)

Windows NT Workstation and Windows 2000 include the AppleTalk protocol for printing to AppleTalk network printers. NT Workstation does not include software for AppleTalk-based file sharing.

Windows NT Server and Windows 2000 Server do include support of AppleTalk protocols and network services: file service for Macintosh clients, and print service for both Mac and Windows clients. These are discussed in some detail in Chapter 11.

In Windows NT Server, the AppleTalk protocol does not appear in the Protocols tab of the Network control panel, as do other protocols. As you'll discover in Chapter 12, the AppleTalk-based services aren't treated as other services are, either. You can access the AppleTalk protocol from the Devices windows of the Control Panel, however. In Windows, protocols are called devices, as is anything that uses a device driver.

TCP/IP on Windows

As mentioned before, the standard Microsoft networking file sharing and printing services can run over TCP/IP, as can remote networking. TCP/IP can be used along with other protocols by using NDIS and ODI drivers.

You configure most of the TCP/IP information in its Properties window, which you bring up by double-clicking the TCP/IP listing in the Network window. Unlike the Macintosh, where you can create multiple settings for different connections (Ethernet, PPP, and so forth) from a single TCP/IP control panel, Windows uses a separate TCP/IP Properties window for each type of connection. There's one TCP/IP Properties window for each network adapter card you might have, and another for a modem connection. (However, TCP/IP properties for dial-up connections are configured in the Dial Up Networking dialog, not the Network Dialog.)

The first tab you configure in TCP/IP Properties is the IP Address tab (Figure 9.7). Here you can choose to manually enter a static IP address by choosing Specify an Address, or you can choose Obtain IP Address Automatically to get an address from a DHCP server or a PPP server.

You'll need to set up the DNS Configuration tab for a TCP/IP connection. A DNS (Domain Name Service) server matches an IP address when a user types in a URL in a web browser or FTP client. You first click Enable DNS in the DNS Configuration tab of TCP/IP Properties. Next, you enter the host, name of your computer domain, and up to three DNS server IP addresses in the field called DNS Server Search Order.

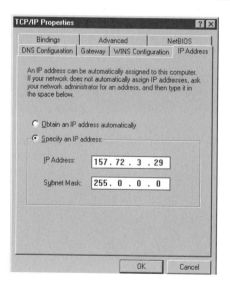

Figure 9.7 The TCP/IP Properties window of Windows 95

NOTE: Configuring DNS in the DNS Configuration tab is equivalent to filling out the "Name Server Address" in the Mac OS TCP/IP control panel.

You'll notice that there's another choice for a naming service: WINS (Windows Internet Name Server). WINS is a TCP/IP service that runs on Windows NT. While a DNS server takes a URL that represents a host and finds an IP address, a WINS server finds an IP address for each computer's NetBIOS name, and also finds a name when given an IP address. You enter a NetBIOS name in the Identification tab of the Network dialog box of each client. The field is labeled simply Computer Name.

Chapter 10 contains more details on TCP/IP configuration issues.

NetBIOS and NetBEUI

The TCP/IP protocol may be older, but NetBIOS and NetBEUI are the venerable old standards in PC networking. NetBIOS (Network Basic Input/Output System) and NetBEUI (NetBIOS Extended User Interface) were created by IBM in 1985.

With NetBIOS in the NetBEUI acronym, there is some confusion about what each does. Technically, NetBIOS is not a network protocol, but a software interface and a naming convention. It interacts with applications to perform functions such as security, name resolution, logging, and administration. But, NetBIOS is not a network transport mechanism and doesn't drive a network interface card. A WINS server running on Windows NT can use NetBIOS to match the Microsoft Windows NT-served computer names with IP addresses. (That is, the WINS server is a NetBIOS name server, or NBNS.)

NetBEUI, on the other hand, is a network transport protocol. IBM created it as a protocol for programs designed around the NetBIOS software interface. It was created so that 1985's DOS programs could access the Sytek network interface card. NetBEUI was once the main protocol in many PC network systems, the AppleTalk of PCs. However, NetBEUI is more limited than AppleTalk, as it is not a routable protocol. This has led to its decline in popularity in favor of TCP/IP.

NetBEUI is much easier to set up for home and small office networks, and it doesn't require a WINS or DHCP server. But a NetBEUI network is not cross-platform. NetBEUI was never implemented on Macs, mostly because Mac applications don't use NetBIOS to interface with a network. Connectivity solutions were based on NetBEUI-to-AppleTalk gateways.

NetBIOS over TCP/IP (known as NBT) provides the NetBIOS programming interface over the TCP/IP protocol, which makes up for the shortcomings of NetBEUI. TCP/IP packets contain NetBIOS modules so that they can travel through multiple levels of network names and addresses. You can also enable NetBIOS to work over IPX/SPX.

There is one Macintosh implementation of NetBIOS over TCP/IP—Thursby Software's DAVE (http://www.thursbysys.com). On top of NBT, DAVE implements the Microsoft client and server file and print sharing on the Macintosh. (See Chapter 14 for more on DAVE.)

IPX/SPX

After NetBEUI's heyday as a top PC network protocol, the king of enterprise networking was IPX/SPX (internetwork packet exchange/sequenced packet exchange). The routable IPX/SPX was the main transport protocol of Novell NetWare. At one time in the early 1990s, IPX/SPX was poised to replace both NetBEUI and AppleTalk as the standard network protocol. Novell even developed an IPX driver for the Mac, MacIPX, which it shipped with its NetWare Client for Macintosh, which is still in use at some sites today. Of course, the Internet boom made TCP/IP the protocol of choice worldwide. Although IPX is still in use today, many NetWare networks use TCP/IP, even though IPX/SPX has advantages over the Internet protocol. Even Novell has admitted that the reign of IPX/SPX is over and has implemented TCP/IP as the native protocol of NetWare 5.

The main advantage of IPX over TCP/IP is that you don't need to configure a network address—IPX is self-configuring. This makes management of IPX easier than that of TCP/IP. Still, there are a few things you need to set up with IPX on Windows. The most important item is to choose the frame type. In the Network dialog box, you select the Properties dialog of the IPX/SPX. If you select Frame Type, you'll see the following list of choices:

- Ethernet 802.2
- Ethernet 802.3
- Ethernet II
- Token Ring

Ethernet 802.2 (an IEEE standards designation) is the default frame type for NetWare 4.x networks. Ethernet 802.3 is the default frame for older versions of NetWare and networks with Macintoshes on them. Ethernet II is an old frame type not used much today. The Mac-

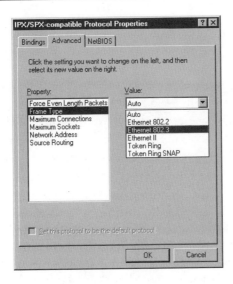

Figure 9.8 Setting the IPX frame type in the IPX Properties dialog

intosh equivalent of Ethernet II is the old AppleTalk (EtherTalk) Phase I used before 1989.

In addition to running NetWare, you can run the Microsoft client and server software over IPX using the Microsoft IPX/SPX drivers that come with Windows. You can "bind" the IPX protocol to the client you want to use in the Bindings tab of the IPX Properties dialog box.

Just as you can run NetBIOS over TCP/IP, you can also enable Net-BIOS over IPX, using the NetBIOS tab of the IPX Properties dialog box. The main reason to do this is for compatibility with older network systems, such as Microsoft LAN Manager and IBM's LAN Server, as well as for the OS/2 operating system. Some network software might require NetBIOS as well.

NOTE: MacIPX and NetWare Client for Macintosh made Macs true peers on NetWare networks, equal with PC clients, without requiring the use of AppleTalk. Microsoft Windows NT Server 4 still has not done this, and neither will Windows 2000. The industry was once so bullish on IPX that several major Mac networking products were IPX-enabled. These included e-mail, network contact forms, and the Claris FileMaker database. (NetWare for Macintosh is discussed in Chapter 13.)

Standard Microsoft SMB Networking Services

Standard Windows file sharing uses SMB/CIFS (server message block/common internet file system), the Microsoft equivalent of AFP (AppleShare Filing Protocol) used in Mac file sharing. A "Microsoft network" uses SMB file sharing just as an "AppleShare network" uses AFP. Windows clients access Windows NT Server volumes using SMB. You can install SMB file sharing over multiple protocols, though SMB/CIFS over TCP/IP is the most common.

Windows comes with the SMB client software, but it also comes with peer-to-peer server software that allows other Windows clients to access files on a peer-to-peer basis. Windows also includes client and services software for printer sharing.

NOTE: Apple's AppleShare IP 6 and later supports Windows clients via SMB (see Chapter 13). This means Windows clients can connect to it without any added software. Mac clients can access SMB servers via Thursby Systems DAVE (see Chapter 14).

Installing and Configuring the Client Software

Windows network client software isn't installed automatically. You usually configure the client software after installing and configuring the network adapter and binding protocols to it.

You install the client software in the Network dialog box. Click the Add button to bring up a dialog box called Select Network Component Type. This box lists the four types of network software available in Windows (Figure 9.9). Select Client and click Add.

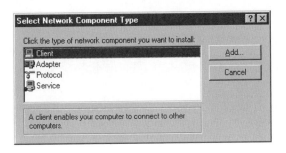

Figure 9.9 Choosing to install client software

The dialog box that comes up lists manufacturers of client software on the left, and the client software for each manufacturer on the right (see Figure 9.10). Some of the software, such as the Client for Microsoft Networks and Microsoft's NetWare client, comes with Windows. For some of the others, you will need the installation disks. In these cases, you would click the Have Disk button to bring up an installation dialog box that would prompt you for the disks.

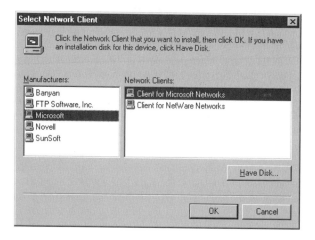

Figure 9.10 Choosing the client software to install

Clicking OK closes the Select Client dialog and brings up the Network dialog box again. You should now see your client in the list of network software. If you select it and click Properties, you'll find some configuration options. The Properties dialog for the Microsoft Client gives you logon options, as shown in Figure 9.11.

If you check "Log on to Windows NT domain," Windows will attempt to log on to a Windows NT domain, which is a group of one or more servers (see Chapter 12). You need to add the name of the domain the PC has been assigned to.

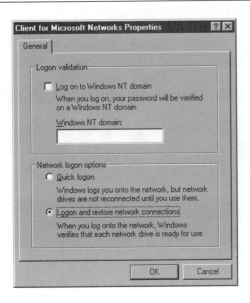

Figure 9.11 Logon options for Microsoft Client software

The selection at the bottom of the screen gives you the option of a Quick logon or a "Logon and restore" logon. The Quick logon will try to log you on to the network resource "on demand," without checking beforehand if the resource is available. The *Logon and restore network connections* option requires the client software to check the network to see if the network devices are available at bootup. Most of the time, you can use the Quick logon option.

You can click OK to close the Properties dialog box, and then click OK in the Network dialog box. If you've installed the Microsoft Client, a dialog box will prompt you to install the Windows CD-ROM, so that Windows can actually install the files on the hard drive. After installation, Windows will ask you if you want to restart the PC. You need to restart in order for the changes to take effect.

Accessing a Network with the Network Neighborhood

Windows 95/98 and NT feature the Network Neighborhood, a browser for finding and logging on to servers and printers on the local network. It can be used for finding Microsoft Network resources, as well as resources on other types of networks, including Novell NetWare.

The Network Neighborhood icon on the desktop (Figure 9.12) behaves as a folder in Windows Explorer, the Microsoft analog to the Mac's Finder. Inside, the Network Neighborhood represents servers and printers of various types as icons or as a text list. One may draw comparisons to the Chooser in Mac OS, but the Network Neighborhood differs from the Mac's Chooser in several ways. For one, the Chooser depicts the network in a flat manner—you either see all the printers and servers on the network at once, or you click on a zone name to see the devices in that zone. The Network Neighborhood presents the net-

Figure 9.12 The Network Neighborhood and My Computer desktop icons are both places to access servers and printers.

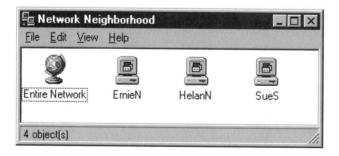

Figure 9.13 The first level of a small Network Neighborhood

Apple's "Network Neighborhood"

Microsoft's Network Neighborhood made it possible for Windows users to easily browse a local area network. Apple once had a similar interface that predated Microsoft's, called PowerTalk. There was a version of Mac OS that came with PowerTalk called System 7 Pro. While Apple deserves credit for coming up with an innovative idea, it also gets the blame for PowerTalk's failure. After spending years developing the technology, Apple completely bungled the launch of the product. For instance, PowerTalk didn't come with all the software pieces a user needed. Apple left out crucial pieces to be created by third-party developers, who weren't all that keen on the idea. The PowerTalk server, called PowerShare, had problems as well. The technology never got off the ground, and Apple eventually discontinued PowerTalk. Microsoft used the concept and successfully implemented it in Windows.

work hierarchically. You may have to access some servers by opening folders within folders, first through the Entire Network icon.

The Network Neighborhood also differs from the Chooser in that it divides network resources into two categories. The first shows devices in your current workgroup or NT domain, which is what you see when you first open the Network Neighborhood icon, as in Figure 9.13. You might see servers or Windows clients with file sharing activated. To see devices in other workgroups or domains, you open the Entire Network icon.

The Entire Network contains a series of nested folders. Click on it once, and you might see some servers, or you might see some Windows NT network domains. Click on a domain icon, and you'll see the servers for that domain. Double-clicking on a server will bring up a prompt for a password, and then a window displaying directories and files that you have been given access to. You can also be prompted for a password as you click on directories and files.

MacWindows Tip

Navigating through the Network Neighborhood can get tedious, as you double-click on icon after icon and open window after window. There are several ways around this. First, you can use the Network Neighborhood's View menu to open successive views in a single Window, displaying all resources as an expanding list.

If you're accessing a particular network directory frequently, you can create a network shortcut—an icon with a link to a network directory or file, similar in function to a Mac OS alias. To create one, right-click on the network directory or file and drag it to the desktop. When you let go of the right mouse button, a pop-up menu will appear with the command Create Shortcut(s) Here.

Accessing a Network through My Computer and Elsewhere

The My Computer icon on the desktop is another way at looking at some of the items you can find in the Network Neighborhood and other places. (For example, the Printers folder shown in Figure 9.14 also appears inside the Control Panel folder itself.) From My Computer, you can access the same servers and printers as you can from Network Neighborhood. However, My Computer is not a network browser—you assign servers to appear here. This process is called mapping. When you map a server volume to a drive letter on the PC, you assign a drive letter to the network server volume, such as G:. The new "drive" shows up in My Computer, and anywhere you access drives, such as the Windows Explorer. You can also type on a path to a file on the network (G:\reports\smith.doc) wherever Windows lets you do so. (This allows older legacy Windows and DOS applications, which can't use a server name in a path, to access network volumes.)

You can map a server or shared directory by right-clicking on its icon. Choose Map Network Drive from the pop-up menu. A dialog called Connect Network Drive will come up, where you enter the drive let-

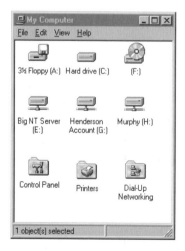

Figure 9.14 Network server directories (center) and printers in My Computer

ter. You can enable the drive to come up a startup by clicking the box labeled Reconnect at Startup.

You can add network printers in the My Computer window as well. In Network Neighborhood, find the server that has the printer attached to it, double-click it, and then double-click the printer. The Printer Wizard will open and ask you what you want to name this printer. When you click Finish, Windows will copy the drivers needed and ask you to perform a printer test.

After the test is finished, the network printer will show up in the Printer Folder window of the My Computer window. Printers attached to the PC also show up here.

Installing File Sharing

To enable other Windows users to access directories and files on a user PC, you go back to the Network dialog box again. In the Configurations tab, see if you have an item called *File and printer sharing for Microsoft Networks.* This is the peer-to-peer service software. If it's not there, you'll have to install it.

NOTE: Macs running Thursby Systems' DAVE will also be able to access the shared directories of a Windows PC.

Installing the services software is very similar to installing the client software, as described earlier. You click Add to bring up Select Network Component Type. This time, click Services. This brings up the Select Network Service dialog. For standard Windows file sharing, click Microsoft under Manufacturers and select "File and printer sharing for Microsoft Networks" under Network Services.

Click OK, and the item will show up in the Configurations tab of the Network dialog. Select it and click Properties. In the Properties dialog box, select the Bindings tab and check the protocols you are going to use. Checking protocols you don't need will needlessly take up processing power and memory on the PC.

Giving the Computer a Name

When sharing files, you need to give the computer a name that will represent the PC in the Network Neighborhoods of other users on the network. (This is the NetBIOS name mentioned earlier, but is the same idea as the Computer Name in the Macintosh's File Sharing control panel.) In the Network dialog box, select the Identification tab (Figure 9.15). The name you type in must be under 15 characters and can't have blank spaces. It's a good idea to use a name that will be meaningful to other users, such as "Edward's PC."

In the Workgroup field, you can type in the NT Server domain the PC belongs to or a local workgroup. The bottom of the Identification tab has a field you can use to describe the computer. This information also shows in the Network Neighborhood of other users, so you should choose one that is useful. You can use a model, such as "IBM Aptiva," or the location of the computer in the building.

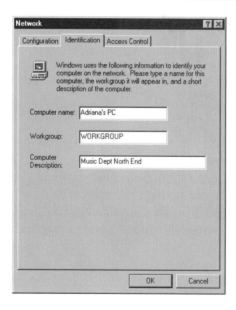

Figure 9.15 Giving the computer a name

Setting Up Access Control

When you enable file and print sharing, Windows allows you to set one of two types of access control: user-level and share-level. You do this in the Access Control tab of the Network dialog box (Figure 9.16). User-level access control is where you give a password to each user, as with file sharing in Macs. Share-level access controls give password protection for each different folder or printer—everyone uses the same password to access a particular item. You can assign two passwords with share-level access—a read-only password, and a full-access password.

Unlike file sharing in Mac OS, file sharing in Windows only lets you specify share-level access control if you have a server on the network. That is, you can't give individual users their own passwords without a server. Windows 95/98 can only obtain a list of users and groups from a server, and doesn't let you create your own users and groups on a client. (Windows NT does let you create users and groups.) When setting up user-level access control, you specify the server holding the user lists in the Access Control tab of the Network dialog box.

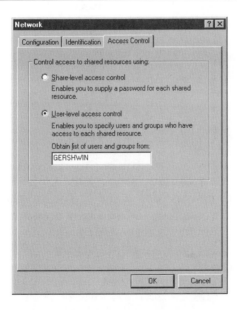

Figure 9.16 Choosing the type of access control in the Network dialog box

Selecting Directories and Printers to Share

You use the same method to share folders and printers connected to the PC. Windows terminology refers to both of them as "shares" when you enable other users to access them. You can use this procedure to share items:

1.   Open My Computer.
2.   Select the folder you want to share, or select a printer from the Printers folder. You'll see printers connected directly to the PC ("local" printers), and network printers, which have a cable icon. You can only share printers connected directly to the PC.
3.   Right-click the local printer you want to share. (You can also share an entire drive or individual folders.) In the pop-up menu, click either Sharing or Properties. Either selection will bring up the Properties window for the folder or printer.
4.   Click the Sharing tab of the Properties window (Figure 9.17)
5.   Click the Shared As button to enable sharing.
6.   Enter a share name, the name by which other network users will see the folder or printer in the Network Neighborhood.

MacWindows Tip

You can also create hidden shares, which don't appear in the Network Neighborhood, by adding the $ symbol to the end of the share name.

7.   Under Access Type, Click Read-Only, Full Access, or Depends on Password. If you choose the last, you can enter two passwords, one for read-only access, and one for full access. (Windows peer-to-peer file sharing does not have a "write-only" option, as does Macintosh file sharing.) Passwords can be no more than eight characters long and can't contain special characters.

If you have user-level access control enabled in the Network dialog box, the folder or printer Properties dialog will have another tab called Permissions. If you want only some users to have access to the folder or printer, click the Permissions tab and unselect Everyone. Click Add and select your users or groups from the list.

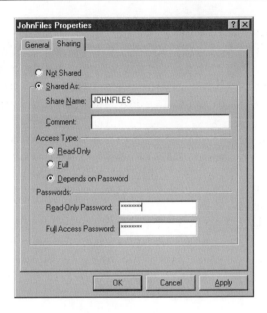

Figure 9.17 Sharing a folder in the folder's Properties dialog box.

The Next Step

This chapter and the previous one described the basic layout of networking for Windows and Macs. We bring the two worlds together in Chapter 10, which goes into more detail about setting up networks with TCP/IP, the most commonly used protocol in cross-platform networks.

Chapter

What's in This Chapter:

- ♦ *IP addressing and configuration, Mac and Windows*

- ♦ *Getting DHCP and BootP to work*

- ♦ *MacIP: TCP/IP on LocalTalk*

- ♦ *Virtual Private Networks*

- ♦ *Proxy servers: problems and solutions*

10

Integrating TCP/IP
on Mac and Windows

The universal network language, TCP/IP, is supposed to be nonpartisan. It was designed for UNIX, a completely open and nonproprietary operating system. Yet as a result of its success, TCP/IP and its associated protocols have been embraced by some very proprietary OS companies, including Apple, Microsoft, and Novell. All three have adopted TCP/IP as their main protocol, a claim that is proven out in their OS and server products of the past few years.

Yet, these companies have also been extending TCP/IP, moving it from the realm of open standards to that of proprietary technology, which has caused some problems. The expectation that TCP/IP and intranet/Internet technologies will work on any platform is tempered by the reality of proprietary implementation of a type of protocol, server or gateway, often running on the popular Windows NT Server.

Even with these limitations, TCP/IP is still the best network transport protocol for cross-platform integration. Every operating system can speak IP natively, as can most client and server software today. TCP/IP is also a fast protocol because it can stream data across a network without interruption and because it can transmit large packets. This is demonstrated in the fact that Macintosh AppleShare-compatible file sharing (AFP) can be several times faster over IP than it is over AppleTalk. (Look in Chapter 13 for a discussion of AFP over TCP/IP.)

This chapter tries to do three things. First, it compares the setup procedures of TCP/IP in Windows and Mac OS, pointing out the differences, similarities, and equivalences. The second task is to describe some of the problems that Mac clients can have with Windows NT-based servers on TCP/IP networks. There's also some information about TCP/IP itself, so that you have enough knowledge to set up a cross-platform TCP/IP network. (Windows NT services are discussed in Chapter 11, and PPP connections and other remote issues are discussed in Chapter 12.)

Differences: TCP/IP Configuration Windows

Operating systems today come equipped with TCP/IP. Mac OS, Windows 95, Windows 98, and Windows NT all come with TCP/IP *stacks*—software supporting the required communications tasks—so there is nothing that needs to be added at the protocol level. For Windows for Workgroups, you can add the Microsoft TCP-32 driver for Ethernet connections, or third-party driver for dial-up connections. There are also third-party TCP/IP stacks for Windows 3.11.

TCP/IP was greatly improved in Macs with the advent of Open Transport a few years ago, after some initial problems (see Chapter 8). Windows 98 improved the TCP/IP stack over that of Windows 95, giving it better performance and compatibility with networking software. For the first time in any Windows operating system, Windows 98 made TCP/IP the default protocol.

Chapter 8 and 9 covered Windows and Macintosh networking separately. Here, we'll start off with a side-by-side summary of TCP/IP settings in Windows and Mac OS. A more detailed look will follow.

NOTE: Running AppleTalk does not rule out the use of TCP/IP. You can run both at the same time, as you would if you were browsing the web while printing a web page to a network printer.

Locating the configuration windows

In Windows, you enter TCP/IP settings in the TCP/IP Properties dialog box, which you bring up by selecting your network adapter bound with TCP/IP entry in the Network dialog box (located in the Control Panel), and clicking Properties. (See Figure 10.1.)

In Mac OS you enter TCP/IP settings in the TCP/IP control panel, accessible from the Apple menu. (See Figure 10.2.)

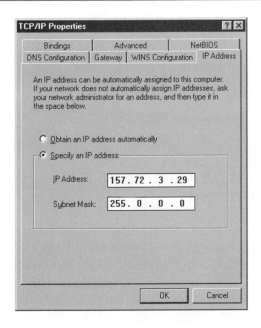

Figure 10.1 The Windows TCP/IP Properties dialog box

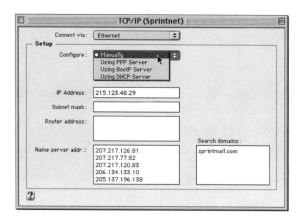

Figure 10.2 The Macintosh TCP/IP control panel

Choosing the network interface

In Windows, you choose the network interface (such as Ethernet or dial-up) from the Network dialog box. Each network interface has its own entry, and its own Properties window.

In Mac OS, you choose the network interface from the Connect Via pop-up menu. You can save multiple setups (such as dial-up and Ethernet) by using the Configurations item in the File menu.

Configuring client or server software

In Windows, you "bind" client or services software to the transport protocol in the Bindings tab of the TCP/IP Properties box. With the bindings set, the user is not aware of what protocols are running.

Mac OS has no concept equivalent to "binding." If the software supports TCP/IP, it will work. (However, unlike Windows, the procedure for using standard file sharing is somewhat different over TCP/IP than on other protocols—namely AppleTalk. Mac users can't use the Chooser to browse for AppleShare-compatible file servers over IP servers. They must type IP addresses in the Chooser to log on.)

Another difference between the two platforms is the NetBIOS tab in the Windows TCP/IP Properties dialog, used to enable NetBIOS services over TCP/IP. Mac OS has no equivalent.

Configuring TCP/IP in Cross-Platform Networks

Now that you know where to enter TCP/IP configuration information, we can get to what information to enter. (If you're still not sure on the *where*, take a look at Chapters 8 and 9.)

The first decision to make is how you assign an IP addresses to the clients. With a smaller network, you might decide to manually type in IP addresses, known as *static* addressing, according to a set of rules. The rules are the same for any operating system.

If you have Windows 98 and Mac OS 8.5 and later, the computers can automatically give themselves IP addresses without a server. Clients can also get their IP addresses from a server, such as one running the Dynamic Host Configuration Protocol (DHCP). This is the easier solutions for larger networks.

Unfortunately, the IP address isn't the whole story to configure TCP/IP. There are other settings as well. Sometimes the settings have the same names in Mac OS and Windows, such as the subnet mask. Other times, Apple and Microsoft have given different names to describe an item. The next few pages compares the settings for both Windows and Mac OS, item by item.

The next section begins with the rules of IP address, which you can use whether you are manually configuring individual computers or setting up DHCP servers.

The Rules of IP Addressing

The IP address consists of four octets separated by periods. The numbers are called octets because each is an 8-bit number, which means you have 28 values to choose from. This lets you assign any number from 0 to 255 for each octet, with a few restrictions.

NOTE: If 2^8 = 256, why is the number 256 illegal in an IP address? The answer is that since you are allowed to use the number 0 in an octet, it counts as one of the 256 numbers. The number 256 would be the 257th number.

Every IP address must be unique. If your local network is not connected to the Internet, then you could pick arbitrary numbers that don't conflict with each other. However, this would get difficult to manage as a network grows. When visible to the Internet, an IP address must be unique. You also need to follow some rules, as the IP address defines a path that routers can use to route data through the network.

Note: There are several ranges of private addresses, which the Internet ignores. You would use these on a network connected to the Internet, but on computers that don't need Internet access. These ranges include 10.0.0.1 through 10.255.255.254 and 192.168.0.1 through 192.168.0.254.

Typically, you get an assigned range of IP numbers, often from an Internet service provider, but you can also apply to a group called InterNIC yourself for the range. If you set up a DHCP or BootP server, the server can assign numbers automatically from this range.

The rules for IP address depend on the range of numbers you have. IP ranges are divided into classes based on the number of values you have in the range. These are called Classes A, B, and C.

A Class C range is small, containing 256 IP addresses. It fixes the first three octets (which must be the same on all the computers), and lets you use the fourth octet. For example, a Class C range might look like 201.5.62.xxx, where the xxx would be a number from 1 to 254. (0 and 255 are reserved for the network itself). All of your computers on the network would have IP addresses that start with 201.5.62. The first three octets therefore define your network on the Internet.

How does the Internet know that your network is a Class C network? The class is defined by the first octet. Class C networks begin with the numbers 192 through 223.

Class B addresses begin with the numbers 128 through 191 in the first octet. In a Class B range, only the first two octets are defined, as in 150.239.xxx.yyy. This gives you 65,534 possible different IP addresses, all starting with 150.239. However, you can't end an address with 0.0 or .255.255, which are reserved for the network.

Class A addresses begin with the numbers 1 through 126. Only the first octet is defined, leaving you with 16,777,214 possible IP addresses. With Class A, you can't use addresses ending in 0.0.0 or 255.255.255.

IP addresses (at least those connected to the Internet) cannot begin with the numbers 127 and 224-to-255. Addresses that begin with 127 are use for testing purposes. Addresses beginning with 224-to-255 are Class D addresses, which are off-limits for use as IP addresses.

Automatic IP Configuration without a Server

A new feature introduced in Windows 98 and Mac OS 8.5 (Open Transport 2.0) enables Macs and PCs to give themselves an IP address and a subnet mask setting without a server. This feature makes TCP/IP nearly as plug-and-play as AppleTalk, though the mechanism differs from the way AppleTalk nodes give themselves AppleTalk addresses. This method is for a local network addressing, not for Internet clients or servers connected to the Internet.

Microsoft refers to this feature as *automatic private IP addressing*, or *IP autoconfiguring*. Apple calls it *self-assigned DHCP addressing*, which is more descriptive. In either case, the mechanism is the same.

In both Windows 98 and Mac OS 8.5 and later, you set the client to accept a DHCP address. In the Mac's TCP/IP control panel, you select Using DHCP Server in the Configure menu. In Windows 98, you select *Obtain an IP address automatically* in the IP address tab of the TCP/IP Properties dialog box.

Both operating systems will send out a packet looking for a DHCP server. If none replies after about 20 seconds, the operating system creates a temporary TCP/IP IP address and subnet mask setting. It randomly chooses an IP address in the range of

169.254.0.0 to 169.254.254.255

With over 65,000 possible IP addresses to choose from, chances are that it won't pick an address already occupied. The operating system also chooses a subnet mask of

255.255.0.0

This configuration is held for 15 minutes. After that, the operating system looks for a DHCP server. If it doesn't find one, it continues to use the same address. It will send out a DHCPDISCOVER packet ever 5 minutes after that.

Autoconfiguration does not include a DNS server or gateway address for name resolution, though you could add this if you had a server.

If you have other Macs and PCs that don't support automatic IP addressing, you can get them to work on the same network by giving them static IP addresses in this 169.254.xxx.xxx range as well as the 255.255.0.0 subnet mask. (More on subnet masks later.)

Dynamic IP Addressing with a DHCP Server

Dynamic IP address configuration is usually done with a DHCP server (dynamic host configuration protocol). You set up a DHCP server with a set of IP addresses it leases to clients as they come on line. The kind of network negotiation is similar to what goes on with AppleTalk, though AppleTalk doesn't use a server. As we've seen, with Win-

dows clients, when you click *Obtain address automatically* in TCP/IP
Properties, Windows will get its IP address from a DHCP server.

*NOTE: Computers being used as permanent servers on the
Internet must have fixed IP addresses.*

There is an optional Macintosh TCP/IP setting that can affect the performance and behavior of a Mac DHCP client. When the TCP/IP
control panel is in Advanced mode (command U), an Options button
appears in the lower right. Clicking it brings up the window shown in
Figure 10.3. When the default setting of "Load only when needed" is
selected, Mac OS loads the TCP/IP stack into memory when the user
makes a connection. When the Mac is not accessing an IP network,
the memory is released, and with it, the IP address obtained from a
DHCP server. This means that the Mac will contact the DHCP server every time it gets on the network, which can slow network access.

On an Ethernet network where use of TCP/IP is more than occasional, it's best to uncheck "Load only when needed" on the Macs. The
trade-off to having TCP/IP loaded all the time is that it takes up memory and can affect overall system performance. Therefore, "Load only
when needed" is a good setting to use with PPP connections.

Macs running Open Transport 1.1 or later can make use of Windows
NT DHCP server on local networks (but not from a dial-up link).
Open Transport 2.0 (which shipped with Mac OS 8.5) introduced a

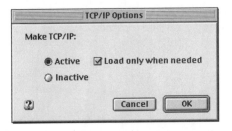

Figure 10.3 The Mac OS TCP/IP options window can affect performance of
the DHCP client.

new DHCP feature in the TCP/IP control panel. When you select DHCP in you get a new field called "DHCP Client ID." (Figure 10.4). The Windows NT DHCP server can make use of the information in this field.

The Mac OS TCP/IP control panel has two other choices in addition to DHCP—BootP and RARP. Both are used for compatibility with existing servers. BootP, short for Bootstrap Protocol, is the predecessor to DHCP. With BootP, you manually preconfigure IP addresses in a database server. You reserve BootP addresses in advance by creating an IP address reservation. The BootP server then doles out the addresses.

DHCP is based on BootP, but is more automatic in its configuration and doesn't require this address reservation procedure. DHCP can also reuse the IP address of computers that shut down, reassigning the addresses to other computers. This is called address leasing. Mac OS 8.5 and later can retain the lease for an IP address when you restart it.

RARP (Reverse Address Resolution Protocol) is useful for Mac compatibility in UNIX environments, where RARP is used by Sun systems and in other UNIX systems. It can assign IP numbers to clients, but has limitations not found in DHCP and BootP. For instance, RARP

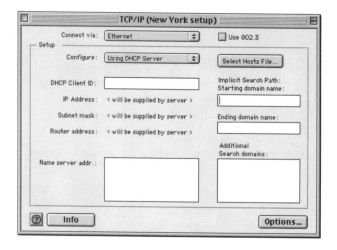

Figure 10.4 The DHCP Client ID field in Mac OS 8.5, useful with NT Server

can only serve a single network segment, and it can't be routed. This means it's not available over a PPP connection.

MacWindows Tip

Each time a notebook computer moves around the network, it must negotiate with the DHCP server. When Macs go into sleep mode, they release the IP address back to the server. The Windows IP stack does not. When you move a sleeping PC laptop to a different part of the network, it's first address is still assigned to the computer. Depending on the lease time set in the DHCP server, you can quickly run out of IP addresses. Shutting down a Windows laptop before moving it will release the IP address.

Configuring Windows NT Server for BootP clients

The DHCP protocol has some backward compatibility with BootP, so that some DHCP servers support BootP clients. One of these is the Microsoft DHCP Server of Windows NT Server 4.0 with Service Pack 3 and later. (Earlier versions do not support BootP.) To enable BootP in NT's DHCP Server, you need to reserve IP address in advance. Microsoft has said that future versions of Microsoft DHCP Server will be capable of leasing dynamic addresses to BootP clients.

To create an IP address reservation in Windows NT Server 4.0, follow this procedure:

1. Open NT Server's DHCP Manager tool in Administration Tools.
2. Double-click on the subnet in which you want to create the address reservation.
3. A window will appear listing the current IP address leases and reservations
4. Click the Add button.
5. Enter the data for IP Address, Client Name, and Identifier.
7. Click OK.
8. A message may appear: "The Unique Identifier you have chosen may not be correct. Use it anyway?" Click Yes.
9. Exit DHCP Manager.

Subnet Mask

In the IP configuration windows of both Mac OS and Windows, there is a field for an IP address, and one for a subnet mask, which helps an IP router to locate a network of computers. Every computer on the same physical network segment needs to have the same subnet mask setting. This is the same on Macs and Windows.

The rules for setting the subnet mask call for using the number 255 in the first few octets, depending on the size of your network. For example, a single Ethernet network of under 256 computers—Class C addressing (described on page 230)—you can set the subnet mask as 255.255.255.0. For a Class B addressing, the subnet can be 255.255.0.0. For a Class A network (a range of 16.7 million address-es), the subnet mask can be 255.0.0.0. (The zeros can change.)

The subnet mask can be supplied by the DHCP server or PPP server during a dial-up connection. (In Mac OS, the subnet mask field is not available unless you select Configure Manually.) The subnet mask is not required information for a point-to-point connection, since inthis case, all packets go to the same destination—the PPP server.

IP Router

If you are manually configuring IP addresses for a TCP/IP network with more than one network segment, such as the Internet or a large intranet, you need to enter the IP address of the IP router that con-nects the network segments. A router receives TCP/IP packets from one network and forwards them to another network, based on the addressing of the packets. For instance, the IP router would take all packets for destinations not on the local network segment, as deter-mined by the subnet mask, and send them on to the Internet.

Mac OS and Windows use different terminology for the IP router in their setup windows. The Mac OS TCP/IP control panel has a field called Router Address. The Windows TCP/IP Properties dialog calls it a Gateway. You enter this address in the Gateway tab.

DNS Settings

A DNS server (for domain name service) matches, or *resolves*, the IP address of a server when a user types in a URL (which contains a domain name for the host). A DNS server address is always required on Windows and Macs connected to the Internet.

A small local network not connected to the Internet doesn't need a DNS server. If you don't have a DNS server on your local network, users will have to type in IP addresses instead of URLs to log on to your local web and FTP servers. An alternative would be to put a Hosts file on each computer that would contain a list of IP addresses and their corresponding URLs.

In Windows, you click the DNS Configuration tab of the TCP/IP Properties dialog box. DNS addresses go in the field called "DNS Server Search Order." Mac OS refers to a DNS server as a "name server." You type in the IP addresses of one or more DNS servers in the "Name server addr" field at the lower left of the TCP/IP control panel.

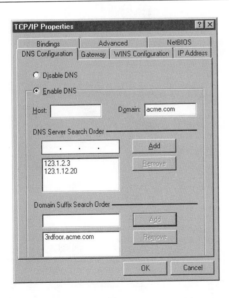

Figure 10.5 Setting DNS information in Windows 95

You can list more than one DNS address on both Windows and Mac. It's useful to identify both a primary and secondary DNS server.

Both platforms also have an area to add the domain names. Domain names can be in the form of "acme.com," but can also have multiple dots, as in "hq.2ndfloor.acme.com.ca.us." In Windows, there are two fields (Figure 10.5). The server's name goes in the Hosts field. You enter the first choice DNS domain in the Domain field. You can add other domains to check in the "Domain Suffix Search Order" field. This enables abbreviation of local URLs. For instance, you could type: `http://intranet` instead of `http://intranet.on.ca`.

NOTE: If the DNS server address is provided by a DHCP server, select Disable DNS in the Windows DNS Configuration tab.

Mac OS does not have the equivalent of the Host field found in Windows. You type the IP address of the DNS server in the "Name server addr" field. You add the domain name in the Search Domains field, when the TCP/IP control panel is in Basic mode (as shown in Figure 10.2). When in advanced mode (as shown in Figure 10.6), this

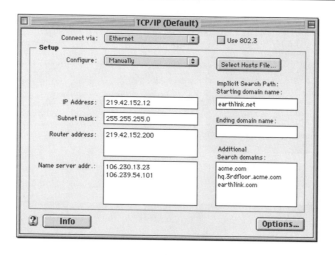

Figure 10.6 Setting DNS information in the Mac TCP/IP control panel (Advanced user mode)

field turns into three fields under the title of Implicit Search Path: Starting Domain Name, Ending Domain Name, and Additional Search Domains. (You can switch between user modes with the Command-U keys.)

The Windows TCP/IP Properties dialog box also includes a WINS tab for specifying address resolution by a WINS (Windows Internet Naming Service) server, which runs on Windows NT (see Chapter 9 for more on WINS). This service is typically used on local networks, not the Internet. WINS is not cross-platform, and there are no implementations of a WINS client for Macintosh. However, Apple's AppleShare IP 6 and later will pass along WINS information to Windows client. (AppleShare IP is discussed in Chapter 13.)

MacIP: Encapsulating TCP/IP inside AppleTalk

MacIP is a method you can use to connect a LocalTalk network of Macs to a TCP/IP network or the Internet without upgrading to Ethernet. You'll need a router that supports MacIP.

MacIP enables Macs to run TCP/IP packets over AppleTalk networks for delivery to a TCP/IP network. MacIP "encapsulates" the TCP/IP network packets inside of AppleTalk packets and sends them out on the AppleTalk network. The encapsulated packets will travel over whatever network interface is selected in the AppleTalk control panel, including LocalTalk, IrDA, and remote AppleTalk connections.

The packets are received by a MacIP gateway on a TCP/IP network. The MacIP gateway function is often a feature in multiprotocol routers. It can also run as software, such as the Apple IP Gateway for Macintosh. The MacIP gateway strips off the AppleTalk encapsulation and places the IP packet on the TCP/IP network. When a user on the TCP/IP network sends packets back to the Mac using MacIP, the gateway encapsulates the TCP/IP packets within AppleTalk.

To enable a Mac to use MacIP, you need to turn AppleTalk on in the Chooser and set up the TCP/IP control panel to use MacIP. In the "Connect via" pop-up menu, select "AppleTalk (MacIP)." A button called Select Zone will appear in the control panel just below the Configure pop-up menu. You use this to specify the AppleTalk zone containing the MacIP gateway, which is seen on both AppleTalk and TCP/IP networks.

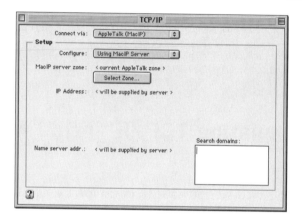

Figure 10.7 The TCP/IP control panel configured for MacIP, automatic IP address

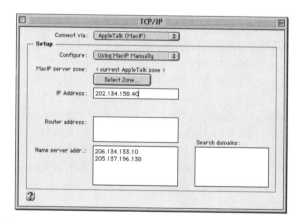

Figure 10.8 The TCP/IP control panel configured for MacIP, manual IP address

A Mac using MacIP encapsulation to send data to TCP/IP network must have an IP address. The Configure pop-up of the TCP/IP control panel gives you two options for IP addressing. If you select Using MacIP Manually, an IP Address field appears in which you can type in an IP address. When you select Using MacIP Server, the MacIP gateway will assign an IP address from a list of addresses entered by the person who set up the server. (See Figures 10.7 and 10.8)

Windows NT Virtual Private Networks

Virtual private networks encrypt information and encapsulate network traffic to create a secure path through public TCP/IP networks, such as the Internet and the public telephone systems. The secure path is sometimes referred as a *tunnel* through the Internet.

A typical virtual private network uses Windows NT Server 4.0 running the Routing Remote Access Service (RRAS) and Microsoft Proxy Server, which contains a firewall. There are also third-party server and client products that implement a virtual private network. Windows NT Server 4.0 uses the Point-to-Point Tunneling Protocol (PPTP), which can be described as a "point-to-point link through TCP/IP." PPTP can also be used for dynamically assigning IP addressing. Microsoft's implementation uses MS-CHAP (Microsoft Challenge-Handshake Authentication Protocol) for authentication. It uses an RSA RC4 algorithm for encryption.

Although Windows 95/98 and NT clients use these protocols, supporting these standards is the main issue for getting Macintosh clients to participate on a virtual private network. Remote Access 3.1 in Mac OS 8.5 supports MS-CHAP, but, like earlier versions, it doesn't support PPTP. Fortunately, you can add a third-party solution that implements the required protocols on a Mac client.

One Mac solution is TunnelBuilder from a company called Network TeleSystems (NTS, http://www.nts.com). TunnelBuilder is a complete virtual private network client for Macintosh, implementing PPTP and MS-CHAP authentication. TunnelBuilder replaces Mac OS's Remote Access or PPP control panel with a control panel called NTS PPP, which enables Macs to connect to Windows NT servers over a VPN, or remotely over NT Remote Access Server (RAS).

NOTE: You'll find an evaluation version of NTS TunnelBuilder on this book's CD-ROM.

TunnelBuilder can also tunnel AppleTalk services through PPTP, letting Mac users access printers and AppleShare file servers on the other side of a virtual private network. To do this, you need to be using NTS's TunnelMaster server, a stand-alone hardware device that can also tunnel IPX through though an TCP/IP network.

Network TeleSystems also offers a version of TunnelBuilder for Windows 3.x; Microsoft does not offer a virtual private networking client for Windows 3.x.

Newer Virtual Private Network Standards

There are some limitations with PPTP. One problem is that it is sometimes difficult to get encrypted information past firewalls. That's because PPTP uses GRE port 47, which many firewalls block. To get around this standard, the industry has developed a new tunneling protocol called the Layer 2 Tunneling Protocol (L2TP). L2TP uses UDP Port 1701, which most firewalls allow to pass more readily than PPTP's GRE port 47.

Windows NT Server 4.0 does not support L2TP, but Windows 2000 does, as does NTS's TunnelMaster Server. Both Windows 2000 and TunnelMaster can support tunneling AppleTalk and IPX over a virtual private network using either PPTP or L2TP.

NOTE: NTS's TunnelMaster server and TunnelBuilder clients also support a proprietary tunneling protocol called NTS-PT. It encapsulates PPTP inside HTTP packets (TCP port 80). This makes it easy to access a VPN from just about anywhere.

Windows clients don't yet support L2TP, but NTS' Tunnel Builder for Windows was the only Windows L2TP client at the time this was written. To get L2TP support Macs, you need TunnelBuilder for Macintosh 5.0. NTS is the only virtual private networking vendor at this time that supports both Mac and Windows clients.

An added feature of the NTS clients is the ability to use both clear (open, unencrypted) and tunnelled traffic at the same time. This is set by the user for each application. For instance, you can choose to have your e-mail client go through the tunnel while you browse the web on the clear Internet.

Another newer virtual private network protocol support by Windows 2000 and NTS TunnelMaster is the IP Security protocol (IPSEC) for authentication. It is supposed to be more secure and less proprietary than MS-CHAP.

MacWindows Tip

With Windows 2000, Mac users can access both AppleTalk and IP networks simultaneously when they're tunneled into Windows 2000 Server running AppleTalk. The AppleTalk access is available over PPTP/L2TP because of Windows 2000's support of the ATCP protocol. The Mac will require a third-party PPTP/L2TP client for Mac, such as Tunnel-Builder 5.0 or later.

Internet Gateways and Proxy Servers

There is a class of software that can let you share one or more Internet connections among a local network of computers. These are generically called Internet gateways, but they are actually a set of tools that run on a Windows or a Mac server, or in stand-alone hardware. You can use Internet gateways on a small scale, to enable one Mac and one PC to share a telephone connection to the Internet.

I said that these products are *generically* called Internet gateways because they go by various different names, including IP routers, proxy servers, and gateways. In fact, most of the products are a combination of one or more of services. For instance, products that call themselves Internet gateways often contain proxy servers and IP routers, and the products that call themselves proxy servers often contain the other services found in the Internet gateway products. These products can contain several of the following components:

- **IP router.** Connects a local TCP/IP network segment to the Internet or other TCP/IP network.
- **Network Address Translator (NAT).** Allows computers on a local network have individual IP addresses, but these are not visible to the outside Internet. They share one IP address.
- **Proxy server.** Allows a local network to connect to the Internet with a single IP address.
- **Firewall.** Blocks access to the local network from the Internet.

The proxy acts on behalf of the other computers. It downloads web pages and other information. Computers on the LAN don't actually contact the Internet directly, but instead contact the proxy server. Most proxy server products contain a cache, so they can download frequently used web pages in advance and store them, thus speeding Internet access for users on the local network.

Whether they run on Windows machines or Macs, the Internet gateways support both machines—at least to some degree. However, some of the Windows products use Windows-specific protocols, which prevents Macs from accessing certain types of Internet servers, such as FTP or e-mail. Some firewall features can also prevent Mac clients from getting out onto the Internet when they use Windows-specific standards instead of UNIX standards. Microsoft Proxy Server has some of these problems, which I'll discuss a little later.

Cross-Platform Gateway/Proxy Products

Internet access features such as proxy services, firewalls, and IP routers are often part of UNIX server systems, but there a number of products that run on Mac and Windows machines. The products described here have reputations for providing good gateway/proxy support of both Mac OS and Windows clients.

Web Update Link: *For the latest product information on these and other Internet gateways and proxy servers, see http://www.macwindows.com/Network.html#Internet*

Vicomsoft Internet Gateway

Vicomsoft
http://www.vicomsoft.com/

Vicomsoft Internet Gateway is software that comes in versions for Windows and Mac. It focuses on workgroups, small networks, and education, and is even used in homes. It lets you share one or more dial-up PPP, cable modem, ISDN, or hardware router Internet connections with Ethernet, token ring, or LocalTalk network segments, or all three. (The software can communicate with a token ring card in the Mac server at the same time as it communicates with LocalTalk and Ethernet ports.) It also can handle dial-up users and includes a DHCP server.

Vicomsoft Internet Gateway includes several security features. It uses a type of firewall called *session filtering*. This type of firewall prevents incoming IP packets from reaching any of the computers on the local network unless a packet is part of a session that one of the LAN computers originated. The IP addresses of the clients are not visible from the Internet, and a protocol blocking feature can restrict access to certain Internet services. Multihosting allows web managers to use a Macintosh to host multiple virtual web sites on one physical server. You can also limit Internet access to individual clients.

Vicomsoft Internet Gateway supports HTTP, POP/SMTP, FTP, telnet, and DNS service for Windows and Mac clients. AppleScript support enables you to automate procedures involving other Mac-based
servers. The Gateway is also known to be easy to set up and manage.

WinGate

Deerfield Communications
http://www.wingate.com

WinGate is similar to Vicomsoft Internet Gate in function and features, except it runs on Windows 95/98 and NT. WinGate contains a
proxy server and firewall, allowing a local network of Macs and PCs
to share a single Internet connection. The connection can be via a
dial-up modem, ISDN, cable modem, DLS, or T1 connection.
WinGate includes a DHCP server and firewall and has the ability to
restrict access by specific clients to specific Internet services. It will act
as a proxy for HTTP, FTP, POP/SMTP, telnet, SOCKS5, RealAudio,
and others, and you can create your own proxies using other protocols.

aVirt Gateway Server

aVirt Gateway Solutions
http://www.avirt.com/

The aVirt Gateway Server is a proxy server for Windows 95 and
Windows NT both on Intel and DEC Alpha. The Gateway Server
supports Macintosh and Windows clients connecting to the Internet.
It includes a proxy server with a firewall. The aVirt Gateway Server
can act as a proxy for SOCKS v4 and v5, caching HTTP and SHTTP
proxy using SSL, SMTP/POP3, NNTP/SNEWS, Telnet, America
Online, Microsoft Network, CompuServe, and others. You can control what protocols clients can use. Bridging capabilities support any
protocol bound to a specific TCP or UDP port. In addition to supporting Macintosh clients better than Microsoft Proxy Server, it is
faster and easier to set up.

Problems with Macs and Microsoft Proxy Server

Microsoft Proxy Server runs on Windows NT Server. Like other proxy servers, it makes Internet connections on behalf of a local network of computers. Unfortunately, Macintosh clients on the local network can have problems connecting to the Internet through Microsoft Proxy Server, particularly with e-mail. These problems are not found with several third-party proxy servers that run on Windows, including the ones mentioned earlier.

Some of the problems have to do with the fact that several features of MS Proxy Server are only activated in Windows clients when you replace the standard winsock.dll file with a special WinSock Proxy Client. This client enables standard Windows Internet programs, which use the WinSock API, to work with MS Proxy server. The WinSock API is not used by the Macintosh Open Transport TCP/IP software.

Fortunately, an upgrade to Microsoft Proxy Server 2.0 can solve some Mac access problems. With Proxy Server 1.0, Macs only have access to browser protocols: HTTP, FTP, Gopher, and SSL (HTTPS SNEWS). There is no way for Macs to access POP3/SMTP e-mail or User Datagram Protocol (UDP) through Proxy 1.0 without running Windows on the Mac via an emulator or coprocessor board. This is because Microsoft Proxy Server 1.0 uses *only* WinSock for e-mail client access, and there is no implementation of the WinSock proxy protocol for Mac OS. Proxy Server 1.0 can't authenticate Mac OS mail and news applications.

Microsoft Proxy Server 2.0 augments WinSock with the SOCKS proxy protocol. With SOCKS enabled on the server, SOCKS-compliant Mac client software can access the Internet through the Microsoft Proxy Server 2.0.

There are Mac e-mail applications that are SOCKS-compliant, including Netscape Navigator and the old Apple Cyberdog (which also does SOCKS Telnet). Microsoft Internet Explorer for Macintosh also supports SOCKS e-mail access, though it has been known to have some trouble running with MS Proxy Server. Other Mac (non-e-mail) clients that work with SOCKS are Fetch 3.0.3 ftp software and the Anarchie and InterNews news clients.

The long-discontinued TCP/Connect by Intercon, which included e-mail, was also SOCKS-compliant. Intercon was acquired by Ascend Communications in February of 1997, and TCP/Connect is now available from VisionSource (http://www.visionsource.com/) under the name tcpCONNECT4.

A good SOCKS-compatible FTP client for Macintosh is NetFinder (http://www-personal.usyd.edu.au/~vtan/sw/NetFinder/), which works well with MS Proxy Server. NetFinder is also very Mac-like, with a graphic, drag-and-drop interface.

The SOCKS proxy settings for Microsoft Proxy Server can be found under Microsoft Internet Service Manager. Ron Volkman of New Age Computers, Inc., once posted a message on a Microsoft news server (microsoft.public.proxy) recommending that one configure SOCKS ports 25 and 110 through the SOCKS proxy, and configure the Netscape client to use the SOCKS proxy on port 1080. (This also works for FTP clients.) However, the Mac clients won't be able to resolve your mail host name through the SOCKS proxy. You have several alternatives:

 ♦ Use a local DNS server inside your proxy. You'll need to enter your local name server address in the appropriate place in the Mac's TCP/IP control panel.
 ♦ Use static IP addresses to configure the Mac client.
 ♦ Use the DNS server on Windows NT to create an entry for your mail host.

You will find certain Windows applications, such as VDOLive and Netshow, won't work with SOCKS proxies because they require WinSock.

What's Next

With TCP/IP and basic networking under your belt, you can move on to providing useful network services to your Mac and Windows clients. Part 4 describes then next level up on the networking food chain—network services. The chapters in Part 4 describe a variety of cross-platfrom servers, as well as using services without servers. Chapter 11 picks up where this chapter left off, describing Windows NT Server.

Part Four

Macintosh and Windows NT and Other Servers

What's in This Section:

- ◆ **Chapter 11 Windows NT Server and Macintosh**

- ◆ **Chapter 12 Remote Access**

- ◆ **Chapter 13 NT Alternatives: Other File Servers**

- ◆ **Chapter 14 Cross-Platform Clients**

- ◆ **Chapter 15 Cross-Platform Printing**

Chapter

What's in This Chapter:

- ♦ *Windows NT Server overview*

- ♦ *Services for Macintosh basics*

- ♦ *Running AppleTalk protocol on NT Server*

- ♦ *Running File Server for Macintosh*

- ♦ *Running Print Server for Macintosh*

- ♦ *Speeding up Services for Macintosh performance*

- ♦ *Dealing with Services for Macintosh problems*

11

Windows NT Server and Macintosh

In recent years, Windows NT Server has caught up to and surpassed Novell NetWare as the most popular network server in the computer industry. In mixed-platform shops, Windows NT Server dominates. Armed with an installation CD-ROM set that includes Windows NT Services for Macintosh, Windows NT Server has also become the single most important piece of technology for integrating Macs into corporate Windows networks. The successor to Windows NT, Windows 2000, will probably play the same role.

Windows NT Services for Macintosh is Microsoft's AppleTalk-based file sharing and print server software. It allows Macs to access the same directories Windows clients can see. NT Services for Macintosh implements the Apple Filing Protocol and Printer Access Protocol (see Chapter 8), which means that Macintosh users can access a Windows

NT Server volume and printer through the Chooser. After Services for Macintosh is set up, the NT server can function as an AppleTalk router, enabling you to setup AppleTalk Zones on NT.

There are dozens of books the size of telephone directories that describe Windows NT in depth. This chapter does not pretend to be one of them. Instead, it gives an overview of the services and features available in Windows NT Server, and whether they apply to cross-platform situations. The chapter then focuses on installation, configuration, and tracking down common problems in NT Services for Macintosh. You can find more detailed information on Mac–NT integration issues that don't apply to Services for Macintosh, including TCP/IP and remote access, in other chapters.

Mac users will find much of the terminology used in Windows NT foreign. Some concepts, such as the registry, binding protocols, and capturing printers, simply don't have any equivalents in Mac OS or AppleShare IP servers. Windows NT is easy to learn for people familiar with Windows 95, but some Windows users may find the Mac networking concepts and client resources unfamiliar. Everyone may find it confusing that Microsoft often uses Macintosh networking terms differently than Apple does. I'll try to point these out.

Windows NT Server Overview

Before jumping into Services for Macintosh, it's worth spending some time discussing how NT Server works, and how Services for Macintosh relates to the rest of the services. It's also useful to know something about the concepts NT Server uses to run a network.

Windows NT Server and Windows NT Workstation are based on the same operating system. (The server and user versions of Windows 2000 are also based on the same, upgraded operating system.) Windows NT Server comes with the extra services and tools used to support clients. Any software that can run on NT Workstation will also run on NT Server. On the surface, the Windows NT user interface looks like Windows 95. But while Windows 98 is simply a new version of Windows 95, Windows NT is a completely different operating system from Windows 95/98. This is true even though Windows NT can run most 32-bit Windows 95/98 software applications (and some higher-level 16-bit software).

The main difference is that Windows NT is a different type of operating system than Windows 95/98. It shares a group of features with other operating systems that are sometimes called "advanced," mature," or "modern." Yet, the term "modern" does not refer to when the software released. In fact, UNIX, one of the oldest operating systems around, is a modern, or advanced, operating system. In addition to UNIX, these so-called advanced operating systems include such old timers as VMS and OS/2, along with newcomers such as Linux, Be OS, and Apple's Mac OS X. Mac OS 8.5 and earlier are not advanced or mature operating systems in this sense. Neither are Windows 95, Windows 98, or Windows 3.x.

The advanced operating systems share certain features, including multi-threading, the ability to run multiple processes at once; pre-emptive multitasking, the ability to prevent one process from hogging the processor or RAM; and protected memory, which prevents an software crash from taking down the whole system. Windows NT is a fairly stable operating system. Yes, NT does crash (as evidenced by the infamous "blue screen of death") and is not as stable as UNIX, but it is more stable than Windows 95/98.

Another benefit of advanced operating systems is efficiency and speed. Windows NT can run Microsoft Office much faster than Windows 95/98 can on the same hardware. Windows NT also has an excellent implementation of virtual memory, and supports symmetric multiprocessing, the ability to use more than one processor at one time.

Another way Windows NT differs from Windows 95/98 is that it can run on non-Intel processors. In the past, there were versions of NT for the MIPS and PowerPC processors (though not in Macs). Today, however, Microsoft and other software vendors only support Intel and Digital Alpha versions in their current releases.

NT Server Features and Concepts

Although it is safe to say that no one gets fired for buying Microsoft, there are strong points about NT Server that have helped it become successful. In addition to the benefits of speed and stability mentioned earlier, Windows NT Server is full of features. It's also easier to set up and manage than Novell NetWare. It takes an average PC network expert half a day to get an NT Server up and running, as opposed to a day or more for a Novell NetWare server. (NetWare 5, released in late 1998, uses a Java-based graphics user interface instead of the old character-based screens. But by this time, NT was already outselling NetWare.)

However, by most accounts, NetWare still has one superior feature— NDS (NetWare Directory Services)—a directory service that keeps tracks of the services and users running on multiple servers. The fact that Microsoft doesn't have anything up to par with NDS has kept NetWare alive today in large networks. Other than that, Windows NT Server offers soup-to-nuts networking.

While Windows NT Server implies that you get a server, the product is actually a set of features that include servers, protocols, and administration and diagnostic tools. Some of the features are installed by default. Others, while included on the CD-ROM set, are separate, optional installations. To the non-Windows-savvy reader, it isn't always apparent that items such as NT domains and the NT registry are features until you understand the concepts behind them.

This section covers some of the basic features and concepts of Windows NT, ending with an introduction to Services for Macintosh, the software that supports Mac file and print sharing clients.

Windows NT Interface

The Windows NT user interface looks very much like that of Windows 95/98 (Figure 11.1). AlthoughWindows 95 users will feel right at home on Windows NT, they will have to learn a few things. The deeper you delve, the more apparent the differences become. For instance, several of Windows NT's Control Panel dialog boxes differ from those in Windows 95/98, even though some of the icons have the same name. There are dozens of differences between the way you do things in Windows 95 and the way you do them in NT. A good book on Windows NT will point these out.

Another difference is that unlike Windows 95, Windows NT does not have DOS running underneath it. You can run DOS programs in NT, but they run in a 32-bit DOS run-time environment called Command Prompt, a program that understands DOS commands. There's no AUTOEXEC.BAT or CONFIG.SYS files for Windows. There are AUTOEXEC.NT and CONFIG.NT files, but they are only used for your DOS applications.

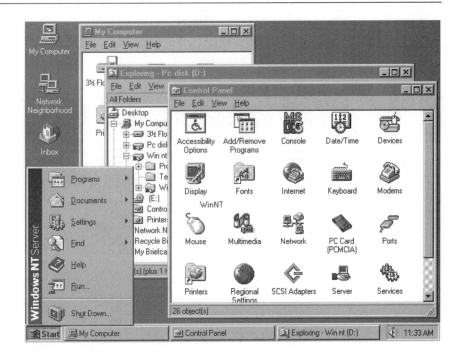

Figure 11.1 The Windows NT desktop

The Registry

The registry is a set of encrypted database files that hold hardware and software configuration information about the server PC. The registry stores information about hardware resource settings, settings of the system and user, and settings of applications. Before Windows NT, there was no central place that stored this information in Windows, and you had to manually configure much of it. Windows 95/98 also has a registry.

When you install software on Windows NT, it registers the file types and three-character file name extensions it uses. This enables Windows NT to open the appropriate application when you double-click it. Windows NT will also hide the three-dot file name extension when you view the icons in Windows.

You cannot make changes to the NT registry with a text editor, but you can view and edit it with the Windows NT Registry Editor utility, known as Regedt32.exe. (I'll refer to Regedt32.exe in the final section of this chapter.) There are plenty of third-party registry editing utilities you can use as well.

Editing the registry brings the danger of damaging or even disabling the system, so proceed with caution. Microsoft usually recommends using other configuration tools rather than editing the registry directly. However, there is sometimes no other way to create a work-around for a bug or to customize a certain aspect of the system.

Although there is no Macintosh equivalent of the Windows NT registry, there is something you can do on the Mac that is almost as dangerous as using Regedit32—opening up and editing the Mac OS System file with Apple's ResEdit. In both cases, you need to be careful what you edit, and make sure you edit it correctly.

NT Server's Protocol Support

Windows NT Server 4 comes with the ability to use four network transport protocols: NetBEUI, IPX/SPX, TCP/IP, and AppleTalk. The first three are native to NT, which means that you can use them for just about anything you can do with NT Server, including running services and administration. However, the natives protocols are used by NT Server to supply file and print services to Windows clients only, even though Mac OS itself can run two of these protocols. AppleTalk is not a native transport protocol in Windows NT Server, and only runs as part of Services for Macintosh.

NetBEUI

NetBEUI stands for NetBIOS Extended User Interface, but is a network transport protocol, not a user interface at all. NetBEUI was created by IBM in 1985 for use in small, PC-only networks of about 50 nodes or less. Its limiting property is that it can't be routed, which means you can only use it on a single network segment. The other three protocols that NT Server supports are routable. NetBEUI is also the only protocol listed here that cannot run on Macs. Windows NT Server supports the SMB (Server Message Block) file and print service protocol over NetBEUI for Windows clients. (See Chapter 9 for more information about NetBEUI and SMB.)

IPX/SPX

IPX/SPX is the protocol of Novell NetWare. IPX networks are easy to set up because the protocol is largely self-configuring. (By comparison, AppleTalk is completely self-configuring.) Back in the early 1990s, in NetWare's heyday, network analysts were talking about IPX becoming the standard networking protocol for computer networks everywhere. Then came the "Information Superhighway" buzz and the web explosion, and TCP/IP claimed the title of number one protocol. Windows NT Server does support file and print services for Windows clients on using the IPX transport.

Macs can run IPX/SPX—Novell's NetWare Client for Macintosh installs an IPX driver in the Mac System folder. Services for Macintosh only work over AppleTalk, and neither Microsoft nor anyone else has ever created an SMB client for Mac OS that runs over IPX. This means that Macs on an IPX network cannot access the services of Windows NT Server. (See Chapter 9 for more on IPX/SPX.)

TCP/IP

Windows NT Server's support of TCP/IP and related protocols and services is extensive. In addition to supporting SMB over TCP/IP for Windows clients, it offers a variety of TCP/IP services, some of which make it easier to implement a TCP/IP network. These are listed in the next section.

As with the other protocols, NT Server 4 does not provide file and print sharing over TCP/IP to Macs. Macs can use TCP/IP to access most standard Internet/intranet services running on NT Server, such as a Web and FTP servers. However, Windows 2000 Server does support Macintosh file and print sharing clients over TCP/IP.

In terms of Macintosh–Windows integration features, the lack of TCP/IP file and print services for Macintosh clients is a serious deficit. Even Apple is focusing on TCP/IP in Mac OS and in its own server products. Fortunately, Windows 2000 will support the Apple Filing Protocol (AFP) over TCP/IP. (AppleShare IP 6 also supports AFP over TCP/IP for Macs and SMB over TCP/IP for Windows clients.) I'll have more to say about Windows 2000 Server later in the chapter.

Even with NT Server 4, there are ways of getting around Microsoft's limitation. You can add SMB client software to Macs that runs on TCP/IP networks. Thursby Systems' DAVE makes a Mac look like just another TCP/IP Windows client. (For more information on DAVE, see Chapter 14.)

Another way around NT Server's lack of TCP/IP Mac support is with Open Door's ShareWay IP, a gateway that runs on a Mac. ShareWay IP enables a Mac AFP client to log into any AFP server—including

NT Services for Macintosh—via TCP/IP instead of AppleTalk. (For more information on ShareWay IP, see Chapter 13).

AppleTalk

The fact that AppleTalk is not native to Windows NT Server means it doesn't support SMB over AppleTalk, so NT Server cannot use AppleTalk to communicate with Windows clients. Nonnative status also means AppleTalk can't be used for administration of the server.

In Windows NT Server 4, Services for Macintosh file and printer servers must use AppleTalk to support Macintosh clients, even though other servers support TCP/IP connections to Macs. Through Services for Macintosh, Windows NT 4 supports AFP file sharing, the Mac's standard file sharing method. In Windows 2000 Server, Services for Macintosh supports Apple's AFP file sharing over TCP/IP—as does Apple's AppleShare IP server. (See Chapter 8 for more on AFP file sharing.)

NT Networking Services

Windows NT Server offers network services, many which are available to both Mac and Windows clients. As mentioned earlier, the file and print services for Windows and Mac clients are separate. Services for Macintosh is actually a set of services that includes file and print sharing. A good chunk of this chapter later on is devoted to this Services for Mac, so I cover some of the TCP/IP services now.

In addition to file and printer sharing, NT Server offers configuration services, authentication and other security services, information services, and remote access. These services provide Windows clients with the ability to browse TCP/IP devices. Mac clients still can't browse unless they are running Thursby Systems' DAVE, but they do get some benefits from these services. (See Chapter 14 for more on DAVE.)

For TCP/IP networks, Windows NT comes with three key services that make TCP/IP networks easier to implement, especially on larger networks:

 ♦ **DHCP Server.** This automatically assigns IP address and other configuration information to Mac and Windows clients.
 ♦ **WINS Server.** This is a dynamic NetBIOS name server for Windows clients. Clients receive the address of the WINS server from the DHCP server, then register their assigned IP address with the WINS server. Macs running Thursby Systems' DAVE can see the network resource names via WINS.
 ♦ **DNS Server.** The Windows NT DNS Server can get the Windows clients' IP address information from the WINS server. This server provides name resolution service for non-Windows clients in a manner known as dynamic DNS.

Macs running Open Transport can get their IP addresses from the Microsoft DHCP Server, since Open Transport includes a full DHCP client. However, there is an alternative. With the release of Windows NT Server 4 Service Pack 3 at the end of 1997, the Microsoft DHCP Server began to support clients using BootP clients, the standard that preceded DHCP and which is sometimes used in the Macintosh world. (Instructions on how to configure BootP on NT Server are included in Chapter 10.)

In conjunction with DHCP, you can use NT Server's Windows Internet Naming Service (WINS). WINS maps IP addresses to NetBIOS names, which are names for Windows resources on TCP/IP. WINS is not supported by Macintosh Open Transport, and NT 4.0 only supports Mac file and print sharing on AppleTalk, which won't run WINS. However, Thursby Systems' DAVE enables Macs to resolve NetBIOS names to IP addresses using a WINS server, which means users don't have to type in IP addresses to access printers and shared files over TCP/IP.

The Windows NT Server Domain Name Service (DNS) is an implementation of the standard Internet service used frequently for web sites. A DNS server maps host domain names to IP addresses of network resources. Windows and Mac clients can access web servers you set up by typing in a name (such as www.macwindows.com) instead of the server IP address.

Of course, if Microsoft went to the trouble of providing a DNS server, they might as well provide a web server. The web server in Windows NT Server is called the Internet Information Server (IIS). Running IIS also provides FTP service, useful for Mac clients if Services for Macintosh is not installed.

Windows NT Server also provides several other services, inlucing the Remote Access Service (RAS), something you can install from the Network icon in the Control Panel. In order for Macs to connect to a RAS server, they should have Mac OS 8.5 or later. It includes the Apple Remote Access client 3.1, the first version to be fully compatible with NT RAS server. You can get Macs clients running software earlier than OS 8.5 to connect to an NT RAS server remotely, but it isn't a straightforward process, and there are limitations. You can find out about Macintosh–RAS issues in Chapter 12.

NT Server also provides connectivity to Novell NetWare networks. The Gateway Services for NetWare is an optional installation.

Windows NT Domains

Windows NT domains are not the same as TCP/IP domains, as in "domain name server." (People often avoid confusion by referring to the latter simply as DNS.) Windows NT domains are a protocol-independent method of enabling a group of NT servers to work together. NT domains are useful in larger networks with many servers.

The user accounts in a domain are kept on one server, which lets the other servers access them. This lets users log on to the domain rather than a particular server. Once a user logs onto a domain, he or she has access to any server in the domain without having to log on to each one. Macs can participate in domains if you install the optional Microsoft User Access Module on the Macs.

A domain also enables you to manage multiple servers from one server, and adds a level of security to the network. On a big network, you can enable separate domains to communicate with each other with the concept of "trust." This enables users with accounts in one domain to log onto to another domain where they don't have accounts.

Basic NT Server Administration Tools

You can find most of the administration tools of Windows NT Server in a single menu, accessible from the Start menu (click the Start button, then Programs, then Administrative Tools, as in Figure 11.2). Here you'll find a little over a dozen tools. Some of them, such as Event Viewer and Performance Monitor, are for administering or troubleshooting the server PC itself. Others, such as System Policy Editor, are used for setting up Windows clients only. The most important in terms of a cross-platform network is Server Manager, which can be use to administer Services for Macintosh as well as Windows users.

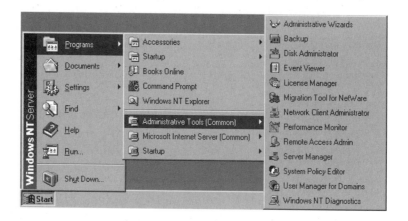

Figure 11.2 Accessing Windows NT Server administration tools

Administrative Wizards. These will guide beginners through certain tasks, such as adding user accounts, setting permissions on files and folders, adding printers, and configuring a modem. More experienced users will go directly to the other administration tools.

Backup. Lets you back up files to tape and restore them to the server.

Disk Administration. This selection provides hard disk drive maintenance tools, including repair and defragmenting.

DNS Manager. Lets you manage the domain name server, a standard TCP/IP service that matches TCP/IP addresses to host names.

Event Viewer. The flight-data recorder of Windows NT, which you might consult after a crash. This troubleshooting utility views the logs of events that NT Server records. Events can be system-level, security-related, and application-related, such as a network backup.

License Manager. Tracks the client licenses you've purchased for Microsoft software, including NT Server and Microsoft BackOffice.

Migration Tool for NetWare. You use this utility to import user accounts from a Novell NetWare server.

Network Client Administrator. This tool creates installer floppies for the Windows 95/98 client software for the NT Server—Network Client for Microsoft Networks. It can also create installer floppies for the Windows 95/98 version of the NT administration tools. Network Client Administrator does not create installer disks for Macintosh clients.

Performance Monitor. A diagnostic tool that presents a real-time graphic of several usage variables of NT Server, including the processor, memory, and disk.

Remote Access Admin. For use with dial-in, ISDN, or other types of remote connections, Remote Access Admin logs who has dialed in and when. It also provide information on remote ports currently in use.

Server Manager. You can manage every Windows NT Server on your network from this utility. You can stop and start services running on other servers, change file sharing configurations, and manage users. If Services for Macintosh is installed on the NT Server PC you are working on, Server Manager lets you configure Services for Macintosh running on other servers. With SFM installed, Server Manager grows a new menu, called MacFile.

System Policy Editor. Policies are standard configurations that apply to all Windows clients. System Policy Editor lets you set the client PCs' Control Panel settings, Network settings, and Desktop items, such as the Start menu contents and screen saver.

User Manager for Domains. You can set up and manage the users on an NT network with this utility. You can create Windows user accounts, set passwords, and create, edit, and delete user groups, as well as a variety of other tasks. You cannot manage Services for Macintosh users here. For these users, you'll need to access the MacFile icon of the NT Server Control Panel. However, Mac clients running Thursby Systems' DAVE will show up in the User Manager.

Windows NT Diagnostics. This tool provides a variety of information, including network statistics, the services running on one or more servers, and the resource configuration of hardware.

Services for Macintosh Basics

Services for Macintosh is an AppleShare-compatible file and print server and an AppleTalk router all rolled into one. It allows Macintosh users to access the same files as Windows users, so both groups can move files to each other. Services for Macintosh doesn't have the benefit of having the Macintosh file system or Mac OS to keep track of the unique aspects of Macintosh files, such as the data and resource forks and type and creator codes, as discussed in Chapter 5. Instead,

Services for Macintosh has its own way of preserving Mac file attributes while allowing Windows users to access them as well.

Services for Macintosh consists of three parts:

1. **The AppleTalk Protocol** provides the AppleTalk transport protocol to communicate with the Mac clients. This part of Services for Macintosh also provides an optional AppleTalk router, which you can use with other AppleTalk routers on the network. As a standard AppleTalk router, Services for Macintosh lets you set up AppleTalk network zones. You change settings for the AppleTalk Protocol through the Network icon in the Windows NT Server Control Panel.

2. **File Server for Macintosh**, also called MacFile, allows you to designate a directory as a Macintosh-accessible volume using the Apple Filing Protocol—AFP, the basis for AppleShare-compatible file sharing. MacFile ensures that Macintosh file names are valid Windows NT file system (NTFS) names. For each volume, MacFile lets you set AFP access privileges, which Microsoft calls "permissions." The installer adds a MacFile menu in the File Manager and the Server Manager, from which you can manage File Server for Macintosh.

3. **Print Server for Macintosh**, also called MacPrint, allows network users to send print jobs to a spooler running Windows NT Server. Windows users can also review the print jobs submitted by Mac users in Print Manager. MacPrint uses Apple's Printer Access Protocol (PAP), so printers connected to the NT Server show in the Mac Chooser. MacPrint enables Macs to print to non-Postscript (PCL) printers, but only at 300 dpi and without color.

Macintosh clients can log on to NT Server printers or volumes from the Chooser, using the standard Apple Filing Protocol (AFP) client built into Mac OS. You can also replace the logon portion of the client, called a *user authentication module* (UAM), with a the Microsoft UAM, which gives you some NT security features. Using the Microsoft UAM enables a Mac client to use encrypted passwords and be authenticated at the NT domain level. It also gives the NT administrator the ability to send messages to the Mac client.

Services for Macintosh has been around for a while, and as of Windows NT Server 4.0, hasn't changed much. Windows NT Server 4.0's support of Macintosh clients is merely adequate and is showing its age. SFM doesn't let the Mac client do everything that PC clients can do, and Mac clients can get more from an AppleShare server, or even from a Novell NetWare server. Services for Macintosh has limitations with printing and remote access, and bugs have been commonplace ever since inception. Windows 2000 (in beta at the time this book was written) addresses many of the issues, but there will still be inequities between Mac and Windows clients.

I don't want to overemphasize the shortcomings—Services for Macintosh does enable Mac users to share files with Windows users connected to the most popular server in business—but people contemplating putting Macs on an NT server should be aware of the limitations. Windows 2000 Server eliminates many of these limitations, despite any issues of it's own it may have.

A Look at Windows 2000 Server SFM

Windows 2000 (originally called Windows NT 5.0) is the successor to Windows NT 4.0. There are three server versions of Windows 2000: Windows 2000 Server, Windows 2000 Advanced Server, and Windows 2000 DataCenter, each featuring more services and capabilities. At the time this book was written, Windows 2000 was in beta and was expected to ship sometime during the second half of 1999. But even in its beta versions, it was clear that Windows 2000 Server offers significant new features and improvements for Mac clients.

Like the versions of Windows NT Server before it, Window 2000 supports file and print sharing for Mac clients separately from Windows clients, using Services for Macintosh. However, administration of Mac users has been integrated with other management tasks, and Mac clients have more capabilities than before.

File Services for Macintosh

One of the most significant enhancements to Services for Macintosh in Windows 2000 is support for the Apple File Protocol (AFP) file sharing over TCP/IP. With Windows NT 4.0 and earlier, Macs can only use AppleTalk. (Other file servers, such as Apple's AppleShare IP and several UNIX servers, have been supporting AFP over TCP/IP for some time now.) AppleTalk file sharing is still supported as well, but TCP/IP can move data faster than AppleTalk. That's because TCP/IP is a streaming protocol, while AppleTalk is not. However, Microsoft claims it has been able to create additional performance improvements to TCP/IP file sharing beyond what the protocol alone supplies. File sharing over AppleTalk on Windows 2000 runs at about the same speed it does in Windows NT 4.0.

A new Microsoft user authentication module (UAM) has TCP/IP built into it (Figure 11.3). If both AppleTalk and TCP/IP are available, the new Microsoft UAM will choose automatically TCP/IP. The

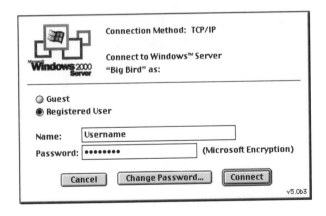

Figure 11.3 The Windows 2000 Services for Macintosh UAM

user can select AppleTalk, if available, with the option key. As with Windows NT 4.0, the Microsoft UAM is optional. Mac clients can also use Apple's encrypted UAM to log on to Windows 2000 Server.

Another file sharing improvement over NT 4 is that Windows 2000 will report the correct size and remaining space of volumes mounted on the Mac client. As is discussed later in the chapter, NT 4.0 Macs accessing volumes over 4 GB won't see the amount of remaining space in the Finder.

NOTE: Windows 2000 Services for Macintosh requires that Macs run at least AppleShare Client 3.8, which ships with Mac OS 8.5. AFP over TCP/IP began in AppleShare client 3.7, but Apple didn't supply a UAM API until version 3.8. Microsoft also warns that a bug in AppleShare Client 3.7.x can cause problems with the old MS UAM when attempting to connect to a Windows 2000 Server—the AppleShare client prevents a TCP/IP connection, and doesn't list an error message.

NTFS Drive Benefits

Like NT 4.0, Windows 2000 Services for Macintosh requires NTFS-formatted network volumes. In Windows 2000, NTFS has several new features, and Services for Macintosh can take advantage of all of them. One feature is system filters, which can process files as they are read or copied to a disk. For example, you can install a file system filter that can encrypt and decrypt data as it is written to and read from your hard drive.

The new NTFS also enables Windows 2000 to use the same security for Services for Macintosh as it does for PC users. In Windows NT 4.0, security for Mac and PC users is separate, even when they share the same data.

Remote Access

Windows 2000 supports the Apple's own AppleTalk Remote Access Protocol (ARAP), as well as the AppleTalk Control Protocol (ATCP), which enables AppleTalk over a PPP connection. Macintosh clients will be able to dial into Windows 2000 Server using the Remote Access control panel of Mac OS 8.5 and of the Apple Remote Access product.

Since UAMs are used for server authentication, Windows 2000 Services for Macintosh supports remote logon to a server using either Apple's native user authentication module (UAM) or the Microsoft-supplied UAM on the Mac client.

(Chapter 12 describes connecting Macs to the Windows NT 4.0 Remote Access Server.)

Virtual Private Networks

Virtual private networks (VPNs) encrypt information and encapsulate network traffic over a TCP/IP link, such as the Internet. Windows 2000 uses the IP Security protocol (IPSEC) for encrypting IP traffic. Windows NT 4 uses Microsoft's Point-to-Point Tunneling Protocol (PPTP) for dynamically assigning IP addressing. Mac clients need to use a third-party client such as Network TeleSystems' TunnelBuilder in order to implement PPTP and the MS-CHAP authentication on the Mac client. (See Chapter 10 for more infomation on VPNs.)

Windows 2000 will add a second tunneling protocol for virtual private networks, the Layer 2 Tunneling Protocol (L2TP), an IETF draft specification. Windows 2000 supports using L2TP to tunnel AppleTalk (as well as IPX) over a VPN. Network TeleSystems TunnelBuilder 5.0 supports L2TP on Mac clients. L2TP has some advantages over PPTP, in that it is easier to get encrypted VPN sessions through firewalls. L2TP uses UDP Port 1701, which most firewalls allow to pass more readily than PPTP's GRE port 47.

Another useful new capability enables Mac users to gain access to both the AppleTalk and IP networks simultaneously when they're tunneled into Windows 2000 Server running AppleTalk. The AppleTalk access is available over PPTP/L2TP because of Windows 2000's support of the ATCP protocol. Again, the Mac will require a third-party PPTP/L2TP client for Mac such as TunnelBuilder 5.0.

Windows 2000 Server Management

In NT Server 4.0, administration of Services for Macintosh is almost completely divorced from the management of Windows clients. Administration for Services for Macintosh is combined with services for just about everything else in a new window called the Microsoft Management Console (see Figure 11.4). The Console combines the administration of users, services, resources, domains, shares, and other

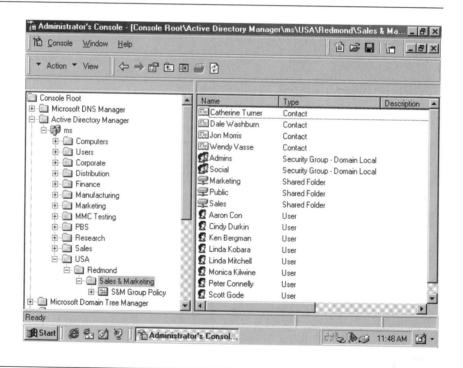

Figure 11.4 The management console in Windows 2000

topics. You select the area you need to manage on the left, and the appropriate related information is displayed on the right.

You won't need to reboot Windows 2000 as much as Windows NT. You no longer need to reboot the server after changing most settings. This includes turning AppleTalk on or off, adding Services for Macintosh, and binding a protocol to a service or network adapter.

Installing and Running AppleTalk on NT Server

The AppleTalk Protocol is the core of Services for Mac and must be installed in order to run the file and print services. Installing the Services for Macintosh software on the NT server does not create shared volumes or printers. Those are separate procedures, covered in the next two major sections, Running File Server for Macintosh and Running Print Server for Macintosh.

Volume size limits

Windows NT 4.0 implements an older version of Apple's Apple Filing protocol, which doesn't support volumes over 4 GB. That doesn't mean that Mac clients can't mount network volumes bigger than 4 GB. In fact, they can. What it does mean is that Mac users will not get an accurate reading of the size of the volume, the amount of data in it, and the free space. So, you can mount a 30 GB volume, but the information might say "4 GB volume, 4 GB used, 4 GB free space." However, you may need to adjust NT Server to enable Mac clients to see volumes bigger than 2 GB. To learn how, see the section called Dealing with Services for Macintosh Problems at the end of this chapter.

To get the AppleTalk Protocol module of Services for Macintosh up and running, you first need to install the Services for Macintosh software. You then have the option of configuring an AppleTalk router on the NT server and creating AppleTalk zones. However, there are good reasons *not* to do this, which are discussed later in this section.

You'll need to install the network interface card that connects the server to an AppleTalk network before you install Services for Macintosh. If you have two AppleTalk networks—LocalTalk and Ethernet, for instance—you can install two different network interface cards and use the AppleTalk router in Services for Mac to connect the networks.

Installing Services for Macintosh

Services for Macintosh is a separate installation that you initiate through the Network window of the Control Panel. Services for Macintosh isn't installed by default, so you'll need to have the Windows NT Server CD-ROM handy. Services for Macintosh won't run on a FAT partition and must be installed on an NTFS partition.

You begin the Services for Macintosh installation the same way you would start installing a lot of other NT services—in the Network window of the Control Panel. This procedure will show you how to install the software, with a quick guide to setting up an AppleTalk router on the server. After the twelve steps, there's some more detailed information on configuring AppleTalk routers.

1. Double-click the Network icon in the Control Panel and select the Services tab. You'll see a list of the network services currently installed. (See Figure 11.5.)

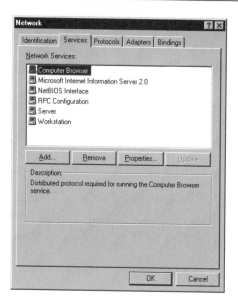

Figure 11.5 The first step in adding an NT network service in the Network windows of the Control Panel

2. Click the Add button to add Services for Macintosh. A Window called Select Network Service will appear. Scroll through the list until you find Services for Macintosh. Select Services for Macintosh and click OK (Figure 11.6).

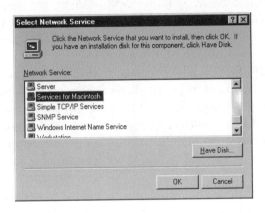

Figure 11.6 Locating and choosing Services for Macintosh

3. The Windows NT Setup program will appear. Insert the Windows NT Server CD-ROM and enter the directory path of the Services for Macintosh installation files on the CD. If the server is an Intel machine, specify the CD drive letter and the i386 directory. If the server has an Alpha processor, type in *alpha* after the CD drive letter. The Setup

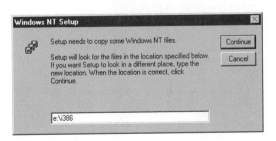

Figure 11.7 Entering the directory of the installation files

software will find the necessary files once you've entered the correct directory. (See Figure 11.7.)

4. Click on the Continue button. Windows will install the Services for Macintosh software.

5. The Network window will return when the installation is finished. Click the Close button, and the AppleTalk Protocol Properties window will appear. Click the General tab. (See Figure 11.8.)

6. From the "Default Adapter" drop-down list box, select the network adapter on which AppleTalk will be run.

7. If your network already has an AppleTalk router, the Default Zone drop-down list box will contain the names of existing AppleTalk zones. Choose the AppleTalk zone in which you want the file server and NT Server–connected printers to appear when Macintosh users select a zone in the Chooser. (AppleTalk "zones" are similar to a Microsoft "workgroups.")

8. If you want the Windows NT Server to act as an AppleTalk router, you need to enable AppleTalk routing. You do this

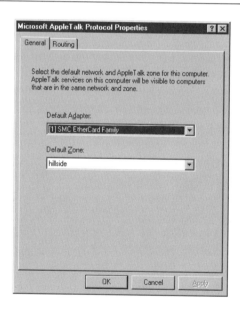

Figure 11.8 Selecting a network adapter for AppleTalk and the AppleTalk zone

by clicking the Routing tab and selecting the Enable Routing check box. If you don't want to use NT Server as an AppleTalk router, skip to step 12. (For more on AppleTalk routing and zones, see the next section.)

9. In the Network Range fields, type in the range for the AppleTalk node numbers (addresses) you'd like to use on this network. (See Chapter 8 for more on AppleTalk addressing).

10. If Services for Macintosh is installed on only one server, or there are no other AppleTalk routers on the network, select the "Use this router to seed the network" check box.

11. Add one or more AppleTalk zones by clicking the Add button naming the zones.

12. Click OK. A dialog box appears prompting you to restart the server. Click Yes to reboot the server (Figure 16.9).

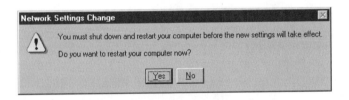

Figure 11.9 A prompting for a reboot after clicking OK in the AppleTalk Protocols Window

Setting Up an AppleTalk Router

If AppleTalk network numbers and zones sound like concepts from an alien world, this section is for you. If you're an old hand at AppleTalk networking, you can skip ahead, but not too far ahead—be sure you read the section called Reasons Not to Run a Router on NT Server.

In the Network Range fields of the Router tab of the Microsoft AppleTalk Protocol Properties window (step 9 above), you assign network numbers to each network cable segment. AppleTalk allows for

254 devices per network number, and you have 65,536 network numbers from which to choose. LocalTalk is limited to one network number per network segment, but Ethernet and token ring can be assigned a range of network numbers.

You can assign numbers randomly, but it makes sense to use some sort of numbering scheme that can give you information about the networks. For instance, the first digit could represent a site, the next digit could indicate the building or floor, the next a department, and so on. This way, if you saw a certain number between 234501 and 234515 in a routing table, it might tell you that you were looking at the Ethernet segment used by the accounting department on the third floor of the San Francisco office.

If there are other AppleTalk routers on the network, you should think twice about designating the NT Server as the seed router. If there is another seed router on the network, the information entered in each must agree. You configure a seed router by telling it what the network numbers are for the segments, and what zones correspond to the network numbers. The seed router then becomes the official spokesman of the state of the network. It and tells the nonseed routers what the network numbers are for the segments, and what zones correspond to the network numbers. If two seed routers on the network are providing differing views of what the network looks like, the nonseed routers will become confused. Mac users might see zones disappearing or changing, or might not see any devices on the network at all.

There's a third type of router—a soft-seed router. You configure it like the seed router, but unlike a seed router, it will check to see if there is a differing view of the network from another router. If there's a disagreement, the soft-seed router will back down, rather than continue to confuse the nonseed routers with a contrary view of the network.

Table 12.1 shows the type of information that AppleTalk routers pass around to each other. Its not a bad idea to keep a list like this yourself as an aid in troubleshooting. Your list should include the router's name, numbers of ports, and physical location.

Table 12.1 An example of a routing table used by AppleTalk routers

Network range	Zone name	Network interface
151	Purchasing	LocalTalk
521–550	Art Dept.	Ethernet
700	Finance	LocalTalk
2200–2300	Lab, 2nd Floor	Ethernet
450–4550	Engineering	Ethernet
500–5050	Customer Support	Ethernet

Creating Zones

You create zones for reasons of convenience. Zones make it easier for users to locate network devices in the Chooser. Creating zones is especially important with large networks; if there were only one zone for a big network, Mac users would have to scroll through a Chooser list of dozens or hundreds of devices just to pick a printer or file server. With multiple zones, a Mac user clicks on one zone in the Chooser to see the devices, as shown in Figure 11.10. Zones can also be created to

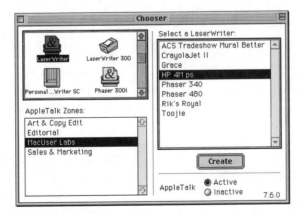

Figure 11.10 AppleTalk zones as they appear to a Mac user

organize nodes by function, or to organize members of a workgroup under a single name, both of which help users physically locate the devices. Zone names like "Accounting," "Engineering," "Fourth Floor," or "West Wing" tell people where printers are located.

Dividing an AppleTalk network into zones does not physically divide an AppleTalk network. Zones don't have anything to do with where nodes are located physically on a network. A single zone can contain devices in multiple network segments, and one network segment can contain multiple zones. AppleTalk allows up to 256 zones in an Ethernet or token ring network. There is no restriction on how many devices can be assigned to a zone.

If you are setting up multiple zones within one network, you'll have to set up a network zone list for the LAN and signify a default zone for each AppleTalk device. The default zone is the zone that automatically selected when a user brings up the Chooser. When a Chooser drivers such as AppleShare or LaserWriter is selected, the Mac polls the network for devices in the default zone.

Reasons Not to Run a Router on NT Server

It is certainly convenient to be able to manage an AppleTalk router and set up AppleTalk zones from an NT Server. As AppleTalk routers go, the one in Services for Macintosh has a good, simple graphical interface for management.

Yet, there are several reasons to ignore NT Server's AppleTalk router feature, particularly if there are other AppleTalk routers on the network. AppleTalk routers can be in other NT Servers, or stand-alone devices, or as part of multiprotocol routers that include AppleTalk. If you are unaware of them, you may configure your router with information that conflicts with the other routers, a situation that can bring down the AppleTalk network.

One reason for having a router in a stand-alone box is that it most likely will remain functional. When the NT Server is shut down or crashes, the router goes with it. This could disconnect two network segments, cause network packets to be lost, or cause zones to disappear. If the router on the NT server is a seed router and the NT goes down, you may have to shut down every AppleTalk router on the network and start up yours first. Otherwise, you could get into a situation of routers with different versions of routing tables.

Another problem with a router-in-a-server approach is organizational: It puts local services and company-wide resources (routing) in one box, each of which can fall under the jurisdiction of a different administrator. Since routers can propagate errors across an entire multi-segment network, large companies with dozens of routers usually have a central organization to handle network plumbing problems. Files servers, on the other hand, are often controlled at the workgroup level by a manager supplying services tailored to local users. The bottom line is, check with your network administrator before installing an AppleTalk router on NT Server.

Stopping and Starting the AppleTalk Protocol

When you install Services for Macintosh and restart the server, the AppleTalk protocol will be running, along with the MacFile and MacPrint services. Stopping the AppleTalk protocol will take MacFile and MacPrint off-line. Similarly, starting either MacFile or MacPrint will automatically restart the AppleTalk protocol. You'll need to restart the AppleTalk protocol if you make any changes to the router.

Windows NT Server doesn't treat the AppleTalk protocol the way it treats other network protocols, so AppleTalk does not show up on the Protocols tab of the Control Panel's Network window. (The Control Panel's Devices tool does show AppleTalk driver along with the other protocol drivers.) You can use the Devices window to stop AppleTalk:

1. Open the Devices item in the Control Panel.
2. Click on AppleTalk Protocol to select it in the list of devices.
3. Click the Stop button.

4. The Stopping window will appear, telling you that File Server for Macintosh and Printer Server for Macintosh will also be stopped. Click OK.

To start the AppleTalk protocol and services, you'll use the Services item in the Control Panel:

1. Open the Services item in the Control Panel.
2. Click on File Server for Macintosh to select it.
3. Click the Start button. NT will start the AppleTalk protocol first, followed by the MacFile file server.
4. If you want to start MacPrint, select Print Server for Macintosh from the list and click the Start button.

Running File Server for Macintosh

With Services for Macintosh installed, you can designate an NT directory to act as an AFP-compatible server volume, which Microsoft calls a "Macintosh volume." To do this, you configure File Service for Macintosh, referred to as MacFile in the software. This directory must be on an NTFS volume, not a FAT volume.

MacWindows Tip

If Services for Macintosh is not installed or enabled, there is a reasonable alternative. You can use a Mac FTP client such as Fetch to share directors via NT Server's FTP server, part of the Internet Information Server. Macs can use an FTP client to retrieve and store data fields, but not application files.

You can also use MacFile to customize the file type associations between Macintosh file types and the PC three-character file name extensions. This allows both Macintosh and Windows users to double-click and launch files that are stored on NT Server.

The installation procedure of Services for Macintosh creates one shared, read-only volume, called Microsoft UAM. You use to this volume to install the optional Microsoft client on the Macs. There are some reasons not to do this, though the Microsoft client software isn't as "dangerous" as the SFM routing software can be.

Creating a Macintosh Volume on Windows NT Server

There are two ways to begin creating your own Macintosh volume—from the File Manager or from the Server Manager administration utility described earlier in the chapter. You can use either on the PC hosting the server; Server Manager can also configure other NT servers on the network that have Services for Macintosh installed, using the utility. Using File Manager is the simpler method.

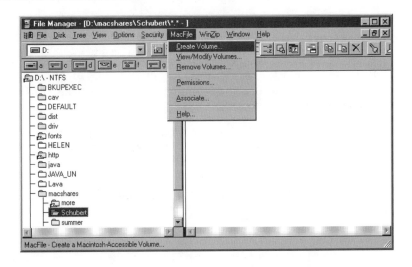

Figure 11.11 Creating a Mac volume from the File Manager

When you installed Services for Macintosh, it created a new Control Panel icon called MacFile. This gives you the same administration capabilities as the MacFile menu described in the following procedures.

Sharing a directory from the File Manager

1. You can bring up the File Manager by typing `winfile` in the Run command of the Start menu.
2. Select a disk or directory from the directory tree on the left side of the File Manager (see Figure 11.11). This can be a directory that is already shared with Windows clients. If you want to create a new directory to share, select the directory (folder) in which you wish the new subdirectory to reside. Then select Create Directory from File menu).
3. With SFM installed, the File Manager has a new menu called MacFile. Open the MacFile menu and choose Create Volume. A dialog box appears where you to enter in the name of the shared Macintosh volume.
4. At this point, you need to assign permissions to the volume. Skip to the section called "Setting Permissions for a Shared Macintosh Volume."

Sharing a directory from Server Manager

1. Open Server Manager and click on the NT Server computer on which you want to create a shared Macintosh volume.
2. Choose Volumes from the MacFile menu (Figure 11.12).

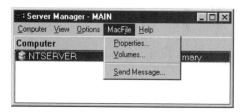

Figure 11.12 The Server Manager MacFile menu

3. A window with a list of Macintosh volumes appears (Figure 11.13). Click Create Volume for a new volume (or click Properties to edit an existing volume.) To unshare a directory, select it and clicking Remove Volume

NOTE: this does not delete the directory—it only unshares it.

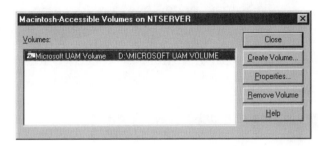

Figure 11.13 Shared Macintosh volumes displayed in the MacFile window

4. When you click Create Volume, a dialog box asks you to enter the volume name and path of the directory you want to share. The volume name does not have the be the same as the directory name (as shown in Figure 11.14). You now need to set permissions.

Figure 11.14 Naming the Macintosh volume and its path on the server

Setting Permissions for a Shared Macintosh volume

1. Click the Permissions button to set user permissions, which are similar to the "access privileges" used in an AppleShare file server or in personal file sharing in Mac OS clients (as described in Chapter 8). If you're familiar with Mac OS, you may notice that this Permissions windows is similar to the Sharing window of Mac workstations before Mac OS 8 (see Figure 11.15). These permissions will only apply to Macintosh users; you need to set Windows users' permissions separately (from the Shared Directories item in the Computer menu of the Server Manager).

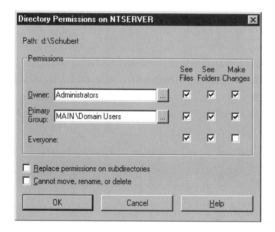

Figure 11.15 Setting directory permissions (the equivalent of AFP access privileges)

2. When you click OK, the directory you just shared appears in the Macintosh-Accessible Volumes window (Figure 11.16). You can add another volume with the Create volume button again, or click the Close button.

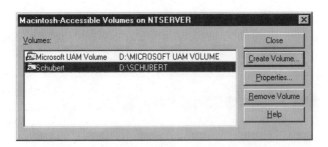

Figure 11.16 The newly created shared volume

3. The directory permissions you've assigned only specify the AFP access privileges for this directory. All users must also have NT File Sharing (NTFS) permissions. To assign NTFS permissions, go to the Windows NT desktop and right-click the directory you just shared. Select the Sharing item in the pop-up menu (Figure 11.17).

Figure 11.17 The pop-up menu you get when you right-click a shared directory.

4.   A Properties window appears with the Sharing tab selected (Figure 11.18). However, these are directory Sharing properties for Windows users, which don't apply to a Mac users. Ignore the Sharing tab and click the Security tab. The Per-

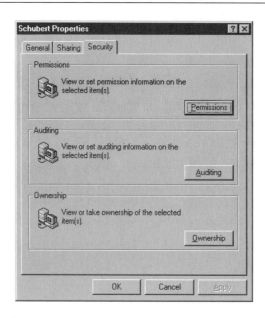

Figure 11.18 The Sharing tab of this Properties window applies only to Windows users.

missions area at the top refers to NT file sharing permissions that always apply to every access folder. Click the Permissions button.

5.   A Directory Permissions window appears (Figure 11.19), where you can set any restrictions you want for both Mac and Windows users. In this case, we've selected Full Control in the Type of Access field, which will enable both Macintosh and Windows users to access the directory.

6.   Click OK. Macintosh users will be able to access the NT directory from the Macintosh Chooser.

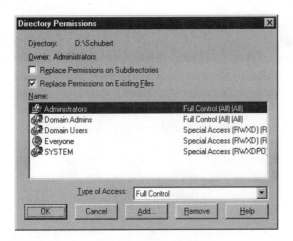

Figure 11.19 Setting Permissions that apply to both Mac and Windows users

Handling Mac Files on NT Server

The differences in Macintosh and Windows files (described in Chapter 5) can cause problems when users of both operating systems are accessing the same file on the same network file server. NT Server goes a long way toward preventing most, but not all, of these types of problems. They fall into four categories:

- ◆ File structure
- ◆ Illegal characters in file name
- ◆ File directory name and length
- ◆ Launching an application from a double-click

File structure

Macs files are made of two parts, a data fork and a resource fork. Windows files systems, including FAT and NTFS, ordinarily ignore the resource fork. In document files, this results in the loss of the icon and type and creator code, which doesn't affect Windows clients opening Windows-compatible Mac files, such as Word, Excel, or PageMaker files. However, Mac applications are destroyed with the loss of the resource fork.

Fortunately, Windows NT Services for Macintosh retains the resource fork of Mac files. This means all Mac files will retain their Mac icons, and Mac users can upload applications to the server without damaging them. Windows clients will still ignore the resource fork of Mac files, which is not a problem, since Windows can't use Mac resource forks or Mac applications.

File names, illegal characters

Windows NT includes an on-the-fly file name translation function that lets Windows users see Mac file names as proper Windows NT file system (NTFS) names. Part of this is an attempt to not to let Windows users see characters that are illegal in Windows (see Chapter 5). However, Mac users still need to learn PC file naming conventions, since Windows NT Server does not fix all file name problems. For instance, Windows doesn't like file names that end in a period or a space. When a Mac user copies a file ending in a period to the NT server, other Mac clients can see and open these files, but Windows clients can't open or copy them. Instead, they'll get an error message that says "Cannot find the specified file. Make sure you specify the correct path and file name." Mac files with names that end with a space may be invisible to Windows 95/98 and Windows NT clients. These files won't be backed up by NT Server's backup software, either.

File and directory name length

NTFS supports file names up to 256 characters long. Since the Mac HFS file system supports file names of up to 31 characters in length, the Mac can't display the entire file name when NT Server's network volumes are mounted on the desktop. To get around this problem, Windows NT Server gives Mac clients a different view of files with long file names. For files names longer than 31 characters, Mac users see only the first six characters displayed, followed by a tilde (~) and a number to indicate that they are not seeing the entire file name. The file name ends with the three-character extension. For example, a file in a shared directory titled "macintosh and windows integration methods.doc" will appear as "macint~1.doc" to the Mac user. This is the same way Windows files on PC disks appear on Macs with Mac OS 8.0 and earlier. It's also the same way Windows NT Server displays file names for Windows 3.x clients.

Mac OS and NTFS also differ in the length of directory paths, but this time Windows NT has the more restrictive requirements. While Mac OS has no restrictions to the length of directory paths, Windows NT cannot make use of paths longer than 260 characters long. This could be a problem if a Mac user uploaded a folder containing many nest folders, each with long names. The Mac users would be able to access directory paths longer than 260 characters, but Windows clients would not. Worse yet, none of the Windows NT services, including virus scans or backup, would be able to access these directory paths.

MacWindows Tip

Want to create dozens of Mac volumes? Be careful in how you name the volumes. Since the AppleShare server supports up to 50 volumes with names of 27 characters or less, the Macintosh Finder was designed to expect no more total characters than 50 times 27, or 1350, on mounted network volumes. When the Finder looks for a mounted network volume, it allocates memory for a string that is 1350 characters long. When the Finder encounters a server whose volumes have a total string length greater than 50x27, the Finder can't handle it and may stop responding.

On a Windows NT server, you can successfully create a few hundred visible Macintosh volumes by giving the volumes very short names, such as A1, A2, B1, B2, and so on.

Launching an application from a double-click

During installation of a Windows 95/98 or NT application, the installer creates an entry in the Registry to tell the system what application to launch when you double-click one of its files. Mac OS does not need a registry, as it has always maintained this type of information itself transparently. The Mac file system keeps track of the file type and creator codes that identify what applications to open when you double-click a Mac file.

Since NT Services for Macintosh doesn't have Mac OS or the Mac file system, it uses a feature in MacFile called *file type associations*. This lets you associate a Mac type and creator code pair to a particular three-character file name extension. This is the same concept as Mac OS's extension mapping, discussed in Chapter 5. Association enables Mac users to double-click on Word for Windows files on the server, for instance, which then launches Word for Mac.

Services for Macintosh comes with a set of associations already installed, but you can add your own.

1. Open the File Manager.
2. Select the MacFile menu and select Associate. The Associate window appears.
3. In the field called Files with MS-DOS Extension, type the file name extension you want to associate.
4. If the file name extension is already associated with a Macintosh file type, it will appear selected in the Creator and Type list box. If you want to change it, scroll through until you find an application want to use.
4. If no application becomes highlighted in the Creator and Type list box, then you'll need to enter the type and create codes manually. (Chapter 5 describes how you can see the type and creator codes of a particular Mac file.) Click Add, and enter the file Type and Creator codes, and click OK.
5. Back in the Associate window, click the Associate button and close the window.

It should be noted that this association is one-way only. That is, it enables Mac users to click on Windows files on the server. It does not work the other way, to add a file name extension to Mac files uploaded to the server. If you want to use the 8.3 file naming convention, you'll have to convince the Mac users to name their files this way, or convert the files with a utility.

Web Update Link: *You can find a list of Mac software that can change Mac file names to Windows-compatible files names at http://www.macwindows.com/filetran#filetools*

Installing the Optional Macintosh Client Software

Mac clients don't need additional software to access shared network volumes and printers on the NT, as they use the AFP and PAP client software that comes with Mac OS (see Chapter 8). The Microsoft client software, the Microsoft User Access Module (UAM), adds some security features, including encrypted NT passwords. However, the encryption is not that hard to intercept with some network monitoring software, as it is sent as clear text. The Microsoft UAM also increases the maximum length of the password from 8 to 15 characters.

Another benefit of using the Microsoft UAM in a Mac client is that administrators can send messages to the Mac user from the NT server, though only when the client is logged on the server.

The major drawback to using Microsoft UAM is that Mac users won't be able to use aliases to log on to an NT network volume. Ordinarily, a Mac user can make an alias of a file or folder on the network volume when it is mounted on the desktop. He can then log onto the server by double-clicking the file, without having to go to the Chooser. The logon window is brought up automatically, and, after typing the password, the volume mounts and the file opens. With the Microsoft UAM installed, this no longer works, as the alias logon mechanism doesn't use the Microsoft UAM logon mechanism.

You install the Microsoft client software from the Mac. From the Chooser, log on to the NT server as a guest and select the Microsoft UAM volume. After it mounts on the Mac desktop, drag the Apple-Share folder (the only item on the volume) into the Mac's System folder. You won't have to restart the Mac.

NOTE: The Microsoft UAM volume is a read-only volume. You can't use it for file sharing.

You can require that a Mac client use the Microsoft UAM to log into the server by using the Control Panel's MacFile tool. Click the Attributes button, and in the window that comes up, click the check box marked Require Microsoft Authentication.

MacWindows Tip: Erratic logging into NT Server by Mac

Unpredictable logon results can occur when a Macintosh user has matching accounts in more than one NT domain, but does not have equivalent permissions on the Services for Macintosh volume that he is attempting to access. In this case, the user has multiple accounts (one for each domain), but access is granted by the permissions of only one account. This means that users can be denied or granted access depending upon which account was found first.

The solution is for the user to log in with the Microsoft UAM Server. In the User Name field, include the domain name and a back slash before the user name—for example, DOMAIN3\RJONES. This forces Windows NT server to validate the user in the specified domain.

Disconnecting Users

The Services for Macintosh installer creates a MacFile tool in the Control panel (Figure 11.20). You can use the MacFile tool for a variety of management tasks. The Users button brings up a list of connected Mac users and the server-resident files that they have open. The Dis-

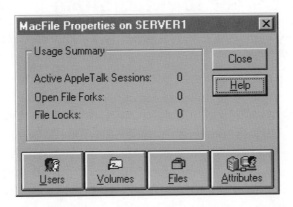

Figure 11.20 The MacFile tool in the Control Panel

connect button in the Users windows lets you kick selected users off of the server.

If you'd like to send the user a message before you disconnect her, click the Send Message button in the Users window after selecting the user from the list. You can then type a short message and send it to the selected user or to all of the Mac users. The users must be connected to the server using the Microsoft UAM described earlier.

In addition to booting a user off of the server, you can disconnect a selected user or all users connected to a single Macintosh volume. You do this by clicking MacFile's Volumes button. The Volumes windows shows the current shared volumes and the users connected to each.

You can even disconnect all Mac clients using a specific file. MacFile's Files button displays a window that lists currently open files that reside on the server. To disconnect the users, select a file and click the Close Fork button. The "fork" referred to here is the data fork of a Macintosh file (see Chapter 5).

Running Print Server for Macintosh

MacPrint has two basic cross-platform functions that serve both Mac and Windows clients.

- Enabling Windows clients to print to AppleTalk Printers. NT will spool print jobs coming from Windows (as well as Mac) clients and print them to AppleTalk PostScript printers. An optional step called *capturing* an AppleTalk printer forces Mac clients to go through the NT server to print.

- Enabling Macs to print to non-Postscript printers connected directly to the NT server.

Unfortunately, MacPrint is the weakest part of Services for Macintosh. It has limitations and bugs that often cause problems. As I'll point out, there are many instances when it is easier to ignore this part of Services for Macintosh. I'll also point out some tricks you can use get around some of these problems.

Enabling Windows Clients to Print to AppleTalk Printers

Although Windows clients can access Postscript printers, PCs on a Microsoft network are not usually running AppleTalk. When Services for Macintosh spools AppleTalk printers, Windows clients see them as if they were connected directly to the server PC.

Sharing an AppleTalk printer with Windows users involves creating a printer port on the server:

1. Select the printer in Printers folder (accessible through My Computer).
2. Right-click the printer and select Properties.
3. Click on the Ports tab (see Figure 11.21).
4. Click on the Add Port button.

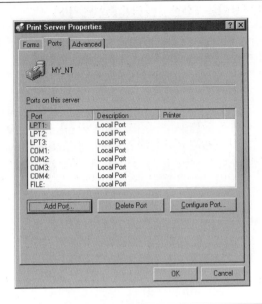

Figure 11.21 The Ports tab of the printer properties dialog

5. From the list of port types select Local Port and click New Port. The dialog shown in Figure 11.22 will appear.

6. When the Printer Ports window appears, choose AppleTalk Print Devices and click OK.

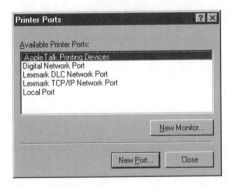

Figure 11.22 Creating a port for an AppleTalk printer

7. A Network Browser dialog box appears listing the printers currently turned on and connected to the AppleTalk network. Select a printer and click OK. NT will create a port with the name of the AppleTalk printer.

At this point, Mac users can now access the printer two ways, either directly over the AppleTalk network or through the server. Both routes will show up as separate printers in the Chooser. However, as is discussed later, it is usually better for the Mac to connect directly to the printer.

Capturing AppleTalk printers and Mac Postscript errors

You can prevent Macs from accessing AppleTalk printers directly by having NT Server "capture" the printer. Capturing an AppleTalk printer makes it no longer directly accessible to Macs over the AppleTalk network. This would be useful if you wanted to monitor usage, as you might for a high-end color printer.

To capture an AppleTalk printer, follow these steps:

1. Bring up the Printer Properties window, as previously described.
2. Click on the Ports tab.
3. Select the port. Click Configure Port.
4. The AppleTalk Printer Configuration window comes up. Click "Capture this AppleTalk printing device" and click OK. To uncapture a printer, bring up this window and uncheck this item.

There are drawbacks to having NT capture an AppleTalk printer, and most network managers recommend against it. For one, preventing Macs from directly sending print jobs to the printer cuts off communications from the printer to the Mac. Ordinarily, AppleTalk printers can tell Mac clients about a variety of errors, including Postscript errors and out-of-paper conditions. Print Server for Macintosh will block these messages from getting to the Mac client.

Even worse, NT's implementation of Postscript tends to generate its own Postscript errors, which the Mac client never hears about. To the Mac user, it looks like the document has printed okay, but at the printer, the user picks up page after page of garbled text, even for graphic images. The Postscript errors that NT Server generates increase in frequency and severity with more complex print jobs with graphics.

The cause of the problem has to do with the assumptions that printers make about Postscript print jobs. Some printers assume that Postscript print jobs received over AppleTalk networks are encoded using standard binary. They also assume that print jobs received over a PC print protocol—such as the DLC or LPR used by NT Server—are encoded using Tagged Binary Core Protocol (TBCP). Microsoft says that this tends to happen only with complex print jobs containing graphics—with simple files, such as a text-only document, the NT server somehow communicates the correct encoding scheme to the printer.

MacWindows Tip

If a Mac user gets Postscript errors when printing files with graphics to an AppleTalk printer through NT Server, try printing a straight text file. If it works, have the Mac user connect to the printer directly. If the user can't access it, uncapture the printer on the server.

When you send the Postscript print job to the NT server, it's encoded in standard binary, but because this printer gets the job from the NT server, it thinks its getting TBCP, and thus generates PostScript errors. If you sent the job directly over AppleTalk, the printer would (correctly) assume it's getting binary. If you still want to print through the NT server, you can encode the print job in a third standard, ASCII text, which most printers can recognize. Some Macintosh applications, such as Quark Xpress, let you choose ASCII as a print data format in the Page Setup dialog box.

However, in situations like this, uncapturing the printer and having the Mac user connect directly to the AppleTalk printer is a simpler resolution to the problem.

Even better, you can actually block all Mac users from accessing shared AppleTalk printers, forcing the users to access them directly over the network. This is almost the opposite of capturing a printer, giving you best of both worlds: Windows users can print to the AppleTalk printers (through the server), and Mac users can print to them directly and can't accidentally access them through the server. I discuss blocking Mac access a little later in the section called Blocking Mac Access to Server-Connected Printers.

Enabling Macs to Print to Non-Postscript Printers

Macs can't ordinarily print to non-Postscript printers, such as PCL printers. After you install Services for Macintosh, which installs MacPrint, Mac clients automatically get the ability to print to non-Postscript printers connected to the server. There's no configuring required. Any printer you share for the Windows users will be shared with the AppleTalk network as well.

To share a printer, right-click the printer from the Explorer and choose Printer Properties. In the Properties window that opens, select the Sharing tab and choose the Shared option.

Despite this simplicity, MacPrint has problems here as well. When you connect a non-Postscript printer to an NT Server and share it, a Mac will see it as a LaserWriter Plus V.38. This is because NT's Printer Services for Macintosh has a Postscript RIP (raster image processor) that intercepts the job and rasterizes it (converts it to a bitmap) and sends out the job to any printer.

One problem here is that the Postscript printer that NT emulates, the LaserWriter Plus V.38, is an ancient black-and-white printer with a maximum resolution of only 300 dpi. That means that even when you print to a 1200-dpi color printer, the Mac will print in black and white and at low resolution.

The way it works is that the Mac client sends a Postscript print job to the server. When the printer doesn't have Postscript, an NT Services for Macintosh print server component (SFMPRINT.DLL) gives it a PSCRIPT1 data type. The SFMPSPRT.DLL print processor then rasterizes the print job at 300 dpi maximum and in black and white. However, if the printer does support Postscript, SFMPRINT.DLL assigns the job the RAW data type, and the SFMPSPRT.DLL print processor passes the print job through to the printer without alteration. By the way, print jobs from Windows clients use the WIN-PRINT.DLL print processor, which does not have the Postscript error problems of SFMPSPRT.DLL.

Another common problem with Mac clients occurs with printer drivers. The Mac user sees that the printer is a Hewlett Packard LaserJet, and selects a LaserJet driver in the Chooser. However, this driver may not work, since the SFMPSPRT.DLL print processor emulates a LaserWriter Plus, which means the Mac should be using a LaserWriter print driver.

If the printer is upgradable, the best solution is to install the Postscript option, available for many Hewlett-Packard printers. In addition to enabling Mac clients to print to the printer's capabilities, it's easier on your NT server—this low-resolution RIP is a processor-intensive task and probably isn't the best use of your server's resources.

Blocking Mac Access to Server-Connected Printers

Although the Macintosh AFP file sharing protocol has a mechanism for requiring password access to folders, the AppleTalk PAP protocol does not. Any Mac on an AppleTalk network can print to any printer or print server. Because PAP does not let client provide names, Windows NT can't restrict access to printers on a single-user basis. It can, however, require passwords and restrict access to all Mac users as a group by applying the standard NT printer permissions to the group.

You can do this because of the peculiar way MacPrint operates on Windows NT—it actually logs in to the server with a user account. The default account it logs into is the Server account, which has the permissions to print on all local printers, those attached to the server. The trick is to create a new user account, give it the permission of No Access to certain printers, and then have MacPrint log in with that account. The Mac users on the AppleTalk network will then have their access blocked to the printers you indicated. To log MacPrint in this way, follow this procedure:

1.   Create a new account for MacPrint to use for log in. You can do this in the User Manager administration tool (click the Start button, then Programs, then Administrative Tools). Name the new user "MacPrint," or some other descriptive name, and give it a password.

2.   Open Services in the Control Panel. Select Print Services for Macintosh and click the Startup button.

3.   You'll now setup the MacPrint services to "Log On As" a user. To pick the user account you just created, click the This Account button.

4.   The Services dialog box will open. Type in the user account name and password you just created. Click OK and close the Services dialog box.

5.   Now you can deny printer access to your new MacPrint "user." Click the Printers icon in the Control Panel to access the Printer Manager.

6.   Select a printer. You might select a LaserWriter if you're sharing an AppleTalk printer with Windows users, but want the Mac users to access the printer directly over the network, not through the server.

7.   Select Security, and then select Permissions.

8.   Add the MacPrint user account. Choose No Access as the permission for the user account. Click OK.

9.   Stop and restart the Print Services for Macintosh to implement the changes.

If the AppleTalk printer is not captured by the server, as previously described, then the Mac users will be able to access it directly, from the

Chooser. Windows clients will still be able to access the AppleTalk printer as if it were attached to the server.

MacWindows Tip

Another reason to log MacPrint on with a user account is when you'd like to enable Macintosh users to send print jobs to printers that forward jobs to other print servers. When MacPrint is logged on using the system account, it doesn't have permission to access other servers' resources. When you log MacPrint on as another user, you can configure the user with permission to print on other print servers.

Speeding Up Services for Macintosh Performance

Services for Macintosh can be a fast AFP file server for Mac clients—it can also be a bottleneck in an AppleTalk network. There are several things you can do to optimize performance for Services for Macintosh. Some of these tips benefit the server as a whole; other times, it's a trade-off, speeding up Services for Macintosh while slowing something else. The next few pages will cover these items:

◆ Add more RAM
◆ Raise the priority of Services for Macintosh
◆ Maximize priorities for network applications
◆ Lower priority of foreground applications
◆ Speed up the Mac Clients with Mac OS 8.5 and later

MacWindows Tip

An OpenGL 3-D screen saver on NT Server can dramatically slow server performance. Ordinary screen savers are fine, but OpenGL takes up as much processor power as possible—taking power away from server functions—in order to smooth out animations.

Add More RAM

Windows NT Server has many advanced capabilities, but in order to perform its many tasks at the same time, it needs RAM, and lots of it. When it comes to memory, don't treat an NT server as you would a workstation or even a Mac server. It's not unheard-of to run over 300 MB of RAM in a server.

If you have been running NT Server and decide to add Mac clients through Services for Macintosh, chances are you will need to add more RAM, or pay the consequences in slower performance. Insufficient RAM will dramatically slow the network server down, and can sometimes bring network activity to a halt, leaving Macs with frozen AFP activity arrows in the upper left of the Finder.

Microsoft says you can run NT Server in 32 MB, but you would never want do that. Technically, Microsoft is correct about this. Rather than giving you "not enough memory" messages, Windows NT is adept at squeezing lots of big software into small amounts of RAM through the use of virtual memory. With too little RAM, NT's virtual memory goes into high gear, continually swapping data back and forth between RAM and the hard drive. To realize how dramatically this slows things down, remember how much slower a hard drive is than RAM. Drive access speed is measured milliseconds, or thousandths of a second. RAM access speed is measured in nanoseconds—*billionths* of a second.

You should consider 64 MB to be an absolute minimum amount of RAM in an NT server—with none of the services running. To the 64 MB starting point, consider adding 8 to 20 megabytes of RAM for each service installed, as a general rule. (Of course, add-on server software will have its own memory requirements.) Running Services for Macintosh certainly requires additional RAM.

The number of users accessing the server also figures into how much RAM should have in the server. Experts recommend adding about half a megabyte of RAM for each user who will be logged on at the same time (not the total number of users).

Because there are certain services that most people always want to run, some network managers say 128 MB is a good minimum for a server running Services for Macintosh. Others say don't go under 256 MB. Whatever figure you come up with after considering the number of services and users, there's one thing that's always true with NT Server—there's no such thing as too much RAM.

Raise the Priority of Services for Macintosh

Windows NT Server 4.0 lets you increase and decrease the priority of individual processes running on the operating system using the Task Manager. Increasing the priority of a process give that task better access to the operating systems, making other process wait longer. If you are not happy with the performance of your Mac file services, you can raise the priority of the Services for Macintosh, or lower the priority of less-used or less-crucial processes. Raising the priority is also something you can do on a temporary basis, in times of heavy usage.

You can access the Task Manager by right-clicking on the task bar and selecting Task Manager from the pop-up menu. When the Task Manager comes up, the Process tab will list processes (and applications) as the file running them, along with the memory and CPU Time used by each. The Services for Macintosh file is SFMSVC.EXE. You can immediately end any process by selecting it and clicking the End Process button. However, this is not a good way to stop AppleTalk. You can raise the priority of Services for Macintosh by right-clicking on SFMSVC.EXE, selecting Set Priority, and then selecting a higher priority. This priority setting is not saved when you shut down or restart the server.

You should approach changing process priorities conservatively, making small, incremental changes in priorities. Big jumps in priority can take their toll on other aspects of server performance, and sometimes disrupt the delicate balance of the processing, possibly making the server less stable. For instance, setting the priority of Services for Macintosh to RealTime will give you very fast file transfer performance, but can cause the user interface of the NT Server console to greatly slow its response to mouse clicks.

Maximize Priorities for Network Applications

Another way to raise the priority of Services for Macintosh is to raise the priority of all network applications. In the Server Services Properties window, you'll have selections for these memory settings:

- Minimize Memory Used
- Balance
- Maximize Throughput for File Sharing
- Maximize Throughput for Network Applications

You might be tempted to choose the setting called Maximize Throughput for File Sharing. However, this applies to file sharing on the Microsoft network, not Services for Macintosh, which is a network application. Choosing the setting called Maximize Throughput for Network Applications will assign a higher priority to Services for Macintosh, as well as other network applications.

Perform these steps to configure the Server Service:

1. Right-click the Network Neighborhood icon.
2. Select Properties, then click the Services Tab.
3. Choose Server, then select Properties.
4. Select "Maximize Throughput for Network Applications."
5. Choose OK, then the Close button.
6. Reboot Windows NT Server to have the changes take effect.

Lower Priority of Foreground Applications

Another way to indirectly improve the priority of Services for Macintosh is to lower the priority given to foreground applications running on the server. Foreground applications are what we think of as user applications, such as a spreadsheet or word processor.

You can do this using the System tool of the Control Panel. When you click the Performance tab, you'll see a slider labeled "Select the performance boost for the foreground application." You can slide the setting from None to Maximum. Using the None setting (for no extra boost in foreground application boost) will increase performance of all server tasks when you run a foreground application. On a server, you won't have foreground applications running very often, but when you do, this setting will minimize their impact on the network services.

Speed Up the Mac Clients with Mac OS 8.5 and Later

If your Mac clients are using a version of Mac OS before 8.5, their AFP file transfer rate is going to be pretty pokey, particularly with large numbers of files. The Finder is the bottleneck here, as moving files with utilities such as Timbuktu Pro is faster. When users copy files to and from a mounted AFP server volume, the Finder of OS 8.1 and earlier can't keep up with either an NT server or the network. You can get a good jump in file transfer rates simply by upgrading them to Mac OS 8.5, which more than quadrupled the file transfer rates of drag-and-drop file copies.

MacWindows Tip

If you don't want to upgrade Mac OS, you can use Connectix Speed Doubler with Speed Copy on the Mac clients. This software makes up for some of the deficiencies of OS 8.1 and earlier, but isn't as fast as OS 8.5.

Dealing with Services for Macintosh Problems

Bugs and bug fixes have been common to Services for Macintosh since it first debuted in Windows NT "Advanced" Server, as it was first known. Most of bugs the bugs are benign, more annoying than anything else, or limited to a specific situation, but occasionally, a bug crops up that can seriously affect how people use the network.

With every new version of NT released, dozens of old bugs get repaired, but change seems to breed new bugs. They can occur with changes with NT Server and with changes in Mac OS. Services for Macintosh bug fixes have been known to create other bugs.

In this section, I've described some of the more common, more serious bugs, and their solutions. (There's also a troubleshooting FAQ in the Appendix.) But before I get to the bugs, I want so say something about the bug fixes.

Web Update Link: *Knowing that a problem is caused by a bug and not by a configuration problem the first step to solving it. MacWindows has several pages with the latest bugs and fixes for Windows NT Services for Macintosh:*

Server Tips page at http://www.macwindows.com/servtips.html.
Service Pack 4 page at http://www.macwindows.com/NTSP4.html.
NT Unsolved Mysteries page at http://www.macwindows.com/NTunsolv.html
MacWindows News at http://www.macwindows.com/

Windows NT Bugs Fixes and Upgrades

Just as Microsoft tests major new releases of Windows NT with large and lengthy beta trials, it also tests bug fixes in a similar manner. A bug fix for Windows NT server begins its journey in the form of a file or set of files called a "hot fix." A hot fix is basically a beta bug fix, released to the public, but deemed as an "unsupported" fix, in that

Microsoft does not guarantee it. Hot fixes are often first available only by calling Microsoft Technical Support (800-936-5900). You have to agree to let Microsoft charge you almost $200 so you can speak to a technician, but the company gives you a refund when you and the technician establish that a known bug is your problem.

After people receive hot fixes, Microsoft discourages people from posting them on their own web sites. This is because before Microsoft posts a hot fix at its own FTP site, it may revise it several times, and doesn't want multiple versions of the same hot fix scattered over the Internet.

It can take a few weeks or months before Microsoft posts a hot fix at it's FTP site (Figure 11.23). At this point in the hot fix's career, it is fairly stable, but is still a beta, equivalent to the "beta2" that major releases get. When Microsoft updates the hot fix update again, the company will sometimes release it in the form of a new hot fix that includes a collection of previously released hot fixes.

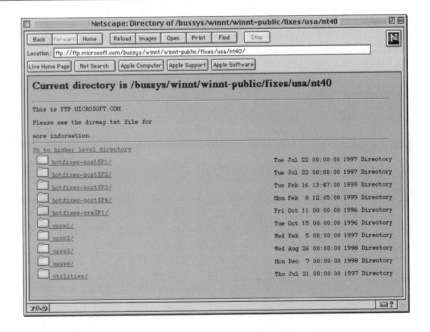

Figure 11.23 Microsoft free FTP site for Service Packs and hot fixes

About every 12–18 months, Microsoft collects the recent Services for Macintosh hot fixes together along with hot fixes for other parts of the server, and releases a supported upgrade to Windows NT Server. Microsoft calls this upgrade a *Service Pack*, which is no longer beta software, but is a supported upgrade. At the time this book was written, NT 4.0 Server was expected to have Service Pack 5 released before Windows 2000 shipped. These updates are simply named *Service Pack 3, Service Pack 4*, and so on. Service packs can contain hundreds of bug fixes, and can sometimes contain new features.

Service Packs can have their own unexpected consequences, so it's a good idea to carefully monitor the effect of a Service Pack on the network after you install it.

MacWindows Tip

When Windows NT 4 Service Pack 4 first came out, it caused a problem with FileMaker Pro 3 running on the NT machine. Service Pack 4 cuts the UDP-signal sent from FileMaker for contacting the server. This prevents clients from seeing the FileMaker server. Users had to type the IP address of the FileMaker server to log on. FileMaker Pro Server NT 3.0v4 Updater fixed the problem.

Downloading hot fixes and service packs

You can download service packs and hot fixes at no cost from Microsoft's FTP site. The exact directory depends on the version of NT Server and the most recent Service Pack you have installed. For instance, the directory for all Service Packs and hot fixes for NT Server 4.0 is:

ftp://ftp.microsoft.com/bussys/winnt/winnt-public/fixes/usa/nt40/

If you have Service Pack 4 installed and need a hot fix released after SP4, a post-Service Pack 4 directory is added to the URL:

ftp://ftp.microsoft.com/bussys/winnt/winnt-public/fixes/usa/nt40 /hotfixes-postSP4/

Downloading a Service Pack can be a time-consuming affair. For instance, NT 4.0 Service Pack 4 comes in eight versions, ranging in size from 450K to 76 Mb. (There are versions for Intel and Alpha, as well as 40-bit and 128-bit security versions.) Microsoft usually offers Service Packs on CD-ROMs for a nominal fee (Service Pack 4 was $19.95 including handling charges). A CD is handy if you ever need to reinstall the service pack.

And now, on to some of the more common bugs that affect Macs.

The Jumping Icons Bug

Macintosh users begin complaining of this debilitating problem when they are upgraded to Mac OS 8.x from 7.x. The file and folder icons in a mounted Services for Macintosh volume constantly "jump" around, making it difficult to select them. The icons move the way they do when a Mac user selects Cleanup in the Finder's view menu — except the icons never stop moving. Some users are also unable to keep the window in list view.

With Mac OS 8, Apple made a change to the way the Finder updates its icon information, which causes the server to fail to update Finder information.When the Finder changes its information, NT Server doesn't save the new information, which causes the Finder to redraw the icons each time it checks on them, producing the jumping effect.

NOTE: The jumping icon problem has been reported with Linux-based AppleTalk servers, though less frequently. The AFP server on Linux is called Netatalk. The problem was fixed in Netatalk 1.4b2 and later, available at Linux sites. Some people have reported occasional jumping icons with NetWare and with Thursby's DAVE logged onto Windows 95 volumes, but with less severity than with Windows NT. There was no fix known for either of these at the time this was written.

The jumping icons problem doesn't occur with Mac-based AFP servers, such as AppleShare IP and Mac clients with File Sharing turned on. Microsoft claims that isn't a SFM bug, but it did issue a bug fix for NT Server nonetheless. The hot fix was incorporated into Windows NT Server 4.0 Service Pack 4, released in October 1998. There is no fix for NT Server 3.5.x.

Before Microsoft released Service Pack 4, it produced a hot fix, which you can still download from the FTP site mentioned earlier. You can use this hot fix if you don't have Service Pack 4 installed. The hot fix comes in an auto-install file called sfm-fixi.exe for the Intel version, and sfm-fixa.exe for the Alpha version. It replaces the sfmsvr.sys file with a new one at this location:

C:\Winnt40\system32\drivers\Sfmsrv.sys

You can run the installer or replace this file yourself.

This sfm-fixi.exe hot fix also contains fixes for nine other less problematic bugs that affect Services for Macintosh. Unfortunately, this hot fix is known to cause another, less severe problem, called "jumping aliases." Macintosh aliases pointing to files or directories on server volumes open the wrong items. The network directories or files that are opened appear to be random. At the time of this writing, there was no known fix for this.

Interestingly, older versions of the jumping icons hot fix don't create jumping aliases. The previous versions of the jumping icon hot fix were called Jump_A.zip and Jump_86.zip. An older version yet was called Hotfix.zip. Both of these replace the Sfmsrv.sys file. You may find these older versions at some Internet sites, but not at Microsoft's site.

Disappearing Icons

There are at various conditions that can cause files on the mounted server volume on Mac clients to disappear from view, but remain visible on Windows clients and on the server PC itself. These conditions are described on the next few pages, along with an effective procedure for recovering the icons.

Bugs in Windows NT 3.51, 4.0

The first disappearing icons bug was fixed with Windows NT 4.0 Service Pack 3. In this case, files would randomly disappear during the course of operation.

The first bug was fixed with NT 4.0 Service Pack 3, and the second was fixed in the June 1998 sfm-fixi.exe hot fix, which also fixes the jumping icon problem noted earlier. In addition to installing the fixes, you may have to apply one of the methods described later to recover the file icons that have disappeared.

Server crashes

Icons can also disappear when the server running Services for Macintosh crashes, even when NT 4.0 Service Pack 3 or later is installed. After rebooting the NT server, Macintosh users may find that random files are missing from the NT volumes, though the files are visible to Windows 95 users who access the same volumes. This bug was fixes in the June 1998 hot fix called sfm-fixi.exe, the same hot fix that fixes the dancing icons problem just described.

Both problems were rooted in the AFP volume indexes used to identify files on the volume. These indexes are stored in RAM on the server and are used by the Services for Macintosh file server. The SFM process manages the indexes for each volume constantly. These indexes are written to disk at shutdown and may be written at other undocumented times. When the server crashes, the RAM-based indexes are lost and the old ones are read from disk. Any files that were recently created and not mentioned in the old index simply disappear from the Macs' view. The June 1998 sfm-fixi.exe hot fix provides a mechanism that enables Services for Macintosh to rebuild the indexes upon restart after a crash. This fix was included in Service Pack 4.

Recovering invisible files

Whatever the cause, you can't recover the files with any NT disk management tool, because it's not a disk problem. The files are actually still there, but Services for Macintosh doesn't know about it. Also, it's a bad idea to attempt to recover the files by moving them off of the server and on to a Windows client. Managers have reported file corruption as a result.

You can recover the files by forcing Services for Macintosh to rebuild the AFP indexes for the volume.

1. Get all users to dismount the volume and unshare the volume.
2. Apply file-level permissions on all subdirectories (from Windows Explorer) with just Administrators full-control.
3. Recreate the Macintosh volumes, setting the permissions as needed.

You don't need to reboot the NT server or the Mac clients. You may lose custom volume icons, however.

Mac Clients "Hang" While Connected to the Server

There are at lease four occasions when Macintosh clients can temporarily "hang" or freeze (showing the AppleShare "network busy" arrows in the upper left of the screen) when connected to a Windows NT server via Services for Macintosh. These are, under special conditions:

♦ During use of the Mac OS Find command
♦ When servers contain multiple Macintosh volumes
♦ When moving data across directories
♦ When there's not enough RAM in the server

Use of the Mac OS Find command

The first occurs when a Mac client uses the Mac OS Find command to search on a mounted Windows NT volume. This causes all of the other Macs connected to the server to lock up temporarily with the AppleShare arrows frozen in the upper left of the screen.

The problem has to do with the way Windows NT 3.5.1 and 4.0 allow the NT server to do the search instead of the Macintosh. The bigger the server volume and the more files and directories it contains, the longer the Macs will be locked up. The Windows NT delays the processing of requests from other Macintosh clients and the Macintosh clients will appear to "hang" while they wait for their requests to be processed.

Windows NT 4.0 Service Pack 2 first addressed the problem by permitting each Macintosh to do its own search, but you can still see the problem with the latest software. If that's the case, you may need to disable a feature called CatSearch, which causes the server to take over from the Mac's Find command.

To disable CatSearch, you need to use the Registry Editor:

1. Run Regedt32.exe and go to the following registry location:

HKLM\System\CurrentControlSet\Services\MacFile\Parameters\Volumes

2. Select the network volume on which you want to disable CatSearch, and then select Multi String from the Edit menu.
3. Add the following text: DisableCatsearch=1
4. Exit the registry editor, and then stop and restart Services for Macintosh.

For more information, see the Microsoft Knowledge Base article Q158796 at:
http://support.microsoft.com/support/kb/articles/Q158/7/96.asp.

Servers with Multiple Macintosh volumes

The problem of Mac clients hanging when connected to a server with multiple Mac volumes was completely fixed with NT Server 4.0 Service Pack 3. Before this version of NT Server, Macintosh clients could temporarily hang when connected to a server with multiple Mac volumes. According to Microsoft, there was a bug that caused NT Server not to release a lock on a particular volume right away. When there are changes being made to multiple volumes, NT puts a temporary lock on the volume while it processes changes to the volume. The bug held on to the lock until more changes were made to the volume, causing the Mac client to hang for varying lengths of time. If you have NT Server 4.0 Service Pack 3, this is not the cause of the frozen Macs.

Moving data across directories

Macs can hang for several minutes when a user selects a Services for Macintosh (SFM) volume in the Chooser when an administrator moves a large number of files in what Microsoft calls a "programmatic traversal of a large NTFS directory tree." Examples include a Ntbackup:*.* or a Dir/s*.xyz operation. Mac and Windows network connections can time out and disconnect. This can occur with NT Workstation and Server 3.51 and 4.0.

The problem is a circular log file that has filled up. This blocks other NTFS operations and makes NT grind to a halt.

You can edit the registry to prevent the circular log from filling. (If you have Windows NT 3.51, you'll need to upgrade to the current NT 3.51 Service Pack before making the change.)

1.   Start Regedt32.exe and go to the following subkey:

```
HKEY_LOCAL_MACHINE\SYSTEM\CurrentControlSet\Control
\FileSystem
```

2.   On the Edit menu click Add Value and edit the following entry:

```
Value Name: NtfsDisableLastAccessUpdate
Data Type : REG_DWORD
Data : 1
```

3. Quit the registry editor and restart your computer.

Not enough RAM in the server

With insufficient RAM in the server, Macs clients can hang when the server gets busy, regardless of the version of NT or Service Pack is installed. (See the earlier section on Speeding Up Services for Macintosh Performance.)

Trash That Won't go Away

There is a bug in Windows NT 4.0 Services for Macintosh that prevents you from deleting a file and folder from the server. Microsoft says the bug does not occur in Windows 2000, because the problem is located in File Manager, which is not used for Services for Macintosh administration in Windows 2000.

The problem starts when a Mac user deletes a file from a mounted NT volume, but doesn't empty the trash. Next, an administrator removes the Mac volume while the Mac user is connected to it. The Mac user will get a Type 51 error message: "A device attached to the system is not functioning." From NT Server, the administrator cannot delete this file.

Web Update Link: *To read about other known bugs in Services for Macintosh that have no fixes, see the MacWindows NT SFM Unsolved Mysteries page at http://www.macwindows.com/NTunsolv.html.*

Macs Can Only See 2 GB of Bigger Volumes

Services for Macintosh volumes residing on the NT server that are 2 to 4 Gb in size can sometimes only be seen by Macs as 2 Gb in size. Though not actually a bug, the problem is caused by the way Microsoft configured Services for Macintosh. Prior to system 7.5, Mac OS did not support volumes bigger than 2018 Mb (just under 2 Gb, which is 2048 Mb). Some versions of Services for Macintosh default at restricting the values SFM reports for total and free space on SFM volumes to 2018 MB, when the actual size of the volume's disk partition is larger. (Windows 2000 fixes this problem.)

System 7.5 raised the maximum volume limit to 4 GB, and System 7.5.2 raised it to 2 terabytes. However, 4 GB is the biggest volume size for which the AFP protocol will report correct total and free space of a network volume. Macs can mount larger network volumes—they just won't see the correct total and free space figures.

To increase the 2 GB volume limit in NT Server, the NT Services registry flag must be edited to raise the default 2018 MB maximum volume size. You'll need to update Mac clients with very old system software to at least System 7.5, or the Finder will crash when trying to mount the SFM volume.

A registry flag controls the maximum volume size and free space reported by the SFM file server. You can raise the maximum reported size for SFM volumes to 4 GB-256 (a flag value of 0xFFFFFF00) by creating the SFM volume, then editing the registry entry.

1. Use the Registry Editor (Regedt32.exe) to access the registry entry at:

```
HKEY_LOCAL_MACHINES\System\CurrentControlSet\Ser-
vices\MacFile\Parameters\Volumes\<VolumeName>
```

```
Properties=xxxxx
```

2. Add 262144 (0x00040000) to the number xxxxx.
3. Stop and restart MacFile to make this change take effect on the Services for Macintosh volume.

In Windows NT 3.51, you can change this value globally to enable all volumes to be 4 GB (or more). To do this, add bit 0x10 to the following section of the registry and every volume will be 4 GB enabled:

```
HKEY_LOCAL_MACHINE\SYSTEM\CurrentControlSet\Services
\MacFile\Parameters
```

```
ServerOptions: REG_DWORD: 0x13
```

NOTE: The ServerOptions value has a default value of 0x03. After you add 0x10 to 0x03, the result becomes 0x13. After this change, every volume will be 4 GB enabled.

Remote Possibilities

Macs aren't limited to file sharing and printing via Windows NT. They can participate in Windows NT TCP/IP networks, taking advantage of services that include web browsing, e-mail, and FTP access. They can also dial into an NT Remote Access Server over a telephone connection.

The next chapter looks at networking with a modem. The discussion isn't limited to Windows NT and Macintosh clients, but includes Windows clients dialing into Macintosh networks. It also includes an old-fashioned modem-to-modem remote access, still an option for individual users in the modern cross-platform world.

Chapter

What's in This Chapter:

♦ *Configuring PPP on Mac OS and Windows*

♦ *Windows remote access of Macintosh networks*

♦ *Mac access to Windows NT Remote Access Servers*

♦ *Dial-up modem-to-modem connections*

12

Remote Access

Extending networking over telephone lines is an important feature of computing, and something that has been available to Mac and Windows users for years. Cross-platform remote access has its own set of issues apart from the standard networking issues. But once understood, both platforms can communicate over telephone lines, share files, and access servers of various types. Solutions exist for a variety of situations, including Macintosh access to Microsoft Windows NT Remote Access Servers (RAS). The Mac's Apple Remote Access has opened up in recent years to support networking standards, weaning itself from its dependence on AppleTalk. There are also strategies for having Windows PCs dial into AppleTalk networks. There's even a dial-up solution that doesn't use any network standards at all—old fashioned modem-to-modem communications.

321

Differences: Remote Access Capabilities on Macintosh and Windows

In order to establish a network link over a modem, you have to use a dial-up protocol. The industry standard is PPP (point-to-point protocol). Mac OS, Windows NT, Windows 95, and Windows 98 include PPP software. For Windows 3.1 and Windows for Workgroups, PPP is available as part of the Microsoft Internet Explorer browser.

Another dial-up protocol, Apple Remote Access Protocol (ARAP), has been enabling Macs to dial into AppleTalk networks for many years, and actually predates PPP. Today, Mac OS provides both PPP and ARAP remote links. A third dial-up protocol, SLIP (Serial Link Internet Protocol) can be installed on any platform with add-software, but the use of SLIP is now rare.

A dial-up protocol connection basically acts like Ethernet to provide basic network communications over a modem link. PPP does this by encapsulating network transport protocols such as TCP/IP and AppleTalk. It does this through the use of *network control protocols*. Table 12.1 lists the network control protocols provided by Mac OS and Windows. The most common is the IP Control Protocol (IPCP) for running TCP/IP over PPP. Both Windows and Mac OS have IPCP built into their remote access software. Windows supports also supports IPX and NetBEUI on PPP, using the control protocols listed in Table 12.1. Mac OS does not support the IPX Control Protocol, so Macs cannot dial into an IPX NetWare network. (They can dial into a TCP/IP NetWare network.)

NOTE: ARAP and ATCP allow you do anything you can do on an AppleTalk network—when you first make an ARAP connection, the standard AppleTalk address negotiations occur over the dial-up link. However, unlike a local AppleTalk connection, ARAP and ATCP don't keep checking the status of the network. This means if a new server or printer appears on the network during a link, the remote client won't detect it.

Table 12.1 Network control protocols run transport protocols over PPP links.

Network transport	Control protocol	Operating system
AppleTalk on PPP	ATCP (AppleTalk Control Protocol)	Mac OS 8.5 & later
IPX on PPP	IPXCP (IPX Control Protocol)	Windows 95/98/NT
NetBEUI on PPP	NBFCP or "NetBEUI over RAS"	Windows 95/98/NT
TCP/IP on PPP	IPCP (IP Control Protocol)	Mac OS & Windows

PPP also facilitates dynamic IP address assignments, an ability that is as responsible as any other technology for helping popularize the Internet.

Apple's support of AppleTalk over PPP via ATCP is a recent development. It began with Apple Remote Access 3.0, which was an add-on product. In Mac OS 8.5, Apple replaced the PPP control panel with Remote Access 3.1, giving every user the ability to connect with either ATCP or IPCP—that's AppleTalk over PPP or TCP/IP over PPP—or both simultaneously if the server supported both. For instance, Windows 2000 Server and Shiva's LANRover hardware remote access server support both ATCP and IPCP over PPP.

If you have a choice, there are several advantages to PPP over ARAP:

♦ PPP is cross-platform.
♦ PPP supports both TCP/IP and AppleTalk, ARAP is AppleTalk only.
♦ PPP is faster than ARAP.

Mac OS 8.5's ARA 3.1 also added support for the Windows NT Remote Access Server's MS-CHAP protocol, described later in the chapter. Unfortunately, Windows NT Server Remote Access Server (RAS) does not support AppleTalk at all, either with ARAP or ATCP. However, Windows 2000 Server RAS supports both ARAP and ATCP connections for Mac users.

Configuring PPP on Mac and Windows Clients

Getting a PPP connection set up is quite different on Mac OS and Windows. On a Mac, the software you need is already installed. In Windows, it may not be.

Getting PPP Ready

On a Mac you start by choosing between the options of using ARAP or PPP, or letting the Mac decide. There is no need to select a network transport protocol. If you select ARAP, you get AppleTalk. If you select PPP, Mac OS 8.5 and later can whether the server you are dialing into supports TCP/IP or AppleTalk, or both. With Windows, you only have PPP, but you can choose which network transport protocol or protocols you're going to use.

MacWindows Tip

If you want AppleTalk over PPP on a Mac but don't have Remote Access 3.0 or later, there are alternative PPP clients for Mac that provide ATCP for Macs. Network TeleSystems' TunnelBuilder (http://www.nts.com) provides ATCP, as well as the ability to dial into Windows NT Remote Access Servers. FCR Software's LinkUPPP! Turbo (http://www.fcr.com/) adds a special feature called multilinking, *which lets you combine two modems to make a PPP connection at speeds of up to 112 kbps over a standard telephone line.*

On the Mac, to switch between ARA's protocol setting between PPP, ARAP, or both, click the Options button of the Remote Access control panel. Click the Protocol tab, and click on the "Use protocol" pop-up menu. As Figure 12.1 shows, you can select ARAP, PPP, or Automatic. The Automatic selection tells the Mac to sense what the server supports, as some do support both. If you want to always take advantage of a faster PPP connection, choose PPP.

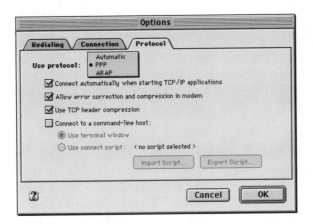

Figure 12.1 Choosing between PPP and ARAP in the Options window of the Remote Access control panel

Mac OS has another step here. If you are using TCP/IP, you have to specify either Ethernet or a dial-up connection in the "Connect via" pop-up menu at the top of the TCP/IP control panel (Figure 12.2). (A third choice for a TCP/IP connection, "AppleTalk (MacIP)," is for "encapsulating" TCP/IP through AppleTalk. See Chapter 10 for more details.) If you are using AppleTalk over the PPP connection, there is no configuration required in the AppleTalk control panel.

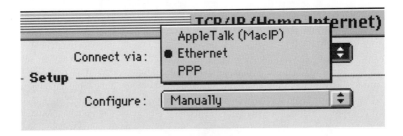

Figure 12.2 Switching between Ethernet and PPP in the Mac OS TCP/IP control panel

MacWindows Tip

If you are using AppleTalk on a Mac, use the Remote Only option in the AppleTalk control panel to disable the Ethernet and LocalTalk ports of the Mac on a network. This lets you dial into this Mac without exposing the AppleTalk network to outside intruders. If you want to enable Ethernet access from the outside, choose Ethernet.

In Windows 95 and 98, you may want to check to see if the modem software and Dial-Up Networking software are installed. If the PC come with a modem, this software is probably installed. Also, if you've run the Internet Connection Wizard, the software is installed. If you're not sure, go to the Control Panel and open Add/Remove programs. Click on the Windows Setup tab. The Communications item should have a check next to it. If not, double-click it to open the Communications window (Figure 12.3). Check Dial-Up Networking and click OK. You may need your Windows installation CD.

You can check the Network dialog box (in the Control Panel) to see if the Dial-Up Adapter card is bound to the network transport protocols

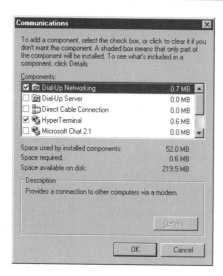

Figure 12.3 Installing Dial-Up Networking software

you want to run on the Dial-Up Adapter, which refers to a PPP connection. Figure 12.4 shows a binding of TCP/IP and the Dial-Up adapter as "TCP/IP -> Dial-up Adapter," and another for NetBEUI. If there are no other network adapters, this choice will just say "TCP/IP." If the Dial-Up Adapter or the network protocol you want to run isn't shown in the Network dialog, you need to add it using the procedures described in Chapter 9. You should now have a Dial-Up networking icon in My Computer.

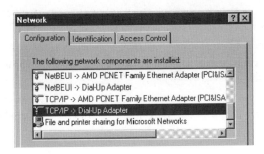

Figure 12.4 Selecting the "Dial-Up Adapter" in Windows 95 to configure PPP

Entering Telephone and Connection Information

The PPP setup windows for Windows 95 and Mac OS are similar, providing places to enter the user name, password, and a telephone number to dial. Both present a button to let you dial and make a connection. With the Mac, you can enter this information directly into the window. In Windows, you enter this data into a Wizard. You can then go directly to the setup screen to change information.

Mac OS has had several different PPP setup windows in the past few years. In Mac OS 8.5 and later or with Apple Remote Access 3.0 or later, you enter this information in the Remote Access control panel. In Mac OS 7.6 to OS 8.1, you enter this information in the PPP control panel. (See Figure 12.5.) In earlier versions of Mac OS (before Open Transport) the control panel was called ConfigPPP, FreePPP, or MacPPP.

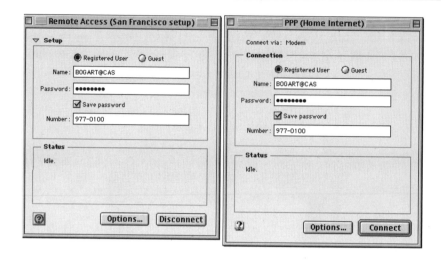

Figure 12.5 The Mac OS Remote Access and older PPP control panels

To enter the connection information in Windows, open the Dial-Up Networking folder in My Computer. (You can also get there by clicking on the Start button, then Programs, Accessories, and Dial-Up Networking.) The Dial-Up Networking window differs slightly in Windows 95 and Windows 98, in that Windows 98 added a Dial button to the Window itself.

Now double-click the Create New Connection icon. This launches a wizard that asks you for the telephone number, a name for the connection, and other relevant information. When finished it creates an icon in the Dial-Up Networking folder with the name of your connection. You can edit it by double-clicking. This launches the Connect To dialog, shown in Figure 12.6.

Windows 95 OSR2 and Windows 98 let you enable auto-redial when a busy signal is encountered. (The Mac OS PPP and Remote Access control panels also have this feature.)

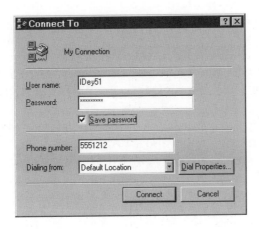

Figure 12.6 Editing a PPP connection in Windows 95/98

Apple Remote Access Servers

For many years, the Apple Remote Access software has provided the remote Mac user with access to files and printers on an AppleTalk network. At first, ARA stood for AppleTalk Remote Access, but Apple dropped the "Talk" from the name when it began to incorporate TCP/IP protocols into the Macintosh overall networking strategy, of which Open Transport is a big part (see Chapter 8).

An ARA server is any machine that can accept modem calls and create network links using the ARAP and/or ATCP protocols. There are ARA servers running on Macs, PCs and other hardware. ARA Personal Server is Mac software intended to enable users to access their own Macs or a small network. ARA Personal Server 3 and later supports PPP and TCP/IP, so Windows users can dial in and access any IP service on the Mac or the network.

Apple Remote Access MultiPort Server is Mac software that supports multiple modems and supports the Simple Network Management Protocol (SNMP) for managing the server over a network. However, at the time of this writing, it hadn't been upgraded to ARA 3.0 and did not work with the AppleShare IP file/web server. You can run the ARA Personal Server on the same server Mac with AppleShare IP.

Windows 2000 Server is an ARA server, as it has both ATCP and ARAP server functionality. You can also get ARA server support in stand-alone remote access server hardware. Shiva (http://www.shiva.com) has been building multiprotocol remote access servers for many years. Other remote access server boxes support ATCP and/or ARAP as well.

Remote Windows File Sharing with Mac Networks

Windows users can dial into an Apple Remote Access server using PPP and TCP/IP, giving them access to standard IP services, such as FTP, web servers, or POP/SMTP e-mail. In this case, the PC can use its native IP over PPP (IPCP) client. With add-on software that provides an AppleTalk over PPP (ATCP) client, Windows PCs can dial into an AppleTalk network. (There are no ARAP solutions for Windows.) As with networking on wires, you also need service software on the PC to enable it to access a file server.

Here are several different strategies for enabling Windows PCs to access Macintosh shared folders or servers through a dial-in connection. The solutions listed here assume there is a remote access server on the Mac network, or running on the Mac, such as ARA Personal Server 3 and later.

Mac OS Personal Web sharing. Activating Personal Web Sharing from a Mac's Web Sharing control panel will allow Windows users to access files on the Mac from a web browser. (See Chapter 8.) Windows uses IPCP to dial in to a PPP server on the Mac or network.

AppleShare IP server via Windows SMB file sharing. If the Apple-Share IP file server is version 6.0 or later, Windows PCs can access files using the native Microsoft file sharing client over the Microsoft Server Message Block (SMB) protocol. There is no SMB support in versions of AppleShare IP before version 6.0. (See Chapter 13 for more on AppleShare IP.)

AppleShare IP server via AFP file sharing. Miramar Systems PC MacLAN Pro is software for the Windows machine that adds an AppleShare client (the Apple Filing Protocol). It also adds an ATCP dial-up client. This enables the Windows machine to access AppleShare IP file servers 5.x and 6.x and later. With PC MacLAN, the PC must have Windows 98 or Windows 95 PC with Dial-Up Networking 1.3 or later. In the Network Control Panel, you can switch the Miramar AppleTalk protocol to bind with the Dial-Up Adapter. (See Chapter 14 for more on Miramar Systems PC MacLAN, http://www.miramarsystems.com.)

Non-IP-capable AppleShare compatible servers via AFP file sharing. In order for a Windows machine to access AppleShare-compatible servers that don't support TCP/IP, such as AppleShare before version 5 or Macs with File Sharing turned on, you can run OpenDoor's ShareWay IP on a Mac. ShareWay IP is a gateway that makes any AppleTalk AFP server accessible over TCP/IP, including dial-up links. The Windows machine would need to run an AFP over TCP/IP client, such as PC MacLAN or CopsTalk (http://www.copstalk.com).

Individual Macs via native Windows SMB. If you want a Windows machine to access files on an individual Mac remotely without installing software on the PC, you can install Thursby Systems' DAVE on the Mac. This turns the Macintosh into a peer-to-peer client and file server using Microsoft SMB file sharing and NetBIOS over TCP/IP. (See Chapter 14 for more information on DAVE or check http://www.thursby.com/.)

Web Update Link: *For current information on the products mentioned in this section, see http://www.macwindows.com/Networks.html.*

Windows Remote Access Service (RAS)

Remote Access Service (RAS) is Microsoft-enhanced PPP, included with Windows NT and Windows 95 and 98. Windows comes with server software as well as the client, which provide dial-up links over PPP using TCP/IP, NetBEUI, or IPX. However, the Windows NT RAS is the most popular and is what is discussed here. Windows NT RAS can use PPP or Microsoft point-to-point tunneling protocol (PPTP) which encrypts data going through the connection. The encryption enables you to send secure messages and data through the Internet to a PPTP server.

Mac PPP Connection to Remote Access Services

There are several methods of enabling a Macintosh to dial in to a Windows NT RAS server. However, Windows NT 4.0 does not allow standard Macs to access file sharing volumes from a remote connection. That's because NT 4.0 only supports AppleTalk, and NT 4.0 RAS does not support AppleTalk. This is changed in Windows 2000 Server RAS, which supports both ATCP and ARAP for AppleTalk connections and supports AFP file sharing over IP.

So why dial up Windows NT 4.0 RAS if you can't access Services for Macintosh? There are several reasons. For one, you can enable a Macintosh to access Windows shared volumes by installing Thursby Systems' DAVE on the Mac. It implements SMB file sharing and NetBIOS over TCP/IP for network browsing on the Mac. (There's more about DAVE in Chapter 14.)

But even with our file sharing, there is a lot a Mac can accomplish by dialing in to an NT 4.0 RAS server. You can access IP services such as local web and FTP servers. If your office network has a link to the Internet, you can use your office NT RAS server as an ISP, dialing into it to connect to the Internet.

Connecting to NT RAS is easiest with Mac OS 8.5 and later, but you can connect with earlier versions as well. To have Mac clients connect to an NT 4 RAS server (or earlier), you'll need to coordinate the authentication protocol is being used by the server with the version of PPP client software on the Mac. Windows RAS can authenticate using three methods that Macs can use:

♦ PAP (Password Authentication Protocol), which transmits passwords in clear text (not a secure method)
♦ CHAP (Challenge-Handshake Authentication Protocol)
♦ MS-CHAP, Microsoft's variation of CHAP. The latter is used most often by default, but is incompatible with many Mac PPP clients. Remote Access 3.1 (which shipped with Mac OS 8.5) and later does support MS-CHAP, as does some third-party software.

A discussion of all three methods follows.

Password Authentication Protocol (PAP) "clear text" authentication

PAP is the lowest common denominator, supported by any Macintosh PPP client, including the older MacPPP and FreePPP. However, it is unsecured, as it is possible to intercept passwords from the data stream. Another security issue with PAP is that it allows a client to make repeated log-in attempts without limit in a trial-and-error manner.

Windows NT RAS refers to PAP as clear text. To set Windows NT 4.0 RAS server for PAP authentication, follow this procedure:

1. Open the Network dialog box in the Control Panel and select the Services tab.
2. Select Remote Access Service and click the Properties button.
3. Click the Network button, and the Network Configuration window opens.
4. Select *Allow any authentication including clear text* under Encryption Settings.

To configure a Mac for a PAP connection to a RAS server, set the TCP/IP control panel settings to *Connect via PPP* and *Configure Using PPP server* (Figure 12.7). Don't use DHCP here.

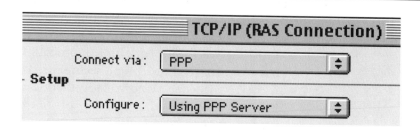

Figure 12.7 Mac TCP/IP control panel settings for PPP access to Windows RAS

Next, you'll need to configure the Mac's Remote Access (or PPP) control panel with the user name, password, and telephone number. If the RAS server resides in an NT domain and is not the master controller of the domain, you'll need to add the NT domain before the user name like this: NTdomain\username. In this case, the server will need to ask the domain controller to validate the user account.

The correct settings in the Options window, the Protocol tab, are the default settings. This is with the following settings enabled: *Allow error correction and compression in modem* and *Use TCP header compression.* The setting *Connect to a command-line host* should be disabled.

Challenge-Handshake Authentication Protocol (CHAP)

The challenge in CHAP is that it authenticates not just at the beginning of the connection, but also during the link. The server sends a challenge message to the client and compares the response it gets with a calculation of what the response should be. CHAP also protects against repeated log-in attempts, as in a trial-and-error break-in "attack."

MacPPP 2.0.1 and earlier do not support CHAP, but the FreePPP, PPP, and Remote Access control panels do. The support problem with CHAP is on the NT side. Windows NT began supporting CHAP with NT 4.0, Service Pack 2. As of NT 4, Service Pack 3, you need to reconfigure the NT, registry to support CHAP. You need to enable what Microsoft calls the MD5-CHAP authenticator. You do this by creating an MD5 key:

```
HKLM\SYSTEM\CurrentControlSet\Services\RasMan\PPP\CHAP
\MD5
```

You need to add account subkeys:

```
[<domain>:]<user>
(REG_SZ)Pw
```

The "Pw" is a subvalue containing the account password. The domain is optional. You'll note that a colon [:] is used instead of the backslash, as is the way with registry keys.

Windows NT Server does not support CHAP on the NT domain level. Each RAS server must be configured separately.

MS-CHAP

Microsoft's version of CHAP, MS-CHAP, is the authentication method preferred by most network administrators and is certainly easier than CHAP to use. Apple only began supporting MS-CHAP in a PPP client with Apple Remote Access 3.1, which shipped with Mac OS 8.5. If you have an earlier version of the Remote Access control panel or the PPP or other control panel, you can upgrade to ARA 3.1 or later, or a one of a couple of third-party products. Ascend's PPP Dialer is part the company's IntragyAccess bundle. (Ascend's web site is http://www.ascend.com/.) It also supports CHAP and PAP.

Another MS-CHAP client for Mac OS is NTS PPP from Network TeleSystems (http://www.nts.com). NTS PPP comes bundled with Ping under the name TunnelBuilder Remote or in a bundle of Internet applications and utilities called TCP Pro. NTS PPP also supports PPTP, as well as AppleTalk over PPP for getting to printers and Apple-Share servers on the network.

Point-to-Point Tunneling Protocol (PPTP)

PPTP uses encryption and authentication provides secure communications through the Internet and the public telephone system. Microsoft calls the use of PPTP a Virtual Private Network, in that two computers can create their own private direct link within a bigger network, such as a WAN or the Internet. Network TeleSystems' TunnelBuilder also supports Macintosh PPTP connections to Windows NT. (None of Apple's Mac PPP clients support PPTP.) A Windows version is available as well.

Using NT's PPTP functions, TunnelBuilder can work without using Microsoft RAS. You can use TunnelBuilder over any ISP. You might want to use PPTP this way if you were accessing a private network through the Internet, and your Internet line was a modem connection.

Chapter 10 has more information about PPTP and TunnelBuilder.

Macintosh Remote Access to NT File and Printer Services

A TCP/IP connection over PPP to RAS will allow a Macintosh to access any IP-based services the Mac client has permissions for. However, unless the server is Windows 2000, Mac clients cannot access file sharing or print services on the NT server. That's because NT 4.0 or earlier only let Mac clients access file service through Services for Macintosh, which is AppleTalk only. Windows NT 5.0 RAS will allow Macs to access Services for Macintosh over PPP connections using two methods—using Apple Filing Protocol (AFP) over TCP/IP, and through direct support of the AppleTalk Remote Access Protocol. If you're not planning on using Windows 2000 Server soon, Thursby Systems' DAVE will allow a Mac to log in as if it were an ordinary Windows client. (See Chapter 11 for Services for Macintosh.)

Old-Fashioned Remote Access: Modem-to-Modem Connections

In this day of sophisticated remote access servers and network authentication protocols, many people forget—or perhaps are too young to remember—that before everyone had an e-mail account, the direct dial-up connection was once a common method of moving files. You don't need to run a server because it's not a network connection. It's also easy to forget that a modem-to-modem connection is still an inexpensive option for moving files between Macs and Windows machines.

The old-fashioned method uses terminal emulation software on one machine to dial the modem of another machine. Unlike the Internet, you have to make and pay long distance calls when connecting to a machine physically distant. Both sender and receiver machines run terminal emulation software to establish a link and to transfer files. On the Mac, you can use the Communications module of AppleWorks (the program formerly known as ClarisWorks; see Figure 12.8) or a traditional terminal program, such as the shareware ZTerm. (I still use an old copy of Microphone from 1988.) Windows comes with a

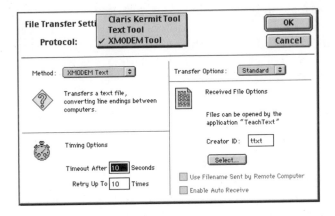

Figure 12.8 Choosing a file transfer protocol in AppleWorks/ClarisWorks

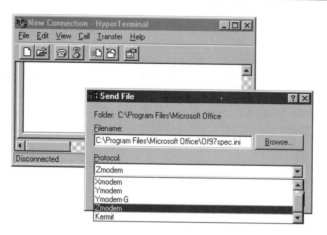

Figure 12.9 Sending a file with Windows HyperTerminal

terminal program called HyperTerminal (Figure 12.9), accessed from the Start button, then Programs, and then Accessories. There are also shareware terminal programs for Windows.

There is nothing Mac-like, or Windows-like, for that matter, about typing at terminal programs, which were invented to allow PCs to access mainframes. (Before PCs, mainframes were accessed from a terminal, hence the name terminal emulation.) A terminal window uses a monospaced font (such as Courier) with 80 characters across a page, often on a black screen. There's no drag-and-drop file transfers—users on both ends of the transmission need to participate. Both sender and receiver need to initiate the connection, and then initiate the file transfer—the receiver sets the software to receive, and the sender sets the software to send. In most terminal software, you do all this from menu commands.

To do the file transfer, the users at each end need to agree on a file transfer protocol to use. This will be either XModem, YModem (or a variation), ZModem or Kermit. You may also need to encode the file if it isn't a text file.

Modem File Transfer Protocols

The key here is that both sending and receiving machines must use the same file transfer protocol. You usually need to talk with the other person on the telephone while setting up the software to be able to get things right. Not all software supports all of the protocols, so you'll have to find one you both have in common. You may also find that one protocol doesn't successfully transfer the file, so you may need to try others.

ZModem is the file transfer protocol to try first when doing a modem-to-modem file transfer between Mac and Windows, as it is the most advanced. ZModem can send multiple files at one time and is the fastest and most reliable of the telecom protocols. ZModem also supports autodownloading, which notifies the receiving telecom software of an impending file transmission and enables the computer to start receiving without user intervention. In addition, it can retransmit data that was transmitted unsuccessfully. If the telephone link is interrupted in the middle of a transmission, the ZModem protocol will allow some software to resume the file transfer where it left off. This is very handy if you're transferring big files that take an hour or more to transmit.

If the terminal software on both machines doesn't support ZModem, or it doesn't work, I recommend trying XModem next. Just about every terminal emulator supports XModem, and it works well for transferring files between Macs and Windows in most cases. Developed in 1977, XModem doesn't have all of the features of ZModem, but it does automatically check for errors, and will correct them by resending incorrect portions of a file.

YModem is a variation of XModem that allows you to send multiple files in one transmission. Another variant called YModem-G is a faster version of YModem, but doesn't have error correction—the transmission is stopped if an error is found. Modems that support V.42 error correction can make up for this.

The fourth file transfer protocol, Kermit, is a specialized protocol used for moving 8-bit data communication paths that only allow 7-bit data, usually text only. It is also very slow. It is a transfer protocol to try if nothing else works for a Windows-to-Macintosh connection.

Encoding

In order to transmit a file using terminal programs, you'll usually need to encode it first. Most terminal programs don't have encoding built in, so you'll have to encode the file with a utility. (See Chapter 6 for information on cross-platform encoding and compression.)

Macintosh terminal programs often have an option to encode in MacBinary format. (In ClarisWorks/AppleWorks, it's in the "Method" pop-up menu.) MacBinary is not a text encoding method, but is a binary encoding method, which folds the file's Mac type and creator codes in.

You should not use MacBinary when sending a file to a Windows PC. The terminal software on Windows may not be able to correctly receive the file. Even if it does, the Windows user will usually not be able to decipher it. You can safely use straight Binary if both terminal programs support it.

Beyond NT

Much of the past 100 pages or so have dealt with using Mac clients with Windows NT Server. Although popular, it isn't the only server for a mixed-platform network. There are servers that run on UNIX and Macintosh that support Windows and Mac clients and can be useful in many situations. In fact, as I mentioned back in Part 1, you can also mix server platforms on your network. Chapter 13 looks at alternatives to Windows NT as a server for Windows and Mac clients.

Chapter

What's in This Chapter:

♦ **AppleShare (AFP) over TCP/IP**

♦ **AppleShare IP server**

♦ **UNIX servers for Macs and Windows**

♦ **Macs and Novell NetWare**

13

NT Alternatives:
Other File Servers

By devoting an entire chapter and many parts of other chapters to Windows NT Server, and then lumping everything else into a single non-NT chapter, I may appear to be making a statement about the worthiness of the server solutions discussed here. This is not the case. While use of Windows NT is widespread, I hope to convey that the server solutions discussed in this chapter and in the next (peer-to-peer and client solutions) are very useful in certain situations. AppleShare IP is easier to setup and manage than Windows NT Server, and therefore has fewer procedures and problems to write about. However, stability is not AppleShare's forte. UNIX servers, more difficult to setup and manage than Windows NT Server, are the fastest, stablest, and most secure servers for Macintosh and Windows clients.

A variant of UNIX, the open-source Linux, has been rapidly gaining popularity during the past few years. International Data Corporation reported that Linux made up 17.2 percent of server operating systems installed in 1998. This was up from 6.8 percent a year ago, which means Linux is outpacing Windows NT as a server platform in terms of growth.

Windows NT Server lacks one feature that's important in business networks: AFP over IP. The key ability of any cross-platform server is support for the Mac and Windows file service protocol—SMB/CIFS (server message block/common internet file system) for Windows, and Apple File Protocol (AFP) for Macintosh. In the best case, these file sharing protocols can run on the same network transport protocol— which is TCP/IP.

The exception to this rule of thumb is Novell NetWare. The NetWare client is built into Windows 95/98/NT, and its support for Macs over IPX or TCP/IP is full-featured. This chapter ends with a discussion of issues particular to Macs on NetWare networks. The chapter begins with the an important feature for most other cross-platform file servers—AFP over IP.

AppleShare (AFP) over IP

AppleShare-compatible service, or Apple Filing Protocol (AFP) service, over TCP/IP has been a boon for Macs on cross-platform networks. Tests results by just about everyone who has run a test show that AFP over IP can be three or more times faster than traditional AFP over AppleTalk. The bigger the file transfers, the bigger the lead AFP over IP has over AppleTalk. The reason has to do with the fact that TCP/IP is a streaming protocol, while AppleTalk is not. AppleTalk waits for a reply after every eighth packet is sent over the network to ensure that the packets were delivered. TCP/IP assumes there is a good connection, increasing its error-checking as a connection with less reliable links. TCP/IP can also send more data at one time because the packet sizes are larger. For networks moving a lot of data, such as in groups working with graphics or prepress functions, running AFP over IP is worth giving up AppleTalk's easy setup and management.

Accessing AFP over IP Servers from a Mac Client

Most of the servers discussed in this chapter can deliver AFP file services over TCP/IP. Mac clients to access them need AppleShare client 3.7 or later, which requires Open Transport 1.1.2 or later. Basically, a Mac running Mac OS 8.0 and later is AFP-over-IP enabled. (The latest AppleShare client is included with AppleShare IP and other AFP servers.) The client software comes in the form of an extension file called AppleShare. With the clients installed, users can choose AFP over IP servers in the Chooser, along with servers on AppleTalk.

AFP URLs

Since AFP is now another TCP/IP service on local networks and even the Internet, it is possible to use AFP URLs to access volumes. The problem is, most client software doesn't recognize AFP URLs. Open Door Networks' AFP Engage! URL Processor (on the book CD; http://www.opendoor.com) enables web browsers, e-mail clients, and other Internet programs to recognize AFP URLs that reside on either TCP/IP or AppleTalk networks. A URL for an AFP server on a TCP/IP network has the general form of:
afp://server-name/volume-name/path
A URL for an AFP server on an AppleTalk network has the general form of:
afp:/at/server-name:zone/volume-name/path
Note that the AppleTalk URL only has one slash after the colon.

Servers that are available over both AppleTalk and TCP/IP show in the Chooser on Macintosh clients, along with servers available only via AppleTalk (Figure 13.1). Apple made TCP/IP the default transport protocol in AppleShare client 3.7 and later. When you choose a file server from the "Select a file server" list in the Chooser, the client tries to connect via TCP/IP first, and then defaults to AppleTalk if it can't make an IP connection. If you want to connect using AppleTalk instead of TCP/IP, you can hold down the Option key while double-clicking the server name or when clicking the OK button.

Servers don't show up in the Chooser if they are available via TCP/IP only. That's because AFP over TCP/IP does not provide Apple's Name Binding Protocol (NBP), which requires AppleTalk. To access AFP servers

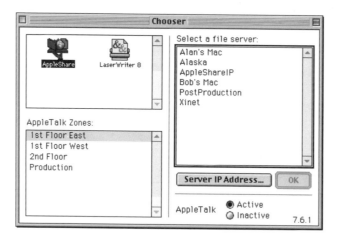

Figure 13.1 AFP servers on IP are visible if both AppleTalk and IP are running.

on TCP/IP only, a Mac user can click the Chooser's Server IP Address button and type in the IP address or the DNS host name (such as *ourserver.acme.com*).

The AppleShare client also lets a Mac user access an AFP server over the Internet by typing its IP address. To reach an AppleShare IP file server behind a firewall, add a colon (:) and the TCP port number (by default, 548) to the IP address or DNS name (as in OURSERVER:548).

MacWindows Tip

Instead of having users remember the IP address for an AFP server on TCP/IP networks, you can make an alias of the mounted server from any Mac. You can then copy the alias and send it to users via e-mail or floppy disk, or post it on a file server. The alias will work from any Mac. This is because the alias contains the IP address of the server as well as any AppleTalk path information. If the server is available over both TCP/IP and AppleTalk, any Mac can use either protocol to access the server when the user double-clicks the alias file.

AppleShare IP

Today's AppleShare IP is a distant relative of the original Apple server for Macintosh. The original AppleShare provided only file sharing to only Mac clients. AppleShare IP today provides file, print, web, e-mail, and DNS services, all of which are accessible by Windows and UNIX clients without having to add client software from Apple. AppleShare IP 6 first added support of Windows SMB/CIFS file sharing. One thing today's AppleShare IP does have in common with the original is simple interface. This makes it a good web and file server for small offices, schools, and workgroups, especially if it's the type of workgroup where the users run the server themselves.

Web and File Server. The file sharing supports Windows SMB/CIFS file sharing over TCP/IP, AFP over TCP/IP and AppleTalk, and FTP over TCP/IP. It supports plug-ins and CGI scripts. Apple claims the web server can handle 25 million hits per day. (A "hit" in this case refers to each graphic and text file used on a web page. If there were 9 graphics element and 1 text element on a web page, this claim would translate into 2.5 million web pages per day.)

Print Server. Supports IP and LPR printing from Mac, Windows, and UNIX clients, as well as traditional AppleTalk printing. (Windows NT supports LPR printing on IP.)

Mail Server. A POP/SMTP server with IMAPv4 support. Small networks that don't want to use TCP/IP can run Mail Server over AppleTalk, using Claris Emailer on the client Macs.

MacDNS. A Domain Name System server for mapping IP addresses to names

PC Net Exchange. A utility similar to PC Exchange on Mac OS clients (see Chapter 5). PC Net Exchange lets you map PC file name extensions to Macintosh type and creator codes. The utility assigns type and create codes to files uploaded by Windows users, so that Mac users can double-click the file to launch the appropriate Mac application. The files appear to Mac users with Mac application icons.

Web & File Admin. Lets you set up folders to share, and manages many of the services together. There is a single administration console for Macintosh and Windows clients, users and groups and their passwords and security.

All the servers share the same database of users and groups, and management of the servers is integrated.

AppleShare IP does not come with a proxy server, a firewall, or a DHCP/BootP address server. You can add these to the server Mac. Developers can add services to AppleShare IP using a database and programming tool called the Registry API.

AppleShare IP supports the multihoming of up to four networks. That is, four different network segments can access one server through the use of add-in Ethernet cards, one card per network segment. However, since there is no routing in AppleShare IP, computers on different networks can't communicate directly with each other. Another limitation allows only one of the four network segments to have access to AFP over TCP/IP. The rest will have to use AFP over AppleTalk or SMB/CIFS over TCP/IP.

AppleShare IP File Access and Security

Apple has adopted the Microsoft use of the word "share" to mean a shared directory or printer—AppleShare IP calls them share points. Share points have access privileges (equivalent to Microsoft's Permissions) that determine the type of access a user or group will have. The privileges are the same as those in Mac OS file sharing (described in Chapter 8). There's read-only access, write-only access, and read and write access. You can apply these to everyone, to a specific group, or user, or to the owner (either the administrator or a user who created the folder). Most users will need a password to log on, but you can enable Guest access, which lets anyone log on without a password, subject to the privileges you assign. (Guest access for Windows SMB/CIFS clients works differently than for AFP clients—but we'll get to that a little later.) Privileges only work over the network, and do not apply to people sitting at the Macintosh server.

The folders inside of a share point also have access privileges. You can set these to be the same as the share point itself, or they can be different. The interface for setting these on the server looks much like the Sharing window in Mac OS clients (as shown in Figure 13.2).

Figure 13.2 Setting access privileges in AppleShare IP looks much as it does in Mac OS peer-to-peer file sharing.

There are several files that keep information about privileges. There's a Users and Groups file, in Mac OS file sharing. AppleShare IP also stores the names of users, groups and folders with an ID number. The database of who has privileges for what folders makes reference to these ID number, and is stored as an invisible file called AppleShare PDS (short for Parallel Data Structure). Privileges for CD-ROM, DVD-ROM, and other read-only disks are stored in separate files called PDF files. The path for these files on the Macintosh server is System Folder/Preferences/AppleShare IP Preferences/Access Privileges.

You can't accidentally delete, move, or rename a file that you can't see. If you do, AppleShare IP creates a new PDS file will all privileges reset to the administrator. In this respect, it works like a Preference file in Mac OS. Like a Preference file, a PDS file can corrupt. Removing it will cause your privilege settings to be lost, but it will also fix a problem.

NOTE: As with Mac OS file sharing, a folder on a network volume with write-only privileges is called a drop box. You can copy files to a drop box folder, but without read privileges, you can't open it to see what's inside. Although you can make almost any other folder a share point (a shared network volume), you cannot make a drop box a share point.

There is a security element here as well. You can't copy privileges just by copying the Users and Groups file. Even if you copied all the data to another hard drive—including the PDS file—you'd still lose privileges, because new ID numbers would be created for the newly copied folders.

Enabling Windows Networking

Windows users can access the same shared volumes (or share points) in AppleShare IP as Macintosh users. On the Windows PCs, you need to enable the Client for Microsoft Networks that comes with Windows (see Chapter 9), using TCP/IP. AppleShare IP does not support NetBEUI or IPX.

You turn on Windows SMB/CIFS file sharing in the same Window you do a lot other setting up, the Web and File Server Settings window in the Web & File Server Admin utility (Figure 13.3). In the pop-up menu at the top, select Windows File Sharing. You'll notice that is looks similar to the Identification tab of the Network dialog box in Windows. Check Enable Windows File Share (SMB).

The AppleShare IP server can register itself with a WINS (Windows Internet Name Service) server running on a Windows NT server on the network. When you check Enable WINS Registration (Figure 13.3), Windows clients can find AppleShare IP servers by their names, which means the AppleShare IP servers appear in the Windows Network Neighborhood.

The log-in behavior of Windows SMB clients differs from that of Mac clients in one respect. In certain situations when a logon fails, Windows clients will be logged in as a Guest if Guest access is enabled. Usually, Guests have fewer privileges than users, so it will appear to the Windows user that he lost his privileges. When Guest access is enabled, AppleShare IP will log the Windows client on as Guest if the account has been disabled, or if either the user name or the password has been typed in incorrectly. When Mac users type in an incorrect name or password, they get a warning message and are not logged in.

Web Update Link: *For current tips, links, and upgrade information about running Windows clients with AppleShare IP, see http://www.macwindows.com/ASIP.html.*

Figure 13.3 Registering an AppleShare IP with a Windows NT WINS server

Handling Naming Conventions

AppleShare IP is aware that Windows cannot access network shares with names longer than 12 characters. To all Windows SMB clients, AppleShare IP automatically presents share point names longer than 12 characters in a DOS 8.3 format. It will truncate the name, removes spaces, and end it with a tilde and a number. The name "In Progress Files" will appear as "InProg~1" to the Windows users.

AppleShare IP isn't as smart about differences in file naming conventions. It doesn't automatically filter out characters that are illegal in Windows (see Chapter 5), so you'll have problems if Mac users include slashes in file names or end names with spaces or periods. However, AppleShare IP includes a batch command you can run. The Short Name command in the Web & File Admin utility will convert file names to the 8.3 convention and strip illegal characters. Since it doesn't run continually, it's best to make the Mac users aware of the naming restrictions of Windows.

Going the other way, the Mac file system cannot view Windows long file names longer than 31 characters. The Web & File Server automatically truncates long file names to 31 characters.

Table 13.1 AppleShare IP's TCP/IP Port Numbers. Each AppleShare IP service has a default TCP/IP port number (on one level, TCP/IP ports are the rough equivalent to AppleTalk zones).

Service	Port
AFP over TCP	548
Domain Name Server	53
FTP	21
HTTP	80
IMAP Admin	626
IMAP	143
POP3	110
SMTP	25

Accessing AFP Servers on IP with ShareWay IP

There are a lot of AppleShare-compatible AFP file servers that don't offer access over TCP/IP. ShareWay IP Gateway from OpenDoor Networks (http://www.opendoor.com) enables Macs to access any AFP file server over TCP/IP. With ShareWay IP installed on a Macintosh, Mac clients can use TCP/IP to access AppleTalk servers, including Windows NT Services for Macintosh, Macs with personal file sharing, old versions of AppleShare (before version 5), Novell NetWare, and Windows clients running Miramar PC MacLAN before version 7. AppleTalk does not need to be running. In fact, with a ShareWay IP Gateway running, you can access these AFP volumes over the Internet. (Look for the evaluation copies of Open Door's ShareWay IP, ShareWay IP Pro, and AFP Engage! on this book's CD-ROM.)

ShareWay IP is gateway software that runs on a Macintosh, either a dedicated machine or a user's machine. It provides an IP address for each AppleTalk AFP server (see Figure 13.4). (ShareWay IP Professional is a version that supports multiple AFP servers. The ShareWay IP Standard addition works with one AFP server.) You can also assign an optional port number to an AppleTalk AFP server. Users on TCP/IP networks refer to the AppleTalk server by this IP address.

ShareWay IP then translates network traffic between the AppleTalk and TCP/IP protocols. It merely passes on the AFP data, translating between underlying protocols, the AppleTalk Session Protocol and Apple's Data Stream Interface over TCP/IP. Data Stream Interface, introduced with AppleShare IP 5.0, is how AFP is delivered on TCP/IP.

ShareWay IP behaves in some ways as an AppleShare IP server, using the same port 548 to communicate AFP over TCP/IP to a client (see Table 13.1 on previous page). ShareWay IP Professional lets you change the port number, should you want the gateway to be accessible from the Internet, and you have a problem getting through a firewall. The gateway also has a logging feature to track activities. ShareWay IP will end a session two minutes after if it detects a break in a connection with either the client or the server.

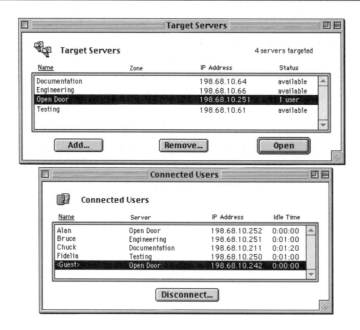

Figure 13.4 ShareWay IP assigns IP addresses to AppleTalk AFP servers.

There are several ways Mac users can access a server. In the Chooser, they can type the IP address that ShareWay IP has assigned to that server. Once the volume is mounted, a Mac user can create an alias of it. The next time you want to mount the volume, double-click the alias to bring up the AFP log-on dialog for that server.

With ShareWay IP 2.0 and later running on Mac Os 8.5 and later, Mac users can browse the TCP/IP network from a list of file servers, much as the Chooser browses AppleTalk networks, and the Windows Network Neighborhood browses TCP/IP (and other) networks. This is accomplished using Mac OS 8.5's built-in Network Services Location (NSL) feature on the server, and an Open Door client utility called AFP Engage!, which is included with ShareWay IP 2.0 and later. Apple's NSL uses the Service Location Protocol (SLP) to enable network services to register with the TCP/IP network, so users can find them dynamically. This is similar to how AppleTalk AFP servers register with the AppleTalk Name Binding Protocol (NBP), and Windows NetBIOS devices register with a WINS server. Mac OS 8.5 contain an extension file called SLP Plugin that implements this feature. ShareWay IP running on OS 8.5 or later automatically registers with the Mac OS using SLP (similar in function to a WINS server.)

TCP/IP browsing is a significant feature that Mac OS has always lacked. It is likely that Apple has added SLP and the Network Services Location feature in preparation for a built-in TCP/IP browser in a future release of Mac OS, and perhaps a built-in NSL/SLP server in a future version of AppleShare IP or Mac OS X Server.

Mac OS X Server

AppleShare IP runs on Mac OS 8.x, and so does not have the benefits of a "modern," kernel-based operating system such as Windows NT, which features preemptive multitasking, protected memory, and quick performance. However, Mac OS X Server (X is pronounced "ten") *is* a modern operating system with all of these features. It is based on the Mach kernel, contains BSD 4.4 (a core set of UNIX code and utilities), and, according to Apple, "uses a UNIX-style process model." UNIX developers were among the first to port software to it, and it delivers UNIX-like performance.

So why is it called *Mac OS X Server*? For one, it's not officially a UNIX variant. It also has a lot of Mac OS 8.5 in it, including the Mac OS 8.5 Finder and interface and the ability to run Mac OS software. However, deep down in its core, Mac OS X Server is more UNIX than Mac OS. Which, for a server, is a good thing.

Mac OS X Server was introduced in March of 1999. It will take several years to build up a market as it matures as software and a development platform. The UNIX-based servers discussed in the next section have a proven track record that Mac OS X lacks at this point.

Mac OS X is initially focused on supporting Mac clients, though you can add limited Windows support yourself. Apple has indicated that support for Windows clients similar to what is in AppleShare IP 6 could be added in time.

A Brief History of Mac OS X Server

Mac OS X is the final chapter in Apple's decade-long quest for a modern operating system. It started with a project code-named *Pink*, which later became Taligent. Apple later spun off Taligent in a joint venture company with IBM, and the project quickly withered away.

The next attempt was a project called Copland. Apple spend several years, thousands of man-hours, and millions of dollars on the project, which never reached completion. And Copland wasn't the final goal—it was only a transition operating system toward a fully modern operating system called Gershwin. Not surprisingly, the period of time in the mid-1990s when Apple was focused on Copland coincided with huge quarterly losses for the company. Many of the interface features developed as part of the Copland project later found themselves into the Mac OS 8.0 and 8.5.

In late 1996, Apple decided to abandon the Copland project in favor of buying an modern operating system and "Macifying" it. Apple purchased NeXT, Inc., for $400 million, acquiring the OpenSTEP operating system—and Steve Jobs with it. OpenSTEP was the current implementation of the NeXTstep operating system. When Steve Jobs went about building a modern operating system, he didn't try to build it from scratch, as Apple had done. He started with UNIX—a Mach kernel and a UNIX core—and added to it.

Apple's plan was to port OpenSTEP to run on Macintosh hardware (it was running on Intel PCs at the time) and merge OPENstep with Mac OS. In an apparent reference to the ill-fated project Gershwin (named after the composer of *Rhapsody in Blue*), the merger project was called *Rhapsody*, and the Mac OS portion was called the *Blue Box*. Existing Mac OS applications were to run in the Blue Box, but without the benefit of multitasking, protected memory, and the other modern OS features. To take advantage of these features, Rhapsody applications had to be written in a new set of APIs based on the NeXT APIs. This was called Yellow Box. The intriguing thing was that the Yellow Box APIs are cross-platform. If a developer wrote a Yellow Box application, it would run on both Rhapsody and, with the addition of some other software, Windows as well.

The problem was that software vendors did not want to completely rewrite their Mac applications with the Yellow Box APIs. With no major developers signed on, Apple abandoned the Rhapsody project in May of 1998. Or rather, it refocused it and called it Mac OS X.

Mac OS X is a further merging of OPENstep and Mac OS 8.x. Apple took the core API set of Mac OS, cleaned it up, modernized it, and renamed it *Carbon*. With the Carbon APIs, a developer can slightly modify current Mac applications instead of rewriting them from scratch, and still get protected memory and the other new features.

What's in Mac OS X Server

Mac OS X Server is built on the high-performance Mach kernel and BSD 4.4. Mac OS X Server was released before Mac OS X (scheduled for late 1999). That's because in this first release, not all of the user services were ready. The Mac OS 8.x Finder interface is only skin-deep, with OPENstep just below the surface. There are some NeXT and UNIX interface items, such as the NeXT File Viewer for looking thought directories, and a UNIX-like Process Panel and Process Viewer for managing user and system processes. There's also a terminal application that lets you access the BSD command-line interface. Mac OS X Server contains the Blue Box for running Mac applications, but it takes its toll on server performance.

File and Print services for Mac and Windows clients

Mac OS X Server's file and print server package is called Apple File Services, similar to AppleShare IP in function and interface, and includes

AFP over TCP/IP services. You configure the services from the Apple menu, from the Services tab of the Network Settings window.

Unlike AppleShare IP, the first release of Mac OS X Server does not include an SMB/CIFS file server for Windows clients, though it has indicated that it might include Windows client support at some later date. Mac OS X can run the open-source SAMBA code, which provides SMB/CIFS file service on UNIX and Linux machines. (To obtain the right version of SAMBA for Mac OS X, see http://til.info.apple.com/techinfo.nsf/artnum/n60172.)

MacWindows Tip

Windows 98 can't log onto SAMBA servers because they use plain text passwords, while Windows 98 sends only encrypted passwords. Microsoft recommends a Windows 98 registry edit that enables plain text passwords. Add the Registry entry Enable-PlainTextPassword (reg Dword) 1 in this Registry location:

```
HKEY_LOCAL_MACHINE\System\CurrentControlSet\Services\VxD\Vnetsup
```

Internet services

Mac OS X Server includes an Apache web/FPT/mail sever (Apache is common in UNIX environments) and the Web Objects development environment and application server for creating dynamic web pages.

NetBoot for Mac clients

A new service called NetBoot lets iMacs and the Blue and White Power Mac G3s boot up directly from the server and run applications from the server. These clients can run without hard drives. The server can support dozens of NetBoot clients at the same time. It's not something everyone needs to do, but Apple thinks education users can make use of the simplified administration NetBoot provides. Users can access their own specially configured desktop, applications, and documents. The clients can access the same system software and applications, so a system administrator only needs to update one copy of each. however, the system software is protected from being damaged by one user. Overall, NetBoot acts a lot like thin-client/server systems (described in Chapter 17), though a different technology.

Management and Administration

Mac OS X Server also has administration and security services and several administration tools. NetInfo is a directory service that allows you to manage a group of Mac OS X Server hosts. NetworkManager (Figure 13.5) is used to add and edit users and groups and shared volumes and printers. The administration tools use much of the the same terminology as AppleShare IP and sport a similar interface.

Mac OS X Server is a johnny-come-lately as a UNIX file server and is still in its early stages of product development. It's likely much of the feature specialization will come as third-party products from UNIX developers. For a full-featured, mature UNIX server, there are several choices that have had a decade of proven experience and more depth in terms of services. Some of these are discussed in the next section.

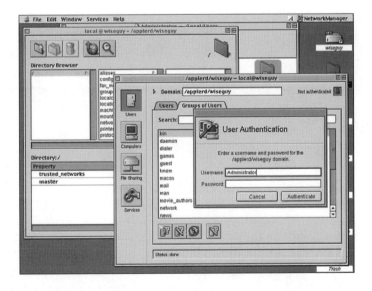

Figure 13.5 Mac OS X Server's Network Manager tool

UNIX and Linux as Cross-Platform Servers

UNIX is an alternative cross-platform server that has been supporting Windows and Mac OS clients for over a decade. Linux is a free variant of UNIX that has been rapidly gaining popularity in recent years for use as a server. You can turn just about any computer running UNIX into a file server. The benefits of UNIX are reflected in its history, which is quite different than that of Windows or Mac OS.

A Brief History of UNIX and Linux

UNIX has been around in one form or another longer than any operating system in use today. Networking has been an integral part of UNIX for several decades. UNIX was created at Bell Labs in the 1960s as a programming environment to use in the development of AT&T's telecommunications systems. Early in the operating system's development, major additions were made at the University of California, Berkeley. These modifications, known as the Berkeley (or BSD) extensions, included programming tools and TCP/IP networking. Later, Sun developed the Network Filing System (NFS) for UNIX file servers. The multitasking, multiuser, and connectivity features of UNIX (as well as an active campaign by AT&T) helped to spread UNIX throughout universities, where several generations of engineering and computer science students helped to develop it and eventually to bring it to the corporate world.

UNIX is scalable, running on all types of hardware, from PCs to supercomputers. Additionally, BSD UNIX is based on open standards, not proprietary technology. Commands that work in one versions often work in other versions. This openness has led to a variety of UNIX implementations from multiple sources, which roughly break down into two classes, commercial UNIX and free UNIX variants. Commercial UNIX software, such as Sun Solaris, HP-UX, and Silicon Graphics IRIS/IRIX uses proprietary versions of UNIX. BSD UNIX commands will run, but the manufacturers have added advanced features, such as symmetric multiprocessing and 64-bit computing. Free UNIX variants, such as Linux and FreeBSD, have been behind commercial UNIX in terms of advanced features.

The appeal of Linux has its roots in the philosophy of Richard Stallman, founder of the Free Software Foundation. Stallman wrote a set of tools in 1984 with the idea of giving them away. Stallman is an advocate of giving away nonproprietary software as a method of advancing the computing industry. This philosophy goes beyond merely advocating open standards; it advocates *open-source* software, which means that no one owns the source code—the programming commands used to create the binary code—and anyone can get it. Whenever you add to open-source software, you have to give away not only the software you create, but the source code with it.

Linux is such open source-software. In 1991, Linus Torvalds, a 21-year-old student at Helsinki University in Finland wrote a new UNIX-like kernel and some device drivers optimized for Intel 386 and 486 processors, which he announced on an Internet newsgroup. A group of people Torvalds had never met added some code to the "beta." This early group began referring to the new operating system as Linus's UNIX, or Linux. Over the next few years, Torvalds coordinated a team of programmers located all over the world to develop Linux. Eventually, networking and a graphics user interface were added. Linux 1.0 was released in 1994. Linux 2.0 in 1996 included support for a variety of processors and the ability to use multiple processors.

Today, you can download Linux for free, or purchase Linux distributions—bundles of the Linux kernel and drivers, GNU tools, and other improvements. Linux distributors also offer technical support plans.

In 1998 there was an estimated 7 million users of Linux worldwide. Large companies, including Oracle, Intel, IBM, Dell, and Netscape, have involved themselves with Linux, by developing software for it, investing in it, or distributing it. Dell, IBM, and other hardware manufacturers will sell you a PC preloaded with Linux.

Even Apple develops (and gives away) its own version of Linux that runs on Macintosh hardware, called MkLinux. However, the most popular and actively developed Linux for Macintosh hardware is LinuxPPC.

Apple sees the future of the Macintosh as being based on UNIX. However, Apple's main efforts in UNIX lie with Mac OS X, which runs on a UNIX Mach kernel, which is similar to the Mach kernel that MkLinux runs on a similar Mach kernel. Mac OS X also has BSD UNIX built into it. (Mac OS X is discussed in more detail in the previous section.)

Web Update Link: *For an updated list of UNIX and Linux implementations for Macintosh, see http://www.macwindows.com/emulator.html#UnixOnMac.*

UNIX versus Windows NT as a Server

Compared to Windows NT, UNIX is generally more stable and is more secure. Depending on the implementation, the performance of UNIX usually exceeds that of Windows NT. Additionally, implementations of AppleTalk for UNIX are faster than Microsoft's implementation in Windows NT 4 and earlier. (The jury is still out on Windows 2000 Server). UNIX servers can often provide better support of Macintosh clients than can NT 4.0, with services including AFP over IP and remote access.

There are drawbacks to using UNIX as a server as well. The most practical is that there isn't nearly as much server software available for UNIX as there is for Windows NT. When a developer releases a piece of server software, there is almost always an NT version, and sometimes the NT version is the only version. Internet and web servers began on UNIX, so you won't have a problem finding one of these, and there are several choices of file and print servers for Mac and Windows clients, but the more specialized servers will be harder to find. Server software used in prepress and print production, document management servers, and web production are more common for Windows NT than UNIX.

The other drawback of UNIX is that it is more difficult to set up and get running than Windows NT, and often requires you to have a UNIX consultant or staff expert on hand. However, a relatively new class of plug-and-play UNIX servers called *server appliances* basically eliminate this drawback. Server appliances are small boxes that come with UNIX and the server software preinstalled—plug it in and turn it on.

Web Update Link: *For an updated list of AFP/SMB file servers for UNIX, see http://www.macwindows.com/Network.html.*

Just as UNIX itself comes in free and commercial versions, so do UNIX file sharing server software packages. The free versions are upgraded through frequent patches, often available from different sources. The commercial versions often include bundles of other types of network services.

Commercial AFP/SMB for UNIX

Commercial versions of UNIX file server software come with the benefits of a software purchase, including technical support and a lower required level of technical knowledge on the part of the person installing the software. Commercial versions of UNIX server software also support more of the commercial versions of UNIX than do the free AFP servers. Some products include support file sharing for both AFP Macintosh clients and SMB Windows clients. Most of the companies also sell image servers based on the Open Prepress Interface (OPI) specification, as well as other servers for the publishing industry. Basically, OPI sends low-resolution versions of images to page-layout programs on the client for screen display. The full-resolution image is embedded when the file is output. Here are just a few of the players, each of which is unique in some way. All of them have been providing these solutions for a number of years.

Xinet K-AShare and FullPress
Xinet
http://www.xinet.com

Xinet is one of the oldest providers of AFP products for UNIX. The company began its AFP product line in 1987, when it released K-Talk, an implementation of the AppleTalk stack for UNIX. K-Talk can also act as an AppleTalk router. Soon after, Xinet released K-AShare (Figure 13.6), which includes K-Talk.

Xinet has made K-AShare and K-Talk the foundation of several high-performance server products for the professional publishing industry. This includes FullPress, a server package that includes a file server, a print and imaging server, and an OPI image server. FullPress also includes an AFP client and PAP print client for the UNIX machine. Xinet's WebNative allows prepress providers to distribute low- and high-resolution images over private Web sites.

Xinet's products run on UNIX computers from Silicon Graphics (IRIX), Sun SPARC (Sun OS and Solaris), and Hewlett-Packard (HP-UX). Xinet has also ported FullPress to Mac OS X Server. Xinet is also a hardware reseller and offers UNIX servers configured with its software.

Xinet has been an innovator and a leader in using UNIX as an AFP server. Xinet was the first company to implement AFP over TCP/IP on a UNIX server. For that, you need K-AShare 9.0 and later, or Full-Press 8.12. Xinet also claims that K-AShare is the fastest AFP server for UNIX. The company says that on 100BaseT Ethernet network with TCP/IP, a beefy Sun server running K-AShare can move data at

Figure 13.6 Sharing UNIX directories over AFP with Xinet's K-AShare

9.5 MB per second in benchmarks, and 5.5 MB per second in "real world" tests. This can be faster than accessing some local hard drives.

If all you need is an AFP file sharing client for UNIX, Xinet offers K-FS, based on the K-Talk protocol stack. K-FS implements a graphical Chooser-like device that displays AFP network volumes. The client can read AFP access privileges and translate them into the appropriate UNIX permissions. You can also use K-FS to setup automatic back-up of Mac disks to the UNIX system.

You can also buy Xinet's Postscript Level 2 print spooler separately. K-Spool uses AppleTalk's Printer Access Protocol to accept print jobs from Mac clients and pass them on to Postscript printers on LocalTalk and Ethernet networks or connected to the server. The UNIX daemon behaves as a virtual LaserWriter, so Mac clients can use the standard LaserWriter driver to print to the server. K-Spool includes the K-ATalk AppleTalk stack and routing capabilities. K-Spool is also has a UNIX print client that can print both Postscript files and ASCII files to Post-script printers.

Object	Type	Zone	Net & Node
ETSPreview Spooler	FullPress OPI	Xinet	11 135
ETSPreview Spooler	LaserWriter	Xinet	11 135
Fa12400pb	Macintosh PowerBo	Xinet	11 74
Fa12400pb	AFPServer	Xinet	11 74
Fa12400pb	ARA - Client-Only	Xinet	11 74
Fa12400pb	Workstation	Xinet	11 74
H-7200	Power Macintosh	Xinet	110 55
H-7200	AFPServer	Xinet	110 55
H-7200	Workstation	Xinet	110 55
head	Echoer	Xinet	110 129
head	K-TalkRouter	Xinet	110 129
head	K-Time Server	Xinet	110 129

Sort network objects by: ◆ Object ◇ Type ◇ Zone ◇ Net/Node [Close]

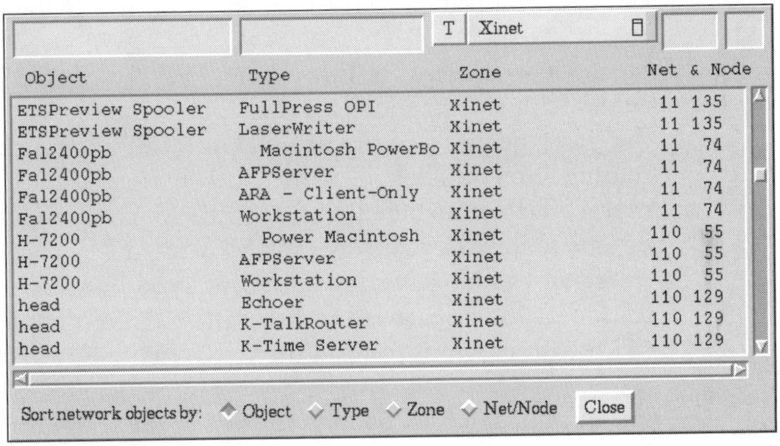

Figure 13.7 Xinet's browser displays both AppleTalk and TCP/IP devices in the same UNIX window.

FullPress includes these lower level services, and lets the server administrator browse for both AppleTalk and TCP/IP devices (Figure 13.7). FullPress also provides a collection of OPI image serving features. It lets you store a single copy of a high-resolution image in a variety of file formats on the server. It creates low-resolution versions for placement when users work with them on Macs, and then inserts the high-resolution image at print time. Mac clients only need the standard Mac OS networking software. FullPress 9.04 added a Java graphical user interface for administration from any platform (including Macintosh), as well as enhancements to security.

Helios EtherShare and PCShare

Helios Software
http://www.helios.com

Helios is another company with a lot of experience in AFP servers for UNIX, with its EtherShare server. Helios also offers PCShare, a UNIX file server for Windows clients. With both PCShare and EtherShare running on a UNIX server, Mac and Windows users can share files with each other.(At the time of this writing, Windows NT clients were not supported.) EtherShare and PC Share runs on hardware from Sun, IBM, Hewlett-Packard, Silicon graphics, and Digital. Ethershare 2.5.1 and later will run on Mac OS X Server, as will PCShare 3.0 and later.

Helios first released its EtherShare AFP server in 1989. EtherShare comes with a print spooler, EtherPrint, which records statistics about the print queue. The AppleTalk protocol stack includes AppleTalk routing for LocalTalk, Ethernet, token ring, ISDN, and X25. AFP over TCP/IP is included with the EtherShare 2.5 CD-ROM CD011 or later. EtherShare also has an NFS-to-AFP gateway, a POP3 mail server, and a font server for Postscript Type 1 and Type 3 fonts. A nice feature of EtherShare is the EtherShare Admin application, a native Macintosh program you can use to configure the UNIX server.

Helios claims that PCShare is the fastest file server for Windows, with file transfer rates of up to 5 MB per second on 100BaseT Ethernet and TCP/IP. With version 3.0 and later, PCShare provides many of the same services as a Windows NT server, including a SMB/CIFS file server. PCShare 3.0 and later includes a WINS and WINS proxy name server and a DHCP main and backup server. PCShare also lets Windows users print to Mac printers via EtherShare queues and access Mac EtherShare volumes. PCShare also allows PCs to print to UNIX spoolers.

Versions of PCShare before 3.0 do not contain a SMB/CIFS server, but use a Helios ODI-compliant client to running on the PCs. Before PC 3.0, Windows users don't use the Network Neighborhood, but instead select network volumes through a Chooser-like interface in the Helios client. The pre-3.0 client presents UNIX directories as PC drivers letters, and Windows applications can access the network through Microsoft's WinSock API.

Helios also offers an optional imaging server module for EtherShare called EtherShare OPI, as well as other tools for professional print and prepress. Helios Print Preview is a proofing system based on the UNIX server. The system previews Postscript jobs as PDF files and uses EtherShare's font server.

TotalNET Advanced Server

Syntax
http://www.syntax.com/

TotalNET Advanced Server (TAS) is both an AFP and a SMB server, as well as a NetWare-compatible server, so you don't need to add anything to the Windows or Macintosh clients. However, TAS focuses more on Windows clients, providing more for Windows clients than the other solutions mentioned, and less for Macintosh clients. TAS provides AFP over AppleTalk, but not over TCP/IP (at the time this book was written). For Windows, TAS provides three types of connections: NetBIOS over TCP/IP and NetBIOS over NetBEUI, both using the Microsoft client; and IPX/SPX using a NetWare client. A print server allows clients to print to UNIX spoolers. TAS runs on the Sun Solaris, IBM AIX, Silicon Graphics IRIX, and HP-UX operating systems.

uShare

IPTech
http://www.ushare.com/

IPTech's uShare is an AFP server for Sun Solaris or IBM AIX. uShare 5.0 and later provides AFP over TCP/IP. The server includes centralized backup software of Mac clients and AppleTalk routing over 10/100BaseT Ethernet, LocalTalk, FDDI, and ISDN. IPTech claims that uShare can handle up to 63,000 simultaneous sessions. There are two optional print modules, uPrint, a print server, and PrintQMgr, an administrative tool for print queues.

IPTech also offers OPI servers, CanOPI for UNIX and CanOPI for Windows NT.

Free AFP Servers for UNIX and Linux

There are two free implementations of AppleTalk and the AFP file server for UNIX: CAP and Netatalk. (These are the AFP equivalents to SAMBA, discussed on page 358.) You can install CAP and Netatalk on Linux and FreeBSD variants, as well as on some commercial UNIX implementations. And with companies such as IBM, Hewlett-Packard, and Compaq offering Linux with their server hardware, you can now purchase technical support.

The Columbia AppleTalk Package (CAP)

http://www.cs.mu.oz.au/appletalk/cap.html, or the Usenet Newsgroup comp.protocols.appletalk

The Columbia AppleTalk Package (CAP) was the first free implementation of AppleTalk on UNIX, originally developed at Columbia University. CAP adds an AppleTalk protocol stack on BSD 4.2, 4.3 UNIX variations, including DEC ULTRIX, Sun OS 3.2 or later and Sun Solaris, SGI IRIS/IRIX, HP Apollo Domain, 386/BSD, FreeBSD 2.0 or later, NetBSD, Linux, and others. An application called AUFS provides AppleShare AFP services. The print server is called LWSRV. Other implementations of AppleTalk on UNIX are more efficient.

However, CAP added support of AFP file sharing over TCP/IP in Patch 199.

The original version of CAP required the encapsulation of AppleTalk packets inside of IP packets and required an IPTalk gateway, such as those implemented in the Shiva FastPath router or a Cisco Router. Current versions support native AppleTalk on Ethernet, though a gateway is still required to connect to LocalTalk networks.

Netatalk

http://www.umich.edu/~rsug/netatalk

Netatalk is a free AppleTalk protocol suite that includes an AFP server and Printer Access Protocol printing. It also includes support for routing AppleTalk using the Routing Table Maintenance Protocol (RTMP). Patches for AFP over TCP/IP did exist at the time this book was written, but were not available from the University of Michigan team where Netatalk originated.

Unlike CAP, Netatalk implements the AppleTalk transport at the kernel-level of UNIX. This makes packet reception and routing more efficient and slightly faster than in CAP. Programmers think of Netatalk as using a coding style that is more "native" to BSD than CAP, which uses programming techniques more similar to Mac OS.

The freeware Linux 1.3, FreeBSD 2.2, and NetBSD 1.4 and later all include Netatalk support in their kernels. You can also install Netatalk on Sun Solaris 2.4.

Server Appliances

Server appliances are designed to remove the biggest drawback to UNIX—complex software installation and configuration that can take days. Server appliances are small boxes with preinstalled operating system and server software. Although you can find server appliances running Windows or proprietary operating systems, it's the devices running UNIX or Linux that are doing the best. The system software often includes AFP and SMB file sharing servers for Macin-tosh and Windows clients, as well as servers for web and mail. Server appliances makes sense in workgroups and can sometimes support up to 100 clients.

Server appliances are the iMacs of the server world—they're inexpen-sive, and you just take them out of the box and plug them in. They usually come with no monitor or keyboard—you can reconfigure or add software from a Windows or Macintosh machine. You usually connect to the server via a TCP/IP and a web browser interface, or sometimes from a serial port. Most have an LED display and a few buttons to push.

Cobalt Qube Microserver

Cobalt Networks
http://www.cobaltnet.com/

Cobalt Networks' Cobalt Qube Microserver is one plug-it-in, turn-it-on server appliance to which comparisons to the iMac go even fur-ther—it's small, inexpensive, and fun to look at. When it first shipped in 1998, the Qube 2700wg sold at an iMac-like price of $1249. Inside is a 64-bit superscalar RISC processor running Linux and file server and intranet server software, all in box smaller than a toaster—7.25 x 7.25 x 7.25 inches. (A rack-mounted version, the Cobalt RaQ, is only two inches thick, but doesn't look anywhere near as cool sitting on a desk.) There's no monitor, keyboard, CD-ROM, or floppy drive, just a few buttons and a small LCD display. You manage the Qube from a Mac or Windows PC on the network with a web browser.

The Qube shares many of the cross-platform and web features of NT Server or AppleShare IP, including SMB file sharing for Windows clients and native AFP file sharing over AppleTalk and IP. The Qube also includes an Apache 1.2 web server, SMTP/POP/IMAP e-mail server, FTP and DNS servers, CGI scripting, Perl 5 scripting, and indexing.

Interjet

Whistle Communications
http://www.whistle.com

The Interjet is an x86-based server appliance running BSD UNIX. It comes preloaded with servers for e-mail, web, DNS, DHCP, firewall, Mac and Windows file servers, and other server software. It comes with one or more modems. The InterJet automatically configures itself through a Whistle-authorized Internet Service Provider. Although the Interjet uses x86 processors, this appliance is not a PC. The Interjet uses neither keyboard nor monitor. Like other server appliances, you administer the server over a network using a Windows PC or a Mac.

Novell NetWare

Novell NetWare has been a cross-platform server solution for many years, preceding Windows NT in its support of Macs. The Macintosh support has been good, with Macs being the equals of Windows clients in many respects, and there are fewer problems with Mac clients than in Windows NT. NetWare also has some features that are superior to that of NT, such as the Novell Directory Services (NDS), which allows users to browse for network services over the entire network on enabled servers.

However, one of the initially appealing aspects of Windows NT Server was its graphic user interface and the relative ease of installation and configuration. The traditional NetWare interface was a mostly command-line interface. NetWare 4.x offered graphics interface elements for configuration as well as the command-line interface. NetWare 5 has a graphics users interface based on Java and is TCP/IP native.

NetWare's once solid lock on the corporate network market was eroded by the onslaught of Windows NT Server at a time when Novell was suffering some of the same lack of focus that Apple had in the mid-1990s. However, the reason Windows NT Server gets more space in this book has to do with the number of Macs being used with each environment. At the end of 1998, there were more new NT networks than NetWare being installed in locations with Macintoshes. A lot of this has to do with the fact that Macintosh often goes into smaller businesses, while NetWare is a product aimed at large enterprise sites.

Additionally, Novell itself is emphasizing Mac OS less. With NetWare 5, Novell stopped its development of a Macintosh client, handing it off to a third party, Prosoft Engineering (http://www.prosofteng.com). The first post-Novell client was the Prosoft NetWare Client 5.12 for Mac OS, and IPX client. In addition to fixing bugs, it offered several advances over Novell's last Mac client,

Novell calls NetWare 5 "pure IP" software, as standardized on Internet protocols. Previous versions of NetWare were based on Novell's IPX/SPX transport protocol, though TCP/IP had been added on. NetWare 5 received generally good reviews when Novell released it in September 1998. With NetWare 5, Novell dropped the NetWare for Macintosh NLM (NetWare Loadable Module) AppleTalk services that had been options on earlier versions. NetWare for Macintosh from earlier versions won't run on a NetWare server.

As of this writing, there was no TCP/IP Mac client for NetWare 5, but Prosoft was developing one. Novell did make provisions for a Mac client or a possible NetWare for Macintosh by including a Mac name space (Mac.NAM) and the AppleTalk stack files (appletlk.nlm and related files). If you enable a NetWare 5 server for IPX, you can use the Prosoft IPX client to access it.

Web Update Link: *For current information on problems with NetWare clients for Macintosh, see http://www.macwindows.com/servtips.html#novell. News about NetWare clients for Mac is posted at the MacWindows home page, http://www.macwindows.com.*

Macintosh Support in NetWare 4 and Earlier

There are two ways a Macintosh client can connect to NetWare networks. One is through the installation of NetWare for Macintosh on the server. NetWare for Macintosh is a NetWare Loadable Module (NLM) that provides an AFP server that runs over AppleTalk. Macs don't need client software to access it, but select NetWare servers from the Chooser. Mac clients do install a NetWare User Authentication Module (UAM) for logging on to the system. (Windows NT Server also has its own UAM, as discussed in Chapter 11.)

The other access method is to install the NetWare Client for Macintosh on the Macs. This is a set of files that enables a Mac to log onto native NetWare file service using IPX, or, in some versions, TCP/IP. The Client software includes the MacIPX control panel (Figure 13.8) and several extension files. There are also several utilities, including Print Chooser for selecting NetWare printers over IPX, Volume Mounter for mounting volumes, and Directory Tree Browser for viewing Novell Directory Services (NDS). The Client for Mac OS gives Mac OS users complete access to NDS, enabling users to locate NetWare file and print services. NetWare Client for Macintosh not only

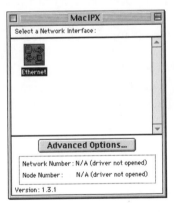

Figure 13.8 The MacIPX control panel

provides greater network access than the NetWare AFP server, but adds more security to the clients.

Client for Mac OS provides easier management as well, because network supervisors can manage Mac clients in the same way they administer Windows clients. With NetWare Client for Macintosh, you don't need to install anything extra on the servers to support Macs.

Prosoft NetWare Client 5.12 for Mac OS and Beyond

The Prosoft NetWare Client 5.12 for Mac OS was an improvement over Novell's NetWare Client 5.11 in several ways. For one, it fixed all of the bugs listed in the next section. But it also made advances in usability. For the first time, Mac users could use the Chooser to access IPX volumes and authenticate to any IPX server, instead of the NetWare Volume Mounter application. You can also select NetWare printers from the Chooser instead of the old NetWare Print Chooser. Mac Client 5.12 also reports the correct volume sizes and file sizes. Previous versions did not. As with previous versions, the Prosoft Client provides Mac access to NetWare Directory Services.

To access NetWare 5, you can use the Prosoft Client 5.12 or Novell's Client 5.11. However, the NetWare 5 server must be IPX enabled, as TCP/IP is now the default protocol in NetWare. The server needs to be configured to load the Mac Name Space (Mac.NAM).

For TCP/IP access to NetWare 5, Prosoft had promised to develop an IP-native Novell client for Mac OS, to ship before the end of 1999. The IP client looks as if it will be the future focus and direction of Macintosh connectivity with NetWare.

For AppleTalk access to NetWare 5, Prosoft is planning to update the NetWare for Macintosh 4.11 NLM to enable it to run on a NetWare 5 server. This would provide the traditionally NetWare AppleTalk services.

Problems with Novell NetWare Client 5.11

Since NetWare for Macintosh has been around longer than Windows NT Services for Macintosh, the bugs and fixes one encounters with NetWare tend to be in the native IPX NetWare client software rather than the AppleTalk NLM on the server. The final NetWare Client for Macintosh that Novell released before handing it off to Prosoft Engineering was the Client for Macintosh 5.11. After 5.11, Novell released several client updates. Novell client updates have 8.3 file names, so that update 5 is called MCLUPD5.BIN, update 6 is called MCLUPD6.BIN, and so on. The updates are available at the Novell web site.

Mac OS 8.0 and 8.1 introduced some problems with the NetWare Client for Macintosh. This was particularly true with Power Macintosh G3 models. Each update to the Client for Macintosh 5.11 fixed some of these problems. Mac OS 8.5 can also clear up some of these problems and is generally a better OS version to use with the NetWare Client.

MacWindows Tip

Novell's web site has a page with articles concerning Client for Macintosh 5.11, the last version produced by Novell: http://support.novell.com/products/nwcmc511/hotissues.htm. These articles discuss the problems with the Client and include Mac OS 8 issues.

The easiest way to get around these bugs is to upgrade to Prosoft's NetWare Client for Mac OS. But in case you haven't, here is a list of some of the more serious problems with the old Novell Client.

Updating NetWare Client for Macintosh, setting frame type

To prevent problems, you should be running the same version and update of the Client for Macintosh on all of the Macs on the network, whether or not they are exhibiting the symptoms of a problem. You should also make sure all of the Macs are set to use the same Ethernet

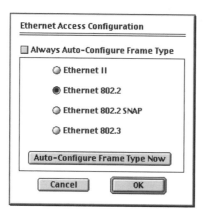

Figure 13.9 Setting the frame type in the MacIPX driver window

frame type. You do this in the MacIPX control panel (Figure 13.9). Double-click the Ethernet driver (in some versions, it's command-click, but not option-click). Then turn off autosensing and choose a frame type. You can use 802.3 for 10BaseT if that's what the servers are using.

MacIPX can't recognize adapter cards

Before update 3 (MCLUPD3.BIN), the NetWare Client for Macintosh 5.11 did not support a PCI network adapter in Macs using Mac OS's Open Transport networking software. (See Chapter 8 for a discussion of Open Transport and "classic" networking in Macs.) There was also a problem with older Macs using Open Transport system software and NuBus Ethernet cards. A work-around in the old Macs was to turn off Open Transport and go to the older "classic" networking. However, more recent Macs don't have the option of using classing networking.

The problem is that MacIPX can't recognize the adapter card with Open Transport installed. MacIPX doesn't have this problem with the Mac's built-in Ethernet port, which works fine. The problem varies with different adapter cards and Macintosh models, but seems to be worse on Power Macintosh G3's. When you try to log on, you'll get one of the following error messages:

- "There may be a problem with your network connection or MacIPX may not be configure properly. Use the MacIPX control panel to configure UPX."
- "The network interface Ethernet could not be selected due to error: -3155. Please configure the Ethernet interface to ensure that the network driver can open properly."
- "No NetWare servers can be found on the network at this time. Please check your physical connection or contact your network administrator."

With some adapters, the Mac can crash when you try to switch the frame type. Update 3 and later fix this problem for Ethernet adapters, but not for token ring. Occasionally, MacIPX doesn't find a network and sets the network address to 0.

This is a different problem. In this case, you can reboot.

NetWare Print Chooser and Mac OS 8.x

Before update 6a (MCLUPD6a.BIN) of the NetWare Client for Macintosh 5.11, there was an intermittent conflict between the NetWare Print Chooser and Mac OS 8.x that prevented the Print Chooser from loading. The Print Chooser will start to load, but will quit during the process. The problem seems to occur when you try to edit or delete a Desktop Printer icon and create a new one. The problem often temporarily disappears after restarting the Mac.

Update 6 fixed the problem. After installing MCLUPD6a.BIN or later, Novell recommends deleting the following preferences files from the System folder's Preference folder: NetWare Prefs, MacIPX Prefer-

ences, Novell Directory, AppleShare Prop, and all of your printer preferences files. Then restart the Mac. As with any Macintosh preference
file, these will be recreated automatically using default settings.

Mac OS 8.x problems

A problem with NetWare UAM prevented Mac OS 8.0 and 8.1 users
from logging in via the Chooser using the NetWare Encryption when
clear passwords were turned off at the server. This was fixed with
update 3 (the MCLUPD3.BIN update).

Another problem occurs with update 6a (MCLUPD3.BIN) and the
LaserWriter 8.5.1 driver, which comes with Mac OS 8.1. Users get an
error message when trying to print to NetWare spoolers over
AppleTalk or to NetWare print queues via IPX. The solution is to
upgrade the LaserWriter driver to 8.4.3 or later. If you are printing to
a Hewlett-Packard printer, you can use the HP LaserJet 8.5.1 driver or
the Adobe 8.5.1 driver.

The problem with LaserWriter 8.5.1 does not occur when you print
directly to an AppleTalk printer through the Mac OS Chooser,
bypassing the server.

Quark Xpress Collect for Output command

The Collect for Output command in Quark Xpress v3.32 generated
an error message, "File is locked [-54]." This error occurred whether
the user choose a Mac hard drive or a NetWare volume when linked
graphics files were stored on the file server. The Collect for Output
command attempts to gather the files used in a document. This was
fixed with update 3 (the MCLUPD3.BIN update).

NetWare Client and AppleShare Client 3.7

The NetWare Client for Macintosh 5.11 before the MCLUPD2.BIN
update contained a UAM that was incompatible with AppleShare Client
3.7 (the first version of the Apple software to support AFP over IP).

Looking Ahead

This chapter was aimed at providing information for people looking for a server to fit their particular situation. The next chapter takes the opposite approach, assuming that you have the server you want—now you want to make your clients talk to it. Or maybe you don't need a server at all.

Chapter

What's in This Chapter:

- ♦ Connecting one Mac to one PC

- ♦ Peer-to-Peer strategies

- ♦ Adding AppleShare (AFP) file sharing to Windows

- ♦ Adding SMB/CIFS file sharing to Macs

14

Cross-Platform Clients

The last few chapters have been focusing on using servers to integrate Macs and PCs, and on picking a server to fit certain groups of clients. There are also solutions that force a client to work with a certain server—you can enable a Mac to masquerade as a native Windows client, and vice versa. These are good solutions if the network administration doesn't want to introduce a second, foreign technology or doesn't want to touch the server. You can turn a Mac into a native Microsoft SMB/CIFS client using PC standards. You can also turn a Windows PC into an AFP client on a Macintosh network.

This client software also lets you do something else—create a cross-platform network without any server at all. Since Mac OS and Windows each has the ability to directly share files without a server, it's no surprise that you can make them share files with each other without a server. In a peer-to-peer network, each user's machine acts as a server to other computers as well as a client. Peer-to-peer file transfer is slower than using a dedicated file server, but is sufficient for smaller networks, or for temporary networks you set up in order to move data from one machine to another.

Before we get to describing this client software, I want to step back and describe some even simpler integration schemes—connecting a single Mac and a single PC together with a cable. Two computers can make a simple network, but you don't actually have to have a network to move files over a wire.

One-to-One Mac–Windows Connections

Moving data between a Mac and a PC has been the driving force behind a lot of sophisticated networking technology, but what if you just want a to move files between your home Mac and a PC, or the laptop you just brought in? It turns out that connecting just two computers simplifies things a bit.

There are two elements you need to assemble: the correct cabling (and sometimes other hardware), and software. This section describes three methods of cabling:

- ♦ **Null-modem cable.** This special cable connects the serial ports of the two machines.
- ♦ **Direct modem-to-modem.** Use a standard telephone cable to directly connect the modems of two computers, without a telephone line.
- ♦ **Ethernet crossover cable.** This method creates a 2-node Ethernet network with a special cable, but without an Ethernet hub.

Moving files over these types of connections can be quite inexpensive, as you can sometimes get away without buying extra software. With the first two methods, you can use some of the same software described in Chapter 12 for a direct-dial connection over telephone lines. Each of these methods has its own benefits and drawbacks.

The software you use depends on the connection method. I'll start with the software first, and then move on to the cabling methods.

Software for a Null-Modem or Direct-Modem Link

The Windows and Mac software you use on for a crossover link is the same software you'd use on a peer-to-peer network, which has no server. Since most of this chapter describes this network software, this section will focus on software used to move files over a null-modem or a direct-modem link.

- ◆ PPP connection and network software
- ◆ Special utilities designed to move over a serial link
- ◆ Terminal emulation software

PPP connection and network software

This is the least practical software to use. You can run a PPP connection over a null-modem or direct-modem link, and then run the TCP/IP protocol. If you have the network software (as described later in this chapter), this will work, but you'll get much better speed with an Ethernet crossover. If you don't have the network software, I recommend one of the serial links.

Special utilities designed to move files over a serial link

The terminal emulators described in the next section are the time-honored method of moving files over a null-modem link, but aren't particularly easy to use. A good alternative is Kevin Raner's shareware Star Gate utility (http://www.home.aone.net.au/krs/). With Star Gate

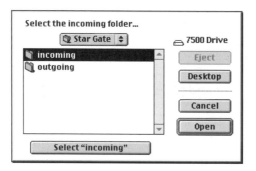

Figure 14.1 Setting up Star Gate for drag and drop file transfers

installed on both the Mac and Windows PC, you can move a file to the other machine by dragging it into a folder called Outgoing. Files arrive in a folder called Incoming.

With Star Gate, you don't have to select a file transfer protocol—you just select the folders you want to use as Outgoing and Incoming (Figure 14.1). From a menu, you then select the port you are using and the baud rate (up to 115,200), and you're done. (You need to connect the null-modem cable first.) Star Gate only works with a null-modem connection, not a direct modem-to-modem link.

Terminal emulation software

A terminal emulation application on the Mac and PC can move files over either a null-modem link or a direct modem-to-modem connection. Terminal emulators are for the most part text-based applications, but a good reason to use them is that you may already have one. Windows comes with a terminal program called HyperTerminal. On the Mac, you can use the Communications module of AppleWorks (older versions were called ClarisWorks), or a traditional shareware terminal program, such as ZTerm or Microphone. This is some of the same software described in Chapter 12 for a direct dial-up connection. You'll find more detail in that chapter, but I'll present a summary here.

Figure 14.2 Setting the file transfer protocol in Windows' HyperTerminal

The settings on both machines must be the same. You can try to use a baud rate of 57,600 or 115200. On the null-modem connection, you may get errors in the data transmission if the baud rate is too high. If you use modems, they will negotiate the baud rate if the rate is too high for the cable to handle. You can set the link to use no parity, 8 data bits and one stop bit. Enable local echo if the software supports it. Don't forget to set both computers to recognize their respective serial ports.

You shouldn't have to go lower than 38,400. If you are going to set the software to use hardware handshaking, make sure both terminal programs are have been launched and turned on at the same time. Otherwise, you can turn off hardware handshaking.

After a link is established, you can use the terminal program to send files from one machine to the next. You have to select a file transfer protocol to use on both machines (Figure 14.2). ZModem should be your first choice if both terminal programs support it, as it will compensate for errors in transmission. After that, try XModem, YModem, and Kermit. Make sure MacBinary is *not* used if you are moving the file from a Mac to a PC. This setting could be under "file transfer method." MacBinary will save the data fork of a Mac file when moving files between two Macs, but will render the file unintelligible to Windows software. (For more on MacBinary, See Chapter 6.)

After the software indicates that a connection has been established, set the receiving computer to receive the file. In ClarisWorks, you do this by choosing Receive File from the Session menu. Finally, send the file from the sending computer. To send a file in AppleWorks (Claris-Works), select Send File from the Session menu. Then you set one computer to send, the other to receive. (For more information on using terminal emulation software to transfer files, see Chapter 12.)

Serial Null-Modem Connection

You can directly connect the serial port of the PC to a serial port of the Mac without using modems with a null-modem cable, which is similar to the crossover cable for Ethernet described later on. The wires in a null-modem cable switch to opposite pins on each connector. However, since a Macintosh and a PC don't use the same connector for their modem ports, a cross-platform null-modem cable will have different connectors at each end.

The benefit to a null-modem method is that you don't need an Ethernet card for the PC, and you don't need to have modems for either machine. It is slower than Ethernet, but is faster than the direct modem-to-modem method. Because it's not a network connection, you can't run standard networking software unless you use PPP, which will slow things down. The main drawback to a null-modem connection is that it requires a nonstandard cabling setup.

Buying a Null-Modem Cable for Mac and PC

Most PCs use a 9-pin (DB-9) connector. Some PCs have a 25-pin (DB-25) connector instead. The Mac modem port uses a round DIN-8 connector.) You have several options in creating a null-modem link.

You can buy a Mac-to-PC null-modem cable, or have one made. Cross-platform null modem cables are not common, however. If you want to use more standard, easier-to-obtain parts, you have a choice of several combinations of cables and gender-changing connectors:

- A standard Macintosh modem cable, a PC null-modem cable, and a DB-25 female–female gender changer.
- A standard Mac modem cable, a standard PC modem cable, and a PC null-modem cable.
- Other cables (camera or printer) that just happen to be null-modem cables with Mac DIN-8 and PC DB-9 connectors on them. You'll also need a gender changer.

There is an alternative to buying a Mac-to-PC null-modem cable or using a combination of standard parts. Oddly enough, this alternative is the simplest. You can find cables used for other purposes that happen to be null-modem cables and already have the Mac DIN-8 and PC DB-9 connectors on them. (This works if the PC has a DB-9 instead of a DB-25.)

One such convienient class of cables are the serial cables that come with some digital cameras (such as Agfa) to connect them to PCs. Some of these will work as a Mac-to-PC null modem cable, with the addition of a DIN-8 adapter. Another source that is close is a Mac 512K ImageWriter printer cable, which has a male DB-9 on one and, and the correct female DIN-8 on the other end. All you need here is a gender changer for the DB-9. Although Mac 512K machines haven't been sold in more than 15 years, you can still buy these cables from cable shops and cable companies on the Internet.

Building your own null-modem cable

If you need to moved data in a pinch or are a bit of a hobbyist, you can build your own null-modem cable. The easiest approach is to start with a Mac modem cable, cut off one end, and connect the wires from a PC modem cable attached to a DB-9 connector. You can twist the appropriate wires together, apply a little solder with a soldering iron if

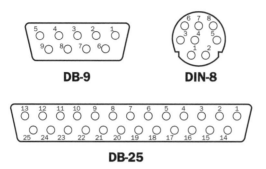

Figure 14.3 The pinouts of the female DB-9 (PC), male DIN-8 (Mac) and female DB-25 connectors from the view of looking at the cable connector

you have one, and cover each connection with electrical tape. (If you are good with a soldering iron, you can connect the wires directly to the connector. However, the leads on the DIN connectors are small and difficult to solder.) The pinouts of the connectors are shown in Figure 14.3.

To build the null modem cable from Mac to PC (DIN-8 to DB-9), use the following pinout connections:

Mac DIN 8   PC DB-9

1 to 8
2 to 4
3 to 2
4 to 5
5 to 3

You can use these pinout connections to build the null modem cable from DIN-8 to DB-25 (Mac to PC):

Mac DIN 8   PC DB-25

1 to 5
2 to 20
3 to 3
4 to 7
5 to 2
8 to 7

If you want to build a PC-to-PC null-modem cable, the pinouts are as follows:

DB-9 to DB-9

1 and 6 to 4
2 to 3
3 to 2
4 to 1 and 6
5 to 5
7 to 8
8 to 7

For software, you can use the Star Gate shareware utility or terminal emulators as described earlier

Direct Modem-to-Modem Connection

You can also transfer data between two computers by connecting the modems to each other. The advantage over the null-modem cable just mentioned above is that you don't have to worry about acquiring a special cable—you simple use a standard telephone cable. The use of modems also adds another layer of error correction beyond that of the file transfer protocol, but slows things down. You would use the same software as with a null-modem link.

The procedure for a direct modem-to-modem connection is very similar to the remote modem connection described in Chapter 12 and uses the same software—terminal emulation programs. The only difference is that modems are not communicating over the telephone system. You connect the modems of the two computers with an ordinary telephone cable with RJ-11 jacks.

Set the connection settings of both computers to be the same. Usually you can go with no parity, 8 data bits, and one stop bit. Set the baud rate at 57,600. The modems will negotiate the speed if needed. You can use a hardware handshake (DTR & CTS).

You can initiate the connection by typing modem AT commands in the terminal window. In ClarisWorks, select Open Connection from the Session menu to enable you to type modem AT commands. On the sending computer, type ATD. On the receiving computer type ATA. You can transfer files using the same procedure described in the previous section.

Making an Ethernet Connection without a Hub

You can create an Ethernet network between one Macintosh and one PC without an Ethernet hub. Not using a hub saves money, but doesn't take away from the fact that this configuration is a real Ethernet network running real networks protocols. It also means that you can run any networking software on the two machines that ordinarily works over Ethernet, including games, backup software, and the peer-to-peer cross-platform file sharing software described later in the chapter.

You create this mini-network by directly connecting the 10BaseT Ethernet ports of the two machines with a special Ethernet cable known as a "crossover cable." You can buy a crossover cable, also known as a "crossed cable," a "patch cable," or a "10BaseT crossover cable," at cable supply companies on the web or at retail stores. These cables have a standard RJ-45 plug at each end, with the pinouts reversed from an ordinary 10BaseT cable. Because you aren't using a hub to boost signals, you should use a heavy grade of wire for the crossover cable. Category 5 twisted-pair cable, the same grade used for 100BaseT, works well. Sometimes these are referred to as a *category 5 crossovers,* or *cat 5 crossovers.* Unlike ordinary Ethernet networks, you can't add any more nodes to this network without adding a hub (or Netopia's EtherWave hardware) and standard 10BaseT cabling.

NOTE: Sometimes both computers must be turned on at the same time, or a computer will see the Ethernet network as "missing."

You can also build your own cable, starting with a standard, category 5 twisted-pair cable and a pair of RJ-45 plugs. Looking at connector end with the cable running away from you and the tab down, the pins are numbered like this, starting from the left: 8 7 6 5 4 3 2 1

The pinouts to create a crossover cable are:

> 1 Tx+ — Rx+ 3
> 2 Tx- — Rx- 6
> 3 Rx+ — Tx+ 1
> 6 Rx- — Tx- 2

That is, pin 1 of one connector goes to pin 3 of the other connector, and so forth. The wire colors can differ, but you can note the colors of the wires by looking through the RJ-45 connector. Cut the cable, strip the wires, and rejoin the wires in the right combination. (Solder would be good, but you can twist the wires together.) If you really want to do it right, you can buy new RJ-45 cable connectors, and insert the wires into the tiny holes. This takes some practice, so buy several RJ-45 connectors.

Since this configuration is an Ethernet network, you configure the Mac and Windows PC to run Ethernet as you ordinarily would, as described in Chapters 8 and 9. And you can use some of the software we will now discuss.

Peer-to-Peer and Client Strategies

There are three client products that enable cross-platform network connections and file sharing—PC MacLAN from Miramar Systems, COPSTalk from Thursby Systems (formerly from COPS), and DAVE also, from Thursby Systems. All three differ from each other, but they represent two basic strategies—running Apple network standards on Windows machines (PC MacLAN) and running Microsoft network standards on the Macs (DAVE). There is no one best solution for everyone. (In fact, before Thursby System acquired COPSTalk, the people at Thursby Systems and Miramar Systems didn't really see each other as competitors. Both companies had told me that they often referred customers to each other if their own product didn't fit.) Which is best for you depend on your situation.

NOTE: You'll fine demo versions of both Thursby's DAVE and Miramar's PC MacLAN on this book's CD-ROM.

If you have mostly Macs and want to connect a few Windows machines, it makes sense to install PC MacLAN or COPSTalk on the Windows machines. This is also true if you don't have experience with Windows networking and are interested in taking advantage of AppleTalk's easy setup and maintenance. Here, you would add Apple Filing Protocol (AFP) file sharing to the Windows machines. AFP over TCP/IP is also an option if you don't want to run AppleTalk, or want faster file sharing.

If you want to support a few Mac clients on a mostly Microsoft network, it makes more sense to go the other way, to make the Macs part of the Microsoft network. This is what DAVE does. This is also a good solution if you don't want to add anything (including Services for Macintosh) to an NT server, or don't want to use AppleTalk on the network. This method installs Server Message Block/Common Internet File System (SMB/CIFS) file sharing on the Mac.

Miramar System's PC MacLAN

Miramar's PC MacLAN (http://www.miramarsystems.com) is an AppleShare compatible (AFP) networking application for Windows 3.x, Windows 95/98, and Windows NT. It provides two-way cross-platform file sharing and printing over AppleTalk, and one-way AFP over TCP/IP in the client beginning in version 7.1. As I've said in some of the previous chapters, AFP over TCP/IP is significantly faster than AFP over AppleTalk.

Over AppleTalk, Macs can access Windows drives or directories, and Windows can access Macs drives or folders as well as AppleShare file servers and printers. Over IP, Windows can access volumes on servers such as AppleShare IP and UNIX, and Open Door's ShareWay IP (see Chapter 13). Macs cannot access Windows machines over IP. (At the time this book was written, Miramar said it had no plans to add an AFP over IP server to PC MacLAN.)

PC MacLAN is a good solution for adding PCs to a mostly Mac network, enabling Windows machines to be full file serving and printing peers on a Macintosh network. However, if you want to be able to access Mac volumes from an NT Server console, you can run PC MacLAN alongside Services for Macintosh on an NT server. This also makes a good interim tool for people migrating from Mac to Windows.

MacWindows Tip

If you've previously installed COPSTalk on the PC, you'll need to completely remove all traces of it before installing PC MacLAN. The two are incompatible. PC MacLAN is compatible with Microsoft's AppleTalk Windows NT software.

Drivers and Clients

Personal MacLAN Connect consists of several pieces: AppleTalk drivers, file and print clients, a file server, and a print server. Starting with version 6.1, PC MacLAN implements the AppleTalk protocol as Windows 32-bit VxD drivers, which means it uses little of the PC's scarce conventional (or "lower") memory. Personal MacLAN Connect supports Windows ODI and NDIS network drivers, which enable the PC to run multiple protocols at once. This means you don't have to remove the PC from a Microsoft, NetWare, or other PC network in order to connect it to an AppleTalk network.

NOTE: On Windows 3.x PC MacLAN truncates Mac file and folder names to standard DOS 8.3 format. You can view the Mac long name and icon in the File Properties option of File Manager.

The PC MacLAN file and print client lets the PC access AppleShare-compatible AFP volumes and Printer Access Protocol (PAP) Postscript printers that are on AppleTalk networks. Although older version of PC MacLAN used a client interface to access Mac networks, the current PC MacLAN integrates the browsing of AppleTalk networks into the normal browsing locations within Windows. A Windows user can log onto an AppleTalk device through the Network Neighborhood. If you click the Entire Network icon, you'll see an icon called Miramar AppleTalk Network. If the AppleTalk network has zones, the Miramar AppleTalk Network window will display them. Clicking on a zone displays AFP volumes and AppleTalk printers, as shown in Figure 14-4. Double clicking on one of these brings up a logon window. You can also access AFP volumes from the Windows Explorer window and from within applications, and you can map Mac volumes to PC drive letters for easier access.

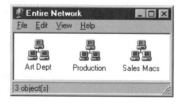

Figure 14.4 The PC MacLAN AppleTalk Network as seen in the Network Neighborhood shows AppleTalk zones.

PC MacLAN Print Client and Servers

When you double-click on an AppleTalk printer icon in the Network Neighborhood, the Windows Printer Wizard will come up to take you through a setup procedure. When finished, the Printer Wizard leaves you with a setup display of the printer, which will behave as a printer on a Microsoft network. PC MacLAN's AppleTalk Printer Utilities offers a number of functions. The utility lets you view fonts on the printer and download new fonts. You can also download Postscript files and change settings. The auto-spooling feature lets you select a directory in which to spool files to an AppleTalk printer. You can access the AppleTalk Utilities for a particular printer in Windows 95/98 or NT by right-clicking on a printer icon from the printer list and selecting "AppleTalk Printer Utilities" from the pop-up menu.

The Print Server allows Mac users to print to any PostScript printer available to the PC, including those attached directly to the PC's parallel port or on a PC network. A Mac user does this by selecting the printer from the Chooser. Print Server also spools print jobs from Mac and PC users. Mac users can print to non-PostScript PC printers with the addition of a printer language translator on the Mac, such as InfoWave's PowerPrint software, or by adding Zenographics' Super-Print to the Windows system. (See Chapter 15 for more details.)

MacWindows Tip

When printing from PC MacLAN on Windows to an AppleTalk printer, you'll get an error message if your document contains fonts not on the printer, and a font substitution will be made. (In Macs, the Printer Access Protocol normally downloads the fonts in a document from the Mac to the printer.) You can prevent this with PC MacLAN's Font Downloading feature. PC MacLAN allows the Windows user to check which fonts an AppleTalk printer has and download needed fonts. The fonts will stay in the printer's RAM until the printer is turned off or restarted. To do this, open AppleTalk Utilities. Select the Fonts tab and click on the "Get Font List" button. After waiting a short while for the fonts to appear, you can add fonts in the window below the font list. Click on the Add button and select the PFB files that you would like to download.

PC MacLAN File Server

The file server allows up to 10 AFP file sharing clients to access a Windows machine simultaneously. You enable file sharing and setup users and access privileges through the PC MacLAN Console (Figure 14.5). File Sharing works much like AppleShare file sharing on Macs (described in Chapter 8) and uses the same terminology. You can share any directory or drive media attached to the Windows PC from a button on the MacLAN Console.

Figure 14.5 The PC MacLAN Console

The security is more beefy than file sharing is in Mac OS, providing a way to set a maximum number of failed logon attempts and password expiration time, as well as an audit trail. You can also assign passwords and AppleShare access privileges much as you would on a Mac. In the PC MacLAN Console window, you access the Shared Directory window, which looks and acts much like Mac Finder's Sharing window (Figure 14.6).

Defining users and groups in PC MacLAN is much like it is on a Macintosh or an AppleShare server or personal file sharing on a Mac client. (It even uses the same icons to represent users.) Users can be Macs and other Windows systems running PC MacLAN.

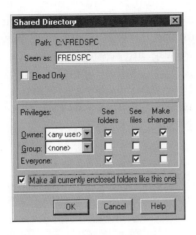

Figure 14.6 Assigning access privileges for a shared directory

Moving Files between Platforms with PC MacLAN

As always when moving files between Mac and Windows, PC MacLAN has issues and provisions concerning type and creator codes and file names (see Chapter 5 for more information). One of these provisions is a file extension mapping feature similar to that of Mac OS's PC Exchange and Windows NT Server's File Type Associations. This allows files created in Windows and moved to a Mac to have the correct type and creator codes, and therefore the correct icon.

In PC MacLAN, you assign a Macintosh type and creator to a Windows file and map it to a Windows extension at the same time. First, right-click a file and select Properties from the menu. When the Properties dialog opens, click the AppleTalk tab. Click the Edit Creator and Type button and type in the Macintosh codes. Click OK, and click the Edit Ext. Mapping button. The type and creator codes will show up with a field for you to type in a Windows extension.

Moving files the other way, from Mac to Windows, usually removes the resource fork containing the Mac type and creator codes. PC MacLAN's file server running on Windows allows Mac files to keep their resource forks by using an Association Index stored in the MacLAN subdirectory. This capability operates only when the Mac sends files through the MacLAN File Server. When a Windows user moves the file from a Mac drive mapped to a PC drive letter to a local PC drive, the resource and data forks will split.

MacWindows Tip

When you move a Mac file with a name that contains illegal Windows characters (? : / \ < > | ") to a Windows machine, PC MacLAN changes the character to its ASCII code value and puts it in brackets. For instance, a slash (/) would appear as [$A3]. Miramar's optional PC Migrator Utility can also help.

This usually isn't a problem, since a Windows user doesn't need the Mac type and creator codes. But if you are backing up Mac files to a Windows machine, you'll want to keep the type and creator codes for when you move the files back to Macintosh.

If you want to back up Mac files to a Windows machine, the Mac should first mount the shared PC MacLAN file server folder on the desktop and copy the data to the PC folder from the Mac. Next, the Windows user can copy the contents of the c:\maclan subdirectory into the backup location. Do not move Mac files and folders from the location from where they were copied.

To restore Mac files from the PC, restore the backup of c:\maclan to the c:\maclan subdirectory, overwriting the existing files. Make sure the directory where the Mac files were backed up is shared, and start PC MacLAN's File Server. From the Mac, mount the PC shared folder containing the files on the desktop and copy the files to the Mac.

To preserve the Association Index file that holds the Mac resource and data fork information, you'll need to exit the PC MacLAN File Server before shutting down Windows. Also, be sure to keep the Mac files in their original directory after backup.

PC Migrator

For moving large numbers of files from Macintosh to PC, Miramar offers an optional plug-in for PC MacLAN called PC Migrator. The software can move one or more volumes of Mac files to a Windows local drive or a file server volume while processing the file names for use on Windows. It cleans up file names, stripping out characters that are illegal in Windows and replacing them with a hyphen. PC Migrator also reads the type and creator codes of the Mac file and assigns the appropriate DOS file name extension. When PC Migrator comes across type and creator codes that aren't in its database, it prompts you to add a Windows file name extension to go with the codes. The extensions you add are then stored in the database.

COPSTalk

COPSTalk is another AppleShare-compatible (AFP) client for Windows 3.x, 95, 98, and NT. Originally created by COPS (and sold by the company for many years, COPSTalk was sold to Thursby Sytems in 1999.

COPSTalk differs from PC MacLAN in that it is not peer-to-peer, but is one way. It installs only an AFP client on Windows. Macs can not access the Windows machine. The printing story is similar— COPSTalk enables Windows machines to print to AppleTalk printers, but does not enable Macs to print to PC printers. COPSTalk is less expensive than PC MacLAN. COPSTalk supports AFP over Apple and also over TCP/IP in version 2.5.1 for Windows 95 and later and in the Windows NT version.

Logging on to an AFP server over AppleTalk or IP is similar to the way you do it in PC MacLAN. Go to the Network Neighborhood, click Entire Network, then AppleTalk Network. You'll be presented with the AppleTalk zones (if any) on the network. If there are no zones, you'll see a single icon. The AFP servers and printers will be listed inside the zone windows or the window of the single icon.

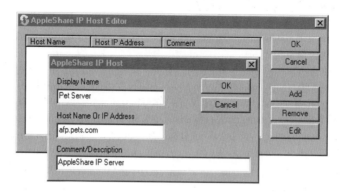

Figure 14.7 The COPSTalk AppleShare IP Host Editor lets you define the location of AFP servers on TCP/IP.

To enable you to log into an AFP server that supports IP or to an Open Door ShareWay IP gateway, you specify its location in a utility called the AppleShare IP Host Editor (Figure 14.7), which you'll find in the COPSTalk program group. When you first launch the Apple-Share IP Host Editor, it will list no servers. Click the Add button and type in an IP address or a host name, such as an AFP URL (see Chapter 13). You'll also want to include a description. Click OK. The utility will attempt to confirm the existence of the IP address and the host name.

The IP servers will now show up in the Network Neighborhood, in the AppleTalk Network window under an icon called AppleShare IP.

If you are accessing an AFP server that is available via both AppleTalk and IP, you don't have to register the server in the AppleShare IP Host Editor. You can browse the server in the network neighborhood (via AppleTalk) and connect to it. COPSTalk will switch the connection to TCP/IP. This is similar to the way the Macintosh AppleShare Client 3.7 and later accesses AFP servers that are available on both protocols.

Chapter 15 has additional information on printing with COPSTalk.

Thursby Systems' DAVE

In one respect, Thursby Systems' DAVE (http://www.thursby.com) is the exact opposite of PC MacLAN. While PC MacLAN turns a Windows PC into a complete Macintosh network peer, DAVE turns a Mac into a complete Microsoft network peer client. DAVE is Mac software that allows Macs to access Microsoft networks using Microsoft's SMB/CIFS (server message block/common internet file system) file and print sharing protocols via NetBIOS over TCP/IP. (See Chapter 9 for more information on NetBIOS.) DAVE also installs a server, allowing Windows PCs to access folders on Macs. Like PC MacLAN, DAVE can coexist with NT Services for Macintosh. (The book's CD-ROM contains an evaluation copy of DAVE.)

DAVE isn't just for peer-to-peer networks, but is a good way to connect Mac clients to a Windows NT Server. DAVE is a good solution for companies that don't want AppleTalk on their networks and don't want to install anything on their NT Server to accommodate Macs, including Microsoft Services for Macintosh. DAVE also has some advantages over Services for Macintosh. Since DAVE Mac clients are standard Microsoft Network clients, their user accounts are just standard NT user accounts, so they're easier to take care of than with SFM. And since you're running TCP/IP, file sharing is faster than it is with NT Server 4's Services for Macintosh. A Mac running DAVE can access network shares over NT's Remote Access Service, something that NT Services for Macintosh does not support. However, DAVE doesn't add MS-CHAP authentication, which isn't supported in Mac OS before OS 8.5. Older versions of Mac OS still can benefit from adding TunnelBuilder from Network Telesystems (http://www.nts.com).

MacWindows Tip

There was a known conflict between DAVE 2.0 and Aladdin's StuffIt Deluxe 4.5 that would cause desktop hard disk icons disappear and the Finder to freeze when you opened an alias of a Windows directory. The source of the problem was a StuffIt control panel called "True Finder Integration" version 4.5.1. Remove this control panel, and the problem disappears.

Installing and Using DAVE

There are a few trade-offs when using DAVE. Installation on the Macintosh is a bit complex and is best accomplished by an administrator trained in Microsoft networking rather than someone from the Macintosh side. After running the one-step installer, you need to configure a Mac's TCP/IP control panel, as well as DAVE's NetBIOS control panel. Though the setup instructions are well documented and explained in the manual, the NetBIOS control panel default settings should only be changed by someone who knows your Windows network. However, this is real Microsoft networking. The NetBIOS control panel (Figure 14.8) even lets a Mac register its IP address with a Windows Internet Name Server (WINS).

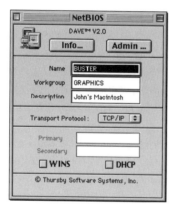

Figure 14.8 DAVE's NetBIOS control panel on a Mac

DAVE also installs a DAVE Access item in the Apple menu, which lets Mac users log in to a Windows NT Domain, a security service that provides authentication for accessing Windows NT Server resources. DAVE Access also lets you participate in Microsoft Messaging, a feature that isn't quite e-mail, in that you can't save, forward, or reply to messages. Microsoft Messaging is meant for sending short messages,

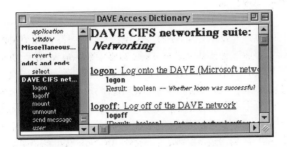

Figure 14.9 The DAVE Access AppleScript Dictionary supports mounting and unmounting shared resources.

such as "We're starting the meeting now." Windows can receive 1600 characters at most, Mac with DAVE can receive 255 characters.

Once DAVE is installed, the Mac user doesn't need to know anything about SMB or NetBIOS. The user logs onto a Windows machine by selecting Dave Client in the Chooser to get a list of Windows servers. Macs can access drives on Windows NT Server, NT Workstation, Windows 95/98, and Windows for Workgroups 3.11 or later. You can use Applescript to automate the process (Figure 14.9) Windows users can access Macs drives or folders via the Network Neighborhood.

Like NT Services for Macintosh and PC MacLAN, DAVE stores file names for Macs and Windows users. That is, it will shorten file names to the DOS 8.3 format required by some Windows applications, and will translate Mac characters that are illegal in Windows.

DAVE Printing

Like Services for Macintosh, DAVE enables Windows users to print to Postscript Macintosh printers. Mac users get access to shared Postscript printers, wherever they are on the Microsoft network. Postscript printers that are configured as shares show up in the Mac's Chooser. DAVE's print client acts as a gateway for the Mac's LaserWriter 8.x Postscript driver. The Windows machines that the printers are connected to do the spooling. DAVE doesn't add a driver for non-Postscript printers, but like PC MacLAN, works with SuperPrint from Zenographics, a Postscript interpreter.

Although DAVE does not use AppleTalk to communicate with printers, the Mac does need the AppleTalk driver installed in order to enable the DAVE print services. Since no AppleTalk packets need to go out over the network, you can use the Remote Only option in the AppleTalk Control panel of Mac OS 7.6 and later, and Open Transport 1.1.1 and later. (This is enabled by a Remote Only extension file.) This setting prevents any AppleTalk packets from being broadcast on the network. However, it is not required. DAVE can coexist with AppleTalk networks if desired.

(See Chapter 15 for more information about DAVE and printing issues.)

MacWindows Tip

DAVE is ordinarily fast, but you can increase the printing speed when using foreground printing as a default when printing through a DAVE print gateway. Normally, foreground printing is slower because it turns spooling off, causing you to wait until the printer becomes available. With DAVE, however, the print data is automatically spooled on the PC server, so there is no waiting involved. Because the print data never gets spooled to the Mac disk, but is sent out over TCP/IP to the PC spooler, printing is much faster than when using background printing.

What's Next

The previous discussion of printing with DAVE just touches on the issue of cross-platform printing, a topic that the next chatper will discuss in some depth. Chapter 15 covers some of the printing tricks you can do with PC MacLAN and DAVE. There are a variety of solutions that enable Macs and PCs to print to the same printers, including network and nonnetwork, Postscript and non-Postscript, AppleTalk and TCP/IP.

Chapter

What's in This Chapter:

- ♦ **Printer drivers**

- ♦ **Postscript and PCL**

- ♦ **Mac printing to PC printers**

- ♦ **Printing over TCP/IP**

- ♦ **Printing over AppleTalk**

- ♦ **Printing over USB and IrDA**

15

Cross-Platform Printing

The simple question, "How can I share a printer between a Mac and a PC?" isn't one that lends itself to a simple answer. It's not that the task is necessarily difficult—it can be as simple as plugging a printer, a Mac, and a PC into the same Ethernet segment. But there can be multiple answers to this question, depending on the type of printer you have, its capabilities, and your setup. And with a few printers, cross-platform sharing isn't practical.

Fortunately, you can boil down cross-platform printing into two basic items that a computer and a printer must have in common—the printer language and the physical connection. This doesn't necessarily mean that all the computers need to be running the same printer language over the same physical connection. Some printers can handle multiple languages over multiple ports.

407

The three most common printer language families are Postscript, Printer Control Language (PCL), and QuickDraw. Postscript is the only one that's actually cross-platform, but there are ways to use PCL in a cross-platform setting. QuickDraw is a Mac-only way to print to certain printers. There are also other printer languages used by specific printer manufacturers.

Physical connections to a printer include parallel, serial (Mac and PC), USB, and network links. A true network connection to a printer is one in which the printer is a stand-alone network node, not directly connected to any computer. However, printers connected directly to a server can appear as network printers. As with most other network devices, you have a choice of network transport protocols to use, depending what the printer or server supports. The printer or server must support the protocols the clients are using. TCP/IP printing is one way to share printers on a mixed-platform network; AppleTalk can be a solution for other networks.

Either way, you've still got to make sure you have a computer printer driver that uses a printer language the printer can understand.

Differences: Printer Drivers and Languages

Like applications, printer drivers are not cross-platform and must be native to one operating system. That is, you can't use Mac printer drivers on Windows and vice versa; you need to use native drivers for each. (In fact, you can't share some printer drivers between Windows NT and Windows 95/98.) Mac printer drivers are extensions files. Once placed in the Extensions folder of the System file, printer drivers will appear in the Chooser (shown in Figure 15.1).

Windows printer drivers are located in the System subdirectory of the Windows directory. Once you install and configure a printer using the Add Printer utility in the Printers window My Computer, an icon for the printer will appear in the Printers window (Figure 15.2). The

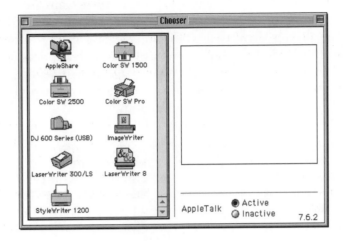

Figure 15.1 The Mac Chooser with printer drivers

driver installation procedure also adds lines of code to the win.ini file. The Windows Printers window differs from the Mac Chooser in that the icon represents an individual printer on a network or attached to the PC, where the Mac Chooser icons represent drivers. In Windows, you can change the printer driver to be used for a particular printer icon by right-clicking the icon to bring up the Properties dialog box.

Figure 15.2 The Printers window in Windows 98

In both operating systems, the printer driver translates an application's request to print a document into a set of commands for the printer. The printer driver tells the printer what's in the document using a printer language, also known as a page description language. Each printer driver uses one printer language, but some printers can understand multiple languages. Printers can also use the printer language to report information back to the computer.

NOTE: Unlike Mac OS, Windows requires you to do a driver installation for each printer you want to connect to. If the driver installation software is on the hard drive, you can use the Add Printer utility to configure additional printers. You will end up with an additional printer icon.

Macintosh printer drivers typically use either Postscript or Quick-Draw printer languages, and therefore use either Postscript or Quick-Draw printer drivers. The Chooser's standard LaserWriter driver is a generic Postscript driver that can print to most Postscript printers. (There is no need to install a different Postscript driver for each model of printer, though this is an option.) QuickDraw drivers, such as a StyleWriter driver, usually work for specific printers. All network printers that Macs can print to are Postscript printers. QuickDraw is used on lower-cost, nonnetwork printers, such as inkjet printers and some laser printers aimed at the home market.

Windows printer drivers typically use either Postscript or PCL (Printer Control Language). PCL is the most popular printer language, used on all types of printers over networks and attached to parallel ports. In fact, every Hewlett-Packard printer supports PCL. Some printers support both Postscript and PCL and can sense which is being used for an incoming print job.

On both Windows and Mac, there are also some proprietary printer languages, used for particular brands of printers. For instance, IBM has an inkjet printer language called IBM Proprinter. Epson uses its ESC/P language in many of its laser and inkjet printers. These printers come with Windows or Macintosh drivers that support the proprietary language. Occasionally, a printer with a proprietary language will also support Postscript or PCL.

Postscript is the best way to share printers in a cross-platform environment, including UNIX workstations. Using a printer that supports both Postscript and PCL can also be a good cross-platform solution in an office situation. However, Postscript is considered the top printer language for professional printers because it tends to yield the best results. It is also the best language for printing graphics.

PCL is a PC-only printer language, and QuickDraw is a Mac-only printer language. There are some ways to enable Macs to print using PCL, but the results aren't always as good as when Macs print with Postscript. Sometimes you can add Postscript to a PCL printer to Mac-enable it. Hewlett-Packard offers Postscript as an option for many of it's printers.

The next few pages take a closer look at Postscript and PCL and discuss how to use them in cross-platform environments.

Using Postscript

The Postscript page description language was invented by Adobe Systems in 1985 to describe the text, graphics, and formatting contained in a document to be printed. Before Postscript, most printers were so-called "line printers" and could only print text. That's because printer drivers would send a printer a list of text characters to print. Postscript was the first printing technology to describe the elements of a page mathematically. A Postscript driver, instead of merely telling the printer what characters or dots to print, gives the printer a mathematical description of an outline. The printer then fills in the outline with as many dots as it is capable of. This enables text to be printed at any size and style, and at different resolutions (dots per inch) on different printers. Postscript enables the easy printing of complex graphical images, including bitmap and vector drawings and scanned images.

MacWindows Tip

One way to enable Macs to access a PCL printer is to add Post-script to a printer that has Postscript as an option. In many Hewlett-Packard printers, you can add a Postscript SIMM, which comes with floppies containing Postscript drivers for Windows. You can find third-party Postscript cartridges for some printers.

There have been two major new versions of the language, Postscript Level 2 and Postscript Level 3. Both added new features for printers and increase the quality of output while retaining backward compatibility. For instance, Level 2 added faster background printing, support for JPEG compressed graphics, and improved color printing. Level 3, introduced in 1997, increased printing speed and color quality again and can produce smoother gradients with less banding.

Postscript drivers are backward compatible, so that a Postscript Level 3 driver can print to Level 1 and 2 printers. Similarly, a computer with a Postscript Level 1 driver will be able to print to a Level 3 printer, but won't get access to the newer features. The first version of the Mac's LaserWriter 8 driver, introduced with System 7.5, is a Postscript 2 driver. The LaserWriter 8 driver version 8.5.1 (which shipped with Mac OS 8.1) and later versions are Postscript 3 drivers.

NOTE: The Postscript page description language is not dependent on Postscript fonts. A Postscript print job can contain both True-Type and Postscript fonts. However, Postscript fonts may look better when printed on a Postscript printer.

Postscript drivers create the Postscript code that is sent to a raster image processor (RIP), also known as a Postscript interpreter, which turns the Postscript outlines into dots. In most office printers, the RIP is in the printer itself. In the publishing and prepress industries, the RIP often runs on a server computer on a network, which passes the "ripped" or rasterized image to a printer.

Though specific drivers for certain output devices can add functionality, many Postscript drivers can print to almost any Postscript output device, including a printer, or a RIP running on a network server, as well as high-end devices such as imagesetters, platesetters, and direct-digital presses. That's because the Postscript language is the same in every one of these devices, whether black-and-white or color. Level 2 and Level 3 just add more commands. Problems with Postscript often originate with the drivers in computers, particularly in Windows NT.

One such problem in a Mac driver is that the Mac version of AdobePS 8.3.1 Postscript driver is incompatible with Mac OS 8.5. The symptoms include a Mac freeze or printing errors. Apple recommends using LaserWriter 8.6 as your Postscript driver with OS 8.5, but you can use a later version of AdobePS as well.

MacWindows Tip

A printer described as "Postscript-compatible" may not actually use the Adobe Postscript language, but instead use a Postscript clone that is actually a proprietary printer language. With these printers, you can encounter Postscript incompatibilities that can result in printing problems with complex graphics.

PPD Files

Postscript Level 2 and 3 drivers for Windows and Mac OS come with a set of Postscript Printer Description (PPD) files. Each PPD file tells the driver about specific features of a particular printer model, such as multiple paper trays and what size paper they can hold and whether they can handle double-sided printing. A PPD file can also tell the driver about the supported resolutions and particular color parameters of a printer. If you don't have the PPD file installed, you won't be able to take advantage of these features.

Mac OS installs PPD files in the Preferences folder in the System folder. You choose a PPD file the first time you select a printer driver from the Mac Chooser for the first time. Select the LaserWriter 8 icon and click the Create button in the Chooser. The LaserWriter driver contacts the printer and chooses the correct PPD file for the printer. (You can also do this from the Desktop Printer Utility, or change the PPD file by clicking once on the desktop printer icon and select Change Setup from the Printing menu.)

A Windows Postscript driver installer will ask you to select a PPD file for the specific model of printer you are configuring. You can choose one from the list. If it's not in the list, click the Have Disk button and insert the floppy that came with the printer to add the PPD files.

Advantages of Postscript over PCL

In addition to working on both platforms, Postscript has a host of other benefits. This is why professional desktop publishing is still based on Postscript output. This could change in the future with the development of PDF (portable document format) and other technologies, but today, Postscript is still the best output format for professionals who need to get quality output, particularly of graphics. This because Postscript can produce superior printing results and give you access to more features than can PCL, particularly with color printing. Hewlett-Packard (HP) and Adobe, who both make Postscript drivers, agree on these points. The degree to which you'll see these benefits varies with the type of printer.

Network independence. Postscript can be printed over a variety of network types, including Ethernet, LocalTalk, and token ring. Postscript data can be transmitted using any network transport protocol, including TCP/IP, AppleTalk, or IPX/SPX. The Postscript driver doesn't care which protocol you use.

Better quality Postscript Type I font results. Postscript printers can give you smoother-looking text when you use Postscript Type 1 fonts, particularly at small and large sizes. Non-Postscript printers may give you jaggy curves with Type 1 fonts.

NOTE: For information about using and converting fonts for cross-platform use, see Chapter 5.

Better error reporting. Some versions of PCL can report printing errors back to the user, but Postscript (particularly Levels 2 and 3) can provide more in the way of messages about paper levels in trays, jamming, and so forth.

More font choices. Some printers support the use of Asian and other nonroman fonts when you print with Postscript, but not with PCL.

Speed. Printing large files with Postscript is faster than printing with PCL. Part of the reason is that Postscript is an efficient language. But Postscript also can compress data when transmitted over a network.

More repeatable colors. Postscript can produce more repeatable color on the same printer, and with less variation between different printers, inks, and paper than does PCL. When a document specifies that a color uses 56 percent magenta, that's how much magenta will be used on any color printing device. Some HP printers offer a Postscript-only feature called closed-loop color to boost color consistency.

Better-quality grays and blacks. On some color printers that use cyan, magenta, yellow, and black (C, M, Y, and K) inks, Postscript prints grays and black with a mixture of the C, M, Y, and K inks. PCL, which uses a set of commands called HP-GL/2 to draw graphics, only uses black ink. The use of multiple colors enables Postscript to deliver darker blacks and smoother grays with less banding than HP-GL/2.

Less visible dots. This varies with the printer, but Postscript delivers graphic images with less visible, more blended dots than does PCL's HP-GL/2, particularly with lighter colors. This is because Postscript's halftoning technology is more sophisticated than that of PCL.

Print effects from vector illustration programs. Vector illustration programs are those that use objects to describe images instead of dots. Adobe Illustrator, Macromedia Freehand, and CorelDraw each have certain effects, patterns, and types of lines that will not print correctly on a non-Postscript printer. Illustrator uses Postscript internally, and is the most affected. Bitmap illustration programs, such as Adobe Photoshop or Corel PhotoPaint, don't have this problem on non-Postscript printers.

Using Postscript on Windows

The Windows installation CD-ROMs come with a variety of drivers for different printers. You select a Windows printer driver from the Printers item of the Control Panel. If the driver you need to use isn't there, you'll need to install it. You can see a list of the drivers included with Windows Add Printer Wizard, which you bring up by double-clicking the Add Printer icon. To add a new driver that didn't come with Windows, click the Have Disk button and insert a floppy disk containing the driver. The exception are Adobe's Postscript drivers, which have their own installer.

NOTE: There is sometimes a problem with Windows NT printing to Postscript TCP/IP printers, where the Postscript code is printed instead of the actual document. This problem is described later in the chapter in the section called Configuring IP Printing on Windows NT.

Ghostscript

One way to enable different platforms to print to the same computer is to run a Postscript interpreter, which rasterizes a Postscript print job and sends it to a printer. Ghostscript is an open-source Postscript-clone interpreter available for Windows, Mac, Linux, UNIX, and OS/2. Ghostscript takes Postscript jobs from these computers and converts them to raster (dots) formats for a variety of printers that don't support Postscript. Ghostscript can also display a print job on screen. Ghostscript can also convert Postscript print jobs to PDF (Portable Document Format) files, which can be viewed on any platform. You can find Ghostscript on the web at:
http://www.cs.wisc.edu/~ghost/
   aladdin/index.html

Both Windows and Macs can benefit from using third-party Postscript drivers. For instance, by using the driver that comes with a printer, a user can sometimes specify trays and otherwise control the printer from the print dialog box. However, Mac OS's generic LaserWriter driver can usually print trouble-free to most Postscript printers. This is not true with Windows, where you can run into printing problems using the built-in Postscript drivers from Microsoft. This is particularly true for Windows NT 4.0 and earlier. In fact, professional publishers have been using more Windows 95 machines than NT because of Postscript problems with the latter.

Postscript print problems occur more often with more complex, larger documents that include graphics images. Complex print jobs can sometimes just stop in the middle of a job, generating Postscript errors. Other problems include fonts not printing and parts of images not printing correctly. Using a different Postscript driver can sometimes alleviate a printing problem. The next few pages describe some of the Postscript choices available for Windows.

NOTE: Windows Postscript driver files are usually called pscript.drv, regardless of the manufacturer.

Hewlett-Packard Postscript drivers

Hewlett-Packard includes Postscript drivers for Windows with its Postscript printers. While Windows comes with Postscript drivers for Hewlett-Packard printers, the HP drivers are sometimes newer than the Microsoft drivers included with Windows and can work better.

Adobe Postscript drivers

Adobe's drivers for Windows and Macintosh are called the AdobePS Printer Drivers. You can download AdobePS drivers from Adobe's web site at: http://www.adobe.com/prodindex/printerdrivers/main.html. The AdobePS drivers sometimes come with printers as well.

Many printing professionals recommend using Adobe Postscript drivers for Windows NT as well as for Windows 95/98. Adobe Postscript drivers will get you closer to trouble-free printing of complex documents, and handle color well. Since Adobe is the inventor of Postscript, the latest Adobe drivers are usually state-of-the-Postscript-art at any moment. Adobe drivers also work well with Adobe applications.

The drivers not only produce fewer printing problems with Windows, but add features, including watermarks and a plug-in architecture that lets you add custom modules to support special printer features. (See Figure 15.3.) AdobePS 4.2.4 was the first version to support Windows 98, and supports Windows 95 as well. Adobe has a separate version for Windows NT. AdobePS 5.0 was the first NT version to provide Postscript Level 3 functionality.

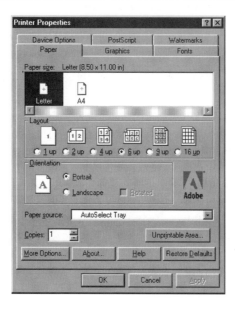

Figure 15.3 Advanced printing features available in Adobe's Postscript driver

Installing an Adobe Postscript driver is a little different from installing a Microsoft driver. You use the AdobePS Setup program (Figure 14.4) instead of the Windows Add Printer utility. Once you install the

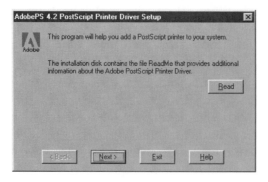

Figure 15.4 Adobe Postscript driver installer for Windows

Adobe driver installation software on your hard drive, you can add a printer with AdobePS by going to the Start menu, to the Programs item, then to the AdobePS item, where you select Adobe PS Setup Utility.

Computer Applications, Inc. (CAI) Postscript OnPage drivers

Most companies that produce printer drivers for Windows also produce printers, but CAI (http://www.caidesign.com) specializes in printer drivers and utilities for Windows and Macintosh. CAI offers Windows Postscript driver packages called OnPage NT and OnPage 95. (A Macintosh version is called OnPage II.) OnPage NT and 95 include a "universal" Postscript driver that uses Postscript Printer Description (PPD) files to basically create drivers for most Postscript printers, which get added to the Windows Print Manager driver list. There, they work as any other driver. The package comes with a printer utility that lets you download fonts and Postscript files to printers and configure the printer.

Zenographics SuperPrint

If you're looking for PC Postscript printing with a non-Postscript printer, SuperPrint (http://www.zeno.com) might be just the package for you. SuperPrint contains a Postscript Level 2 interpreter that rasterizes print jobs on the PC and then sends the jobs to non-Postscript printers. SuperPrint costs less than a raster image processor (RIP) server, yet gives Windows the quality and control of Postscript printing. Zenographics claims that SuperPrint replaces the printing architecture of Windows with a faster, higher quality one.

SuperPrint lets you preview print jobs, a handy feature that enables you to catch such surprises as a bad font substitution. You can also adjust the color to change the sharpness, contrast, saturation, grayscale, and dot gain, among other things. SuperPrint also has image filters that can make adjustments to graphics files automatically. In addition to the standard version, there are versions of SuperPrint specifically for more specialized output devices, such as film recorders, large format printers, thermal printers, and continuous tone devices.

In a cross-platform setting, SuperPrint can work together with Miramar's PC MacLAN software to enable Macs to print to non-Postscript printers. This procedure is described later in the chapter.

Using PCL

Today, all Hewlett-Packard printers include the PCL printer language, as do printers from many other printer manufacturers. Postscript comes with some of these printers and is an option on others. Even some Apple printers support PCL, which enables PCs to print to them.

Hewlett-Packard first created PCL for its character-based dot-matrix and inkjet printers. Since then, PCL has undergone a number of revisions. Hewlett-Packard introduced PCL 3 with its first laser printer in 1984, the LaserJet. In 1990, PCL 5 included HP-GL/2, a set of PCL commands for describing vector graphics. (HP-GL/2 is sometimes referred to as a printer language, but is a part of PCL.) PCL 5e boosted the resolution above 300 dots per inch (dpi). Today, PCL print jobs can travel over both network links and parallel ports.

Printers that support both PCL and Postscript are cross-platform printers, usually laser printers. These bilingual printers can sense what type of a print job has been sent and automatically switch between the two interpreters. Some older bilingual printers need to be told what printer language is being used through a manual setting. Auto-sensing PCL–Postscript laser printers are available from Hewlett-Packard, Apple, and many other vendors.

MacWindows Tip

Laser printers can run out of available RAM during a large or complex print job, which can cause the printer to stop without an error message. Most laser printers have expandable RAM in the form of SIMM or DIMM slots. This kind of printing problem can be harder to diagnose on non-Postscript printers, which generally don't have error reporting capabilities as good as those of Postscript printers.

Mac Printing to PC Printers

Macs can't ordinarily print to PCL printers that don't also support Postscript. However, there are software products you can add to the Mac that are enable Macs to print to PCL printers. These products include sets of Macintosh drivers and other support software for devices that normally don't support Macintosh. Usually, this software works by translating QuickDraw code to PCL commands.

Some of these PCL-for-Mac products can print over networks, while others come with cables or connectors to connect a Mac to a printer ports that don't exist on a Mac—the parallel port or PC serial port.

The quality of the output varies with the software and with the printer and generally isn't as good as Postscript. The QuickDraw-to-PCL translation also makes for a slower printing process. Plain text documents usually print okay, but the more complex and graphical the document, the more of a chance that you'll be unhappy with the print quality. Using Macs to print to PCL-only printers is not a practical solution for people in the professional publishing industry. However, for people printing memos, letters, reports, and other general office output, using PCL-enabling software on Macs can save you the cost of buying another printer for a Macintosh.

> **Web Update Link:** *For the latest information and URLs concerning these and other non-Postscript printing software for Mac, see http://www.macwindows.com/Network.html#Peer2Peer.*

PowerPrint

InfoWave
http://www.infowave.net

PowerPrint is the granddaddy of PCL print drivers for Mac. It wasn't the first tool for non-Postscript printing for Macs, but it has been around for over a decade, longer than any other similar product still in existence. Originally sold by a company called GDT, PowerPrint has been offered by InfoWave for several years. PowerPrint is a collection of Mac printer drivers and connecting hardware that enables Macs to print to more than 1400 types of non-Postscript PC-printers, including laser and inkjet, 32-bit color printers, and specialty printers, such as wide-carriage dot matrix printers and barcode printers. It can also print documents containing TrueType and Postscript fonts.

PowerPrint can print to PCL printers, such as HP LaserJet printers, as well as printers that use proprietary languages, including those from Epson. PowerPrint enables the Mac to speak these languages through a set of drivers for different printers. Using a particular driver, a Mac can print to that particular printer, or to a printer that emulates the original—that is, uses the same printer language or a clone. (A printer's manual often will list an emulated printer.) For laser printers, PowerPrint uses the PCL in HP's many LaserJet series printers. PowerPrint also supports inkjet printers, including HP DeskJets, Epson LQ, Canon BubbleJets, and printers that emulate them. PowerPrint even supports Epson dot matrix printer and printers that emulate them, including the Epson FX, LQ, and ESC/P2.

MacWindows Tip

To see if PowerPrint supports your printer, check InfoWave's Printer compatibility List at
http://www.infowave.com/print/infowave_printer_compatibilitylist.htm.

Some of the PowerPrint printer drivers let you choose the dot resolution of the output. Every driver supports the printer at its maximum resolution. On some printers, PowerPrint supports some advanced features, such as tray selection and handling, duplex (double-sided) printing, and scaling from 20 to 400 percent. On the HP DeskJet 890C, for instance, PowerPrint supports watermarks and color calibration through Apple's ColorSync. The PowerPrint drivers don't support nonprinting functions, such as fax, copy machine, or scanning features on multifunction machines.

There are three versions, PowerPrint and PowerPrint USB for a direct printer connections, and PowerPrint Networks (formerly PowerPrint Pro) for sharing a parallel printer over a network. PowerPrint comes with cable that converts a PC parallel port to a Mac serial port. The cable is intended for use with a single Mac, though you can share the printer using a standard parallel-port printer switching box. Power-Print USB comes with a USB-to-parallel cable for Macs with Universal Serial Bus ports, such as the iMac. PowerPrint Pro comes with a LocalTalk-to-parallel port connector that lets you share a parallel-port printer over an AppleTalk network.

The PowerPrint software runs on the Mac, but also uses RAM in laser printers. For 300 dpi print jobs, PowerPrint requires 1 MB of available printer RAM. It needs 4 MB of printer RAM for 600 dpi print jobs.

MacJet

Computer Applications, Inc. (CAI; part of Software 2000 Ltd.) http://www.caidesign.com and http://www.sw2000.com/

MacJet comes with a QuickDraw-to-PCL driver (translating Mac OS QuickDraw calls into PCL), as well as with some handy utilities. Unlike PowerPrint, which installs a separate driver for each different type of printer, MacJet puts a universal driver in the Chooser for all printers, but has a few versions for different types of physical connections. The MacJet driver prints to non-Postscript network printers, while the MacJet/S driver prints to PC serial and parallel printers. (The converter cables are not included with MacJet.) On Macs with a USB port (such as the iMac), MacJet/USB supports printing to USB printers that don't ordinarily work with Macs, such as the Hewlett-Packard DeskJet 895c. (CAI also sells MacJet/USB as a separate package.) MacJet also works over USB-to-parallel cables, though a cable isn't supplied.

MacJet can print with TrueType and Postscript fonts. The included Font Maker utility speeds the printing process by converting the fonts to HP-compatible printer fonts and sending them to the printer. You can set print resolutions from a control panel. You can preview a print job before you send it using a print-to-screen driver called Preview. MacJet includes Echo Utility, which lets you send custom commands to a serial or parallel printer. The utility will also store commands.

OnPage II

Computer Applications, Inc. (CAI; part of Software 2000 Ltd.)
http://www.caidesign.com and http://www.sw2000.com/

OnPage II is actually a Postscript Level 2 driver, but lets you print to
Postscript printers that are ordinarily PC-only, with only parallel ports
and PC serial ports. Like the Windows version, OnPage II for Macs
uses PPD files. An included utility lets you send Postscript files to a
printer.

Using PC MacLAN to Share PC Printers with Macs

Running Miramar's PC MacLAN networking software on Windows
can help Macs access non-Postscript printers as well as printers with
only parallel ports. PC MacLAN enables two-way cross-platform file
and print sharing between Macs and Windows over AppleTalk. With
PC MacLAN running on the Windows machines, and with the PC
connected to an AppleTalk network, Macs can access a PCL printer
connected to the PC's parallel port.

(See Chapter 14 for a more general description of PC MacLAN, and
look on this book's CD-ROM for an evalution copies of PC MacLAN
for Windows 95/98 and Windows NT.)

An advantage to this approach is that it enables both the Mac and
Windows machine to access the printer. However, PC MacLAN does
not provide PCL driver software for Macs, so you will still need software. There are two choices: You can run InfoWave's PowerPrint Pro
on the Macs, or you can run Zenographics SuperPrint on the PC.

Using PC MacLAN and PowerPrint

As mentioned earlier, InfoWave's PowerPrint enables Macs connected
to an AppleTalk network to access a non-Postscript PC printer. When
you use PowerPrint Pro on the Macs with Miramar's PC MacLAN on
the Windows PCs, then both Macs and Windows machines can also
access the printer over AppleTalk.

Miramar Systems has certified that InfoWave's PowerPrint Pro (the network version) is compatible with recent version of PC MacLAN. This includes PC MacLAN Pro for Windows 95/98 v7.0 and v7.1; PC MacLAN for Windows 95/98 v6.1 and v6.2; and PC MacLAN for Windows NT v4.0. It should also work with later versions as well.

The first thing you need to do is to create a new spooler in the PC MacLAN Print Server. Here's how you do that:

1. In the PC MacLAN Print Server, click the Spooler menu and select Create New Spooler.
2. Give the printer a name.
3. Type `Printer_Adapter` in the Type field.
4. Check the Windows Printer radio button.
5. If the printer is connected directly to the PC, select either LPT1 or LPT2. If it is a network printer, capture the printer to an LPT port and then select it.
6. Select the file defprtr.ppd as the PPD file.
7. Save the spooler.

You now need to configure the Macs so that print jobs are sent to this PC MacLAN spooler. In the Chooser, select the PowerPrint Pro LT driver. Now select the printer and close the Chooser. (The PC MacLAN spooler must be running.)

Using PC MacLAN and SuperPrint

As described earlier in the chapter, SuperPrint is a Postscript interpreter for Windows clients that enables PCs to print Postscript jobs to non-Postscript printers. If the Windows PC is also running the PC MacLAN Print Server, then SuperPrint will accept Postscript print jobs from Macs and other Windows PCs and pass them on to non-Postscript printers. The PC MacLAN Print Server (located in the PC MacLAN program group) is an AppleTalk Printer Access Protocol (PAP) server for Windows 95/98 and Windows NT. You'll need PC MacLAN 6.0 or later.

To set up the packages to use together, you should install PC MacLAN first on the PC. When you install SuperPrint, make sure SuperPrint's Masquerade Postscript conversion program is part of the installation process. Masquerade is included in the full installation of SuperPrint. During the installation procedure, you'll select a non-Postscript "SuperDriver" for your printer. SuperPrint non-Postscript drivers have a "(Z)" after the printer name. This non-Postscript driver will communicate with the printer in its native printer language (such as PCL).

NOTE: If you have SuperPrint 5.0, Miramar Systems recommends you also install a Zenographics patch file called 4update.exe. You can download it from http://www.zeno.com/tech/sp50upd.html.

You will also need to configure a Postscript driver with SuperPrint. Basically, SuperPrint uses Masquerade to accept a Postscript print job from the Postscript driver, convert it to the printer's native language, and pass it off to the non-Postscript printer.

Configuring the Postscript driver for use with SuperPrint and PC MacLAN requires several steps. You start installing a standard Windows Postscript driver using the standard Windows Add Printer command. (From the Start button, click Settings and then Printers.) When you get to the list of drivers, select the Apple LaserWriter driver, and click Next. (You'll later need to insert the Windows CD-ROM.) You should choose not to print a test page. Because you aren't actually going to print to a Postscript printer, you need to delete the Apple LaserWriter printer without deleting the Postscript driver. You do this in the Printers window by selecting Apple LaserWriter and hitting the delete button. A message box will come asking you if you want to delete files that are no longer needed. The files the message is referring to include the pscript.dvr driver file, which you actually do need. Click the No button in the message box.

You now have to configure Masquerade to create a new Postscript driver that will convert the Postscript print jobs for the non-Postscript driver you've installed. Launch Masquerade from the SuperPrint program group in the Windows Start menu. You'll see the pscript.dvr file you just installed highlighted in the Postscript Drivers box. In the Non-Postscript Printers box, select the non-Postscript SuperPrint driver you installed—the one with the (Z) at the end of the name. Click the Install button. Masquerade will create a new Postscript driver ending in (Z) (PSCRIPT), such as "HP LaserJet 4MP (Z) (PSCRIPT)." This driver, and the non-Postscript SuperPrint driver will now show up in the Printers window.

Masquerade also creates Postscript Printer Description (PPD) files that appear in the Windows System directory. To enable the PC MacLAN Print Server to work with SuperPrint, you need to copy the these PPD files (ending in "Z.PPD") to the MACLAN directory.

Next, you'll need to create a new spooler within the PC MacLAN Print Server. Here's how:

1. In the PC MacLAN Print Server, click the Spooler menu and select Create New Spooler.
2. Give the printer a name. (The Type field displays the word "LaserWriter." You can leave this as it is.)
3. Scroll the Printer box until you see the SuperPrint Postscript driver you created, the one ending with (Z) (PSCRIPT). Select it.
4. Scroll the PPD File box until you see the .PPD file for your printer. (This is one of the files you copied from the Windows System directory to the MACLAN directory.) Select the PPD file.

The PC MacLAN Print Server window will display the printer's name and the (Z) (PSCRIPT) driver "on port ZPS1" and will designate the printer as running. Macs can now send Postscript jobs to this PCL printer.

NOTE: There is a problem with certain versions of PC MacLAN for NT that requires a patch for use with SuperPrint. The patch is called ATSPOOL.EXE and is available at:
http://support.miramarsys.com/techsupp/patches.htm.

Printing to PC Printers with Thursby's DAVE

Thursby's DAVE software for Macintosh enables Macs to print to Postscript printers connected to Microsoft networks and PC servers, but it does not allow Macs to print to PCL printers. Unlike PC MacLAN, DAVE does not work with add-on PCL drivers for the Mac. That's because the DAVE Print Client can use only the Mac's LaserWriter 8 driver, a Postscript driver.

(As is explained a little later, DAVE is useful for printing over TCP/IP networks.)

QuickDraw Printers and Windows

QuickDraw printers don't have a rasterizing engine of their own. The Mac does the rasterizing, using QuickDraw, the same basic Mac OS technology that draws screen images. On a Mac, each QuickDraw printer has a specific printer driver that translates the QuickDraw calls into commands for the printer. Apple's StyleWriter inkjet printers are QuickDraw printers, as are the old dot-matrix printers, the ImageWriters. There are some older Apple LaserWriter models that are QuickDraw printers only and that don't support Postscript or PCL. Many of these begin with the word Personal, as in *Personal LaserWriter SC.*

Unfortunately, there is no way to enable a PC to print to a QuickDraw printer directly. There aren't any drivers or utilities that can create QuickDraw-compatible printer commands on Windows, and most Quick-Draw printers don't have network ports or PC parallel ports. The interface is usually a Macintosh serial port.

A NeXT QuickDraw

QuickDraw printers aren't the only devices to rely on the computer and operating system to create the image of the page. LaserMaster's WinPrint-ers, which are Windows-only printers, work in a similar way. So did Steve Jobs's old NeXT laser printer, which was not a home printer. As NeXT computers were almost always networked, and the NeXT laser printer put a heavy load on the host computer, the NeXT printer usually ended up on a computer dedicated to the task. In a sense, the real cost of this printer included that of the host computer.

You can share some Apple QuickDraw printers with other Macs through the use of the Printer Share extension file, which comes with Mac OS. When you make a QuickDraw printer available over a network, the Mac it is connected to will be called to do work every time someone sends a print job to the printer. Unfortunately, although there are ways to enable Windows machines to access AppleTalk printers (Windows NT Server, for instance), there are no Windows drivers for QuickDraw printers.

The Apple printers that can't be shared with Windows PCs because they are QuickDraw-only include the StyleWriters, the LaserWriter IISC, Personal LaserWriter LS and SC, Personal LaserWriter 300, and LaserWriter Select 300.

TCP/IP Printing

Just as the TCP/IP and its related Internet protocols are cross-platform, so are the most popular printing protocols for TCP/IP. The Line Printer Remote/Line Printer Daemon protocols (LPR/LPD) were originally created for BSD UNIX. Today, LPR/LPD has been implemented in Mac OS, Windows, and most other operating systems though an industry specification known as RFC 1179. Windows can print to TCP/IP printers using other methods, but LPR/LPD is how Macs print over TCP/IP. The term LPR is usually associated with the client print command, and LPD refers to the software that receives the print commands, either on a printer server or on a printer. LPR print jobs can use either PCL or Postscript printer languages, or pass along straight text (as in a line printer). Along with the print job, an LPR computer also sends a control file to the LPD printer or server.

Both the printer and the computer operating system need to be able to support LPR/LPD and IP. On the operating system side, most flavors of UNIX support LPR and LPD. Windows NT Workstation and Server support LPR printing. Windows NT Server also acts as a LPD server. Windows 95 and Windows 98 don't include LPR/LPD printing, but it can be added with third-party software.

Mac OS 8.1 was the first version of Mac OS that could print using LPR because it included LaserWriter 8 driver 8.5.1, the first driver to supports both LPR over TCP/IP and the Printer Access Protocol over AppleTalk. You can use the LaserWriter driver version 8.5.1 on versions of Mac OS dating back to 7.5, except for Mac OS 8.0. That is, LPR printing does not work in Mac OS 8.0, even with LaserWriter 8.5.1 installed. The LPR solution for OS 8.0 is to upgrade to OS 8.1.

On Macs, there are some drawbacks to LPR printing on IP. These entail giving up some features that are available with printing on AppleTalk via the Printer Access Protocol (PAP). First, Mac users won't be able to browse IP printers. That is, IP printers don't show up in the Chooser. To connect to an IP printer, Mac users have to know its IP address. However, you can create a desktop printer manually. Fortunately, you only have to enter the IP address once, as you do in Windows NT. Another drawback to LPR is that it doesn't have the features of PAP printing, such as the ability to report status information. This includes errors such as out of paper, missing paper tray, and the status of the printer, such as busy or idle.

NOTE: There are methods of using LPR over IP to print to printers that support only AppleTalk and PAP. These methods are discussed later in the section on AppleTalk printing.

Setting Up TCP/IP on a Printer

Most laser printers from Hewlett-Packard and other manufacturers support IP printing. Even Apple's more recent LaserWriter printers support IP printing, including the LaserWriter 8500, 16/600 PS, and 12/640 PS, and the Color LaserWriter 12/600 PS and 12/660 PS. (These printer support both Postscript and PCL.) You can also print to print servers using LPR. If your printer has both Ethernet and LocalTalk ports, you must use the Ethernet port for LPR/LPD print jobs, since LocalTalk does not support TCP/IP.

Just as with a computer, a printer connected directly to the network needs an IP address. Some printers start with a default IP address, such as 0.0.0.0. You can add or change an IP address manually, or you can enable the printer to get an IP address using a DHCP server. However, it is usually best to assign a static IP address to the printer, considering that Mac users have to know the IP address to print to it. If the printer is connected directly to a print server, it sometimes uses the IP address or domain name of the server.

To set or change an IP address of a printer, you usually use software on a Mac or PC with the printer connected to a parallel or serial port. (With Apple IP printers, you usually use the Apple LaserWriter Utility on a PC or Mac.) With printers that have a default IP address or can use DHCP, you can often telnet to the printer from any computer to set a static IP address. You can also often use a utility that came with the printer.

MacWindows Tip

Some TCP/IP software requires you to enter a socket number for the IP printer. The LPR/LPD specification, RFC 1179 calls out the number IP socket number 515 for printers. Some printers (including Apple LaserWriters) use 515 as their default.

Configuring IP Printing on Mac

To configure IP printing on Mac OS, you need the LaserWriter 8.5.1 driver or later. This extension file comes with Mac OS 8.1, but works with older versions of Mac OS, except for Mac OS 8.0. You can download LaserWriter 8 drivers from the Apple web site at http://til.info.apple.com/swupdates.nsf/search. (LaserWriter 8.5.1 can also print to AppleTalk printers.)

Configuring printers on a TCP/IP network in Mac OS has some similarities to "installing" printers on Windows clients. Because TCP/IP printers don't appear in the Mac's Chooser, you have to create a icon for each printer. (Unlike Windows, you don't have install a different driver—LaserWriter 8.5.1 and later can print to most Postscript printers, regardless of what network they're on.) You'll need to know the IP address of the printer before you can create the printer icon, called a Desktop Printer. The Desktop printer icon first appears on the Finder desktop, but you can move it to any folder.

The printer and the Mac both need to be connected to the network and running when you create the Desktop Printer icon. You create desktop printer icons for one or more IP printers using Desktop Printer Utility. You can usually find it in a folder called Apple LaserWriter Software, which is installed in the Apple Extras folder.

1. Open Desktop Printer Utility and select "Printer (LPR)" from the list. Click OK. (See Figure 15.5.)
2. A new window will open. In the top section, "Postscript Printer Description (PPD) File," click the Change button.
3. A list of printers will appear. Select your printer from the list. (This will select a Postscript Printer Description (PPD) file in your system folder.) Click the Select button. Your printer will be displayed, as in Figure 15.6.
4. Click the Change button next to *Internet Printer.*
5. In the Printer Address field, type in the IP address or domain name of the printer (Figure 15.7).
6. You can enter a queue name if you have one, or leave the field blank.

Figure 15.5 The first step in creating a TCP/IP desktop printer with the Mac's Desktop Printer Utility

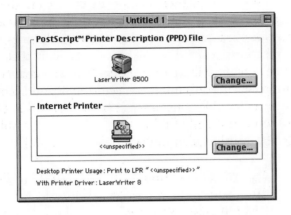

Figure 15.6 A selected PPD file in the Desktop Printer Utility

7. Click the Verify button. The utility will attempt to send a message to the printer. It will display an error message if it can't find the printer. Click the OK button.
8. Select Save from the File menu.
9. The Save dialog appears. The IP address of the printer will appear in the name field. You can keep this as the desktop printer's name, or type in any name you want. Click Okay.
10. An icon for the printer will appear on the desktop. You can now quit the Desktop Printer Utility.

```
┌─────────────────────────────────────────┐
│           Internet Printer               │
├─────────────────────────────────────────┤
│ Specify the Internet printer you are printing to │
│ (using domain name or IP address)        │
│                                           │
│ Printer Address: │159.143.162.002│       │
│        Queue: │                 │        │
│ The printer cannot be verified.           │
│                                           │
│    ( Verify )    ( Cancel )   ( OK )      │
└─────────────────────────────────────────┘
```

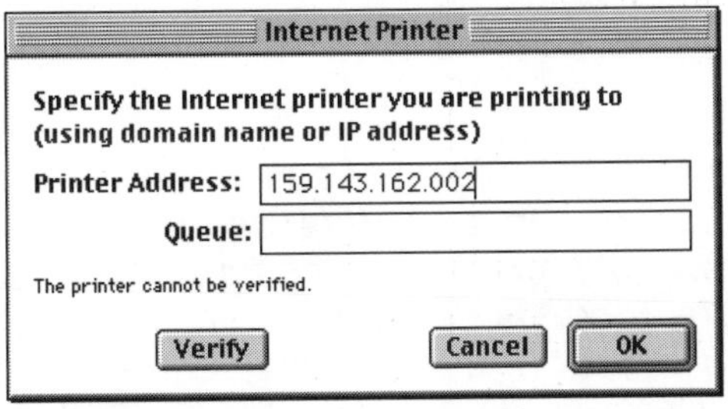

Figure 15.7 Entering a printer's IP address in the Desktop Printer Utility

Enabling TCP/IP printing does not affect AppleTalk printing. You can still create desktop AppleTalk printers if needed. You can print files to any desktop printer icon by dragging the files to the printer icon. Applications will print to the printer icon that is the default printer. The default desktop printer icon has a thick line around it. To make a printer the default printer, select its icon and hit command-L.

IP Printing with DAVE on Macintosh

If you have a Windows network, Macintoshes running Thursby's DAVE will have access to Postscript printers on the Microsoft network over TCP/IP. As discussed in Chapter 14, Thursby's DAVE is Mac software that uses NetBIOS over TCP/IP to give Macs access to Windows network resources. DAVE includes a Print Client that is a kind of gateway that interacts with the Macs' LaserWriter 8 driver and spools Postscript print jobs to shared Windows printers. The Print Client displays the Windows printer in the Chooser, which ordinarily only displays AppleTalk printers, and handles Postscript Printer Description (PPD) files in the standard Mac OS manner.

The DAVE Print Client does not include LPR functionality, but can give Macs access to LPD printers through a PC running Windows NT Workstation or Server. In this setup, you would configure Windows NT to access an LPD printer or print server, and then set the printer as a shared device. (This configuration is described in the next section.) The Macs running DAVE would then send print jobs to the NT machine using Microsoft protocols, and the NT machine would then send the print job to the printer using LPR.

MacWindows Tip

Because the DAVE Print Client uses the LaserWriter 8 driver, it cannot print to non-Postscript printers. This also mean that in order to print to Windows printers, the Macs must have AppleTalk turned on, even though TCP/IP is being used. Fortunately, you can keep AppleTalk off of your Ethernet network. In the AppleTalk control panel, set the Connect Via pop-up menu to Printer Port, Modem Port, or Remote Only. The last choice blocks the Mac from accessing any LocalTalk printer directly.

Configuring IP Printing on Windows NT

Windows NT Workstation and Server (and Windows 2000) can print to LPD servers and printers using LPR. Windows NT Server comes with an LPD server. You can add LPR/LPD printing to Windows 3.x, 95, and 98 with a variety of add-on utilities. You can also use Windows NT to share an LPD printer with Windows 3.x, 95, and 98, as well as with Macs running Thursby's DAVE (for Postscript printers) through the standard Microsoft network. When adding the printer in Windows NT, you would select Share This Printer on the Network. In this case, Windows NT acts as a Microsoft network print server (as opposed to an LPD server) for other PCs.

To enable LPR/LPD printing on Windows NT, you need to install the basic TCP/IP protocol with the service called Microsoft TCP/IP Printing. You can then create a TCP/IP printer in NT using the Printer item of the Control Panel, just as you would create any other printer on a standard Microsoft network. After you create the printer in NT, you'll need to use NT's LPR utility at the command line to print Postscript jobs.

To create a TCP/IP printer in Windows NT 4, follows these steps:

1. Open the Printer Window in the Control panel and click Add Printer.
2. Select My Computer to manage the printer. Click the Next button.
3. Click the Add Port button.
4. Select LPR Port from the list and click the New Port button.
5. In the box called Name Or Address Of Host Providing LPD, type the IP address or the DNS name of the printer (if it is a stand-alone network printer) or of the computer to which the printer is connected. (The DNS name can be specified in the Hosts file if necessary.)
6. In the field called Name of Printer, type the name of the printer or of the print queue on the server.
7. Click the OK button.
8. Click the Close button to close the Printer Ports window.

9. Click the Next button.
10. From the list of drivers, choose printer manufacturer and the printer model. Click the Next button.
11. Type a Windows name for the printer and click the Next button.
12. If you want to share this printer with other Windows machines that don't have LPR functionality (and Macs running DAVE, if the printer supports Postscript), click the Shared radio button. If not, make sure it's unchecked.
13. Click the Next button, and then click the Finish button.

You can also use the Windows NT LPR Connectivity Utility at the NT command print to print a file to an LPD server or printer. The command looks like

```
LPR -S<server> -P<printer> [-oOptions] [-CClass]
[-JJobname] filename
```

where `-CClass` contains the content of a banner page, and `-JJobname` is the name of this particular print job.

You can run into a problem with Postscript jobs, where the Postscript code is being printed instead of the document. In this case, you should use the "l" option of the o switch (`-ol`) to specify that the print file be passed on to the printer. Otherwise, NT's LPDSVC service prefaces the print job with a reset command, which can sometimes cause the LPD printer or server to interpret the Postscript job as a text file. The command would look like this (without the brackets):

```
LPR -S <server> -P <printer> -ol <filename>.PS
```

LPR/LPD Printing for Windows 3.x/95/98

Windows 3.x, 95, and 98 don't come with LPR printing, but can access an LPD printer through Windows NT. If you don't have Windows NT, you can add LPR functionality through third-party software. Utilities that enable Windows 3.x, 95, and 98 to print over TCP/IP using the LPD/LPR protocol run the gamut from public domain (free) utilities, to inexpensive shareware, to complete connectivity packages costing over $500. Generally, you will find LPD/LPR functionality in software that connects Windows to UNIX, including NFS and FTP tools. The main thing to look for in a Windows LPR-enabler for a cross-platform network is compatibility with the RFC 1179 specification. Compatible packages will often list adherence to the spec as a feature.

There are dozens of packages available. I'll just list a few of them. This is by no means meant to be a list of the best LPR enablers for Windows, but is instead a sampling of what's available.

Public domain

There are web sites and FTP sites that contain free Windows utilities for LPR printing. An LPR/LPD utility called WINLPD for Windows 95, 98, and Windows NT is available at
http://www.winsite.com/info/pc/win95/netutil/winlpd.exe/

Another utility called WLPRSPL v4.0c (the file is called wlprs40c.zip) is a WinSock-based printer/spooler for Windows 3.1 and Windows 95/98. It's at ftp://ftp.cdrom.com/pub/win3/winsock/wlprs40c.zip.

Remote Print Manager

Brooks Internet Software, Inc.
http://brooksnet.com/

Remote Print Manager is a shareware LPD print server for Windows 95, 98, and NT that uses TCP/IP networking. The server allows you select any printer that Windows can see. It also includes the LPR printing to send jobs to other IP printers. After you set up Remote Print Manager, it can run in the background by itself.

Omni-Lite

XLink Technology
http://www.xlink.com/

Omni-Lite is a relatively inexpensive package available for Windows 95, 98, and NT that adds an NFS (UNIX file sharing) client as well as an LPR/LPD client and server. The LPR client gives you a graphic interface for printing jobs, and the LPD server accepts print jobs for printers connected to the PC.

AppleTalk Printing for Windows

As enticing as the benefits of TCP/IP networks are, there are situations when you might want use AppleTalk for printing. For instance, you might want Windows PCs to print to Mac network printers that don't support TCP/IP. People adding a few PCs to an established AppleTalk network might prefer to stick with the easy setup and maintenance of AppleTalk. Mac clients can get better feedback from printers (in the form of error messages about printer jams and paper levels) on AppleTalk than on TCP/IP. This might be a reason not to switch everything to TCP/IP. Or, you might want to enable the PCs to print to AppleTalk printers while you transition the network to TCP/IP.

Whatever the reason, there are several strategies for printing from Windows to AppleTalk printers. One way is with a print server. In this case, the Windows PCs might communicate with the server using Microsoft protocols, and the server communicates with the printers via AppleTalk. Another strategy is to enable Windows to print directly over AppleTalk, using either PC MacLAN from Miramar Systems or COPSTalk from Thursby Systems. This entails using AppleTalk's Printer Access Protocol (PAP), the rough equivalent of TCP/IP's LPR/LPD. When you enable Windows to print directly to PAP printers, users get the benefit of the printer status reporting of AppleTalk. Keep in mind that all AppleTalk printers are also Postscript printers, so the Windows PCs will need the appropriate Postscript drivers.

Print Servers

A print server can act as a network gateway, allowing a Microsoft network of Windows computers to access printers on an AppleTalk network. One of the most popular platforms for this type of printer server use is Windows NT Server. Chapter 11 describes how to set up the MacPrint print server in NT Services for Macintosh to enable Windows machines to print to printers on an AppleTalk network connected to the server. (In this case, Services for Macintosh is actually providing a service for the Windows clients.) There are also a number of print servers for Windows NT that can provide the same access to AppleTalk printers. Print servers for other platforms are also widely available. These include Novell NetWare, AppleShare IP running on Mac OS, and several UNIX-based systems (see Chapter 13 for further information).

As well as providing cross-platform printing connectivity, higher-end print servers can provide other features, such as Postscript RIPs (raster image processors) and OPI (Open Prepress Interface) servers. Because of its superior speed, the TCP/IP protocol tends to be used in prepress and professional publishing environments, but support of older AppleTalk-only printing devices is common.

Built-in AppleTalk Printing in Windows NT/2000

Windows NT Workstation, NT Server, and Windows 2000 come with the AppleTalk transport protocol and PAP support, enabling them to print directly to AppleTalk printers. (Windows NT Workstation supports only PAP printing over AppleTalk. It not include an AppleTalk file sharing client or server.)

Setting up Windows NT Workstation to print involves installing the AppleTalk protocol and printer. To add the protocol, you need to be logged in as an administrator. The procedure in NT Workstation 4.0 is this:

1. Right-click the Network Neighborhood icon and select Properties from the pop-up menu. The Network dialog will appear.
2. Click the Protocols tab and click the Add button.
3. Click on AppleTalk Protocol in the Select Network Protocol field. Click OK. Windows will install the protocol.
4. Click the Close button in the Network dialog. A dialog box called Microsoft AppleTalk Protocol will appear.
5. As the default AppleTalk zone, select the one that contains the AppleTalk printer you want to print to. Click OK.

You will have to reboot Windows NT in order to use AppleTalk printing. After that, you can install the printer. As usual, you will need to log on as an administrator. Installing an AppleTalk printer is similar to installing other printers, but you do need to add a port:

1. From the Start button, select the Printers item from the Settings listing.
2. Double-click the Add Printer icon in the Printers window to launch the Add Printer Wizard.
3. Click the radio button labeled My Computer. Click Next.
4. Click the Add Port button.
5. Select AppleTalk Printing Devices in the Printer Port window. Click the New Port button.
6. Select the printer you want to print to from the list of available AppleTalk printers. Click OK.
7. A message will ask you if you want to capture this device. You'll probably want to click No. If you click Yes, the printer becomes unavailable to any other computers on the network, including Macintoshes.
8. Close the Printer Port dialog. This returns you to the Add Printer Wizard, where you can continue as usual.

PC AppleTalk Printing with DAVE for Macintosh

In addition to enabling Macs to access Postscript printers connected to PCs (as noted earlier in the chapter), Thursby's DAVE running on a Macintosh allows Windows to print to a Postscript printer on an AppleTalk network. DAVE doesn't put AppleTalk on the PCs, but puts Microsoft networking protocols on the Macintosh, and even uses the Microsoft terminology of "shares." It also acts as a gateway, allowing a Mac to designate one AppleTalk printer as a Share printer on the Microsoft network. Each Macintosh running DAVE can share one AppleTalk Postscript printer at a time. The Windows machines run the standard Microsoft Client and access the AppleTalk printers as they would any other printer.

To share an AppleTalk printer with the Microsoft network, the Mac running DAVE must be able to display the printer in the Chooser using the Apple LaserWriter 8 driver. To share the printer, open the DAVE Sharing control panel and follow these steps:

1. Click the Print button in the DAVE Sharing control panel. The Share a Printer dialog box will open (Figure 15.8).

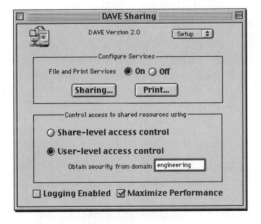

Figure 15.8 The DAVE Sharing control panel

2.   Click the Add button. (If you have a printer shared, there will be an Edit button instead.) A list of AppleTalk printers will appear.

3.   Select a printer from the list and click the OK button.

As in Windows, DAVE lets you assign share-level or user-level security to a printer. However, as in Windows, a read-only password for a printer is meaningless. You choose between share-level and user-level access for the entire Mac in the DAVE Sharing control panel. (Share-level security is where everyone uses the same password to access a particular printer or file server directory. User-level access gives different passwords to different users.) To assign passwords in DAVE, you use the Sharing button of the DAVE Sharing control panel.

See Chapter 14 for more information on DAVE.

AppleTalk Printing with PC MacLAN for Windows

PC MacLAN from Miramar Systems, AppleTalk software for Windows, was mentioned earlier as way for Macs to access PC printers. It also enables Windows to access AppleTalk printers. AppleTalk printer and file access is enabled through the PC MacLAN Client. With the Client installed, AppleTalk printer will appear in the Network Neighborhood, inside a Window called Miramar AppleTalk network. (The printer must be turned on.) When you select a printer, Windows will launch the standard Add Printer Wizard, which you will use to set up the printer. (You'll need to know the manufacturer and model of the printer in order to select a Postscript driver.)

PC MacLAN also provides an AppleTalk Printer Utility that provides some of the capabilities Mac users have with Apple's printer utilities. The AppleTalk Printer Utility lets you view printer properties, look at the fonts on the printer, and download fonts, as well as download Postscript files to the printer. You access the AppleTalk Printer Utility from pop-up menu that appears when you right-click the printer icon in the Printers window.

To keep track of PAP messages from an AppleTalk printer, PC MacLAN adds an AppleTalk tab in the Properties dialog of a printer (accessible by right-clicking the printer). Here you can enable PC MacLAN to keep a log file that records messages and events from the printer. You can also use the AppleTalk tab to create a directory that will be used spool files for the AppleTalk printer.

See Chapter 14 for more information on PC MacLAN.

MacWindows Tip

With either PC MacLAN or COPSTALK, you should set up Post-script to send print jobs as binary data. You do this in the window for a particular printer. Choose Properties from the file menu and select the Postscript tab. Change the output format to Archive format. Press the Advanced button, and select Pure Binary Data as the data format.

AppleTalk Printing with COPSTalk for Windows

Like PC MacLAN from Miramar Systems, COPSTalk from Thursby Systems is an AppleTalk-based file and printer sharing packages for Windows. Unlike PC MacLAN, COPSTalk does not enable Macs to access PC printers. COPSTalk is one-way, enabling Windows PCs to access Mac file and print services.

Once you've installed COPSTalk, you can create printers by selecting them from the Network Neighborhood and using the Windows Add Printer Wizard. Before COPSTalk 2.1, only Apple LaserWriters would show up in the Network Neighborhood. COPSTalk 2.1 and later come with a COPSTalk Utility that lets you define the types of printers that you want displayed in Network Neighborhood. However, you still need a Windows Postscript driver to print to the printer—COPSTalk doesn't provide drivers.

NOTE: COPSTalk will display forwards and backwards slashes in printer names as underscores. Slashes are illegal characters in Windows printer names.

COPSTalk works with the Microsoft drivers provided with Windows, as well as with Postscript drivers from Hewlett-Packard and Adobe. However, you can get a Postscript error with HP drivers that requires that you modify the .SPD file for the printer you've installed. Thursby provides a utility called hpfix.exe that will modify the file for you.

COPSTalk also has an issue with Adobe drivers that may cause a problem when you're installing an AppleTalk printer in Windows, due to the fact that Adobe has its own driver installer that is used instead of the Add Printer Wizard. There is a work around that involves installing a "dummy" Adobe driver, and then changing the printer's driver:

1. Create the printer with the Add Printer Wizard.
2. Run the Adobe installer. When you're asked whether the printer is a local or network printer, choose local.
3. After you select the appropriate PPD file, you need to select a port. Choose "FILE: creates a file on disk."
4. Choose not to make this a default printer or print a test page.
5. When you're finished, open the Network Neighborhood and double-click the printer for which you want to use the Adobe driver.
6. Open the Properties dialog box for the printer and click the Details tab.
7. In the box called "Print using the following driver" select the Adobe driver. (It will start with "AdobePS.") Click OK.

COPSTalk displays some of the printer status information provided by the AppleTalk Printer Access Protocol. This is the same information Mac users can view in their desktop printer windows, including "busy," "waiting," "idle," "out of paper,"and "printer error." COPSTalk displays this information in the title bar of the printer's window after the name. (This is the standard window that appears when you open a printer in the Printers folder in My Computer.) For instance, if the printer's name was "Bob's Laser," the title bar of the printer window might say "Bob's Laser—Waiting." This PAP status information is in addition to the information that Windows provides in the Status column of this window, which displays the status of the print job in Windows—"off-line," "printing," "spooling," and so forth. (See Chapter 14 for more information on COPSTalk.)

Special Printer Connection Methods

There are two cross-platform connection standards that aren't normally thought of in terms of printing applications, but that are nevertheless used on some printers. These are Universal Serial Bus (USB) and the wireless IrDA standard (both of which are supported on iMacs).

USB Printing

Universal Serial Bus (USB) is a 12 Mbit cross-platform interface with 25 times the bandwidth of a Mac serial port running LocalTalk. With a driver for Macintosh and Windows, the same USB printer, drive, mouse, keyboard camera, or other peripheral should work on either platform. Through the use of USB-to-parallel-port cables and drivers, USB offers an opportunity for cross-platform use of lower-end printers. Most of these are inkjet printers. USB (along with the appropriate drivers) can help Macintoshes connect to printers that they might not ordinarily have access to. The two leading inkjet providers, Hewlett-Packard and Epson, provide USB printing solutions for both Mac and Windows. At this time, these most of these printers have parallel ports as well, so USB hasn't been as helpful to Windows printing.

The iMac was the first Mac model to have USB ports. Apple has said that it intends to have USB ports on every Macintosh model. Since Microsoft included support for USB in Windows 98, USB ports began to appear on PCs. USB is not likely to completely replace the parallel port in PCs for many years, because of backward compatibility concerns in a competitive market. However, Apple, which has a degree of control over Mac hardware that PC manufacturers don't, has said that USB will eventually replace the serial and ADB (Apple Desktop Bus) ports in all models, as in the iMac.

MacWindows Tip

USB printing differs from parallel port printing in two major ways. First, a USB lets you connect multiple USB printers to one computer through the use of a USB hub. Second, you can't share a single USB printer with multiple computers through the use of a switch box, as you can a parallel printer. (You can share USB printers with networking software.)

Because of this, Hewlett-Packard is basing its support of Macintosh for lower-end inkjet printers mostly on USB, and is not likely to produce another inkjet printer with a Mac serial port. HP once had a line of Macintosh QuickDraw, serial-port inkjet printers, called the DeskWriters. In a technology deal in the mid-1990s, HP provided the DeskWriter technology to Apple, which renamed them the StyleWriter 4100, 4500, and 6500, and dropped its own Macintosh line. Apple dropped the StyleWriters in 1997, leaving Mac users with no HP inkjet products.

Hewlett-Packard restarted its support of Macintosh in its inkjet printers when the iMac began shipping in 1998, this time with USB. Its first USB product for Macintosh was the HP Printer Cable Kit for iMac, which consists of a USB-to-parallel port cable and a Mac driver for the DeskJet 670 and 690 series printers. (These are inkjet printers that have parallel ports and no Mac port.) The driver takes Quick-Draw calls and converts them to PCL. Hewlett-Packard also has printers with a built-in USB port, such as the LaserJet 895C, that don't come with Macintosh drivers. In this case, you can use third-party packages, CAI's MacJet USB and InfoWave's PowerPrint USB (discussed earlier in this chapter), to enable a Mac to print (Table 15.1).

MacWindows Tip

Early iMacs had some USB printing problems with Epson printers under Mac OS 8.1 that produced horizontal white bands. This was corrected with Apple's iMac Update 1.0 patch, released in September 1998, and was also fixed in Mac OS 8.5.

TABLE 15.1 USB Cable/driver packages for Macs with USB ports

Company	Name	Printers supported
Epson	USB/Parallel Port Adapter Kit	Epson Stylus Color and Stylus Photo
Hewlett-Packard	HP Printer Cable Kit for iMac	HP DeskJet 670 and 690 series
Infowave	PowerPrint USB	A variety of printers
CAI	MacJet/USB	A variety of printers

Epson also has a USB Parallel Port Adapter Kit for its Epson Stylus Color and Stylus Photo inkjet printers. However, most of these printers have a Mac DIN-8 serial port and Mac drivers, so USB isn't the only option for Mac users. Some Epson inkjet printers, such as the Epson Stylus Color 740, have a built-in USB port in addition to a parallel port and a Mac serial port. Epson supplies drivers for both Windows and Macintosh.

You can find the Epson's most recent USB drivers posted at http://www.epson.com/support/pdcip.html.

MacWindows Tip

USB isn't the only printing option for iMacs. iMacs can print to LocalTalk printers using an Ethernet/LocalTalk converter or bridge, such as Farallon's iPrint.

Adding USB to your computers

Macs and PCs that don't have USB ports can print to a USB printer via an add-in card for the PCI slot. As with other PCI card, the same card will work in both PC and Mac as long as you have a driver for each. Keyspan offers both Windows 98 and Mac OS drivers with its USB PCI Card. The card provides two USB ports. USB cards are inexpensive, going for well under $100 at the time this book was published (http://www.keyspan.com/products/usb/).

IRDA Printing

IrDA is a type of physical connection that can be used for printing on some PCs and Macs, but uses line-of-sight infrared communications instead of cables. IrDA is a cross-platform standard, used in some printers (including the HP LaserJet 5P, 5MP, and 6MP), as well as in some laptop PCs and Mac PowerBook models and in hand-held Windows CE devices. Some desktop computers, including the iMac, also have an IrDA Infrared (or IR) transmitter/receiver that can be used for printing. However, IrDA printing can be impractical in desktop models, since the printer needs to be within 3 to 4 feet of the computer. IrDA can also be used a method to connect to a network (as described in Chapter 7), in which case the standard rules of networks apply.

Although IrDA printing is usually a one-to-one connection, it is similar to a 4 Mbit-per-second network connection. These means your computer needs to be running a network transport protocol and an appropriate printer driver. You also need the appropriate IrDA driver software for the computer.

MacWindows Tip

Since sunlight contains infrared wavelengths, direct sunlight shining on an infrared transceiver can interfere with a connection.

IrDA printing on Macintosh

The iMac, PowerBook 2400, PowerBook 3400, G3, and PowerBook G3 Series support IrDA printing. Some older Macs—the Power-Books 190, 1400, 5300—support an older Apple technology called IRTalk that isn't compatible with IrDA printers. Some of the later models support both IrDA and IRTalk and let you switch between them in the Infrared control panel via the Options button.

There are three system files needed for IrDA communications: the Infrared control panel and the IrDALib and IrLanScannerPPC extension files. You need to have AppleTalk turned on in the Chooser. (TCP/IP can also be used over an IrDA link to a network.)

MacWindows Tip

The USB mouse that comes with the iMac uses an optical sensor that can interfere with an IrDA connection. The interference can occur when the Apple USB mouse is positioned directly in front of the infrared transceiver.

After you position the computer and printer within a few feet of each other, the Infrared control panel will indicate that a connection has been established. In the AppleTalk control panel, you'll then need to select Infrared Port in the Connect via pop-up menu.

Macs use a Postscript driver, such as LaserWriter 8, for IrDA printing. However, you can't select an IrDA printer using the Chooser. Instead, you need to create a desktop printer, just as we did in the earlier section on IP printing.

Open the Desktop Printer Utility (in the Apple Extras folder) and choose New from the File menu. Select "Printer (Infrared)" from the list (Figure 15.9). You'll next select a PPD file by clicking the Change button and selecting your printer from the list, and clicking Select. This PPD file tells the Mac that the printer supports IrDA. Next, the printer will appear in an Untitled window. Choose Save As from the File menu and save as a desktop printer. The desktop printer icon will appear on the Finder's desktop.

Figure 15.9 Choosing IrDA in the Desktop Printer Utility

IRDA printing in Windows

IrDA printing on Windows began with Windows 95 Service Pack 1 in 1995. (You can also download IR communications software from http://support.microsoft.com/download/support/mslfiles/W95IR.EXE.) Windows 98 and Windows 2000 also come with infrared drivers, including an IrLPT driver. When Windows is installed, it should detect the IrDA hardware. If it doesn't, or if you add the hardware later, you can install the IrDA software using the Add Hardware Wizard.

Once installed, you'll see an Infrared icon in the Control Panel. This is used for configuration tasks, such as turning on infrared communications and "searching," which enables the PC to look for the infrared device. You'll also need to select the infrared printing port (called a "virtual LPT" port) as the printer port. For the printer driver, it's best to try using the drivers that came with the printer first.

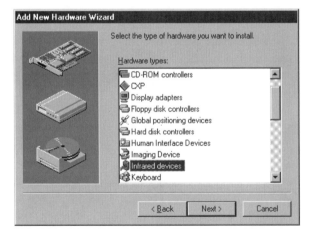

Figure 15.10 Installing the IrDA drivers in Windows 98

Looking Ahead

Sometimes file translation, e-mail, file sharing, and printing aren't enough—you need to run Windows on a Mac. Or you need to run a Mac program on a PC. Part 5, Using Foreign Operating Systems, looks at several variations of a theme. The next chapter looks at putting a foreign operating system directly on your computer using a software emulator or coprocessor board. Chapter 17 describes two more indirect methods that let you operate a foreign application that is running on another computer over a network—remote control and thin-client/server solutions. Chapter 18 describes sharing a monitor and keyboard between a Mac and a PC. This lets you run either operating system from the keyboard of your choice.

Part Five

Using Foreign
Operating Systems

What's in This Section:

Chapter

What's in This Chapter:

- ♦ **Reasons to run Windows on a Macintosh**

- ♦ **Pros and cons of emulators and coprocessor cards**

- ♦ **Using PC emulators**

- ♦ **Using coprocessor hardware**

- ♦ **Macintosh emulators for PCs**

- ♦ **Emulators on UNIX and other operating systems**

16

Operating Systems: Using Emulators and Coprocessors

In some respects, the ultimate step in integrating Windows and Macintosh is running software created for one platform on the other. Running foreign software is sometimes the only solution when none of your native applications can open a foreign file, no translators are available to convert the file, and no version of the software is available for your platform. Installing Windows on a Macintosh can also be a viable solution to enable a Mac to participate on a PC network.

There are two types of solutions for running one operating system environment on another. There are software-only solutions called emulators, which translate calls between Intel and the PowerPC processors. The other solution is hardware. A coprocessor card, sometimes called a "compatibility" card, is basically a PC motherboard on a PCI expansion card that sits inside a Mac. The basic trade-off between the two types of solutions is cost versus performance. The more you spend, the faster the foreign environment will be.

Most of the solutions discussed in this chapter run Windows on Macintosh. That's because the state-of-the art of running Windows on Mac is more advanced, with more capabilities than running Mac OS on PCs. There are several reasons for this, which are described later on. This chapter also looks at some solutions for running Windows and Mac on UNIX operating systems.

With the Windows-on-Mac products, compatibility with Windows software is very good for both low-cost emulators and more expensive coprocessor cards, and you can run multimedia and sound. Some products are limited to running DOS, Windows 3.X, and Windows 95/98, while others can run also run Windows NT/2000, or any other PC operating system. Compatibility with DOS and Windows networking from within the Windows environment is also good. By sharing files, ports, and peripherals, these products also allow you to use the Mac and Windows environments with each other.

Web Update Link: *For the latest information about emulation and coprocessor products for both Mac and Windows, see http://www.macwindows.com/emulator.html.*

Why Run Windows on a Macintosh?

A common question about running Windows on a Macintosh is "why?" With emulators not as fast as a real PC, and some PCs costing less than coprocessor cards for Macs, what's the advantage over an actual PC? The answer is integration (Figure 16.1). Running Windows on a Mac lets you work in both platforms together. Maybe you do mostly Macintosh activities, but need to run a special piece of software that doesn't exist for Mac. In this case, running Windows on a Mac can prevent you from having to replace a Mac with a PC. Or, you might want to see how a web page you've created on the Mac looks in Windows, or check out the latest version of an Intel-based Linux. Or you might be a Mac user who wants access to PC games.

Keep in mind, however, that emulators and Pentium cards are platform integration solutions, not replacements for real PCs. For instance, if you need the fastest Windows environment money can buy, or need to run a PC server, you'd be better off buying a real PC.

What follows is a list of some of the benefits of running Windows on a Mac. If none of these are important to you, then you might think about buying a PC and networking it to your Mac.

File sharing and copying without a network. Running Windows on Mac lets you can access Mac folders and files from within Windows and access Windows files from the Finder. You can copy files between

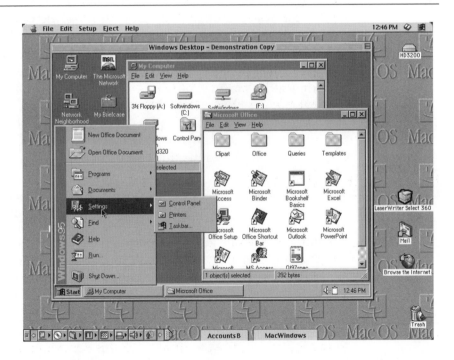

Figure 16.1. Running Windows on a Mac gives you the benefits of integration.

the two environments using drag and drop, from within Save dialog boxes, and from command lines.

Cut and paste. With Macintosh and Windows applications open at the same time, you can cut and paste data between documents.

Share peripherals. Both Mac and Windows environments can share the same printers, CD-ROMs, Zip drives, floppy drives, network ports, and other peripherals. In general, the Pentium cards are compatible with more PC peripherals than the emulators.

Save Desk space. Running two operating systems on one computer is a convenient solution for people who don't have room for two computers.

Faster and easier installation of Windows. Installers for emulators and coprocessor cards create a preconfigured Windows system on your Mac, skipping most of the configuration dialog boxes that you have to go through when you install Windows from a Microsoft CD-ROM.

Easier maintenance. Because these products use a lot of the Mac's hardware, problems such as hardware conflicts are much less common than on real PCs.

Low cost of software. Starting at about $30 for versions without an operating system, emulators are less expensive than a PC, though much slower. Including Windows, the cost of an emulator is under $150.

Web Update Link: *The MacWindows web site often posts comparative analysis and tests results of current versions of emulation software and coprocessor cards. To find the most current review, check the MacWindows home page at http://www.macwindows.com.*

Differences: Emulators vs. Coprocessor Cards

For the past several years, there have been three lines of products that run Windows on Macintosh—SoftWindows from Insignia Solutions, Virtual PC from Connectix, and the OrangePC cards from Orange Micro. Many people still use the discontinued cards from Apple, Reply, and Radius as well. A newer PC emulator for Macs, Lismore Systems' Blue Label Power Emulator emerged in in 1999 as a shareway product. There are also several Macintosh emulators for PCs.

Despite all these products, your first choice is between just two paths: emulator or coprocessor card. Deciding between the two is basically a task of choosing between a slower, cheaper solution and a faster, more expensive one. Which one is the better alternative depends on your situation. Generally, the less frequently you need to access Windows, the more practical the software solution is. There are other factors that you should consider as well, such as the Mac model you have and what you want to do with Windows.

Table 16.1 (page 160) summarizes the pros and cons of each type of solution. These issues are discussed in more detail over the next few pages.

Costs

An emulator will cost less than a Pentium card, but just how much less depends on a lot of factors. There are a range of prices for each product line. Additionally, the retail price of an emulator or Pentium card doesn't give you whole story, as there are sometimes hidden costs.

The least expensive way to run Windows on a Mac is to buy a DOS-only version of an emulator and install your own copy of Windows. (The DOS version of Insignia's SoftWindows is called Real PC. Connectix offers Virtual PC–PC DOS.) The installation will be more complicated, however, as you won't get a preconfigured version of Windows.

Table 16.1 Emulators versus coprocessors

	Software emulators	Coprocessor hardware
Cost	+ $30 (without OS) to under $200 with Windows	From several hundred to over a thousand dollars
Performance	Varies with the Mac's processor, but significantly slower than most coprocessors	+ Independent of Mac processor; will work in older Macs
Software Compatibility	Very good	Very good
Windows Networking	Very good	Very good
Peripherals Compatibility	Limited I/O for devices such as dongles, cameras, PDAs	+ Some cards have PC ports (parallel, serial, etc.). Others work through Mac ports.
Effect on other Mac software	Takes RAM away from Mac. Can slow Mac software	+ Negligible
RAM	Uses about 6-to 8 Mb more RAM than coprocessor cards. Best on Mac with 48 Mb or more	+ RAM on card Runs on Macs with low RAM
Effect on Mac Expansion	+ No effect	Takes up PCI slot. Draws a lot of power, which can limit other expansion options
Noise	+ No extra noise	Adds a fan. Extra power draw can increase the pitch of Mac fan in some Mac models.
Run Windows in a Mac window	+ Yes, but slower than full-screen	Full-screen only, but can run Windows in a second monitor

When comparing costs, keep in mind that the cost of some RAM is usually included in a coprocessor board, but not emulation software. With either solution, you need RAM to run Windows in, but emulators need about 8 Mb more RAM than coprocessor boards for the emulation software itself. Of course, you'll be able to use this RAM to run Mac software when you aren't running the emulator.

This is a similar issue with 3Dfx graphics cards, which emulators can use to speed up graphics performance for 3Dfx-compatible Windows software (mostly games). When you add the cost of the 3Dfx card to that of the emulation software, the total can come close to that of a low-end Pentium card. However, you can use a3Dfx card for some Mac games as well. If you plan on using 3Dfx on the Mac side, then it's a bonus.

Performance

I've already said that coprocessor cards run Windows on Macintoshes faster than emulators do. This is true as a general rule, but the issue of speed is more complicated than this simple statement implies. The performance will vary with each version of SoftWindows, Virtual PC, and OrangePC card, but there are three facts about speed that remain constant over the years:

1. Emulation speed mostly depends on the Mac's processor.
2. Emulators are much slower than coprocessor hardware.
3. You cannot compare the speed of either emulators or coprocessor cards to that of "real" PCs.

Let's look at these points in more detail.

Emulation speed is mostly processor-dependent

A big difference between coprocessor cards and emulators is the effect that the host Mac they are running on has on performance. The speed of Windows running under emulation depends on the Mac it's running on. There are a lot factors that play a part in emulation performance, including the Mac's bus speed, the hard drive, and how much RAM it has. However, the results of thousands of real-world tests I've performed on PC emulators make it clear that the Mac's processor is the biggest factor in how fast Windows software will run. In tests where one varies the processor on a Mac, and then with each processor, varies the amount of RAM, the processor always proves to be the more important factor. For instance, on a Power Mac 7500, going from a 132 MHz PowerPC 604 to a 250 MHz G3 processor can double Windows performance.

The effect of RAM on emulators, while significant, is nowhere near as important as that of the processor. Increasing the amount of RAM allocated to the emulator from 24 Mb to 64 Mb in a Mac gives you at most a 40 percent speed boost, though the average is more likely to be in the 20 percent range. Once you get above 48 Mb, the percentage speed gain for every 32 Mb RAM added drops into the single digits. (All of these figures hold for average business tasks, such as using Microsoft Office for Windows.)

Moving to a Mac with a faster system bus can also affect the speed of an emulator. Generally, you can see that emulators run 3 to 4 times faster on a 300 MHz Power Macintosh G3 with a 66 MHz bus than on a Power Mac 7500 with a 132 MHz Power 604 processor and a 44 MHz bus.

Coprocessor cards, on the other hand, run at pretty much the same speed on different Macs. The performance of Windows will be similar whether the Mac has a 100 MHz 601 processor or a 400 MHz G3. (You can make Windows run faster by upgrading the Pentium-compatible processor on the card.) The amount of RAM in the Mac is also not a factor, as the cards contain their own RAM. The speed of the Mac's system bus also has only a small effect on Windows perfor-

Processors and Speed

It's important to remember that the speed of a processor is not determined solely by its clock rate, measured in megahertz (MHz). Although an indication of speed, megahertz is not a universal measure, as is the horsepower rating in cars. Comparing megahertz ratings is only meaningful when you're talking about the same model of processor, such as PowerPC G3. For instance, at the same megahertz rating, PowerPC 603e processors yield about two-thirds the performance of PowerPC 604e processors. If all the PowerPC processors used in Macs were running at identical speeds, you'd see a progression in performance like this, starting with the slowest and moving to the fastest: 601, 603e, 604, 604e, G3 (also known as the PowerPC 750), and G4 (expected in late 1999).

mance, since the coprocessor card has its own system bus and only goes to the Mac's motherboard for disk and other I/O. Both emulators and coprocessor cards are equally affected by a slow hard drive.

Emulators are slower than hardware

Because emulators depend on the Mac's processor for their Windows performance, emulators gain significant performance with each new generation of Macintosh hardware. Speed gains from faster Macs are usually more significant than improvements in the emulators themselves. (Historically, a 25 to 30 percent performance gain in a new version of an emulator has been about the upper limit.) With every new batch of PowerPC processors, there are claims from enthusiastic users that emulators have caught up with hardware. The problem is that every time PowerPC processors get faster, so do the Pentium-compatible processor available in compatibility cards.

I once found that SoftWindows and Virtual PC running on a 300 MHz Power Macintosh G3 to run at approximately the same speed as a 166 MHz OrangePC card, then Orange Micro's slowest, cheapest card. The problem was that as soon as I had published the test results at MacWindows.com, the lowest available Pentium compatible on the Orange PC card became 200 MHz, which once again outperformed the emulators. (At the time of this writing, 400 MHz Pentiums-compatibles were available for the OrangePC card.) This pattern has continued, with emulators running on the fastest, highest-priced avaible Macs models just about reaching the speed of the the slowest, cheapest Pentium card.

On the higher end of the OrangePC line, the coprocessor cards can yield more than 10 times the speed of emulators on the fastest Mac. This also has been true for many years now, and trends indicate that emulators will be slower than most Pentium cards. The x86-to-PowerPC translation step simply devours processing power.

This doesn't mean that coprocessor cards are a superior integration solution—the low cost and simplicity of emulators make them valuable in many situations. What is "fast enough" depends on the Windows software you are running. I'll have more to say about optimizing emulators and coprocessor cards for speed later in this chapter.

You can't compare speeds to "real" PCs

The data presented in the last section give rise to some questions. Is it fair to say that emulators on 300 MHz G3 Macs run Windows at the speed of 166 MHz PCs? For that matter, does a 300 MHz Pentium coprocessor card run at the same speed as a real 300 MHz PC? The answer is yes—and no.

There are several problems with comparing running Windows on a Mac with running Windows on an "equivalent" PC. In fact, such a comparison is misleading and one that should be avoided. There are two basic reasons for this. First, it turns out there really is no such thing as "an equivalent PC." Second, different tasks run at different speeds on real PCs, emulators, and coprocessors.

Generally, I've found that Orange PC cards do have some processing overhead, and do run slightly more slowly than many PCs with the same processor. However, they also have tested as running faster than other PCs with the same processor. The reason is that even with the same processor and amount of RAM, PCs from different manufacturers can run at vastly different speeds. You can sometimes see these speed differences in reviews of systems in magazines. I have tested many PC systems and found significant differences in brands. For instance, in one review I once wrote for clnet, I found systems with 100 MHz Pentiums running faster than other systems with 150 MHz Pentiums.

With Macintoshes, a faster processor means a faster machine. This isn't true with PCs, which can differ greatly inside the case. Among PC brands, you'll find significant differences in the PC's system bus, the BIOS, the drive subsystem, and other subsystems. The lack of a "standard" PC system to compare against is one reason I no longer test real PCs along with emulators and coprocessor cards.

Macs with the same processor can vary a little as well. On a Mac with a fast UltraSCSI card, emulators and coprocessors might run database lookups faster than some given PC model. If you have a Mac that's a few years old, database tasks could be slower than that same PC.

The other reason is that not all tasks scale equally. An emulator or coprocessor card might run at 80 percent of the speed of a given PC model for one particular task, but run at 140 percent for another task. For example, emulators tend to perform graphics-intensive tasks more slowly than other tasks when compared to coprocessor cards and some PCs, but they can perform disk-intensive tasks well. Typical performance for one user will be faster than typical performance of another.

When you add all this up, saying that "Acme Emulator runs as fast as an XXX MHz Dell PC" doesn't provide a lot of useful information.

Similarities: Running Windows on Mac OS

Despite the differences in price, performance, and features between emulators and coprocessors, the various Windows-on-Macintosh products have much in common. Connectix' Virtual PC, Insignia Solutions' SoftWindows and Real PC, and Orange Micro's OrangePC cards all install an application named after the product (for instance, "Virtual PC" or "OrangePC"), which you can see in Figure 16.2. For an emulator, this application is the emulation engine itself. For an OrangePC card, this is a small facilitating application used to launch Windows. (The now-discontinued Apple-based cards used a control panel called PC Setup to launch Windows. Lismore Blue Label Power-Emulator takes a modular approach, with a set of software.) When Windows is in full-screen mode, you can use a key combination to access the Mac menu bar to return to the Mac environment or to change settings.

All of these solutions recreate the basic components of a PC on your Mac, including processor, RAM, and boot hard drive. When you start one of these programs, the PC environment "boots" using these and other PC components. Emulators create a "virtual" x86-class processor in software, while the coprocessor cards add an actual Pentium or

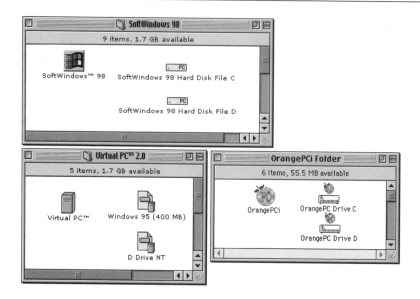

Figure 16.2 The virtual C: drive file common to Windows-on-Mac products

Pentium clone. The emulators use the Mac's RAM, while the cards contain their own RAM. With either type of solution, it's important you set aside enough RAM for Windows. This should be at least 16 Mb for Windows 95/98, and at least 32 Mb for Windows NT.

When it comes to recreating the PC boot drive, all of these products, both emulators and coprocessors, use the same method pioneered by Orange Micro. The installer software for each of these products will create a large Macintosh file that acts as a virtual boot drive, the C: drive. (This file is sometimes called a "drive container file.") If you want a 500 Mb C: drive, you create a 500 Mb virtual drive file. Inside this virtual drive file goes all of the Windows software, including the Windows operating system and application software. Practically speaking, you need a minimum of about 350 Mb of free hard disk space in order to run Windows with any of these products on your Mac. You can also create a second virtual drive, the D: drive.

MacWindows Tip

Be sure to defragment your hard drive with a drive optimizing utility (such as Norton Utilities) before installing any emulator or coprocessor card. A fragmented virtual C: drive file can greatly diminish the performance of Windows on your Mac.

From within Windows, you can use virtual drives as you would the C: and D: drives on a PC, saving files to them from within Windows and running Windows applications from them. You can also defragment the virtual drives from within Windows using the Microsoft defragmenting tool. If your Mac crashes while you are running Windows, the PC environment will ask you if you want to run the Microsoft ScanDisk utility on the C: drive when you reboot the PC (Figure 16.3).

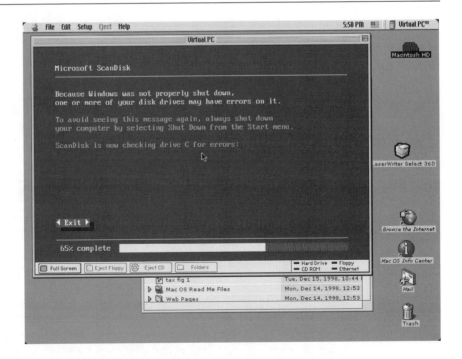

Figure 16.3 Running Microsoft Scan disk on a virtual C: drive

You can also peer into the virtual drive files from the Finder. All of the current versions of the shipping Windows-on-Mac products include a method of mounting the virtual drives on the Finder desktop. With the virtual drive mounted, you can peer into the Windows directories (as shown in Figure 16.4) to check for missing files or do drag-and-drop file copies between Windows and Mac. If Windows is running, the mounted drive files are read-only.

The method of mounting the virtual drive differs with each product. With Virtual PC, you double-click the drive file to mount it. With Insignia's SoftWindows and Real PC, you drag the drive file on top of a utility to mount it. With OrangePC, you use a specially modified version of Apple's DiskCopy utility. With Blue Label PowerEmulator, you use the included PC Disk Mounter utility.

Figure 16.4 The volume called "SoftWindows" is a mounted virtual C: drive file, giving you access to the Windows System directory. The same can be done with Virtual PC and OrangePC.

MacWindows Tip

If you ever need to edit some of the system configuration files in Windows 95 or 98, you can bring them all up at once without knowing their location. Simply select Run from the Start menu and type "sysedit." This launches the System Configuration Editor and opens the system.ini, config.sys, autoexec.bat, win.ini, and protocol.ini. files.

Connectix, Insignia, and Orange Micro products also let you access Mac folders and files from within Windows. You can map Mac folders to drive letters as if they were network volumes. You can then access the Mac folders from Windows' My Computer (Figure 16.5), from within applications, and from anywhere else you can access drives in Windows. (You also can do this with Lismore's BlueLabel Power Emulator, but it is more difficult than with the other products, as you need to modify the autoexec.bat file and use a component called HFS Redirector.)

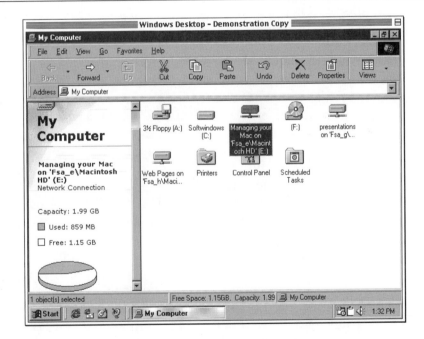

Figure 16.5 A folder on the Macintosh hard drive appears as a network drive to Windows running on the same Mac.

Using PC Emulators

When you run Connectix Virtual PC and Insignia's SoftWindows and Real PC (the DOS version), they look and act very much alike. However, there are differences that can make one product better than the other for some users (Table 16.2). With software changing once or twice a year, it's not my intention to review the products or recommend one or the other. However, I can point out differences that have been fairly consistent over the life of the two products. You'll also find that this section contains techniques for the effective use of emulators.

NOTE: *Lismore's BlueLabel PowerEmulator was released after this book was finished, so I couldn't cover it as thoroughly as I did the other emulators. You should know that it doesn't come with a pre-installed operating system, which makes it more difficult to setup and use than the other emulators, and it isn't any faster. Like Virual PC, it can run any PC operating system.*

SoftWindows has always been a little more expensive than Virtual PC, but includes more in the way of cross-platform and network utilities. SoftWindows has always been the faster of the two emulators, particularly on older Macs. Virtual PC's biggest virtue is that it can run Windows NT, Linux, and any other PC operating system.

Insignia's SoftWindows is the older of the two PC emulators and has always been the faster of the two. The progenitor of SoftWindows was SoftPC, which ran on Macs with 680x0 processors. (At this time, there are no longer any PC emulator solutions available for 680x0 Macs.) SoftWindows comes with Windows, the version of which is reflected in the full product name. (SoftWindows 98 comes with Windows 98, while SoftWindows 95 comes with Windows 95.) Connectix introduced Virtual PC 1.0 in 1997. Version 2.0 delivered a significant speed boost and was the first mature version. The biggest difference between Virtual PC and SoftWindows is that Virtual PC can run Windows NT, Linux, or any other PC operating system. At this time SoftWindows can only run Windows 95/98, Windows 3.x, or DOS. Although Virtual PC will run NT, you can't buy a preconfigured version of Windows NT with Virtual PC that integrates with the Mac environment, as you can with an Orange Micro card.

Both Insignia Solutions and Connectix offer versions of the emulator with DOS instead of Windows. Insignia calls its DOS version RealPC, which comes with Microsoft's MS-DOS. Virtual PC–PC DOS comes with IBM's PC DOS. Some DOS-o-philes may have a preference for one or the other, but if your intent is to install Windows, the version of DOS is irrelevant. If you already own a copy of Windows, you can save about $100 by purchasing one of these the DOS versions and installing your own copy of Windows. Performance will be the same as if you had bought the Windows version, but you'll lose the one-step, preconfigured installation of Windows that comes with the emulators.

Table 16.2 A brief comparison of SoftWindows and Virtual PC

	SoftWindows	Virtual PC
Speed	+ Faster on most Macs. Much faster on pre-G3 Macs	Slower than SoftWindows, though close on Macs with G3 processors
Operating systems supported	Windows 98, 95, 3.x, and DOS	+ Windows 95/98/3.x, DOS, Windows NT, Linux, or any other PC OS
Cost	Slightly more	+ Slightly less
RAM for emulation engine	9–10 Mb	+ Approximately 8 Mb
Maximum RAM that can be used	No limit	128 Mb for the PC environment
Gaming	Faster DirectX	Better compatibility with some DOS games
Software bundle	+ More in the way of cross-platform and networking utilities	
Memory configuration+	Requires memory to be set from a special window	No additional configuration other than the Get Info window
DOS version	MS-DOS (Microsoft)	PC-DOS (IBM)
Networking	+ Mac and Windows can share IP addresses. Supports Token Ring	No sharing of IP address. Ethernet only

Compatibility with PC Software

Insignia uses the same emulation engine in SoftWindows and Real PC, one that differs slightly from the engine Connectix uses in Virtual PC. Connectix says Virtual PC can run any PC operating system because it more completely emulates a PC's hardware than does Soft-Windows. Virtual PC emulates hardware subsystems where SoftWindows routes the I/O to Mac subsystems. For instance, to connect Windows to Ethernet through the Mac's Ethernet port with Virtual PC, you select the DEC 21041 PCI Ethernet adapter in the Windows Network dialog box. Virtual PC emulates this adapter. With Soft-Windows, you choose the Insignia Solutions Ethernet Driver as your network adapter to connect to Ethernet from Windows.

NOTE: Mac OS 8.5 is incompatible with earlier versions of Virtual PC and SoftWindows. If you are running OS 8.5 or and later, you need Virtual PC 2.1 and later, or SoftWindows 95 5.0 or later.

Emulating the subsystems does seem to takes more processing power, however, which may account for SoftWindows' performance advantages. Connectix says its approach is aimed at providing better compatibility with PC software, but one doesn't see this with Windows application software, which has a high degree of compatibility on either emulator. Virtual PC is more likely to run off-the-shelf software that works at a lower level, such as drivers. I have also seen some DOS software run on Virtual PC but not on SoftWindows, but I've also seen a smaller number of DOS programs that ran on SoftWindows and not on Virtual PC.

One type of software that no emulator can yet run is speech recognition. The problem isn't compatibility, but limits in sound input. The top speech recognition software require 16-bit sound input, but the emulators only support 8-bit sound input.

Web Update Link: For current informtation about software compatibility with Lismore's Blue Label PowerEmulator, see http://www.macwindows.com/lismore2.html.

Mac Processors and Emulation Speed

SoftWindows has always been faster than Virtual PC. Just how much faster depends on the Mac. As I mentioned earlier in the chapter, the Mac's processor is the biggest factor that will determine how fast your emulator will run Windows. The slower the processor, the more Virtual PC will lag behind SoftWindows. On a Power Macintosh G3, however, Virtual PC can come within single-digit percentage points of SoftWindows, and surpass it in some tasks. (For instance, SoftWindows 95 5.0 has better floating-point speed on G3 processors, but Virtual PC 2.0 had better disk access speed. SoftWindows also has better performance with DirectX games.)

This means that the older your Mac's processor is, the bigger the superiority of SoftWindows over Virtual PC. Of course, this could always change with future versions of either product, but this has been the case so far over the history of both emulators.

Connectix recommends a 180 MHz 603e as the minimum processor for Virtual PC running Windows 95 or less, and a G3 for Windows 98. Insignia says SoftWindows will run on any PowerPC processor. For either emulator, I recommend at least a 604 processor at bare minimum. However, if you can manage it, a G3 processor will give you the most usable Windows environment.

(For more on the effect of processors on emulation performance, see the previous section titled Emulation Speed Is Mostly Processor Dependent.)

Web Update Link: *For current test results of emulator performance, check for a link to the most current special report at http://www.macwindows.com.*

18 Tips for Optimizing Emulator Speed

Optimizing the speed of PC emulators can squeeze extra performance out of a Mac. Individually, these items don't turn an emulator into a speed demon, but together, they can make a significant difference.

Web Update Link: *For tips on optimizing the performance of specific versions of emulators for certain Macs, see http://www.macwindows.com/emultips.html.*

Tip 1: Keep the virtual C: drive file defragmented

Run a Mac disk optimizer such as Speed Disk in Symantec's Norton Utilities on the Mac drive periodically (once a month if you use the Mac daily) to keep the emulator's virtual C: drive in one piece. Disk optimization will also help your Mac software, but emulators in particular are adversely affected by a fragmented virtual drive file.

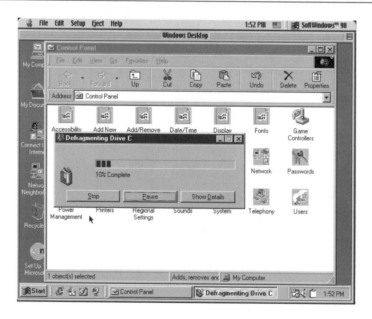

Figure 16.6 Defragmenting the virtual C: drive within Windows

Tip 2: Keep the virtual drives defragmented within Windows

You also need to occasionally run the Windows Defrag utility (Figure 16.6) on your C and D drive. (Select Run from the Start menu, and type DEFRAG.) This isn't as important as optimizing the Mac drive, but it helps.

Tip 3: Leave a few megabytes on the virtual C: drive empty

Windows 95/98 and NT/2000 need some empty space for Windows' virtual memory. Windows will slow if the empty space grows too small, and eventually will report that there isn't enough disk space.

Tip 4: Make sure your Mac has a level-2 RAM cache

Most Macs of the past few years, including all G3 models, included a level-2 cache. On older Macs, such as the Power Mac 7600, the level-2 cache was optional. If you have an older Mac with an empty level-2 cache slot, adding a cache card is an inexpensive method of getting a 30 percent speed boost for the Mac. If you have a G3 processor in one of these older machines, it has backside cache with the processor.

It should be noted that although they're fast, Apple's top Power Macintosh G3 models do not use the fastest PowerPC hardware design. That is, the speed of the backside cache is only half the clock rate of the processor. Connectix says that if Apple were to increase the cache speed from 2:1 to 1:1, the emulator speeds would improve by another 20% or so.

Tip 5: Make sure your Mac has enough RAM

A lot of RAM can increase emulator speed a little, but too little RAM can really slow speed a lot. If you are running Windows, make sure you have enough RAM to allocate at least 32 Mb to emulator application. (More on how to do this later in the chapter.) The biggest jump in speed is when you increase allocated RAM from 24 Mb to 32 Mb. With more RAM than that, speed only increases are small. Below 24 Mb, Windows crawls.

Tip 6: If you're short on RAM, turn down Disk Cache

If you can't find enough RAM to give your emulator 32 Mb, you can squeeze a little more by turning down the Disk Cache setting in the Mac's Memory control panel, shown in Figure 16.7. (You can't turn Disk Cache off, and the minimum setting varies with each Mac model.) The Disk Cache comes right out of RAM and is added to the amount of memory used by Mac OS, as reported in About This Computer. Turning down the Disk Cache setting slows hard drive performance, but if you have less than 32 Mb available for your emulator, you'll do better allocating the RAM to the emulator.

Tip 7: If you have RAM to spare, turn up Disk Cache

If you enough RAM to give your emulator at least 32 Mb, the slowdown you get from turning down the Disk Cache setting will be greater than any speed increase you get from more RAM. Apple recommends setting 32K of disk cache for every megabyte of RAM you have in the Mac. However, going above this wastes RAM. For example, if you have 64 Mb, the your setting would be 32 x 64 = 2048K. Ordinarily, you shouldn't go below a setting of 1024K.

Figure 16.7 Disk cache and virtual memory in the Memory control panel

Tip 8: Turn the Mac's virtual memory off

Emulators tend to suffer (more than ordinary Mac applications do) from the inherent slowdown that Mac OS's virtual memory brings due to a heavier use of the hard drive, which is slower than real RAM. Virtual PC and SoftWindows are compatible with virtual memory, however, so you can trade performance for the extra RAM if you need to. Unlike most other applications, however, emulators don't use a lot less RAM with virtual memory turned on.

One of the reasons that emulators are particularly affected by virtual memory is that the emulated Windows system also uses its own virtual memory. Windows usually grabs most of the available RAM in a low-memory system and pages part of itself to a swap file if a Windows application needs more RAM. If some of that memory, which Windows thinks is real, is actually virtual on the Mac side, then the performance can be unpredictably slow at times.

Tip 9: Don't run RAM Doubler

As with virtual memory, Connectix RAM Doubler increases the use of the hard drive and adversely affects emulation performance.

Tip 10: Configure memory properly

Configuring memory properly is important to getting optimum emulation performance. This is particularly true with SoftWindows, as is described in the next section.

Tip 11: Run Windows and the Mac in 256 colors

Adding more colors slows the graphics performance of an emulator. In addition, having the Mac's Monitors and Sound control panel set at a different color depth than in Windows will also slow the emulated environment. So if you need to bump up the number of Windows colors, make sure you set the Mac colors to the same level.

Tip 12: Run Windows 95 instead of Windows 98

Windows 98 takes up more RAM and processing power than Windows 95, and there are few programs that require it.

Tip 13: Turn off the Windows 98 Active Desktop

If you do run Windows 98 on an emulator, you can help speed things up by turning off the Active Desktop, which is on by default. From the Start button, go to Settings, then Active Desktop. Make sure the View as a Web Page item is turned off.

Tip 14: Turn off processor cycling in PowerBooks

PowerBooks have a semi-sleep mode called processor cycling. It slows down the processor when you aren't typing or moving the cursor. This is fine for a word processor, but is takes a toll on an emulator, which is always running. PowerBooks are usually set in processor cycling mode by default. Processor cycling is intended to save battery power, but is also in effect when you are using AC power.

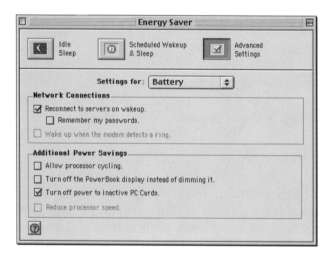

Figure 16.8 Turning off Processor Cycling in the Advanced Settings window of a PowerBook's Energy Saver control panel increases emulator performance.

The Quit-the-Finder Myth

One of the many myths perpetuated by the Internet tells us that running an emulator (usually Connectix Virtual PC) without the Finder greatly increases the speed of Windows. Usually, this information is accompanied by information on how to prevent the Finder from loading so that the Mac boots right into the emulator and Windows. Some versions of the myth credit Apple cofounder Steve Wozniak (or sometimes his son) for inventing the technique. The described procedure does work in one respect—you can actually prevent the Finder from launching. The problem is that this doesn't speed up the emulator, a fact that has been confirmed by engineers at Connectix. Quitting the Finder will make a couple of megabytes of RAM available for use by the emulator, which might improve performance a few percentage points on Macs with 32 Mb of RAM or less. For Macs with more RAM, there is no speed improvement.

With Mac OS 8.0 and later, you can tell if processor cycling is turned on in the Energy Saver control panel. (In older versions of Mac OS, it's called the PowerBook control panel.) Click the Advanced Settings button. At the left of the window (shown in Figure 16.8), click Processor Cycling off.

In older versions of Mac OS, you open the PowerBook control panel, set the switch to Easy, and then hold the option key while dragging the toggle switch from Easy to Custom. An item called Allow Processor Cycling will appear. Uncheck the box to turn it off.

Another way to find out if you are in processor cycling mode is to set the Mac's display clock to seconds. If the clock starts skipping seconds, then the Mac is in processor cycling mode.

A warning: Although turning off processor cycling speeds up emulator performance, it will cause the battery to drain much faster.

Tip 15: Don't run Mac applications in the background

Some Mac applications that are active in the background will steal processor cycles from the emulator you are using. A Mac word processor open in the background isn't going to do much damage, but something that is actively crunching numbers or accessing the hard drive or a network will. One simple offender is the Chooser, which, if left open, will poll the AppleTalk network regularly and slow the emulator.

Tip 16: Avoid multitasking under Windows

Run one Windows application at a time, for the same reasons as Tip 15.

Tip 17: Don't use wallpaper on the Windows desktop background

Wallpaper requires a little graphics processing power, something emulators don't do quickly. It also takes some RAM.

Tip 18: Turn off unnecessary MS Office startup utilities

Again, these are items that will take up RAM and processing power.

Configuring Emulator Memory

Configuring memory is an important part of setting up an emulator, since too little RAM for Windows will restrict performance. The first thing to do is to make sure your Mac has enough RAM to operate an emulator comfortably.

A Mac with 32 Mb RAM is the bare minimum needed to launch an emulator with Windows 95 or 98. Keep in mind that you are running two operating systems on your Mac, as well as an 8-to-10 Mb emulator and Windows applications. Depending on your version of Mac OS, 10 to 16 Mb will go to the System software, leaving 16-to-22 Mb for the emulator. About 8 to 10 Mb of that is used by the emulation engine and an internal cache, leaving only 6 to 14 Mb for Windows and your Windows applications. This is really below what you should have for Windows 95 and will affect Windows performance.

If you are running Windows 95/98, I recommend a Mac with 48 Mb minimum for either emulator, or a minimum of 32 Mb of RAM assigned to the emulator software. (With Windows NT on Virtual PC, I recommend a Mac with 64 Mb minimum.) Increasing RAM assigned to the emulator increases performance, but the greatest increase occurs when going from 24 Mb to 32 Mb, where you can see a speed difference of up to 15 to 20 percent. After these levels you get single-digit percentage performance increases with further increases in RAM. All of these figures are with standard business software. Obviously, if you are using Windows software that requires more RAM than, say, Microsoft Office, you will need more memory in the Mac.

MacWindows Tip

You can squeeze more RAM out of a low-RAM Mac by turning off unused extensions and control panels in the Extensions Manager control panel.

You allocate RAM in the emulator application's Get Info window (Figure 16.9) as you would with any Mac application. (In Mac OS 8.5 and later, you access the Memory Requirements section of Get Info by choosing Memory from the Show pop-up menu.) The Preferred Size is the amount you'd like the emulator to take if it is available. The Minimum Size is the least amount of memory you would like the emulator to open in. If there is less free memory available on the Mac than indicated in the Minimum Size field, the emulator won't launch. In this case, you can free up memory by closing other applications, or you can lower the amount in the Minimum Size field.

These numbers should include that total for the emulator engine and for Windows. That's about 8 Mb for the Virtual PC emulation engine,

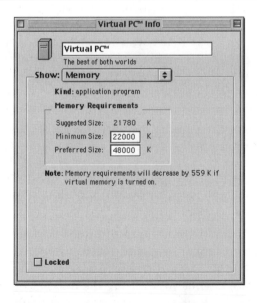

Figure 16.9 Allocating emulator memory in an emulator's Get Info window

or 9 to 10 Mb for SoftWindows' engine. The rest goes to Windows. Therefore, your memory allocation shouldn't go much below 24 Mb (16 Mb for Windows, 8 for the emulation engine) if you want to accomplish anything substantial in Windows. If you need to open Windows 95/98 just to take a look or to move a file, you can allocate as little as 16 Mb in the Minimum Size Window, though performance will be quite slow, and I don't recommend it for a normal work or gaming session. (If you are using DOS only, and not Windows, you can go with a Get Info box memory allocation of as little as 16 Mb— 8 Mb for DOS and 8 Mb for the emulation engine.)

NOTE: Virtual PC has an upper limit of 128 Mb of RAM that the PC environment can use. If, in Virtual PC's Get Info box, you assign more than 136 Mb (128 Mb for the PC and 8 Mb for the emulator engine), any memory above this figure will go unused and will be wasted.

At this point, you are finished configuring memory with Virtual PC, and you can launch it. SoftWindows has one more setting you must check to ensure the best performance. In a Mac with plenty of RAM (64 Mb or more), you'll probably only have to deal with this setting once. In Macs with less RAM, you may have to change this setting every time you start the emulator, if the amount of available RAM changes. These means beginning to boot Windows, resetting the RAM configuration, and rebooting Windows.

The procedure for configuring memory from within SoftWindows or Real PC is as follows:

1. Launch SoftWindows.
2. While still in the DOS screen, Select SoftWindows 98 Setup from the Setup menu.
3. Click the Memory button in the Setup window. You'll see a screen similar to Figure 16.10.
4. Use the arrows at the top to fill the red line labeled CPU Memory, while maximizing the number in PC Memory.
5. Click the Restart button to begin booting Windows (or DOS) again.

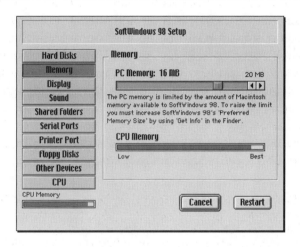

Figure 16.10 Configuring memory within SoftWindows and RealPC

Gaming and 3Dfx Cards for Emulators

A big boost in performance for running PC games is to add a 3Dfx, 3-D graphics accelerator card to the Mac. These cards are not expensive, but must be specifically supported by the software, which is usually games. The support is also known as Voodoo 1 and Voodoo 2, the name of the 3Dfx graphics chip sets. The card can also accelerate some Mac games as well as Windows games under emulation.

A 3Dfx card can accelerate games that use Microsoft's DirectX standard, which is used in a lot of Windows games, but not DOS games. More specifically, 3Dfx cards accelerate a 3-D subset of DirectX called Direct3D. Other aspects of DirectX, such as 2-D, game controller input, and sound, are not affected by 3Dfx cards. A 3Dfx card can also accelerate non-DirectX games, such as those using OpenGL or the native 3Dfx "Glide" API. (For all you Mac gamers, DirectX on Windows is analogous to Apple's Game Sprockets on Mac. Direct3D is analogous to RAVE on the Mac.)

The emulators support DirectX without 3Dfx (in SoftWindows 4.0 and later, RealPC 1.0 and later, and Virtual PC 2.0 and later, Blue Label PowerEmulator 1.0 and later). Without a 3Dfx card, SoftWindows runs DirectX action faster than Virtual PC. If you are running DirectX on Virtual PC without 3Dfx, you really needs a G3 processor to make it usable. (SoftWindows 5.0.2 and RealPC 1.0.2 fixed some DirectX problems that were in SoftWindows 5.0 and RealPC 1.0.)

Not all 3Dfx cards are compatible with both PC emulators. Check with Connectix or Insignia Solutions before you purchase a card.

MacWindows Tip

When installing a DirectX game in SoftWindows, it's important that you choose "yes" if asked to install DirectX, but choose "No" if the installer asks to overwrite your display driver.

Both emulators support joysticks. Virtual PC can access analog joysticks, but not digital devices. SoftWindows also supports Plug and Play joysticks in Windows and displays the type of joystick being used.

Emulator Ease of Use

The two emulators offer the option of skipping the Windows startup procedure and delivering you right into Windows, with the same applications open that you had been using the last time you ran the emulator. SoftWindows calls this feature TurboStart, while Virtual PC asks you if you want to save the PC state when you quit. In both emulators, when you select this option when shutting down, it saves the state of Windows memory, including what applications, files, and windows were open. The next time you start the emulator, you're returned right to this spot, as if you'd never left. It doesn't work if your Mac has less available RAM the next time you start the emulator. In this case, Windows will simply go through the boot procedure.

SoftWindows has a feature called Easy Launch that lets you launch the Windows environment and a Windows application by double-clicking on a PC file in the Finder. The file needs to have originated from Windows—that is, you saved to a Mac folder from within Windows. (Within SoftWindows, you can map a drive letter to any Mac folder or Drive, as you can with Virtual PC and Orange PC.) For instance, when you double-click on a Microsoft Access document in the Finder, SoftWindows will launch, load Windows, and open Access and your file. SoftWindows is AppleScriptable, letting you create AppleScripts that include key commands in Windows applications.

Virtual PC has the very convenient feature of letting you copy files from the Finder to the Windows desktop via drag-and-drop when you're not in full-screen mode (see Figure 16.11). Virtual PC also has handy buttons for ejecting floppies and CDs. Configuring memory is also easier in Virtual PC, as was described earlier.

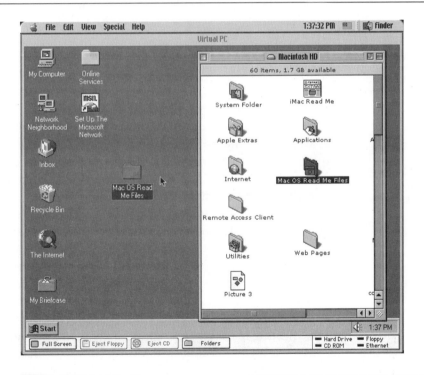

Figure 16.11 Connectix Virtual PC lets you drag and drop files from the Finder to the Windows desktop.

Peripheral Device Support

SoftWindows, Virtual PC, and Blue Label PowerEmulator (BLPE) all let you print to a Mac printer from within Windows and use the Mac's CD-ROM and floppy drive. SoftWindows automatically supports Mac or PC SCSI device connected the Mac, including scanners and removable drive cartridges such as Zip. BLPE also supports any SCSI device—after you perform a significant amount of configuration. Virtual PC can support Mac SCSI devices if you make them available as shared folders, but does not support SCSI scanners. Virtual PC does, however, support the synchronization of PDAs with Windows software.

Except for 3Dfx cards, Ethernet adapters, and token ring adapters (SoftWindows and Real PC only), the emulators don't support expansion cards in a PCI or the older NuBus slot.

Networking from an Emulator

A Windows emulator can sometimes be a good solution for connecting a Mac to a Windows network. Emulators use a lot more RAM than any client software alone would, but enable connectivity from a Mac when there are no Mac clients available. SoftWindows and Virtual PC come with the standard Microsoft network client and file and print sharing software (BLPE does not, but you can add it), and you can add third-party Windows networking, database, or other connectivity software. SoftWindows and Virtual PC can also print to the AppleTalk (or nonnetwork) printer selected in the Mac's Chooser.

Setting up networking in an emulator begins with plugging the Mac into an Ethernet network. With Virtual PC, you'll need Open Transport networking (see Chapter 8) on the Mac. SoftWindows can use either Open Transport or the older "classic" networking, including MacTCP. Both emulators will configure basic networking for you during installation if you choose to do so, but you can also configure it manually in Windows and install third-party Windows networking software. As was mentioned earlier, Virtual PC use the Mac Ethernet port by emulating a DEC 21041 PCI Ethernet adapter, which is what you select in the Windows Network dialog box. In SoftWindows, you select the Insignia Solutions Ethernet Driver as your network adapter. The SoftWindows Ethernet driver requires you to use Insignia's special NDIS and ODI drivers for DOS networking. This difference between the emulators doesn't affect compatibility with networks.

However, SoftWindows' networking features go further than those in Virtual PC. For instance, SoftWindows supports token ring as well as Ethernet. Another networking advantage SoftWindows has is that you don't need a separate IP address for Windows—you can run simultaneous Macintosh and Windows IP sessions over a single link. Soft-Windows enables the Windows session to share the Mac's IP address whether it's manually entered or obtained by DHCP, PPP, or another method. (SoftWindows also allows simultaneous IPX connections using the Novell MacIPX driver, which Insignia provides on the CD-ROM.) With either emulator, you can use separate IP addresses for the Windows and Mac environments, though you can't have both operating systems accessing DHCP servers to obtain their addresses.

Setting up networking in an emulator is just like configuring a PC. Chapter 9 can help you get started with Windows networking.

Sharing an IP address in SoftWindows

In order to use the same IP address for both Mac and Windows environments, SoftWindows uses a special version of the winsock.dll file created by Insignia Solutions. This file was created to work with three instances of the Mac's TCP/IP protocol stack: those supplied by Open Transport, by MacTCP (so-called "classic" networking), and the Novell TCP/IP.

The winsock.dll resides in the C:\windows directory. If this file has been replaced by Microsoft's default winsock.dll file (or another version), you won't be able to share an IP address between Mac and Windows. It is possible that you may have accidentally replaced the Insignia winsock.dll file with another during the installation of networking software. If you have replaced the Insignia file, or just aren't sure, you can delete the current file and replace it with the Insignia winsock.dll file. You also need to delete the winsock.old file. To do this, perform the following procedure:

1. Make sure your Winsock-compatible network application software is installed. (This can include web browsers and FTP software.)
2. Enable Show All Files by selecting Options from the View menu of the Windows Explorer (click the Start button then Programs).
3. In My Computer, open the SoftWindows C: drive, select the Windows folder, and select winsock.dll. Delete the file.
4. Select winsock.old and delete it.
5. Open the Insignia folder and make a copy of the winsock.dll file by selecting it and choosing Copy from the Edit menu.
6. Select the Windows folder and select Paste from the Edit menu. The file will be copied to the C:\windows directory.
7. Open the C:\windows\sysbckup directory and select the winsock.dll file.
8. Select Rename from the File menu and change the name to winsock.ms.
9. Restart Windows.

When Windows comes back up, you should now be able to run simultaneous IP connections over one IP address.

Installing and Running Windows NT on Virtual PC

You can install Windows NT, Linux, or any other PC operating system on Virtual PC, but you can't buy these operating systems from Connectix. These operating systems will run independently from Mac OS, without the Mac OS integration features that are found when you run Virtual PC with Windows 95 and Windows 98. For instance, you won't be able to access Mac files from within Windows by mapping a drive letter to a Mac folder, you won't be able to copy and paste between environments, and the Eject CD and Eject Floppy buttons don't work (Figure 16.12). The OrangePC coprocessor cards, on the other hand, do include Mac integration features. Installation of Windows NT on Virtual PC is also a more manual process than with Windows 95/98, or with NT with an OrangePC board.

There are two methods of installing Windows NT on Virtual PC. The first is a "dual-boot" configuration, with Windows 95 or 98 installed on the C: drive and Windows NT installed on the D: drive. The second is a single-boot configuration, where you have one virtual C: drive with Windows NT installed on it. In either case, the virtual drives will be formatted as FAT 16 drives. Virtual PC does not support NTFS-formatted drives.

Before you begin installing either configuration, you need a copy of Virtual PC with Windows 95 or 98 already installed on the Mac.

Figure 16.12 Windows NT runs on Virtual PC, but doesn't get the Mac integration features found in the Win 95/98 version, or with NT on OrangePC.

490   PART FIVE • USING FOREIGN OPERATING SYSTEMS

You will need a full keyboard to install Windows NT, as the Microsoft installer requires the Page Down key and some of the function keys.

Dual-boot configuration (Win 95 on C:, Win NT on D:)

The procedure for installing a dual-boot Windows 95 (or 98) and Windows NT configuration in Virtual PC is to create a virtual D: drive file that is 250 Mb or larger.

1. Start Virtual PC and select Preferences from the Edit menu. (You don't have to wait until Windows boots.)
2. Select the D Drive item from the list (as shown in Figure 16.13) and click on the New Hard Drive Image button.
3. Choose a location for the new virtual drive file, give it a name (such as D Drive NT), and type in the size of the new drive file. Click Create.
4. Click the Restart button and let Windows 95 or 98 load.
5. Insert a Microsoft Windows NT CD-ROM. Click the Windows NT Setup button in the Window that appears.

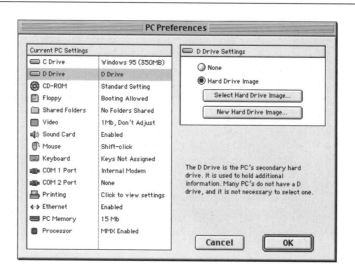

Figure 16. 13 Creating a new D: drive in Virtual PC's PC Preferences window

6. A Window will appear showing the path (E:\I386) to the Windows NT files on the CD-ROM. Hit the Return key. Windows NT Setup will copy installation files to the hard drive.

7. A message will ask you to restart your computer. Hit the return key. If Virtual PC doesn't restart, choose Restart PC from the Control menu.

8. Virtual PC will load in DOS mode into the Windows NT Setup program. At the Welcome to Setup window, press the Return key.

9. The Setup program will locate hardware and emulated devices. Use the Return key to accept the default settings, accept the licensing agreement. (Here you will need a Page Down key on your keyboard.)

10. At one point, the Setup program will ask you to choose a partition on which to install Windows NT. (See Figure 16.14.) Press the down arrow key to highlight the D: drive. Hit Return.

11. The next screen will ask if you want to format the D: drive and will give you a choice to format in FAT or in NTFS, or to make no changes. Highlight the default selection of

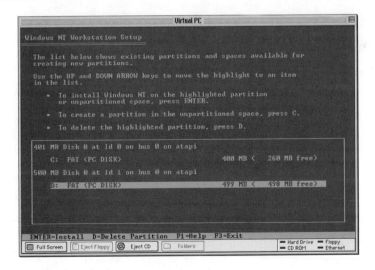

Figure 16.14 Choosing the D drive to install NT in the NT Setup program

"Leave the current file system intact (no changes)." Hit Return for this and for the next screen.

12. A screen will ask to examine your hard disk for corruption. Choose the option "skip the exhaustive examination" by pressing the ESC key.

13. After the Setup program copies files to the D: drive, it will ask you to remove the CD-ROM. Click Virtual PC's Eject CD button and press the Return key.

The emulated PC will reboot into Windows NT and Windows NT Setup will appear. At this point, the configuration procedure for the dual-boot is the same as that of the single-boot installation. See the section called Setting Up after Installation on page 494.

Single boot option (Win NT on C:)

The first step in installing Windows NT on the C:\ virtual drive within Virtual PC is to create a boot floppy.

If you don't have one, you can format a Mac diskette as a PC boot floppy by selecting Run from the Windows start menu and typing:

```
format A: /s
```

If you want to be prompted for a volume label, then enter:

```
format a: /s /v
```

If you have a DOS-formatted floppy without system files (that is therefore not bootable), you can make it bootable by typing:

```
sys a:
```

You now need to boot from the floppy and create a new virtual C: drive file that is 250 Mb or larger:

1. Launch Virtual PC and Windows 95 or 98.
2. Insert a DOS-formatted floppy diskette.
3. Copy the cdrom.sys and mscdex.exe files from the C:\cntx directory to the floppy.
4. Copy the autoexec.bat and config.sys files from the C:\ directory to the floppy.
5. Open the Notepad utility (Start button, Programs, Accessories). Open the config.sys file on the floppy. Delete all lines except the one that reads as follows:

```
DEVICE=A:\CDROM.SYS /D:IDECD001
```

6. Open the autoexec.bat file on the floppy from within Notepad. Delete all lines except the ones that read as follows:

```
@ECHO OFF
SET BLASTER=A220 I5 D1 T4
A:\MSCDEX.EXE /D:IDECD001 /L:E
```

7. Shut down Windows 95/98. With the boot floppy still in the drive, launch Virtual PC again. Select Preferences from the Edit menu.
8. Select the C Drive item from the list and click on the New Hard Drive Image button.
9. Choose a location for the new virtual drive file, give it a name (such as C Drive NT), and type in the desired size of the new drive file. Click Create.
10. Click the Restart button. When the command prompt appears, unlock the new C: drive by typing:

```
lock C:
```

11. Insert the Microsoft Windows NT CD-ROM. At the A: prompt, type E: and press Return.

12. When the E: prompt appears, type:

```
cd i386
```

13. When the E:\i386 prompt appears, type:

```
winnt /b
```

The Windows NT Setup program will copy the installation files to the hard drive.

14. A message will ask you to restart your computer. Hit the Return key. If Virtual PC doesn't restart, choose Restart PC from the Control menu.

15. Virtual PC will load in DOS mode into the Windows NT Setup program. At the Welcome to Setup window, press the Return key.

16. The Setup program will locate hardware and emulated devices. Use the Return key to accept the default settings, accept the licensing agreement. (Here you will need a Page Down key on your keyboard.)

17. A screen will ask to examine your hard disk for corruption. Choose the option "skip the exhaustive examination" by pressing the ESC key. Accept the other default settings by pressing the Return key.

The emulated PC will reboot into Windows NT and Windows NT Setup will appear. At this point, the configuration procedure for the single-boot is the same as that of the dual-boot installation. See the next section.

Setting up NT after installation.

At this point, you've installed Windows NT as either the dual-boot or the single-boot option in Virtual PC. The emulated PC has rebooted into Windows NT and Windows NT Setup has appeared. To finish configuration, perform the following steps:

1. Continue through the installation windows. If you are on a network, click the Start Search button in the window that asks you to select a network adapter. The DEC PCI 21014 Ethernet Adapter should appear. Select it and hit Return.

2. At the Finish Setup stage of installation, the Setup program will detect a generic S3 video card. You can click OK to this. Virtual PC emulates an S3 928 PCI SVGA Card. If you want to install these specific drivers, you can download them from http://www.s3.com.

3. At some point, you will need to restart again. After restarting, Windows NT will ask you to log on by pressing Ctrl+Alt+Delete. Use the Option key for the Alt key, and the Control key for Ctrl.

4. To set up sound, open the Multimedia window in the Control Panel, click the Devices tab, select Audio Devices, and click the Add button.

5. Click Creative Labs Sound Blaster and click OK. The Install Driver window will appear (Figure 16.15).

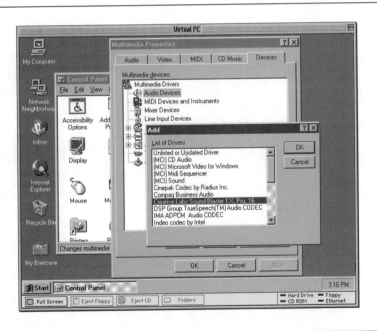

Figure 16.15 Configuring audio when setting up Windows NT on Virtual PC

6. Insert the Windows NT CD-ROM and click the Browse button. Open the following directory: E:\drvlib\audio\sbpnp\i386. Click OK.

7. Click OK in the Install Driver window.

8. A series of configuration windows will appear. The correct settings should be as follows:

```
I/O Address 220
Interrupt 5
DMA Channel 1
```

9. The System Setting Change dialog will appear. Click the Don't Restart Now button.

10. To set the Startup menu delay to 0, click the Start button, select Run, and type Regedit to open the Registry Editor.

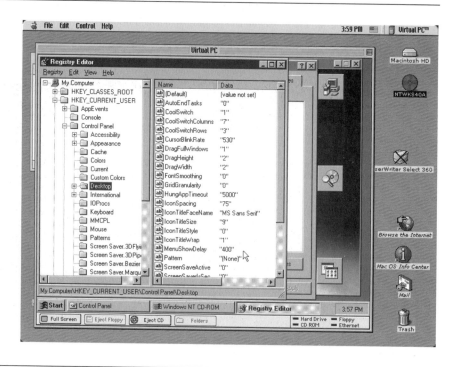

Figure 16.16 Setting NT's Startup menu delay to 0 with Regedit in Virtual PC

11. Click the plus sign next to HKEY_CURRENT_USER, click the plus sign next to Control Panel, and select Desktop (as shown in Figure 16.16).
12. Double-click MenuShowDelay on the right window and change the setting from 400 to 0.
13. Exit the Registry Editor and restart Windows NT.

Switching between Windows 95/98 and Windows NT

If you've installed Windows NT on a Virtual PC D: drive in the dual-boot configuration, you can choose which operating system to boot when you first start or restart Virtual PC. The first screen you'll see (Figure 16.17) will give you a choice between Windows NT and Windows (which can be 3.x, 95, or 98). Use the arrow keys to select one and press the Return key. The default setting is Windows NT. If you don't touch the keyboard within 30 seconds, Windows NT will boot.

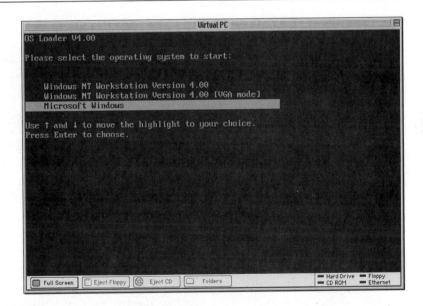

Figure 16.17 Choosing between Windows 95 and NT at startup time in Virtual PC in a dual boot configuration

Virtual PC and NT Service Pack 4

Virtual PC 2.1.1 and earlier are not compatible with Windows NT 4.0 Service Pack 4. When you reboot Windows NT after installing Service Pack 4, the boot-up procedure stops at the logon screen. When you attempt to log on, an error message appears telling you that the NetLogon Service isn't running, even if you aren't on a network. Virtual PC does work with NT 4 Service Pack 3.

If you've already installed Service Pack 4 and are stuck, you can rescue any data you need by creating a new C: drive file (without Service Pack 4) and booting from it. You can then copy your data to the new C drive file.

Using Coprocessor Cards

Running Windows on a Mac through the use of a coprocessor card is a little like running an emulator, and a little like running a PC. You are running Windows on a Macintosh, printing to your Mac printer, and saving files to your Mac hard drive in the same manner you would an emulator. (See the section called "Similarities" earlier in the chapter.) You're also accessing PC networks, using a modem within Windows, and you are running doing real-world tasks in actual Windows applications at several times the speed that you could in an emulator.

However, just because it uses hardware doesn't mean it is a replacement for a PC. It isn't. It won't run Windows as fast as the fastest PCs. And though you have essentially put a PC motherboard inside the Mac, it is rather nonstandard PC hardware. Rather than a PC replacement, you should think of a coprocessor board as the method of integrating a Windows inside a Mac that gives you the best performance. (Some of the reasons to integrate are discussed earlier in the chapter in the section called "Why Run Windows on a Macintosh?".)

As with an emulator, a coprocessor card comes works with a virtual C:\ drive file, where the Windows operating system, applications, and documents reside. The coprocessor card also uses a Mac application that you use to launch Windows, which means that Mac OS must be running in order to run Windows. In this case, the application is not an emulation engine, but a facilitator between the Macintosh and Windows environments.

The coprocessor card contains many of the elements of a PC mother-board. To start with, there's an x86 processor, such as a Pentium MMX or clone, usually with a cooling fan. (Older cards have a 486 proces-sor.) The processor is often upgradable. There's also RAM in one or two DIMM slots (SIMM slots in older cards), as well as level-2 cache, video RAM, and sometimes graphics accelerator chips. The board has its own system bus running at a clock rate independent of the Mac. (For instance, the OrangePC 660 from Orange Micro has a system bus running at 100 MHz.) Unlike with emulators, running Mac applications doesn't have a lot of effect on the Windows applications unless both are accessing the hard drive at the same time.

With hardware as well as software going into your Mac, a coprocessor is a more complex solution than a software-only emulator. Installation of a coprocessor card is more complicated than that of emulators, though installing the Windows OS software is just as easy as it is in emulators. (In the case of Windows NT on an Orange PC board, it's easier.) Since you are basically running a PC inside of a Mac, you can run into the same configuration problems that PCs owners run into, plus some they don't often see.

Today, the only company making Pentium cards for Macintosh is Orange Micro of Anaheim, California. For several years, Apple sold a line of coprocessor cards called Compatibility Cards and licensed the design to Reply and Radius. All of the Apple-based cards have now been discontinued.

Web Update Link: *You can check a list of current and dis-continued coprocessor cards at http://www.macwindows.com/emulator.html#Coprocessor.*

Using Orange Micro's OrangePC Cards

Orange Micro is one of Apple's oldest developers. Its first Apple product, introduced in 1980, was the Grappler, a printer interface card for the Apple II computer. The company's first coprocessor card was the Mac286, an 8 MHz Intel 80286 processor card for the NuBus expansion slot. Today, Orange Micro's line of 7-inch and 12-inch OrangePC cards fit into PCI slots and can sport Pentium, AMD, and other processors running at over 400 MHz. Some models have a single DIMM slot for RAM, while higher-priced models have two slots.

Orange Micro offers a choice of Windows 95, 98, and Windows NT with its cards. (You can't buy a card without an operating system.) Windows is included on an Easy-Install CD-ROM, which contains a preconfigured version of Windows. As with the emulators, installing Windows form the Easy-Install CD is basically a one-button procedure. Windows NT is also available in an Easy-Install version, making it much easier to install than it is with Virtual PC (see previous section). OrangePC boards are the only Windows solution for Mac that integrates Windows NT with the Mac environment. As with Virtual PC, OrangePC can only work with FAT volumes, not NTFS. Orange Micro does not support non-Microsoft operating systems on the OrangePC cards.

MacWindows Tip

When the "Blue and White" Power Macintosh G3s were released in 1999, they were incompatible with most OrangePC cards, including including the OrangePC 400 and 500 series and 600 series cards released before early 1999. Fortunately, an Apple software fix enabled the Series 500 and 600 OrangePC Windows compatible cards to run in the Blue and White Power Mac G3. Users only need Apple's G3 Firmware Update 1.0.2 or later (http://asu.info.apple.com/swupdates.nsf/artnum/n11361).

Although Windows is contained on the OrangePC Easy-Install CD-ROM, you also get a standard Microsoft CD-ROM as well. This is useful for installing drivers or making other changes to your Windows configuration.

After plugging in the card, you use a supplied cable to connect the Mac's monitor port to the card. You then plug the monitor into the card. This enables the board to pass-through Mac video and display Windows video when it needs to. Windows running on an OrangePC card requires an entire screen, so you can't run it in a Mac window. If you have two monitors, you can put Windows on one and Mac OS on the other at the same time.

OrangePCi software

OrangePC cards come with software on both the Mac and Windows sides. The Mac application you use to launch Windows is called OrangePCi. An important feature of OrangePCi version 3.1 and later is support for Windows 32-bit drivers. (The Apple, Reply, and Radius cards do not support 32-bit drivers.) These drivers include NDIS Ethernet support via the Mac's Ethernet port, 32-bit drivers for drive mechanisms, which enables support for long file names, and a Windows 95/98 Plug and Play SCSI driver. The last can detect enabled SCSI devices connected to the Macintosh SCSI port.

Several years ago, OrangePCi was a very small application, taking about a megabyte of RAM. More recent versions have grown to about 8 Mb because of new Mac–Windows integration features and the addition of some software emulation used in more recent OrangePC cards to reduce the cost of an all-hardware solution. The OrangePC PCfx!, 620, and 660 models emulate WAVE, MIDI, and DirectX audio (using the Mac processor), as well as PC ports. This selective emulation hasn't affected all-around performance, though the Mac's virtual memory can make some audio choppy.

Older versions of the OrangePC boards, including the 500 series, used actual SoundBlaster chips on the board and included a multiport connector cable that provided actual PC ports (including serial, parallel, and joystick ports).

You launch Windows with OrangePC as you would with an emulator, by double-clicking the C: drive file or the OrangePCi program. Your display is then filled with the PC booting and Windows launching.

If you are using a single monitor with the Mac, you can switch back and forth between the Mac and Windows environments with the click of a mouse button. From Windows, you can click on the Switch to Mac button on the Windows task bar to immediately switch the screen to the Mac (or hit command-D). When the Mac comes up, Windows is still running at this point, though you can't see it. If you are running a macro or some other process in Windows that will take some time, you can switch to the Mac and run Mac software without affecting the Windows performance.

The Snap Shot window is a view of the other environment: that is, it lets you see Windows from the Mac (shown in Figure 16.18), and the Mac from within Windows. It's not a live view, but a still screen shot of the other environment that is updated periodically. You can use it to monitor the progress of some activity (such as a rendering or a macro) that is going on in the other environment.

Figure 16.18 Orange Micro's Snap shot from the Mac side

OrangePC processors

Orange Micro offers a choice of processors on some of its models. At the time of this writing, Orange Micro was offering Pentium MMX and compatible processors with its OrangePC cards—Pentium II processors were not available. This means that the OrangePC boards are not going to be as fast as the fastest PCs. This could change with the introduction of a new OrangePC model, but the size and shape of the Pentium II package would make it difficult to fit on an add-in card. Additionally, the power requirements of the current Pentium II are a bit high for a coprocessor. More likely to be used by Orange Micro are newer generation of Intel Celeron processors that are going back to a socket-based design, which would work on an add-in card. (The newer Intel socket is not the same as the older Socket 7 used in the first-generation Pentiums, so an older OrangePC card could not be upgraded to these Celeron processors.) However, another processor being used in OrangePC cards, the AMD K6-3, is close to the Pentium IIs in performance.

Of the processors available, the AMD processors are the fastest, followed by Cyrix processors. At publishing time the AMD K6-3 processors were the fastest available for OrangePC cards. Intel processors come in third. Orange Micro sometimes offers IDT Winchip processors, which are about as fast as Intel Pentium MMX, and Cyrix processors, which are slightly faster than Pentiums. Compatibility with Windows business software seems about the same with any of these processors.

Most models have upgradable processors, though some lower-cost models (such as the OrangePC PCfx!) don't. One strategy to save some money is to order an OrangePC card with the slowest processor available, then shop around the web for a good deal on a high-end processor, and upgrade it yourself. Some OrangePC models have limits on the clock rate they'll support, so it's important you check your documentation before buying a new processor.

You can upgrade a processor yourself, as an upgradable processor usually sits in a standard ZIF Socket 7 slot. OrangePC models with an upgradable processor also have a voltage regulator. (Nonupgradable cards lack the voltage regulator.) When you upgrade a processor, you'll need to reset the voltage regulator using a set of jumper switches on the board. The exact setting of the switches depends on the card model and the processor you're putting into it. The OrangePC card's manual (in electronic .PDF format) includes tables of jumper settings for different processors.

Power considerations

Coprocessor cards do require a lot of power. Power consumption can vary from 10 to over 20 watts, depending on the card and the processor. It is important that you not exceed the power output of a Mac by adding too many expansion cards. For instance, some lower-end Mac models have a limitation of three 15-watt PCI expansion cards or two 25-watt cards. (You can find this information in the documentation that came with the Mac.) An example of another high-power card would be a fast graphics accelerator containing a large amount of graphics RAM. The type and number of drives in the Mac also contribute to the power usage.

A Mac with a weak power supply may have problems with a coprocessor card that you might not otherwise see. For instance, voltages output by the power supply can temporarily drop below required levels, causing Windows to freeze or the whole Mac to crash. This kind of behavior can be difficult to troubleshoot, since the Mac will seem to act okay when you use Mac software or when the card is not installed.

One symptom of a weak or bad power supply is a frequently changing pitch coming from the Mac's fan. For instance, if scrolling or some other screen action raises or lowers the pitch of the sound produced by the fan, the power supply may be straining. You may also hear the fan's pitch temporarily rise when you insert a CD. The fan in many Mac models is variable, spinning faster when there is more heat being output, but a healthy power supply should not change pitch in response to minor screen actions. Another way to test a power supply is to install the OrangePC card in another Mac. If you see the same problem on another Mac, you probably have a defective card. Replacing the Mac's power supply is the best course of action if you discover it to be a problem.

Tips for Optimizing OrangePC Cards

There's not much you can do on a Mac to affect the performance of an OrangePC card, which isn't usually a problem anyway. The most trouble people tend to run into are with peripherals, such as modems, scanners, and printers. Fortunately, there are some things that you can do to prevent or solve problems.

Tip 1: Trash the OrangePC prefs file when upgrading
When upgrading the OrangePCi application, throw away the OrangePC preference file in the Preference folder of the System folder. This can prevent potential conflicts.

Tip 2: Have enough RAM on the card for Windows NT
Windows NT takes a big jump in speed when going from 32 Mb to 64 Mb, even on a PC. Graphics-intensive tests nearly doubled in performance with the added memory. Windows 95 also benefits from adding the memory, but only by a third to half as much.

Tip 3: Turn off the Mac's virtual memory for game sounds
This is particularly important for cards that use emulated sound. You can get choppy sound (and sometimes animation) with games when the Mac's virtual memory turned on. However, virtual memory doesn't seem to affect ordinary business applications.

Tip 4: Use the correct graphics rendering when configuring games
If you have a PCfx! or an OrangePC 660, use the nVIDIA (RIVA) 128 rendering option when setting up your games. Do not use a 3Dfx option.

Tip 5: Try a generic 28.8 modem driver for modem problems
If you are having trouble using a 56K or 33.6K modem from within Windows, a generic 28.8 modem driver is likely to give you reliable connections.

Tip 6: Use recent OrangePCi versions with InfoWave's PowerPrint
If your Mac is connected to a PC printer using PowerPrint's serial cable, you'll need at least version 3.2 of the OrangePCi software in

order to access the printer from Windows. You can get an upgrade at http://www.orangemicro.com/updates.html. OrangePCi 3.2 also cleared up some general printing problems.

Getting Windows to read a SCSI device

Windows on Orange PC cards can access SCSI drives and scanners. You'll need OrangePCi 3.1 or later. You'll also need to configure the software to enable it to see the drives.

In the OrangePCi Setup menu, select which SCSI devices you will access from Windows. When you restart Windows, the Mac's SCSI Manager will become available to PC. Windows automatically installs drivers and may ask for the Windows CD-ROM.

For a Zip or Jaz drive, you also need to perform the following procedure (I'll describe Windows 95 here, but it's not much different for Windows 98):

1. With the SCSI Zip or Jaz connected to your Mac turned on, install the ASPI Manager (aspi.sys) from the Windows Setup CD-ROM. This allows Windows to access the Mac's SCSI port.
2. In My Computer, open the C: drive icon, open the File menu, and select New and Folder. Name the folder *Iomega*.
3. Insert the Iomega floppy disk. Copy the file guest.exe (not guest95.exe) to the Iomega folder you created in the last step.
4. Selection Run from the Start menu, type `sysedit`, and click OK. The Windows system configuration files will open.
5. In the autoexec.bat file, add the following line after C:\windows\mscdex.exe:

```
C:\IOMEGA\GUEST.EXE
```

If you'd like to map a drive letter to the Zip or Jaz drive, add LETTER=F (or another drive letter) after the line you just typed, as in:

```
C:\IOMEGA\GUEST.EXE LETTER=F
```

6. In the config.sys file, add the following line to the end of the file:

```
LASTDRIVE=H
```

7. Save and close the configuration files and restart Windows. The Zip or Jaz drive will shop up as another drive letter.

You can't use Iomega's Windows drive utilities, since OrangePC uses the DOS compatibility mode file system in Windows 95 and 98.

Apple, Reply, and Radius Coprocessor Cards

The discontinued coprocessor cards from Apple, Reply, and Radius are all based on Apple's design and use Apple's software. Apple had two lines, the original DOS Compatibility card and the PC Compatibility cards. Apple also included some of the cards with some Macs, such as the "Power Macintosh 7300 PC Compatible." Apple also licensed the PC Compatibility design and software to Reply, which later sold the cards under the name of DOS-in-Mac. Reply then sold the product to Radius, which produced it for a short time.

The cards were made for the older NuBus slots and later for PCI slots, and there were 7-inch cards and 12-inch cards. Some of the last cards shipped had a 166 MHz Pentium processor and 16 Mb RAM. Cyrix 586 or 6x86 processors were also used. Some models had a PC game port. The later cards produced SoundBlaster compatible audio output and supported Ethernet networking.

Despite the old processors, many have found these Apple-based coprocessor cards to be useful, running Windows at speeds faster than emulators on many Mac models, including recent models.

Apple DOS/PC card software

Installing the software for one of the Apple-based cards is a multistep procedure. Since Apple never distributed Windows (just DOS), there's no one-click installation as found in the OrangePC Easy Install and the software emulators. First you have to install System 7.5 Update 2.0, if you don't already have it. Then you install the PC Compatibility software from an Apple CD-ROM. You then install DOS 6.22 from the supplied Microsoft floppies. You're not done yet. Now you install some driver software from an Apple floppy disk. If you want to use Windows 3.1 or Windows 95/95, you install it from your own copy of Microsoft software. (The cards don't support Windows NT.) Finally, if you want to use the SoundBlaster-compatible sound, you need to install special SoundBlaster drivers from Apple's PC Compatibility Card PC Utilities CD-ROM. The installation procedure is similar with the Reply/Radius cards as well.

The Apple/Reply/Radius cards don't launch from an application as with Orange Micro's cards, but use instead a control panel called PC Setup (Figure16.19). Here, you can create and select virtual C: and D: drives, select a Mac folder to share with Windows, and set up COM ports for a modem connection. You also startup and switch to DOS or Windows by pressing buttons at the bottom of the control panel.

MacWindows Tip

With PC Setup, you can enable Windows to access a PC-formatted SCSI hard drive to your Mac, but you can't boot Windows from it. You need to boot from a virtual C: drive file and select the PC-formatted hard drive as drive D: in PC Setup.

In November 1997, Apple released its final version, PC Setup 1.6.4. It runs on all versions of the DOS and PC Compatibility Card except the old Quadra 610, which requires PC Setup 1.0.2. The PC Setup

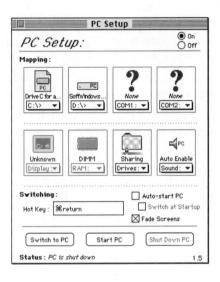

Figure 16.19 Apple's PC Setup software configures a PC Compatibility Card.

software has several deficiencies, some of which have work-arounds, some of which don't. The main problems are lack of support for 32-bit Windows drivers, conflicts with Mac OS 8.5 and later, and problems with expanding RAM. Some people also have problems getting audio to work. The next few pages will take up these issues one at a time.

You can download both versions of PC Setup from Apple's web site:

♦ PC Setup 1.6.4:
   http://til.info.apple.com/swupdates.nsf/artnum/n10766
♦ PC Setup 1.0.2:
   http://til.info.apple.com/swupdates.nsf/artnum/n10768

Lack of 32-bit drivers for Apple-based cards

After installing Windows 95 on a Mac with one of the Apple-based cards, you may see the message that the hard drive, floppy drive, and CD-ROM drive are running in "Compatibility Mode," and that the computer is not running at optimal performance. This indicates that 16-bit drivers are being used instead of 32-bit drivers. Windows 95 runs 16-bit drivers in protected mode.

The lack of support for 32-bit drivers is the biggest limitation of PC Setup and the Apple/Reply/Radius cards if you are running Windows 95. (It's not a problem for running DOS only or Windows 3.x, however.) Without 32-bit support, the Compatibility Cards don't support long file names of Windows 95/98. Because Windows 95 can't access 32-bit drivers, you may have problems with some Windows 95 software that may require 32-bit protected-mode drivers.

In this respect, the Apple-based Compatibility Cards and DOS-in-Mac boards are not completely compatible with Windows 95, and are even less so with Windows 98. The lack of 32-bit driver support also makes the cards completely incompatible with "pure" 32-bit operating systems, including Windows NT and Linux.

Web Update Link: *MacWindows News at http://www.macwindows.com has been following the story on 32-bit drivers for Apple-based coprocessor cards. Another resource is a small web site called Apples and Oranges (http://www2.bc.edu/~fonneman/apple.html), run by Boston College student Mark Fonnemann, class of 2000. Fonneman has been lobbying for 32-bit compatibility for the old cards.*

Since Apple announced that it would no longer update the PC Setup software, several companies have attempted to pick up where Apple left off and developer there own 32-bit PC Setup. The first was Orange Micro, which picked up much of Apple's Pentium card business when Apple discontinued its line. However, the company abandoned the project in mid-1998 when Apple would not reveal the source code for PC Setup and the accompanying software. In late

1998, Fraser Valley Distributed Computing Systems (FVDCS), a consulting company in British Columbia, Canada, said that it would produce a PC Setup 2.0, which it hoped to sell at around $25. However, it ran into the same problem with Apple that Orange Micro had. As of spring of 1999, the project was on hold, but FVDCS was still hopeful that it could work out its differences with Apple.

Mac OS 8.5 conflicts

When Apple released Mac OS 8.5 in 1998, one sentence in a file called "Installing Mac OS 8.5" worried owners:

> Apple DOS Compatibility cards do not work with Mac OS 8.5. After you install the software, you will no longer be able to use your DOS Compatibility Card to run DOS or Windows software.

It turns out that this isn't quite true: You can run DOS and Windows on the DOS Compatibility Card and PC Compatibility Card, but networking doesn't work. With Mac OS 8.5, Apple decided to stop supporting the discontinued cards, which means it was no longer testing the cards with new operating system versions.

However, there is an unofficial solution to the networking problem. Jason Linhart of Summary.net wrote a patch that enables networking with Apple PC Compatibility cards and Mac OS 8.5. The readme file promises partial networking, but many users have found the patch to restore fully functional networking. You can find the patch at:

http://summary.net/soft/PC-CardOS8.5NetPatch.sit.hqx

Expanding RAM

Most of the Apple-based coprocessor cards included RAM in the form of DIMMs (dual in-line memory modules). There is a problem with some cards that prevented the software from being able to use the 12-inch PC Compatibility cards with 32 Mb or 64 Mb DIMMs. The symptom is that when you switch to the PC, the screen goes black after the PC memory test in DOS. Apple has a software fix called the *PC Setup DIMM Patch*. You can find this patch at Apple's software update web site at:

http://asu.info.apple.com/swupdates.nsf/artnum/n10769

Additionally, there are some types of DIMMs that don't work with the PC Compatibility Card and DOS-in-Mac boards. You need to use the older Fast Page Mode memory for these cards, not EDO (extended data output) memory. Older cards that use SIMMs (single in-line memory modules) require noncomposite memory.

Some of the older Apple cards give you the option of sharing the Mac's RAM with Windows software. I don't recommend this, as it greatly slows performance of both Windows and Macintosh.

Audio problems

There are also some problems with PC Compatibility Card cards producing sound. In some cases, this is a matter of configuration. For instance, the audio from some PC cards comes through the CD connection on the motherboard (via a cable put in during installation). In order for the PC sounds to play though the Mac, the Sound Input setting of the Monitors and Sound control panel must be set to "Internal CD," not "Microphone" or "None."

Serial and parallel card problems

Another problem with 12-inch PC Compatibility Cards exists when you have a serial/parallel board in the Mac. When you have the Mac port assigned to the coprocessor card through PC Setup, the Mac doesn't have access to it any more. This is true even when DOS or Windows isn't running.

Running Mac Software on PCs

The state of the art for running Mac software on PCs is many years behind that of Windows emulators for Mac, mostly because of difficulties in emulating Macintosh hardware in software. The main limitation at this point is that none of the products emulate a PowerPC processor. (At the time of this writing, several companies had promised to deliver PowerPC emulation, but none had yet delivered.) That means all of the Mac emulators for PCs are 680x0 emulators, which means that they can't run PowerPC-native software, including Mac OS 8.5 and later. One reason for this is the technical difficulty in emulating a RISC chip (reduced instruction set chip), such as a PowerPC processor, on a CISC chip (complex instruction set chip), such as the Pentium.

This is not to say that the Mac emulators aren't fast. On a fast Pentium II PC, these emulators run old Mac software dozens of times faster than the original Macs did. In fact, Mac emulation on PCs can run significantly faster than Virtual PC or SoftWindows runs on Macs. This is because compared to the Pentium, the 68040 is a relatively simple processor to emulate. For this reason, several of the Mac emulators for PCs can be seen as an upgrade path for old 68040 Macs. People replacing old Macs with Windows machines can use their old Mac software.

Another problem with Mac emulators for Windows is that they must rely somehow on Macintosh ROMs, which are required to run Mac software. More specifically, Mac software needs the Macintosh Toolbox code that is in the Mac's ROM chips. Apple doesn't sell Mac ROMs, so the only source of ROMs that work with these emulators are old Macs. The emulator products deal with this in different ways. One emulator puts Mac ROMs on an inexpensive card in the PC. Two others require you to "download" a Mac's ROM into a file used by the emulator, which requires that you have access to a sufficiently old Macintosh. Another company has "reversed engineered" the Apple ROM code, but is limited in software compatibility.

Starting with the iMac, however, much of the Macintosh ToolBox code was moved out of ROM chips and into a "ROM file" that resides in the System folder. Having access to one of these files would simplify the task for Mac emulators. But none of the Mac emulators can use this file because of the lack of PowerPC-native code. This could change soon, as one company, Emulators, Inc., has promised to demonstrate an iMac emulator in July 1999.

Emulators, Inc., is one of four companies producing Macintosh emulators for PCs. You have to supply your own copy of Mac OS with all of them. The next few pages offer a discussion of these four products. They are listed in order of the abilities, with the most advanced emulator first and the least advanced last.

Web Update Link: *For current information on Macintosh emulator products for Windows, including contact information see http://www.macwindows.com/emulator.html#Maconother.*

Gemulator

Emulators, Inc.
http://www.emulators.com

Emulators, Inc., has been producing emulators longer than any of the other companies, starting in 1986 with Atari emulators. It has been shipping Gemulator, its Mac emulator, since 1993. Gemulator 98 and the newer Gemulator Pro run on Windows 95/98 and Windows NT.

Gemulator solves the ROM issue by providing old Mac ROMs on an ISA card for the PC. Even with the hardware, Gemulator is inexpensive, costing about as much as Virtual PC. If you have your own Mac ROMs, such as from an old Mac or a used hardware dealer, you can get Gemulator for even less. Gemulator can use ROMs from almost any 680x0 Mac. If you find ROMs from a later Mac model, you can upgrade.

Gemulator offers the best compatibility with Mac OS and Mac software. This is partly due to the fact that it uses real Mac ROMs, but

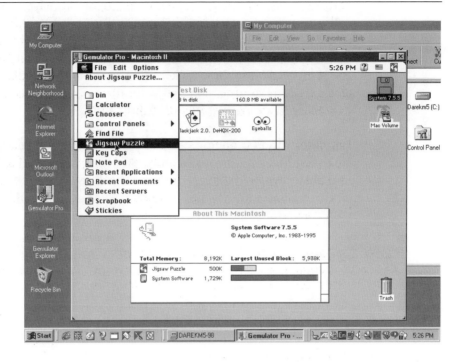

Figure 16.20 Gemulator runs Mac OS in a Windows window or full-screen.

Gemulator also has some advantages in its processor emulation. It is the only Mac emulator so far that lets you select the 680x0 processor you want to emulate, including the 68000, 68020, and 68040. This means it's compatible with software written for all of the processors. At this point, Gemulator can run up to Mac OS 7.6.

At the time of this writing, Emulators, Inc., was promising to demonstrate a version of Gemulator that would emulate a PowerPC processor at the July 1999 Macworld Expo show. (There was no promised shipping date for the product, however.) This would make it the first PowerPC emulator for Windows. The company also promised to demonstrate an iMac emulator, and one that would run Mac OS 8.5.

Emulators Inc. says that running Mac OS in emulation on a Pentium 200 is 20 times faster than a Mac Classic. It claims that running old 680x0 software on Gemulator on a PC is faster than running it on some Power Macintoshes. The company claims that its 680x0 emulator is faster than the one in Mac OS.

Gemulator can run Mac OS either in full-screen mode, or in a window (as shown in Figure 16.20). Unlike some other emulators, which take over the PC, Gemulator lets you run Mac OS at the same time you run Windows programs. You can access Macintosh disks, including Mac-formatted Zip cartridges and HFS-formatted SCSI hard drives, as well as 1.44 Mb floppy disks and Mac CD-ROMs.

Fusion

Microcode Solutions
http://www.microcode-solutions.com/

Fusion emulates Macs with 68040 processors. (Fusion has promised PowerPC emulation in mid-1998, but still had not delivered it by the time this book was published.) Fusion uses a Mac ROM image, a file created by saving the ROM code into a file using a special Mac utility. Since it is illegal to sell a Mac ROM image, Microcode Solutions can't provide you with one—you have to create your own using a utility that comes with Fusion. This means you have to have access to an old Mac that works. Legally, you must own the Mac. Copying the ROM code from a Mac that you don't own is software piracy.

There are several disadvantages of Fusion compared to Gemulator. For one, you must start Fusion from the DOS prompt. More significantly, Fusion takes over the entire PC, preventing you from running Windows or Windows applications while you use Mac OS.

One advantage of Fusion is that it will run Mac OS 8.0 and 8.1 with a 1 Mb ROM from later 68040 Macs, including Mac Quadras, Centris, Performas (the non-PowerPC models), and PowerBooks (again, the non-PowerPC models; if you aren't sure, PowerPC Macs and PowerBooks have four-digit model numbers, as in "Performa 6400"). Fusion supports serial devices, modem communications, and TCP/IP networking, but does not support AppleTalk. You can print from the Mac environment if you have an appropriate Macintosh driver for the particular printer. It also works with InfoWave's PowerPrint PCL drivers (see Chapter 15). As with Gemulator, Fusion supports Mac-formatted SCSI drives and CD-ROM disks (with MSCDEX running).

vMac

The vMac Project
http://www.vmac.org

vMac is a free Macintosh emulator for PCs and is definitely not in the same class as Gemulator and Fusion. vMac emulates a 68000-based Mac Plus, and as such, runs in a black-and-white, 9-inch screen. Like Fusion, it requires that you download the contents of a Mac ROM, and doesn't supply the ROM. Unlike Fusion, vMac requires a Mac Plus ROM—and working Mac Pluses (it has to be working in order to do the download) are pretty rare at this point. The vMac Project plans to add emulation for other 68000 machines, including the Mac SE and Mac IIs. vMac does not access Mac disks, as do Gemulator and Fusion. It does run up to System 7.5.5 on Windows, UNIX, OS/2, and NeXT OpenStep.

ARDI Executor

ARDI
http://www.ardi.com

ARDI Executor is a 680x0 emulator that uses ROM code that was reverse-engineered. Because of this, it is the least compatible Mac emulator of the four, running about 60% to 80% of Macintosh 680x0 applications, according to ARDI. It doesn't support any INITS or CDEVs or most Desk Accessories. It can't access serial ports or use a modem, and works best with System 6.x. It does support 1.44 Mb floppies. Additionally, it costs as much as Gemulator, and more than Fusion, though it is less capable than either. ARDI Executor doesn't require you to have access to a Mac as do Fusion and Vmac, but for the same cost, you can get the much more advanced Gemulator with Mac ROMs. Executor is less advanced than the free vMac.

The one advantage ARDI Executor has is speed, because it runs the Mac OS calls natively on a PC rather than emulated. ARDI says that Executor on a 75 MHz 486DX4 will run as fast as a 25 MHz 68040. Because of this, Executor might be a good choice for old PCs, but on a modern Pentium, the more advanced Mac emulators are plenty fast.

One other unique aspect of ARDI Executor is that there is a version for Linux on x86 platforms, the only Mac emulator for that operating system.

Emulators on UNIX and Other OSs

This chapter ends with an eclectic collection of software products that don't have a lot in common other than they are out of the mainstream, but are worth mentioning. Apple's Macintosh Application Environment is a now-discontinued product that ran Macintosh software on UNIX. Apple discontinued it after it began working on Mac OS X, which is basically a UNIX-based OS that runs Mac software. SheepShaver is not an emulator, but a run-time environment that runs Mac OS natively in BeOS for PowerPC. There is also a version of SheepShaver for LinuxPPC. I end the chapter by getting away from Macintosh completely with Insignia Solutions' SoftWindows for UNIX, a Windows emulator for several UNIX environments.

NOTE: Two other Mac emulators for Windows described in the previous section, vMac and ARDI Executor, are also available for for UNIX and Linux.

Macintosh Application Environment (MAE)

Apple's Macintosh Application Environment (MAE) was the most complete Mac environment for another platform, more complete than any of the Mac emulators for Windows described earlier. MAE ran in UNIX X Window on Sun SPARC workstations and HP 9000 and 700 workstations. The final version was MAE 3.0, which emulated a 68LC040 processor and let you run off-the-shelf Mac software with good compatibility. MAE 3.0 was based on System 7.5.3 and included AppleTalk and TCP/IP networking, AppleScript, Drag and Drop, PC Exchange, and AppleGuide.

Apple discontinued MAE on June 1, 1998, right after it had announced Mac OS X. Clearly, Apple saw MAE as somewhat of a competitor to Mac OS X, which is based on UNIX.

Web Update Link: *For current information on emulators for UNIX and other operating systems, see http://www.macwindows.com/emulator.html#Maconother.*

SheepShaver

by Marc Hellwig and Christian Bauer
http://www.sheepshaver.com/

BeOS for PowerPC completely takes over the Macintosh, preventing you from running Mac OS or Mac software. SheepShaver is an inexpensive run-time environment for BeOS for PowerPC that lets you run Mac OS 7.5.2 through Mac OS 8.1. A run-time environment means that the operating system code runs natively on the processors, not requiring the translation steps of emulation. The creators say that Mac OS runs on top of BeOS on a Mac about as fast as Mac OS would normally run. SheepShaver is not available for BeOS for Intel.

SheepShaver is a full-featured Macintosh environment, running both 680x0 and PowerPC code. It supports printing via AppleTalk, Ethernet networking, disk access, and sound in/out from within the Mac OS environment. You can copy and paste text between Mac OS and Be OS sides. Compatibility is with Mac software is very good. You can even run a Windows emulator, such as SoftWindows 98 or Virtual PC, to get the best of three operating systems.

SheepShaver 2.0 was the first version to work reliably on BeOS Release 4. It added an icon on the Mac desktop that allows you to access files on BeOS volumes, and has the ability to detect removable media.

SheepShaver for LinuxPPC

by Marc Hellwig and Christian Bauer

http://www.sheepshaver.com/

As with BeOS, LinuxPPC running on Macintosh takes up the whole Mac and doesn't let you run Mac OS. SheepShaver for LinuxPPC allows you to run Mac OS in a window. At the time of this writing, SheepShaver for LinuxPPC wasn't finished, but was planned for release in mid 1999. The developers say SheepShaver for Linux will have all of the capabilities of the BeOS version. SheepShaver for LinuxPPC requires LinuxPPC Release 3 or later and runs on most PowerPC Macs.

Figure 16.21 SheepShaver for LinuxPPC running Mac OS in Linux on a Mac

Windows for UNIX: SoftWindows for UNIX

Insignia Solutions
http://www.insignia.com

SoftWindows for UNIX doesn't have anything to do with Macintosh, but it is worth mentioning here. SoftWindows for UNIX is a Windows emulator for UNIX and is the UNIX version of the SoftWindows for Macintosh described early in the chapter. The UNIX version has capabilities similar to the Mac version in terms of Windows software compatibility, networking, and drive access. As with the Mac version, it comes with Windows preinstalled.

Insignia actually offers three SoftWindows products that run on UNIX. SoftWindows 95 for UNIX runs on HP HP-UX 10.20, Sun Solaris 2.5, SunOS 4.1.4, and IBM AIX 4.1.4. SoftWindows 95 for Solaris runs on the UltraSPARC workstation, and SoftWindows 95 for Silicon Graphics runs on the IRIX 6.3 operating system.

It's interesting to consider that Insignia once had a version of SoftWindows for the NeXT operating system, which was based on UNIX. As was mentioned in Chapter 13, NeXT became the basis of Mac OS X. In a way, Insignia Solutions was there with a Windows emulator before Apple added the Blue Box—the portion of Mac OS X that runs traditional Mac OS software.

Another Approach

Emulators and coprocessors make your Mac or PC truly cross-platform. However, there is another way to operate a foreign operating system from your computer that doesn't actually install Windows on a Mac. Chapter 17 goes back to the topic of networks one more time to describe using cross-platform remote control software and a high-end solution call thin-client/server computing.

Chapter

What's in This Chapter:

- ♦ *Application sharing with Netopia's Timbuktu*

- ♦ *X Window application sharing*

- ♦ *Windows NT thin-client/server solutions based on ICA clients*

17

Network Application Sharing and Thin Clients

The previous chapter looked at ways to use one machine's processor and RAM to run software written for another. Network application sharing takes a different approach, but gets you the same result—using Windows software on a Mac, or the other way around.

Consider a network link. On one end, you have a host machine actually running the software. Somewhere else on the network is another machine—running a different operating system—where the user is controlling the application on the remote machine. To the user, it appears that the application is running in his or her machine. What's actually happening is that the host receives only the mouse clicks and keyboard signals from the client machine. The host does the processing, and sends back only changes to the display. The network traffic generated by the application sharing is small.

This is network application sharing, and there are two general strategies. You can use a so-called "thin-client" solution such as those based on technology from Citrix. These types of solutions are centered around Windows NT Server acting as an application server, though UNIX can sometimes be used. The second method of sharing applications over a network is using a remote control program, which can be thought of as providing a peer-to-peer application server. With either of these types of solutions, the user application doesn't actually run on the client machines' RAM and processor.

There are a lot of things that you can do with application sharing technologies. These uses include providing information services and computer maintenance, training, and running public kiosks. This chapter focuses on using network application sharing to enable Windows and Macintosh to run applications from the other platform.

The thin-client solutions tend to make the most sense in larger organizations. For a while, thin clients—also called "network computers," (or "NC" if you were really in the know)—were hyped as the Next Big Thing to take over corporate computing. They haven't and they won't. But thin-client solutions still offer cross-platform benefits that may work for some people.

Fortunately, there is a solution for smaller organizations as well. There's only one remote control program that works on both Windows and Macs—Netopia's Timbuktu Pro.

Web Update Link: *For the latest information on cross-platform application sharing solutions, see http://www.macwindows.com/emulators.html#NTappservers.*

Using Timbuktu Pro

Farallon Computing created Timbuktu almost a decade ago. A few years ago, Farallon spun off its intranet/Internet products into a new company, Netopia, which also got Timbuktu Pro. The software was originally for Mac OS, but has been cross-platform for many years. It is now available in versions for Windows 95, Windows NT, Windows 3.1, and Macintosh. Timbuktu Pro is a benign piece of Windows software. Unlike some of the Windows remote control products, Timbuktu Pro is independent of the PC hardware, so it doesn't replace video drivers or load TSRs. This prevents conflicts with Windows applications and with the Windows operating system itself.

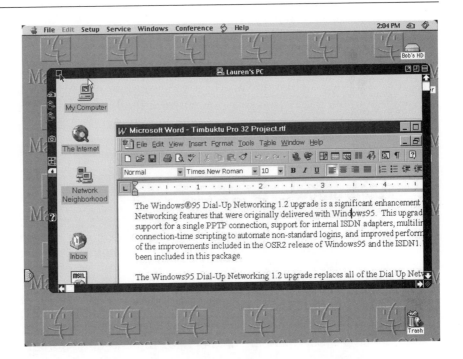

Figure 17.1 Controlling a Windows PC from a Mac with Timbuktu Pro

You can set Timbuktu Pro to enable users to control a machine or to just observe it. You would use Control mode to run Windows software from a Mac (or vice versa). You would use Observer mode to demonstrate some software to a group of Mac and Windows users. In the latter case, you'd have to use a Mac, since, the Mac version of Timbuktu Pro can have many observers at the same time. At this time, the Windows version can only host one Control or Observe session at a time.

With a copy of Timbuktu Pro on a Mac or a PC, each machine can control the other machine and access its software over the network, either in a special Timbuktu window or over the full screen. You can also display a portion of the remote screen and scroll around within the Timbuktu window, or shrink the entire screen to fit in the Timbuktu window. Performance is good, generally better than an emulator, because the software is running natively on the host machine, not the local machine—only keystrokes and screen updates are sent over the network.

You copy and paste between Mac and Windows applications using the clipboard icons on the left side of the Timbuktu window, as shown in Figure 17.1. You can also use Timbuktu to move files across the network. This enables a Mac user running MS Access on a PC via Timbuktu Pro to take a data set from the Mac, move it to the PC over the network, and then import it into an Access database. The user could then save the file to her Mac. The same is true for a Windows user controlling a Mac with Timbuktu Pro.

MacWindows Tip

To log onto Windows NT from a Mac, you'll need Timbuktu Pro 3.0.2 or later. The PC will ask you to enter Control+Alt+Delete. You can log on with the Mac equivalent of Control+Option+Delete. To logon to NT from another Windows PC, open screen-sharing window, go to the menu in the upper left corner, and select "Send Ctrl+Alt+Del to Remote Computer." Occasionally, a NT 4.0 host won't respond to the "Control+Alt+Delete" command from either PC or Mac. In this case, you need to stop and restart the Timbuktu Remote Control Assistant service. You can do this from the host's Service control panel item or using Server Manager from another NT 4.0 over a network.

Timbuktu Pro's Intercom feature that lets you transmit full-duplex sound, enabling you to speak and listen, as on a telephone (Figure 17.2).

More recent versions of the Mac software lets Windows users access Mac software by using Microsoft's NetMeeting (or any other T.120 application sharing software) instead of Timbuktu Pro. Timbuktu for Macs lets Mac users access Windows machines running this software. However, using Timbuktu Pro on the Windows machines does give you more features. There's also a bundle called Timbuktu Enterprise that includes some extra management and security features and tools.

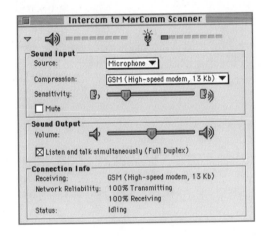

Figure 17.2 Timbuktu Pro's Intercom features provides full-duplex voice communications between users.

When to Use Timbuktu

In order to use Timbuktu Pro as an alternative to an emulator, there are certain conditions that have to be met. First, it doesn't make sense to have another user controlling a computer that someone is working at. Timbuktu doesn't add any multiuser capabilities to a host computer the way Citrix WinFrame and MetaFrame software do to Windows NT. If a Macintosh user is controlling a Windows 95 machine with

Timbuktu, someone sitting in front of the PC will see the applications launch, menus open, and words getting typed. The same is true with a Windows user controlling a Mac.

This means you have to be able to share a machine, and share it one user at a time. The machine can be a Mac or PC dedicated to the task of letting Timbuktu users access it, or it can be a machine that isn't currently being used. In the right situation, Timbuktu Pro can be used as an alternative to an emulator. Here are some example scenarios that show when Timbuktu Pro is useful for cross-platform access:

Spare machine

You have a spare PC, and Mac users occasionally need to use a Windows program. This might be an older machine that used to be a user's PCs, but was replaced by a faster model.

Migration to Windows

Have you moved to mostly PCs, but still have some special-purpose Mac software? By keeping one or two of the old Macs and installing Timbuktu Pro, users now on PCs can still access the older software.

Cross-platform telecommuters

Timbuktu Pro can also be a good solution for a telecommuter who has a Mac at home and Windows at work, or vice versa. The software works over TCP/IP and the Internet, as well as over direct dial-up connection. There are some limitations here that are discussed later.

Use of part-time workers' computers

Macs or PCs set aside for part-time workers can be used by Timbuktu Pro users when the part-time workers aren't in the office. If your part-time worker comes in 3 days a week to enter data in a Microsoft Access database, the Mac users can access the PC the other 2 days to run Access or other Windows software.

Training

Timbuktu Pro is useful for training a group of Mac and Windows users on software that exists on both platforms, such as a web-based application, a Microsoft Word macro, or a Photoshop filter. Users of both platforms could watch a demonstration on machines in different rooms or buildings, since Timbuktu also includes real-time audio conferencing.

Conferencing

With multiple Mac and Windows users controlling a Mac, you can hold a virtual conference over the network.

Cross-platform network management and administration

Windows NT Server requires that certain administration tasks be performed at the NT console. Timbuktu Pro allows you to control Windows NT servers from Macs or Windows 3.x/95/98 and NT from any local or remote location. In fact, from a single computer, you can maintain all of your servers—NT services, AppleShare IP on Macs, web servers on NT or Macs—as well as configure users' computers.

Connecting with Timbuktu Pro

Timbuktu for Windows can communicate with Macs or other PCs over TCP/IP and IPX (though the Windows NT version does not work with IPX). Macs can communicate over TCP/IP, IPX, and AppleTalk. The TCP/IP connections include the Internet, so a Mac and PC don't even have to be in the same building to control each other. However, Timbuktu does not work through proxy servers.

You may also have some problems making a Timbuktu connection through a firewall. You can enable firewalls to let Timbuktu work if you allow the firewall IP router to open UDP port 407 and TCP ports 1417 through 1420. Table 17.1 shows how Timbuktu Pro uses each port. If you'd rather use different ports for Timbuktu, you can change

Timbuktu's port assignments with the Timbuktu Pro Administrator's Toolkit that comes with Timbuktu Pro for Enterprise. The dynamic ports are those greater than port 1023.

Table 17.1 Timbuktu Pro default UDP and TCP ports

Feature or purpose	Port number
Connection (handshaking)	UDP port 407
Control	TCP port 1417
Observe	TCP port 1418
Send Files	TCP port 1419
Exchange files	TCP port 1420
Chat	Dynamic TCP port
Notify	Dynamic TCP port
Intercom	Dynamic TCP and UDP port
Ask for permission	Dynamic TCP and UDP port

You can use Timbuktu Pro to control another computer over a remote connection. The Windows version can communicate over Windows Remote Access Server (RAS) connections, and the Mac version can communicate over Apple Remote Access (ARA) connections. Both versions support PPP connections using TCP/IP or IPX. The PPP server can be running on a Mac or PC, such as RAS or the ARA Personal Server 3.0, or a stand-alone box such as a Shiva LAN Rover.

Macs also have the ability to directly dial into each other using Netopia's Direct Dial protocol. (Unfortunately, Timbuktu Pro for Windows does not have this ability, so you'll have to stick with PPP.) With Timbuktu Pro running on both Macs, the incoming call will be recognized as a request for a Timbuktu session. However, the Direct Dial service can't answer calls if you also have fax software set to answer calls at the same time. Most fax software doesn't have this problem when you use ARA to answer an incoming call.

NetMeeting Application Sharing

Timbuktu Pro for Macintosh gained the ability to join in Microsoft NetMeeting conferences with version 4.8, the full title of which is Timbuktu Pro 4.8 with Microsoft NetMeeting Compatible Application Sharing. (Figure 17.3) This means that with this version of Timbuktu on the Macs, the Windows machines don't need Timbuktu at all, but can run any T.120 application sharing software (including NetMeeting) for Macs and Windows users to access each other's software.

Timbuktu Pro 4.8 with Microsoft NetMeeting isn't a Mac version of NetMeeting—it just implements the T.120 Invitation and Conference Services. The Invitation Service lets you invite other Timbuktu Pro with NetMeeting or NetMeeting users to connect to and control or observe the Mac. The Show My Screen utility will immediately dis-

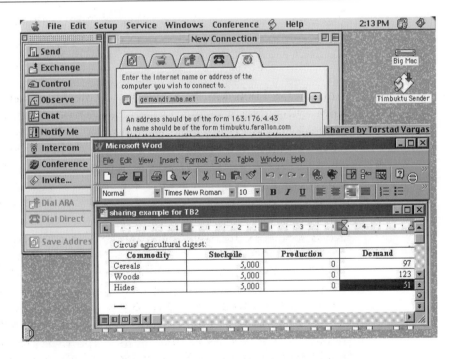

Figure 17.3 Timbuktu enables Mac users to participate in a Microsoft NetMeeting collaborative conference.

play your desktop to another user. The Conference Service provides the T.120-compatible application sharing.

Timbuktu Pro with Microsoft NetMeeting does not implement Net-Meeting's whiteboarding feature or its H.323-based video and audio capabilities. (You can add an H.323 audio and video client for Mac with White Pine's CUCMe if you also have a CUCMe server.) Computers running Timbuktu Pro can use Netopia's Intercom feature for transmitting audio.

Administration and Windows NT Networks

Timbuktu Pro has some abilities that can make it fit in with Windows NT networks. For instance, you can use Windows NT's users and groups to assign Timbuktu access to an NT host instead of creating a separate users and group list in Timbuktu. You can also use Windows NT security to authenticate users trying to control a host. However, both situations apply only to Timbuktu Pro 32 for Windows, and not to Macintosh clients. This is becuase of the way Windows NT handles Mac users; Netopia has not added any additional support for Macs, which will have to gain access through Timbuktu itself. In fact, Timbuktu Pro 32 for Windows services uses Windows NT's security the same way that Windows NT File and Print services do. Timbuktu Pro 32 also supports Windows NT password encryption and event logging. Other security features include screen blanking, password aging, and automatic log off when disconnecting

To use Windows NT's users and groups to grant Timbuktu Pro 32 access to an NT host, you open the "NT Users" tab of Timbuktu's Security dialog. This lists the Windows users and groups with check boxes to assign access to specific Timbuktu Pro services, such as control and observe. You can add or remove users here. This window will let you browse NT domains databases that have trust relationships with other domains to located users. NT will handle the authentication, so Windows users can log on to the host without seeing a Timbuktu logon dialog.

Of course, giving a lot of users permission to control to a lot of NT servers isn't a task most groups will want take on. But it may be useful to give a group of administrators access to a server. Or, you may want to give groups of users access to a shared Windows NT machine.

Enterprise Edition

Aimed at networks of 100 nodes or more, Timbuktu Pro Enterprise is a bundle of the versions for Windows NT, Windows 95/98, Windows 3.x, and Macintosh and management and security features and tools. It comes with the Timbuktu Pro Administrator's Toolkit, which lets you manage security, users, and networking from one location.

Multiuser Application Sharing Solutions: Thin-Client/Server

When multiple clients log onto a server to run control applications, it makes sense to dedicate a server to the task of sharing applications. This type of system is also known as a "thin-client/server" system. The clients—Windows, Macintosh, and UNIX—are called "thin" because they don't need a lot of processing power, RAM, or hard disk space, since the processing and file storage is done on the server. The ultimate thin client is called a Windows terminal, because like the text-based terminal connected to mainframes years ago, everything the user sees and manipulates on a Windows terminal originates on a host.

Diskless PCs haven't gone over as big as some had predicted, so the "thin" aspect of this technology isn't as important as it was once thought to be. But running software on a server does have some management benefits, and it does give Mac users the ability to view and control applications running on Windows NT and UNIX, the two main application-sharing platforms. Additionally, users with old machines can run the latest application software via the network.

Windows NT is by far the most popular application server platform. There are few application server solutions for Mac OS, mostly because of the lack of protected memory. However, as a UNIX-based operating system Mac OS X Server is a potential platform for X.11 servers or other application-sharing products that might enable Windows users to run Mac OS applications over networks.

There are two types of thin-client/server technologies. The first uses X.11 (also called X Window or X Terminal) technology, which comes out of the UNIX world, but is also available for Windows NT. There's even one solution for Mac OS servers. The second and more popular is the Independent Computing Architecture (ICA) client technology from Citrix Systems. The Citrix server technology is called WinFrame and MetaFrame, which run on Windows NT. There are also some application server products that support both X.11 and ICA clients.

Differences: X Window and WinFrame/MetaFrame

The X Window and Citrix WinFrame/MetaFrame thin-client solutions differ in a number of ways. First, X Window comes from the open software movement of UNIX, where the source code is freely available. The Citrix-based thin-client solutions are proprietary.

Another difference between the two approaches is that X Window has its own interface and can only run applications written to work for a particular X Window system. Citrix WinFrame and MetaFrame look like Windows and run off-the-shelf Windows applications. This makes it more practical as an alternative to emulators.

The Citrix ICA client is also a "thinner" client than an X.11 client, in that, like Timbuktu, the host does all of the processing. With the X Window system, the user's machine is responsible for producing the display. The X Window user often has a slower experience than a Win-Frame/MetaFrame user. The X Window protocol also moves more data over the network, making it nearly unusable over a modem connection. ICA generally works well over a modem.

NOTE: There is a technology called Low Bandwidth X (LBX, also called X.Fast) that can improve X Window's performance by a factor of 10 using compression and caching. You use it instead of PPP. However, it is a relatively new technology, and there isn't any Mac LBX software yet.

However, the "thinness" of the Citrix technology and its low bandwidth can make it slower than X Window in some cases. Thin-client servers are not good for Windows applications that use frequently changing, large bitmaps. For example, when running AutoCAD for Windows over the ICA protocol, the on-screen cursor often becomes sluggish. A 3-D game would run poorly over the ICA protocol.

There is a trade-off between the low-bandwidth ICA protocol and the high-bandwidth X Window protocol. You can run a CAD program over the X Window protocol on an Ethernet network and get good results because the graphics processing is done locally by the user's computer.

X Window Solutions

X Window, or simply "X," started as a graphical display standard for UNIX computers, but host implementations of X have been created for other operating systems as well. These include VMS, Windows NT, and even Macintosh. On multiuser operating systems, such as UNIX, multiple users can access applications over the network.

X is basically a windowing standard originally developed by a group called the MIT X Consortium. X first enabled the character-driven command-line UNIX operating system to run graphics software that could be controlled with a mouse. X Window can run directly on the host machine, or can be used on another computer over a network to access the host. An application with a graphic interface appears on the remote user's machine, but most of the processing is done on the host. (Still, an X Window client isn't as "thin" as a Citrix WinFrame ICA client. With X, the processing for the interface is handled by the local computer, not the host.) An X system operating over a network uses the X.11 protocol.

To confuse matters, traditional X Window technology uses the words client and server in exactly the opposite way that the terms are used in describing other network services. In traditional X Window lingo, the shared computer running the application software which most people would think of as the "host" is the one running the client software. The X server, or display server, is software that always runs on a user's machine. The display is considered a server because it is shared by the applications running on what we would call the host. Some vendors of X Window products use these older meanings, while others don't. I will take a more modern approach, referring to the user's machine as an "X.11 client," "X terminal," or "X display," and to the computer running the applications as the "host."

X user interfaces

Different implementations of X Window can have different user interfaces. This is due to a piece of X software called the window manager, which usually runs on the user's machine as part of the X terminal. Window managers determine the exact look and feel of the interface, including what the scroll bars look like, how the windows are resized, and how various icons act.

Traditional X Window managers such as Open Look from Sun and Motif from the Open Software Foundation provide a more UNIX-like look and feel, while others are more like Mac OS or MS Windows. Applications running on the host are sometimes written for a specific window manager, while others have the ability to switch between window managers. In order to ensure compatibility with multiple hosts, X display software contains multiple window managers.

MacWindows Tip

If you have the choice of using a local window manager or a remote one, choose a local window manager running on your machine. It puts more processing on the user's computer, but results in faster performance.

X display software for Mac users

There are several X.11-compatible clients for Mac that have been around for many years—Apple's MacX, eXodus from White Pines Software, and XTen from Tenon Intersystems. They run differently from ordinary Mac applications because of the oddities of the X Window system. For one, X.11 uses its own X screen drawing techniques instead of Mac OS's native QuickDraw routines. X display programs also come with their own fonts.

eXodus
White Pine Software
http://www.wpine.com/

White Pine Software's eXodus is the top X.11-compatible X display utility for Macs. eXodus supports FTP file transfers, keyboard mapping, and 24-bit color display. With eXodus 7.0 and later, you can add the optional OpenGL for eXodus by Conix for access to 2-D and 3-D applications running on X hosts.

eXodus comes with a variety of window managers for a compatibility with a wide variety of hosts and software, and for choices in interface. It supports both rootless windows, which can be moved around the desktop like standard Macintosh windows, and rooted windows, in which all other X windows are run inside the first window, similar to the way Windows 3.x worked. The windowing is handled by the included window manager, eXene (named after the lead singer of the rock group X from the early 1980s). The eXene window manager provides a Mac-like window with well-designed menus and easy-to-use scripts, and was always more elegant than Apple's old MacX. For better performance, you can configure eXene to run in rootless-motif mode, which gives you a look somewhat similar to the old Motif window manger.

eXodus also comes with a Motif Window Manager (MWM), which produces a more traditional UNIX interface. With MWM, you have a choice of two rooted mode versions: a standard, full-screen rooted mode, and an invisible rooted mode which gives you access to the Mac desktop. You can also run MWM at the same time you're running eXene or another window manager, such as Open Windows (olwm) or HP-VUE (vuewm).

White Pine has discontinued eXodus for Windows, replacing it with WebTerm X, a product that provides X sessions from within a web browser.

MacWindows Tip

You can optimize the speed of eXodus with some attention to graphics settings. For instance, you can reduce the pixel resolution to improve performance. Also, when setting the color matching tolerance, turn off Exact Match in the Screen Editor command in the Settings menu. Increasing the amount memory allocated to eXodus in its Get Info box can also help performance.

MacX
Apple Computer
http://www.apple.com/networking

Apple's MacX is a simple, easy-to-use, and quick X.11 system. It is a simpler X Window display program than eXodus. MacX and eXodus are both long-lived programs, but through the years, Apple hasn't upgraded MacX as much as White Pine has upgraded eXodus, so it doesn't have a lot of extra features. However, MacX been modernized enough to support PowerPC processing and Open Transport. Like eXodus, it runs over Ethernet, PPP, and the Apple Remote Access protocol.

MacX comes with a window manager that can display rooted or rootless windows. It can give you familiar-looking X windows with standard Mac title bars and close boxes. MacX also runs less Mac-like window managers, such as Motif, Open Look, and twm (short for Tom's Window Manager), and so is compatible with a good amount of X Window host software.

XTen
Tenon Intersystems
http://www.tenon.com/products/xten/

XTen is different than eXodus and MacX, in that in addition to a full-featured 24-bit color X display system, it also includes an X host for running X applications on the Mac. Tenon Intersystems, makers of MachTen, a BSD and Mach UNIX environment for Macintosh, have embedded enough of UNIX in XTen to enable Mac users to run X applications, as well as view and operate them. To clarify, XTen does not make Macintosh applications available to other platforms—the XTen host runs X applications, for the purpose of the local user. You can also run Mac applications at the same time you run local or networked X applications.

Like other X terminals for Mac, XTen includes Motif, OpenLook, and other window managers, letting you display and control applications running on a variety of UNIX and non-UNIX X hosts, including Sun, SCO, HP, IBM R/6000, Silicon Graphics, NeXT, and VAX.

You can configure XTen with a web browser. For network, you have the choice of use the Mac's Open Transport or Tenon's own multi-homing, IP aliasing TCP/IP stack.

VNSviewer
AT&T Laboratories Cambridge
http://www.uk.research.att.com/vnc/start.html

VNCviewer for Macintosh is a not a general-purpose X display package like the packages previously described, but is a special piece of software that can only be used to view applications running on AT&T's Virtual Network Computing (VNC) servers, described in the next section. VNC is based on X, but uses a special VNC protocol instead of X.11. VNC viewers and servers are available for variety of platforms, including Windows NT, UNIX, and Macintosh, and are free.

X Window host software for Macintosh and Windows

You'll find X Window host software built into many UNIX systems. With X.11 display software, Macs, Windows, and multiple UNIX users can view and control applications written for X Window. For Mac and Windows hosts, there are some packages related to X Window that do a similar function, though not exactly.

For Windows, there is WinCenter from Network Computing Devices, described in the next section on thin-client computing. It layers X.11 on top of the Citrix WinFrame-based servers, so that multiple Mac, Windows, and other clients can access Windows software by running the X display software described earlier. The host looks like an X Window host to the user software, but actually is not.

Another approach is the Virtual Network Computing (VNC), a free, open source system from AT&T. VNC lets you view and control UNIX, Windows, and Mac applications from multiple platforms, but is only multiuser on UNIX hosts.

There used to be several other X-like host systems for Macintosh: XGator from Cayman Systems, and PlanetX from Intercon Systems, now defunct. The problem is that Mac OS 8.x and earlier isn't as robust as UNIX and isn't multiuser. This may change as use of Mac OS X spreads, since OS X has UNIX BSD 4.4 built into it.

Virtual Network Computing System
AT&T Laboratories Cambridge
http://www.uk.research.att.com/vnc/start.html

The Virtual Network Computing (VNC) system was created by Olivetti Research Laboratory (ORL) of Cambridge, England, founded in 1987. AT&T acquired the lab in January 1999, and VNC became a project of AT&T Laboratories Cambridge.

The Virtual Network Computing (VNC) system calls its host software VNC servers, and its client software VNCviewers. Both servers and viewers for multiple platforms and the source code are freely available at AT&T's web site. Both servers and viewers are very compact, fitting in small amounts of RAM. At the time of this writing, the Mac version of both the viewer and the server were considered beta. The Windows and UNIX versions have been "golden" for some time. There are also VNCviewers for Java and Windows CE.

VNC is a unique system, somewhat of a cross between an X Window system and Netopia's Timbuktu Pro. When running on UNIX machines, the VNC server can act like an X Window host, running X Window application and sending the display to VNCviewers running on other platforms (Figure 17.4). However, with a VNC server running on Windows or Mac, the VNCviewers can display and control the entire Mac or Windows desktop, not just applications written for X Window. In this respect, it is more like Timbuktu Pro than an X Window host. As with other systems, the servers can be set to allow only viewing.

Figure 17.4 VNCviewer for Mac accessing a Windows PC running VNC Server

Another difference from standard X-ware is that VNCviewers don't use X.11, but AT&T's VNC protocol. This means that VNCviewers can only access VNC servers, and VNC servers can only be accessed by VNCviewers.

While VNC servers on UNIX are multiuser, VNC servers on Windows NT or Mac OS are not. Although Windows NT does allow different users to log on at a console, it doesn't have the capability of having multiple, different graphic interfaces distributed to different users. (This is a capability that Citrix' MultiWin adds to NT, as described in the next section.)

Citrix WinFrame/MetaFrame ICA Solutions

Citrix Systems is the leader in thin-client/server technologies based on Windows NT. Multiple Mac, Windows, and UNIX clients can view and control any Windows application running on the server. (Figure 17.5 shows a Mac client accessing a WinFrame server.)

The Citrix client technology is called Independent Computing Architecture (ICA). Citrix has two servers, the older WinFrame and the newer MetaFrame, which can both be accessed by ICA clients. Other companies, including Microsoft, have licensed portions of Citrix technologies to create their own server software, some of which uses X.11 (described in the previous section) for client access. WinFrame-based solutions are usually cross-platform. The exception is Microsoft's Windows Terminal Server, which supports only Windows clients.

The Windows NT host running WinFrame and MetaFrame provides all of the processing, sending the user interface to the clients at the beginning of a session. Then, only screen updates, keyboard signals, mouse clicks, and audio are sent over the network. The resulting bandwidth used is low enough to make modem connections practical. ICA traffic uses much less bandwidth than when a user simply launches an application from a file server. In the latter case, the file server sends large chunks of application and document code over the network for processing by the client CPU.

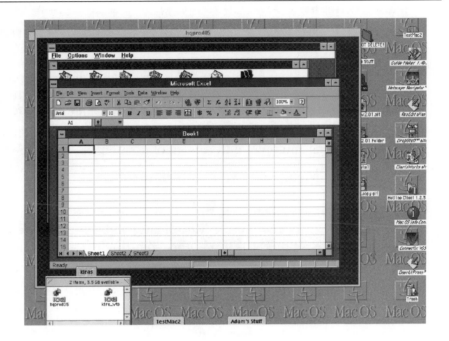

Figure 17.5 This Windows program on a Mac is actually running on a Citrix WinFrame server on Windows NT.

With ICA software, a Mac user controlling a 32-bit Windows application via ICA can expect better performance than running an Windows emulator. That is, if the server and network aren't overloaded. Generally, one Windows NT Server running WinFrame or MetaFrame can support about 15-to-20 simultaneous thin clients without performance degradation. WinFrame or MetaFrame can also run side-by-side with on Windows NT Services for Macintosh for traditional file and print support of Macs. For more clients, you can add Citrix' load balancing option, which distributes the host duties to other NT servers on the network.

Users of ICA clients can save files to the server or locally and can access local hard disks, CD-ROMs, floppy drives, and printers. Network administrators can restrict access to these items as well.

MacWindows Tip

One way to give Macs access to UNIX servers via Citrix servers is to install a Windows client for a UNIX service, such as an SQL database client, on the NT machine running WinFrame or MetaFrame. With multiple users, this strategy reduces network traffic, since the SQL commands and data are only transmitted between the UNIX and NT servers. The clients send and receive only screen updates, mouse clicks, and keyboard strokes.

WinFrame versus MetaFrame versus Terminal Server

So far, I've mentioned three thin-client servers for Windows NT: Citrix WinFrame, Citrix MetaFrame, and Microsoft Terminal Server. There are products from other companies as well, but these are based on WinFrame technology licensed from Citrix. In a nutshell, the differences between the three major thin-client servers are thes:

- ◆ **WinFrame, Citrix' older server.** Multi-platform client support, uses ICA.
- ◆ **Microsoft Terminal Server.** Based on multi-user technology from Citrix, but clients are Windows only and don't use ICA.
- ◆ **MetaFrame, Citrix' newer server.** Runs on top of Microsoft Terminal Server. Adds support for non-Windows clients.

Of course, there is more to these products than can fit in a nutshell, so lets take a closer look.

WinFrame

Citrix started its corporate life in 1989 as a developer of a multiuser version of IBM's OS/2. It first shipped WinFrame for Windows NT in 1995. Citrix used its expertise in multiuser operating systems to create a component of WinFrame called MultiWin that enables multiple users to run the same or different applications. MultiWin can be seen as an add-on to the NT operating system itself that enables NT to share off-the-shelf 32-bit Windows applications among ICA users.

At first, Citrix did not have a Macintosh client for WinFrame. The first Mac ICA client was created by a WinFrame licensee, Insignia Solutions, makers of the SoftWindows emulators for Mac and UNIX. Citrix had licensed the WinFrame/MultiWin server technology and the ICA client technology to several developers, most of whom are no longer in the thin-client business.

Insignia's Mac ICA client was part of a product called NTrique, a WinFrame/MultiWin-based server for Windows NT with ICA clients for Macintosh and UNIX. In addition to supporting the ICA clients, the NTrigue server also supported X.11 clients, so that any machine running standard X Window software could access the NTrigue server. NTrigue networking was over TCP/IP protocols.

Insignia sold NTrigue to Citrix in January of 1998. Based on the Insignia software, Citrix released a free Macintosh ICA client for Win-Frame in March of 1998. Citrix did not add Insignia's X.11 support to WinFrame.

There were other third-party products that let you access WinFrame with X.11 software on the client to see and operate Windows applications on a WinFrame server. Today, however, there is just one left, WinCenter from Network Computing Devices (NCD). There are versions of WinCenter for both WinFrame and MetaFrame servers. NCD doesn't offer an X.11 client for Macintosh, but any X terminal software, including White Pine's eXodus (described earlier), will work. In 1998, NCD purchased and discontinued a competing product, Tektronix WinDD, which also supports Mac X.11 clients.

Windows Terminal Server

While WinFrame is still major server for thin clients, the market changed when Microsoft introduced Windows Terminal Server. In 1997 Microsoft licensed Citrix' MultiWin, the low-level portion of WinFrame that added multiuser capabilities to Windows NT. On top of MultiWin, Microsoft developed its own application-sharing server and client software, Windows NT Server Terminal Server Edition. For the clients, the Windows Terminal Server does not use ICA, but uses Microsoft's RDP (Remote Desktop Protocol) and is only available for modern versions of Windows. RDP runs only on TCP/IP, not the wide variety of network protocols supported by ICA (TCP/IP, IPX, NetBEUI, and PPP). Windows Terminal Server also does not offer the load balancing feature of WinFrame.

MetaFrame

Citrix MetaFrame fills the holes in Windows Terminal Server by running on top of Windows Terminal Server. MetaFrame uses ICA for clients, so enables clients of many platforms to access Windows applications. The clients include Macintosh, DOS, Windows 3.x, UNIX, and Java. MetaFrame also restores the multiple protocol support of ICA, and adds direct dial-in access to Terminal Server. For larger network, the server load balancing feature of WinFrame is also available for MetaFrame. MetaFrame can also be accessed over a web browser. The ICA clients can access both WinFrame and MetaFrame.

A MetaFrame solution costs more than WinFrame, because it also requires you to buy Microsoft Windows Terminal Server. However, if you already have Windows Terminal Server, MetaFrame is a viable add-on to enable Macintosh participation.

NT Services for Macintosh and WinFrame/MetaFrame

Windows NT Services for Macintosh can coexist with WinFrame or MetaFrame servers. In fact, running a WinFrame-based server simplifies administration. Instead of separate user accounts for Mac and Windows users, you can convert Services for Mac accounts and security for use with WinFrame. This gives you a single set of users with consistent file-level security.

You need to convert Services for Macintosh volumes for use with WinFrame with a Citrix utility called sfmconv. The utility creates new volumes equivalent to the old ones while retaining volume passwords. If a Guest account is enabled, the sfmconv utility duplicates file and directory access permissions for the Guests group and gives them to the Everyone group.

Looking Ahead

Throughout this book, I've attempted to break down the real and perceived barriers to integrating Macs and Windows. But when it comes down to it, computing is just typing on a keyboard and looking at a monitor. When you run an emulator or a network application sharing client, you have created a situation that enables you to use one keyboard and monitor to operate Mac OS and Windows software.

There's another way to do that—physically connect a keyboard and monitor to two or more Macs and PCs. Or, maybe you just want to use your favorite keyboard and mouse. This is the topic of the next chapter.

Chapter

What's in This Chapter:

♦ **Differences in Mac and PC monitors and keyboards**

♦ **Sharing monitors with switch boxes**

♦ **Cross-platform use of keyboards and mice**

♦ **USB keyboards and mice**

18

Sharing Monitors and Mixing Keyboards

Running or controlling software from the "other" platform can solve major integration problems, but there are situations when some people need to run both a real Mac and a real PC directly. With one person using two ore more computers, there isn't always a need for multiple sets of monitors, keyboards, and mice. Using a single set for multiple machines can save money and desk space. But even people with one machine might want to use a favorite PC keyboard with a Macintosh, or an Apple keyboard with a Windows machine. Fortunately, there are three types of devices you can use to share these basic input and output devices or to use the "wrong" keyboard:

- ◆ Monitor switches
- ◆ KVM (keyboard, video, and mouse) switches (no converter)
- ◆ ADB-to-PS/2 keyboard converters (no switch)

Compared to some of the topics in previous chapters, the solutions here are fairly low-tech involving switch boxes, cables, and connector adapters. These items can be low-cost as well and are easily obtainable from multiple sources. You can shop for all of these at one of dozens of web sites as well as many computer stores.

However, it's easy to buy the wrong cables and adapters, especially if you are ordering from the Internet or a catalog. So before you buy anything, it's a good idea to take an inventory of your equipment. Note the types of connectors on your computers and monitor, how many pins they have, and whether they are male or female.

As in previous chapters, we'll start by pointing out the differences in the monitor and keyboard technology before moving on to discussing the solutions.

Web Update Link: *For current product and contact information on specific keyboard and monitor sharing devices, see http://www.macwindows.com/keyboard.html.*

Differences: Monitors, Keyboards, and Mice

There is little difference between current Mac and PC monitors other than the connector at the end of a cable. And in Apple's newer "Blue and White" monitors introduced in 1999, Apple adopted the same cable connector used in the PC world.

Keyboards have been a different story, as Macs and PCs use different methods of communicating with their input devices. This is changing, however, with the advent of USB (Universal Serial Bus) input devices, which are the same on both platforms. (USB is discussed at the end of the chapter.)

Monitor Differences

Monitors created in the past few years can run on either PCs or modern Macs. Today, the only difference between some Mac and PC monitors models is the connector at the end of the cable. Both have 15 pins, but the traditional Mac connector is arranged in two rows, while the pins in PCs connectors are arranged in three rows. The latter is called a 15-pin mini D-sub connector, also known more simply as an HD-15 connector. Some Macs, such as PowerBooks and some of the old Mac clones (Power Computing and Motorola StarMax), use the three-row mini D-sub connectors. You can take care of this with a simple converter adapter. A third type of connector called a 5-BNC is sometimes seen on graphics cards and monitors. It works the same for Macs and PCs.

You can run into problems with older hardware. Older Apple fixed-frequency RGB monitors will not run on PCs. In order to work with PCs, you need a VGA/SVGA monitor that can scan at multiple pixel resolutions, variously known as multiple scan, multiscan, multisynchronous, or multisync monitors. Fortunately, multisync VGA/SVGA monitors make up the vast majority of monitors—single-scan RGB monitors have not been sold for many years.

If you have an old Apple monitor and aren't sure what type it is, you can find out by plugging it into a working Mac. If you go to the Monitors and Sound control panel and you only have one choice of pixel resolution (such as 640 x 480), then you have an old RGB monitor that won't work with a PC (or with a PC coprocessor card in the Mac).

MacWindows Tip

If you don't have a Mac to connect to the monitor, you can check to see if it is a multisync montor by looking it up on the web. Griffin Technology, a manufacturer of monitors and video adapters, has a Net Monitor Database web site (http://www.nashville.net/~griffin/monitor.html). It doesn't list every monitor ever made, but there are more than 2000 monitors from hundreds of vendors.

Computers and video cards sense the type of monitor from lines in the connector. You may run into problems with very old Macs or video cards, or with old PC monitors. With some older Macs (made well before the first Power Macs), you'll only get a single 640 x 480 resolution when you plug in a multisync monitor. Old PC monitors may require a special adapter or software utility to help the Mac sense the resolution of the monitor.

In most modern monitors, computers, and graphics cards, the auto sensing lines comply with the VESA Display Data Channel and Extended Display Identification Data standards. (VESA is the Video Electronics Standards Association, at http://www.vesa.org.)

Keyboard and Mouse Differences

Traditional keyboard and mouse ports (that is, non-USB ports) on Macs and PCs are vastly different and not interchangeable. Most PCs use a type of serial port usually referred to as a PS/2 port, named after an old IBM PC model. (The older, less common AT-type mouse port is named after an even older IBM PC model.) A PC mouse plugs into its own RS-232 port on the PC. Joysticks also have their own port.

Since the Macintosh SE and Macintosh II of 1987, the Apple Desktop Bus (ADB) has been the traditional Mac keyboard and mouse port. ADB is a serial bus that allows you to daisy-chain one device into another, such as plugging a mouse into a keyboard. ADB supports keyboards, mice, trackballs, joysticks, and other input devices.

WARNING: ADB and PS/2 devices are not hot-swappable. You should shut of the computer before plugging or unplugging any ADB or PS/2 keyboard or mouse directly into the computer. Failure to do so can damage the motherboard.

Switching boxes that convert singles between ADB and PS/2 are more complex than the simple monitor switch boxes. This complexity translates into higher prices for the boxes and more problems that can crop up.

Aside from the keyboard interface, there are a few minor differences in Mac and PC keyboards themselves. For instance, the latter often have special keys for Windows 95/98, which won't work when used with a Macintosh. And then there are minor naming differences, such as the ALT key on a PC key board and the Option key on the Mac. The Mac Return key is Enter on PC keyboards. Other than these differences and some small rearrangements in key placement, most keyboard functions are the same.

Mice differ a little more than keyboards. The PC standard mouse has two buttons; the standard Mac mouse has one. (UNIX mice often have three buttons.) In some software, holding down a Mac mouse button has the same effect as pressing a PC right mouse button.

Sharing Monitors with Switch Boxes

Since you can use a multisync VGA/SVGA monitor on both Macs and PCs, using a Mac monitor on a PC is virtually a non-issue with modern hardware. The only task that we need to discuss here is sharing a monitor between computers. Sharing a monitor between one Mac and one PC can be accomplished easily and inexpensively with a switch box. You can also get switch boxes that support more computers for a lab or for rooms with servers. In fact, there are switch boxes that can share a monitor with dozens or even hundreds of computers.

There are two types of switch boxes available. The first are simple monitor switch boxes, with two or more input ports to receive cables from the computers' graphics cards, and one output port for a monitor. The second type are the more complicated KVM switches, short for keyboard, video, and mouse. These devices let you use one set of monitor, keyboard, and mouse to control multiple computers.

The simple monitor switches are significantly cheaper then the KVM switches and can be had for under $25. KVM devices can run several times that, not including the keyboard converter box usually required for switching between Macs and PCs. There are often special cables required for these devices, at extra cost. The addition of keyboard switching to the device also adds a great deal of complexity. (See the next section for more on keyboard sharing.) Because of this, you might want to consider sharing only a monitor between a Mac and PC, and sticking to using separate keyboards for each.

Ghosting Problems and Cables

Other than getting the right cables and connectors to fit the Mac and PC ports, there really aren't any cross-platform issues with either KVM or monitor-only switches. The main issue with monitor sharing is one of image quality. The main image quality problem is ghosting, where you see shadowy duplications of images and text on screen. More than just annoying, ghosting can cause eyestrain.

MacWindows Tip

Try to get away with as few adapters and cables as possible. Each additional connection can add more noise that can degrade the monitor signals.

The less you spend on a switch box and the cables, the more likely you are to run into ghosting problems. Particularly important are the cables. You can often get away with a low-cost switch box if you invest in the best VGA cables you can buy. The switch box itself can be a source of ghosting, so it might be prudent to not buy the absolutely cheapest box you can find. However, with a good cable, you won't have to spend a lot for the switch. The thickness of a cable is a good indication of quality: thicker is usually better.

Cheap VGA extension cables use twisted-pair wires inside and are not suitable for anything more than a 640 by 480 display at 60 Hz VGA. These are likely to cause ghosting (due to impedance problems.)

The best cables go by various names, including *super-shielded, coax, mini-coax,* or *75-ohm.* These cables include three "mini-coaxial" cables inside the overall sheath. In super-shielded cables, each interior cable is individually shielded. A good cable should be rated as having 75-ohm impedance.

You should also try to use the shortest cables you can get away with. However, with super-shielded cables, you can get away with longer cables without image problems than with less expensive cables.

BNC cables can also reduce ghosting effects, but have drawbacks as well, as discussed in the next section.

Web Update Link: *For links to cable company web sites that sell high-quality, super-shielded, and BNC cables, see http://www.macwindows.com/keytips.html. These companies often sell video switch boxes as well. One of the best is Cables Unlimited at http://www.cablesun.com.*

Monitors with Built-in BNC Switches

Some higher-end monitors have a built-in switch and two input connectors—one for a standard 15-pin mini sub-D VGA/SVGA plug, and another for a coaxial connector known as 5-BNC. If you can use the BNC connector for one of the computers, you can use the built-in monitor switch to share the monitor between a PC and a Mac. Using this option is most useful if the graphics card in the PC or the Mac has a BNC output port. If not, you can use a converter cable to go from the standard 15-pin mini D-sub VGA/SVGA to 5-BNC.

Because a BNC cable has better electrical transmission characteristics than a 15-pin mini D-sub cable, taking advantage of a BNC connection can give you a sharper image that is less prone to ghosting.

However, you should not look at a BNC solution as a cost-saving measure. BNC cables are more expensive than standard mini D-sub VGA/SVGA cables and can easily cost several times more than a simple monitor switching box.

PART FIVE • USING FOREIGN OPERATING SYSTEMS

There are other potential drawbacks as well. With 15-pin-to-BNC switches that are built into monitors, the monitor will experience a delay of several seconds between switching as the monitor readjusts. With a KVM box or monitor sharing device, the new display comes up nearly instantaneously when you switch between computers. You should also be aware that on some monitors, the control switch is located on the back of the monitor, which can be difficult to reach on large monitors. Fortunately, you'll find several display brands, including Sony, with the switch located on the front of the monitor.

Use of BNC can often prevent a monitor's "plug and display" features from working, since the BNC cable doesn't use the pins that 15-pin connectors use to convey information about the monitor. In this case, you may have to do some manual configuration on the PC.

Cross-Platform Use of Keyboards and Mice

There are two different goals with mixing keyboards and platforms. One is to share a particular keyboard (Mac or PC) between two or more PCs and Macs. The other use is to use a PC keyboard that you happen to like on a Mac, or a Mac keyboard on a PC.

When sharing a keyboard between PC and Mac, you need two types of devices—a switch and an ADB-to-PS/2 keyboard converter. If you're just using a PC keyboard on a Mac, you just need a keyboard converter.

Keyboard Switching

There are plenty of reasons to use the same keyboard to control both Mac and PC. Besides saving space, it is advantageous to the typist to have the same keyboard layout, size, and ergonomics when hopping back and forth between Windows and Mac OS.

If you want a keyboard switch, you'll usually have to buy a KVM (keyboard/video/mouse) switch, as discussed in the pervious section. A pure keyboard switch is rare, because most people sharing a keyboard between two or more computers are also sharing a monitor.

NOTE: Some KVM switch boxes also support UNIX machines. Usually they support controlling a UNIX workstation, such as a Sun, with a PS/2 keyboard.

Unfortunately, KVM boxes are not usually cross-platform when comes to keyboards and mice—they don't convert between a PS/2 and ADB signals. In addition to handling video, they either have ports for PS/2 keyboard/mouse or have ADB ports. You'll find that most KVM boxes switch PS/2 keyboard signals, which means with most products, you have to use a PC keyboard and mouse. A few, such at the MoniSwitch from Dr. Bott, switch Mac ADB signals. (MoniSwitch comes in versions for two and four computers.)

To control a mixture of Macs and PCs, you'll also need a keyboard converter box for each machine that is different from the keyboard you are using. That is, if you are using a box that accepts input from a PC keyboard, you'll need a converter box for every Mac; if you're using a Mac keyboard, you'll need converter boxes for every PC. Many of the KVM switch manufacturers also offer keyboard converters. It's not a bad idea to buy the PS/2-to-ADB converter and the KVM switch from the same company, since the company should guarantee that they will work together.

MacWindows Tip

One way to use a Mac keyboard with PCs is to convert to USB. Griffin Technology's iMate ADB-to-USB converter box, which lets you connect standard Mac keyboards, mice, tablets, etc., to iMacs, also supports Windows 95 OSR2 B and Windows 98, according to the Griffin web site. In addition to letting you use a favorite Mac keyboard on a PC with a USB port, it can also be used to add a PC to an existing Mac KVM switch, such as Dr. Bott's MoniSwitch. For further info on the iMate, check Griffin's web site (http://www.griffintechnology.com/imac/sysreq.html).

When to use KVM boxes

The cost of KVM and keyboard converter boxes and the required cables doesn't need to be high, though it can be. A setup with two-to-four Macs and PCs can be quite economical However, if the number of computers grows much beyond six, you should seriously consider the alternative of networking the computers together and running Netopia's Timbuktu Pro remote control program, described in the previous chapter. This won't work if you're using the computers to test networking products, but a Timbuktu Pro solution will be less complex and expensive when you start to get into dozens of Macs and PCs.

At its simplest, a KVM switch box has one set of input ports for keyboard and mouse, and two sets of output ports to connect to the two computers, as well as the video in and out ports. To one of the sets of output ports, you'd connect an ADB-to-PS/2 keyboard converter box. The complexity of a cross-platform setup seems to increase exponentially as you increase the number of Macs and PCs, and the problems seem to multiply. Cables for monitors, keyboards, and mice, which need to be extra long for a large number of computers, are more prone to interference and impedance problems. They also cost significantly more than Category 4 or 5 Ethernet cabling. Timbuktu Pro does require a graphics card in some computers, even when they don't have monitors, so you won't save that cost, but you won't need the ADB-to-PS/2 converter boxes.

KVM keyboard features and problems

The more you spend on a KVM switch, the more fancy features you'll get. This can include the option of a foot pedal switch to select the computer to control and view. However, you should also look for required options not included in the price. For instance, though you can expect use a PS/2-to-ADB converter with Macs, you may not expect that some KVM switches require you to purchase a small dongle to plug into a PC port. This is related to the fact that many PC systems won't boot properly without a keyboard. If the KVM doesn't trick the PC into thinking there is a keyboard, then you may need the dongle. You can also configure some systems to bypass the keyboard check at boot time. You do this from the setup program at the beginning of the boot procedure. The setting usually has a name like "keyboard disconnect at boot."

A similar boot-up issue occurs with some KVM switches when you are running Windows NT. With these switches, you can only boot Windows NT when the NT system has been selected to be controlled by the keyboard and monitor. That is, Windows NT won't boot if you are controlling another machine with the keyboard. (The video image problem of ghosting is discussed earlier in the chapter in the section called Sharing Monitors with Switch Boxes.)

MacWindows Tip

Although you probably won't find a KVM switch that has built-in PS/2-to-ADB conversion, you will find some that convert between PS/2 and the older AT keyboard signals. If your KVM box doesn't support this, you can use external PS/2-to-AT converters.

Most KVM switches add a "hot-swapping" ability not found in either ADB or PS/2. That is, you can disconnect and plug the keyboard and mouse into the KVM switch without having to shut down or restart the computers. This is sometimes useful in solving a problem of the keyboard or mouse not working properly to control a PC or Mac. Unplugging and replugging in the keyboard or mouse can sometimes resolve this. However, don't assume the box is hot-swappable—check with the manufacturer first.

You might want to ask a KVM box manufacturer about the ability of a switch to transmit certain mouse features to PCs. Standard features, such as the right mouse button, will work with Windows through a KVM switch, but more exotic features, such as a thumb wheel or scroller roller, may not. Support of these mouse features is even less likely for Macs. However, PC mouse functionality for Macs is provided mostly by the ADB-to-PS/2 converter box, as discussed in the next section.

Finally, high-end users might want to consider a multiuser KVM switch, which enables several users, each with a monitor, keyboard and mouse, to control one of many computers. On the extreme high end, you can have four users connected to any four of 256 computers through the KVM box.

Keyboard Converters

An ADB-to-PS/2 converter is necessary to use with a KVM switch box, but you can also use it with a single Mac to use a PC keyboard or for Mac users who don't want to give up their Mac keyboard when they move to a PC. More often, people want to type at a Macintosh using one of the large variety of keyboards available for PCs, including keyboards that are wireless (infrared), waterproof, or ergonomic.

Converters that plug into the back of a PC and provide ADB ports are rare. To use a Mac keyboard on a single PC, consider adding a USB card to a PC and using a USB keyboard (described in the next section).

Typical keyboard converters include the AppAdapt from USAR (http://www.usar.com) and the Kinesis Mac Interface II (http://www.kinesis-ergo.com/). Both plug into a Mac ADB port and provide three ports: one for a PS/2 keyboard, another for a PS/2 mouse, and the third for a standard Mac ADB device. (If you were going to use a wireless keyboard, you would simply plug the infrared receiver into the keyboard plug in the converter.) Like many similar keyboard converters for Mac , the AppAdapt and Mac Interface II are both powered by the ADB port.

Where these and other converters sometimes differ are keyboard mapping features. Most automatically map Alt to Option, and the PC Backspace to the Mac Delete. However, some use keyboard combinations to represent the Mac keys, which isn't as natural. Also some converters support the Mac keyboard's Power-On button, used to turn the Mac on and off. For instance, the Kinesis Mac Interface II has a button on the converter box to first turn the Mac off. When the Mac is on, you can use the PC keyboard's Scroll Lock key to restart or shut down the Mac. Some converters don't provide a Mac startup key at all, which means you have to use the button on the Mac itself. These kinds of features are sometime built into the hardware itself, while some converters use Mac software, such as a control panel on Mac OS.

You'll have less luck with mapping PC mouse functions over to the Mac. Only a few keyboard converters support the use of more than one button on the Mac. Any that do use Mac software to implement a driver for the PC mouse in Mac OS. One that does is Keystone from Silicon Valley Bus Company (http://www.svbus.com/). More exotic PC mouse features usually won't work on the Mac side, mostly because they require support at the application level.

All this being said, it is much easier to move keyboards and mice from Mac to PC using USB devices, which is where we now go.

USB Keyboards and Mice

The Universal Serial Bus (USB) is a boon to cross-platform integrators, as it implements the exact same hardware standard on all platforms that adopt it. As with PCI expansion slots, the same USB device can plug into a Windows PC or a Macintosh. Unlike ADB keyboards and mice, you can "hot swap" USB devices are "hot-swappable," which means you can plug them in or disconnect them without shutting down or restarting the computer.

There is a catch, however—you can't share a single USB keyboard directly between two machines, as you can with an ADB or PC serial keyboard, or with FireWire devices, for that matter. Although all ADB, FireWire, and USB are all bus technologies, USB differs from the other two in that it controls peripheral devices in a master/slave relationship in which there can only be one master. (Keyboard sharing would be possible with an USB-to-ADB converter device.)

MacWindows Tip

When plugging a keyboard into a USB hub, the hub must provide power to the USB ports. Hubs that do not are unpowered hubs.

USB's low cost, relative high speed, and large number of devices supported per computer (127) makes it likely that it will become the dominant method of connecting keyboards to computers. Apple has made it clear that USB is the future of all Apple keyboards and mice, as well as for third-party trackballs, joysticks, and game pads. The iMac was the first USB Mac, followed by the "Blue and White" Power Mac G3. Microsoft jumped on to USB with Windows 98 and Windows 95 OSR 2.1, which has spurred the growth of USB ports (and BIOS support) in PCs. You can USB-enable Macs and PCs that don't have USB ports by adding a USB expansion card in a PCI slot.

USB Drivers

USB devices require a driver for a particular operating system. However, with USB keyboards, mice, and trackballs you don't need to add a driver, as the standard drivers that come with Mac OS and Windows will support the basic functionality of most USB mice and keyboards. This means that a Mac user can plug in keyboards and mice not aimed at Mac markets, including the standard Microsoft Natural Keyboard Elite, which comes with both USB and PS/2 connectors, and the standard Microsoft IntelliMouse USB. You can also use a standard Strawberry iMac keyboard with a Windows 98 PC with a USB port.

The price you pay for the lack of a specific driver for a USB keyboard is no functionality beyond the basics. This is more of an issue for using Windows keyboards and mice on Macs, as the Windows versions often offer more features. Without a Mac driver specifically for a PC keyboard, there may be special keys that won't work.

A driver is even more important with mice with multiple buttons or special features. For instance, the IntelliMouse has a feature called a *scroller roller*, a little wheel that lets you scroll down a document without having to move the mouse. With these special-feature mice, you should look for a company that offers a Macintosh driver. Joysticks, game pads, and track pads, which go well beyond the basic functionality of a mouse, usually do require a device-specific driver for Mac OS or Windows.

Appendix

Troubleshooting
Frequently Asked Questions

I used to write a column called *BackPanel* in MacWeek magazine, which became eMediaweekly in mid-1998 and ceased publication in February of 1999. BackPanel was a list of questions and answers to common problems with getting Macs and Windows PCs to work together. Much of the topics focused on Mac clients and Windows NT Server. With permission of the publisher, I've taken the best of the BackPanel columns and organized them into an FAQ list geared towards troubleshooting. The questions are listed in five categories:

- Problems with Files
- File Sharing Problems
- Mac Printing with Windows NT Server
- Networking Problems
- Emulation

Problems with Files

Batch file name conversion

Q: We have hundreds of Mac files that were on an AppleShare server that we now want to share with Windows users using Windows NT Server. The problem is that many of the file names use characters that are illegal in Windows, such the slash "/" use for dates, as in "reports 4/13/98." Also, Windows 95 clients can see files on the server that end in a period, such as "reports, etc..." but can't open or copy them. Is there any way to change the names automatically?

A: The problem of file names ending in periods and spaces was supposed to have been fixed with NT 3.5. However, there are several Mac shareware utilities designed for converting Mac file names to legal DOS and Windows formats. Sig Software's NameCleaner ($20, http://www.sigsoftware.com/namecleaner/index.html) uses filters to alter Mac file names to fit DOS "8.3" formats, and can strip out illegal characters. It can also automatically give the files the proper file name extension based on the file's Mac Type code. A Find and Replace command would let you remove multiple periods on a batch of files. You can change the names of a folder full of files by dragging the folder on top of NameCleaner. Drop Rename 3.5 from Chaotic Software ($10, http://www.chaoticsoftware.com/ChaoticSoftware/) lets you create custom self-running scripts that do some of the same type of rename tasks. Drop Rename also has wild card searching and removing.

Originally published in MacWeek 07.6.98

Mac application damage in transit

Q: We often copy Mac applications to our Windows NT Server running Services for Macintosh. The Macs on the network then download it without a problem, icon and all. However, when a Mac tries to download the application the server through FTP or the web, the file does not come through as an application. The file size is also much smaller.

A: The Mac resource fork is being lost. Unlike Windows files, Mac files consist of two parts—the data fork and the resource fork. Applications keep most of their code in the resource fork. With data files, most of the data sits in the data fork, with some icon information in the resource fork, including the Type and Creator code.

Windows NT Server Services for Macintosh is smart enough to know that Mac files have two forks. However, FTP is not—it loses the resource fork, and most of the application code, and the application can no longer function.

The solution is to compress the file before uploading it, using StuffIt or another utility. Compressing puts both forks in one archive file. When you download the archive from FTP, it may not have an icon, and double-clicking it may not open it. But you should be able to decompress it by opening it from within StuffIt.

By the way, the same thing happens when you attach a file to an e-mail message. Attaching a file encodes the file, putting both forks together, so the servers handling the files don't have a problem. The recipient's e-mail software then decodes the message, restoring both file forks.

Originally published in MacWeek 07.6.98

Fonts in Mac OS and Windows

Q: Our Mac group creates Microsoft PowerPoint presentations for use on Windows machines, but the fonts always come out looking very odd on Windows—nothing like the fonts we specify.

A: Because you don't have the same fonts installed on the Mac and Windows machines, PowerPoint substitutes fonts. Buy the same font sets for Macs and Windows PCs, and use only those fonts for creating presentations.

If you don't have the same fonts installed on both platforms, you can predict how PowerPoint will substitute fonts from this list of TrueType fonts:

- Avant Garde on the Macintosh will become Century Gothic on Windows.
- Bookman on the Mac will be read as Bookman Old Style in Windows.
- Helvetica Mac will become Arial in Windows;
- N Helvetica Narrow will be Arial Narrow.
- New Century Schlbk will become Century Schlbk; Palatino will become Book Antiqua;
- Times will be Times New Roman;
- Zapf Chancery will become Monotype Corsiva;
- Zapf Dingbats will become Monotype Sorts.

If the Windows machine has a font with the same name as a font specified by the Mac, PowerPoint uses that font. But fonts with the same name on Macs and PCs don't always look alike, unless you bought them as a set. If PowerPoint for Windows doesn't recognize any of the fonts, Windows takes its best shot at a substitute.

In a pinch, the Windows user can easily replace the missing fonts with those installed on the PC. In PowerPoint's Tools menu, select Replace Fonts. In the appropriate fields, click on the font to replace and the new font to use.

Microsoft offers several font sets for Mac and Windows that can be downloaded free from its Web site at http://www.microsoft.com/truetype/fontpack/mac.htm. The fonts are supposedly designed for the Web, but they should do the job for on-screen PowerPoint presentations.

Originally published in eMediaweekly Aug. 24, 1998.

Mac and Windows images

Q: We created a full-screen image on a Mac, but when we move it to Windows, it looks slightly stretched-out vertically. We've tried exporting it in different formats, and transferring the file to the PC over the network and with a disk, but we get the same result whatever we do.

A: Mac OS and Windows PCs have slightly different screen aspect ratios, even at the same pixel resolution. (The aspect ratio is the ratio between the height and the width of the screen.) This is because pixels are not as tall as they are wide. On a Mac, the pixels are slightly less tall than they are on Windows machines. When you move a Mac graphic to Windows, the latter's taller pixels can make the image appear stretched vertically or compressed horizontally. The difference between aspect ratios is small, but can be noticeable in images with a lot of detail, particularly on full-screen images.

To prepare a Mac-created image for display on a PC, you need to scale the vertical length to 83 percent of the original. This is easily done in both Equilibrium's DeBabelizer Pro 4.5 for Windows and DeBabelizer 3.0 for Macintosh, which can scale an image from Mac to Windows and back. In the Image menu, select Scale and choose Mac to PC Aspect Ratio. The PC to Mac Aspect Ratio command scales the width of an image created in Windows to 83 percent of its original width.

Originally published in eMediaweekly Sept. 21, 1998

Generic Mac icons with NT Server

Q: We recently changed the Windows NT 4.0 file server permissions for some of our Mac users. Now the mounted server volumes on these Macs are represented by generic icons instead of the NT icons they used to have.

A: This effect can be caused by the Access Control List permissions settings that you may have set for the Mac client's user or group account. An Access Control List for a specific directory would list the users and groups as well as the permissions each has for that directory. (This is in the Directory Permissions window you can access by right-clicking a file or directory, selecting Properties, and then selecting the Security tab.)

By default, the Access Control List uses NT file system permissions for directories and files that look like this:

```
Special Directory Access: READ (R) EXECUTE (E)
Special File Access: N/A
```

You can modify the user or group permissions to enable the group's read access on the volume. This will bring back the volume's icon when it is mounted on the Macintosh desktop. Change the Special File Access permission to match the Special Directory Access:

```
READ (R) EXECUTE (E)
```

The Read permission lets users open a file and see a list of directory contents. The Execute permission lets users run an application in the directory. For a directory, an Execute permission lets users access a directory that is nested within other directories, without having access to those higher-level directories.

Originally published in eMediaweekly Sept. 21, 1998

Generic icons on Windows NT Server

Q: Whenever I go to the Windows NT server and download a Windows QuarkXPress file to my Macintosh, it has a blank icon. When I double click on it, XPress doesn't open it, even though it is supposed to open the Windows version. When I use Find File to look at the type and creator codes, it says the type is text and the creator is LMAN. What am I doing wrong?

A: You need to map the extension of the file name—in this case .QXD—to the Macintosh type and creator codes for QuarkXPress. The type is XDOC and the creator is XPR3. You can do this one of two ways: either on your Macintosh or on the Windows NT server (text and LMAN are the default type and creator codes that NT Services for Macintosh gives a file when a Windows user uploads the file). On the Mac, use the PC Exchange control panel to map the type and creator codes to the name extension. Click on the Add button, type in the extension (.QXD) and select QuarkXPress from the list. Finally, choose the file icon from the pop-up menu.

On NT Server, this task is called "association." Open the File Manager, click on the Mac File menu and choose Associate. Type in the extension, click on the Add button and type in the correct type and creator codes in the dialog box that appears.

One benefit to mapping on the server is that all the Macintosh users will get the benefits. One benefit to doing it on the Macs is that it doesn't matter when the files were created. On the server, only the Windows files stored after you did the association will get the correct Quark type and creator codes.

Whether you do the mapping on the Mac or on Windows, the result only works one way: with Windows files moving to Macintoshes. When moving files created on the Mac over to Windows, you'll have to make sure you use the correct extension in the file name itself.

Originally published in eMediaweekly Oct. 26, 1998

Moving ligatures to Windows

Q: Whenever we use the ligatures "[fl]" and "[fi]" in a Macintosh document and move it to Windows, the characters are replaced by a space. It doesn't seem to matter what application we use. Is there any way to convert Mac ligatures to Windows ligatures?

A: The PC keyboard doesn't support ligatures, so Windows will substitute another character in place of the ligature. Sometimes this substituted character is invisible.

However, you can use a font's so-called expert set, a set of special characters. Instead of using an actual ligature, which merges the two characters typographically, you use one of the special characters in an expert set that represents the ligature as a single character.

Another workaround if you need to distribute a read-only file is to create a PDF file of the Macintosh file using Acrobat PDF Writer or Distiller and embed the font in the document. Acrobat Reader can view a PDF file identically on Macintosh and Windows machines when the fonts are embedded.

Originally published in eMediaweekly Oct. 26, 1998

File Sharing Problems

NT Services for Macintosh error

Q: Our NT 4.0 server with dual Pentium processors stops sometimes when it gets busy, showing the following error: STOP 0x0000000a.

A: This a known bug in Services for Macintosh caused by a network interface card driver that is written as a "full NDIS driver" for better performance. This causes a synchronization problem in Sfmsrv.sys. Microsoft offers a fix which involves new versions of Sfmatalk.sys and Sfmsrv.sys; call (800) 936-5900 to get it.

Originally published in MacWeek June 15, 1998

Windows clients on AppleShare IP

Q: Our Windows users get the message "I/O error" when trying to save a file from within some applications to any of our AppleShare IP 6 servers. It doesn't happen with all applications, and it never happens with the Mac clients. How can we fix this?

A: Get AppleShare IP 6.1, due this month. Apple says it will fix this known bug. AppleShare IP 6.0 automatically disconnects a Microsoft SMB (Server Messaging Block) file-sharing session after four minutes of inactivity. In a normal SMB session on a Microsoft network, Windows applications can automatically re-establish an SMB session when a user saves to a file on the server. With AppleShare IP 6.0, some Windows applications can't reconnect.

One workaround is to save the file on the Windows machine and then manually copy the file (via drag-and-drop) to the mounted AppleShare IP volume.

AppleShare IP 6.1 is supposed to fix a minor bug that affects Windows clients. On Windows, when you bring up a Properties dialog box (right-click) of a file on an AppleShare IP server volume, the server will not show the correct date and time stamps for the file. Mac clients have a similar problem with the Get Info window of files on the server. In this case, AppleShare IP doesn't report all of the text in the Comments field.

The new version of AppleShare IP will also be compatible with Mac OS 8.5; AppleShare IP 5.x and 6.0 are not. You can check the AppleShare IP update page at:
http://www.apple.com/appleshareip/text/downloads.html.

Originally published in eMediaweekly Nov. 16, 1998

Mac OS 8.5 freezing when connected to Windows NT volumes

Q: Since we installed Mac OS 8.5 on some of our Macs, they are having problems transferring files to mounted Windows NT volumes. Usually, the Mac freezes for a while and then reports that the volume has been disconnected. Another problem occurs when volumes are mounted on the Desktop: Users can't open 8.5's Network Browser. Occasionally, the Macs will also freeze or crash. Our Macs with earlier versions of Mac OS don't have this problem.

A: The problem is not a conflict between Mac OS 8.5 and Windows NT Server but between OS 8.5 and some Mac virus protection programs, including Symantec's Norton AntiVirus (NAV) Version 5.0.2 and earlier as well as with Network Associates' Virex. It also occurs with AppleShare and other AppleShare-compatible volumes. Symantec's NAV 5.0.3 upgrade fixes the problem. This upgrade (available at http://www.symantec.com/nav/nmac503.html) also fixes other problems with Mac OS 8.5 that aren't related to file sharing. Network Associates doesn't have a fix for Virex yet. However, a workaround can disable the Scan Files When Opened function. To do this, open the Virex control panel, go to Preferences and select File Access. Disabling Scan Files When Opened will let you keep network volumes mounted on OS 8.5 without problems.

Originally published in eMediaweekly Jan. 25, 1999

Mac Printing with Windows NT Server

Macs can't print in color

Q: Our Windows users have no problem printing color to our HP Color LaserJet connected to our Windows NT Server, but the Macs always print in black and white.

A Installing the PostScript option (called the "HP Adobe PostScript Level 2 SIMM") in the printer should fix this problem. When the printer doesn't have PostScript, the NT Services for Macintosh print server component (SFMPRINT.DLL) gives it a PSCRIPT1 data type. The SFMPSPRT.DLL print processor then rasterizes the print job at 300 dpi maximum and in black and white, even though the printer may support higher resolutions and color. When the printer supports PostScript, SFMPRINT.DLL assigns the job a RAW data type, and the SFMPSPRT.DLL print processor passes the print job through to the printer without alteration. Print jobs from Windows clients also use the WINPRINT.DLL print processor and are not affected by problems with SFMPSPRT.DLL.

Originally published in MacWeek June 6, 1998

Macs can't print to AppleTalk printers

Q: We just replaced our old AppleShare server with Windows NT Server. We set up the MacFile and MacPrint services with the NT permissions, but now the printers on the AppleTalk network don't show up in the Chooser on the Mac. The PCs can print to the AppleTalk printers just fine. What did we do wrong?

A: There are two ways you can let Macs see AppleTalk-based printers: directly over AppleTalk and through the MacPrint server on the NT machine. Your setup has probably disabled both methods.

Macintoshes are prevented from accessing AppleTalk printers by configuring NT Server to "capture" the printer. You can configure NT Server to "uncapture" a printer in the Ports tab of the Printer Properties window. Choose Configure Port and unselect "Capture this AppleTalk printing device." You will have to do this for each printer. Windows users will still have access to the AppleTalk printers as long as the printers are shared (that is, added as a port in Printer Properties).

The reason your Macs can't access the printer through NT Server is that you must have set the permissions for MacPrint. Because the Apple Printer Access Protocol doesn't allow password log-in of printers, NT lets you log into MacPrint as a "user." You then give or deny access to printers for the MacPrint user. Because Macs access printers through an NT server via MacPrint, permissions given to MacPrint apply to all Mac users. In your case, the network administrator has not given MacPrint the permissions it needs to see the printers.

If you give MacPrint log-in permissions and uncapture the printers, then an AppleTalk printer will show up twice in the Chooser, which is no doubt confusing to users. I recommend uncapturing each printer and leaving the MacPrint blocking permissions intact. This solution has a side benefit: Having the Macintoshes directly access AppleTalk printers bypasses Windows NT's buggy PostScript.

Originally published in eMediaweekly Sept. 21, 1998

Poor print results

Q: Last month, you recommended setting Windows NT Server's MacPrint so that Macintosh clients print directly to the printer over AppleTalk (see 09.21.98, page 20). Why would you get poor print results by sending print jobs to the Windows NT spooler? Doesn't the Mac's own driver create the PostScript code for the print job, and doesn't Windows NT just spool the file that the Mac generated?

A: The problem has to do with the assumptions that printers make about the encoding scheme used in PostScript print jobs. Some printers assume that PostScript print jobs received over AppleTalk are encoded using standard binary. They also assume that print jobs received over a PC print protocol—such as the DLC (Data Link Control) or LPR (Line Printer Remote) protocols used by Windows NT Server—are encoded using Tagged Binary Core Protocol (TBCP).

Windows NT Server is supposed to know this about the printers. With simple files, such as a text-only document, NT Server communicates the correct encoding scheme to the printer. But in other cases it often transmits the job using the wrong encoding scheme.

Microsoft says that this tends to happen only with complex print jobs containing graphics. When you send the PostScript print job to the NT server, it's encoded in standard binary, but because this printer gets the job from the NT server, the printer thinks it's getting TBCP and thus generates PostScript errors. If you sent the job directly over AppleTalk, the printer would (correctly) assume it's getting binary. The problem varies with different printers.

If you still want to print through the NT server, you can encode the print job in a third standard, ASCII text, which most printers can recognize. Some Macintosh applications, such as QuarkXPress, let you choose ASCII as a print data format in the page setup dialog box.

Originally published in eMediaweekly Oct. 26, 1998

Windows NT print error

Q: When we print to Windows NT's print server, we sometimes get an error message saying that spoolss.exe has generated an application error.

A: The spooler in Windows NT stores a print job as a pair of files ending in .SHD and .SPL. If a lot of these files collect in the spooling directory, NT will generate the spoolss.exe application error. You can get NT printing again by removing these files from the directory systemroot/system32/spoolprinters. You should also delete any old .TMP files that may have accumulated in the temporary directory. After this, restart the spooler.

The .SHD and .SPL files can accumulate if too many print jobs are being submitted to NT at the same time, but it is more likely that jobs are being corrupted. There are several reasons why print jobs can get corrupted. One cause is a flow-control problem that was fixed with Service Pack 4. This is a case when the server can send the print job to the printer faster than the client can queue the print job to the printer spooler. In this case, the .SPL file will contain 0x00 in addition to the print data.

Originally published in eMediaweekly Nov. 16, 1998

Networking Problems

NT Server and BootP

Q: Is there any way to get NT Server to assign IP addresses to Macs using BOOTP?

A: Microsoft Service Pack 3 for NT adds BOOTP, with some limitations, to the Microsoft Dynamic Host Configuration Protocol (DHCP) Server. You need to reserve BOOTP addresses in advance by creating an IP address reservation in MS DHCP Server. Microsoft has indicated that future versions of Microsoft DHCP Server will assign IP addresses dynamically to BOOTP clients. The Macs must be running Open Transport 1.1 or later.

Originally published in MacWeek April 13, 1998

Mac dial-in to Windows NT Remote Access Server (RAS)

NOTE: Since this was published in MacWeek, Mac OS 8.5 was released, which can log on to the Windows NT RAS, because of added support for MS-CHAP authentication in the Remote Access control panel (see Chapter 12 for more information). This FAQ item does apply to versions of Mac OS before 8.5.

Q: Is there any way I can use my home Mac to dial into our Windows NT Remote Access Server (RAS)? Our IS people say it can't be done.

A: The problem is usually authentication, but there are ways to make a Mac–RAS connection. One method is to set the Windows NT RAS server to use the Password Authentication Protocol, which is used by the Mac's Point-to-Point Protocol (PPP) control panel and FreePPP:

1. Go to Control Panels and select the Network icon.
2. Under Installed Network Software, select Remote Access Service, then click on the Configure button.
3. In the Remote Access Setup window, click the Network button to bring up the Network Configuration window.
4. Under Encryption Settings, select "Allow any authentication including clear text."

In the Mac TCP/IP control panel, you'll select Connect via PPP and Configure Using PPP Server. Enter one or more DNS server IP addresses. You'll also need to enter your NT domain user name and password in the PPP control panel. (In some cases, you may have to enter domain\username instead of just username.)

If your IS people are unwilling to reset the NT RAS server, you can enable a Mac to use the more popular MS-CHAP (Challenge Authentication Protocol) by replacing PPP or FreePPP with an MS-CHAP-enabled PPP client. Network TeleSystems Inc.'s (http://www.nts.com) TunnelBuilder is a Mac PPP client that is capable of MS-CHAP authentication. However, TunnelBuilder doesn't support call-back, if that function has been enabled on the RAS server.

In addition, Ascend Communications Inc.'s IntragyAccess (http://www.ascend.com/2401.html) includes the Ascend PPP dialer, which supports PAP, CHAP, and MS-CHAP authentication.

Originally published in MacWeek June 1, 1998

Mac Access to NT RAS via PPTP

Q: Is there any way to connect a Mac to a Windows NT-based server over Point-to-Point Tunneling Protocol (PPTP) using Windows NT's Remote Access Service (RAS) software? With a Windows client, this lets you create a "dial-up" networking connection that does not use the modem, but instead uses Microsoft's virtual private network (VPN) adapter over an Ethernet network. You can't use Point-to-Point Protocol (PPP) over Ethernet on a Mac; is it possible to connect with a Mac this way?

A: Yes, it is, but it's not simple. Network TeleSystems Inc. (http://www.nts.com) has the only VPN solution for Mac: Tunnel-Builder for $99. A control panel called NTS PPP replaces the OT PPP control panel, and "NTS PPP TCP/IP" appears as an option in the Connect via: pop-up menu in the TCP/IP control panel (you need Open Transport 1.1.2 or later). This lets the Mac connect to VPNs using Microsoft's PPTP and MS-CHAP protocols. PPTP creates a secure, encrypted "tunnel" over the Internet to your LAN, while MS-CHAP is Microsoft's authentication protocol for Windows NT RAS machines. Of course, as a TCP/IP connection, you can't get to the NT file service unless you also run DAVE from Thursby Software Systems Inc., which lets Macs access Windows file servers using NetBIOS over TCP/IP.

AppleTalk can access NT Services for Macintosh, but there's a catch. TunnelBuilder's NTS PPP supports AppleTalk over PPP for getting to printers and AppleShare servers on the network. But Windows NT RAS won't route AppleTalk, so you can't get to the network through NT RAS. If you are willing to replace NT RAS, you can use Network TeleSystems' TunnelMaster, a hardware VPN server that can route AppleTalk over PPTP. Macs can then access Services for Macintosh through a VPN.

Originally published in MacWeek July 20, 1998

Mac FTP through Microsoft Proxy Server

Q: Whenever I try to use Fetch 3.0.3 (the latest version of the freeware FTP client) to upload or download files to an Internet FTP server through Microsoft Proxy Server 2.0, I get the message, "Error number -1." What's up?

A: You should probably try another FTP utility, or another proxy server. When Fetch tries to Put or Get files through the server's SOCKS proxy, it rejects Fetch's request because Fetch doesn't send a destination port with its bind request.

A partial workaround enables Fetch to download files through the SOCKS proxy. You need to configure Fetch's fire-wall settings to use a PASV mode connection to the FTP server. The Put command is a different story. While the transfer seems to work, the server will abort a transfer before it's complete. Fortunately, not all FTP utilities have this problem with Microsoft Proxy Server.

Originally published in eMediaweekly Aug. 24, 1998.

MS Outlook and Exchange

Q: Whenever a Mac-based Microsoft Outlook user receives an e-mail message that contains blind carbon copies (BCCs), and embeds that message in another e-mail message, the BCC names become visible.

This doesn't happen with our Windows 95 and NT users. Is our Mac user doing something wrong?

A: No. This is a newly recognized bug in Microsoft Exchange Server 5.0 and 5.5. Microsoft recently posted a fix called PSP2STRI.EXE for Intel-based systems, or PSP2STRA.EXE for Alpha platforms (ftp://ftp.microsoft.com/bussys/exchange/exchange-public/fixes/Eng). The solution requires that you have Exchange Server 5.0 Service Pack 2 installed. The problem occurs with Exchange Client 5.0 for Mac or Windows 3.x, or with Outlook 8 for Mac or Windows 3.x. The clients for Windows 95 and 98, as well as NT Exchange and Outlook, are immune to this particular malady.

Originally published in eMediaweekly Aug. 24, 1998.

FTP and Microsoft Proxy Server 2.0

Q: A few months ago, you said that the Fetch FTP client had a problem getting through to the Internet past Microsoft Proxy Server 2.0. Is there another FTP client that doesn't have this problem?

A: You need an FTP client that works well with the SOCKS proxy protocol. One that works well is the shareware NetFinder (http://www.personal.usyd.edu.au/~vtan/sw/NetFinder). It displays an FTP site like the Finder shows a volume, as folders and files.

Originally published in eMediaweekly Oct. 26, 1998

Emulation

Running Windows NT on Virtual PC

Q: I've been running Windows NT on a Mac using Connectix's Virtual PC 2.0.1. It worked until I upgraded Windows NT to Service Pack 4 and the Mac to OS 8.5. When I tried to launch Virtual PC, it froze. I thought Mac OS 8.5 was the problem, so I reinstalled OS 8.1. Now Virtual PC launches, and then Windows NT launches, but I can't log on. I get an error message that the NetLogon Service isn't running. But I'm not on a Windows network, so I can't run NetLogon. What's up?

A There's good news and bad news. The good news is that you can run Mac OS 8.5. The bad news is that you can't run NT Service Pack 4.

First, Virtual PC versions 2.0 and 2.0.1 are not completely compatible with Mac OS 8.5. Upgrading Virtual PC to Version 2.1 or 2.1.1 will fix the problem (http://www.connectix.com/html/vpc_updates.html). The problem that's keeping you from logging into Windows NT is an incompatibility between Windows NT Service Pack 4 and Virtual PC. Connectix does not yet have a fix for this, and it recommends you run NT Service Pack 3.

Originally published in eMediaweekly Jan. 25, 1999

The material presented in this appendix is reproduced with permission from Mac Publishing, LLC. eMediaweekly and the eMediaweekly logo are trademarks of Mac Publishing LLC.

Index